THE STANDARD SERIES.

THE
POPULAR HISTORY OF THE TRANSLATION
OF THE
HOLY SCRIPTURES
INTO THE ENGLISH TONGUE.

WITH SPECIMENS OF THE OLD ENGLISH VERSIONS.

BY

MRS. H. C. CONANT,

AUTHOR OF TRANSLATIONS OF NEANDER'S PRACTICAL COMMENTARIES.

REVISED EDITION,
CONTINUING THE HISTORY TO THE PRESENT TIME.
By REV. THOMAS J. CONANT, D.D.

No other Christian people can show a vernacular Bible with such a history as ours; so consecrated by high purpose and noble sacrifice, so baptized in the tears and blood of faithful souls, so linked with the inmost life and history of the people.—*Preface to the first edition.*

Wipf and Stock Publishers
EUGENE, OREGON

Wipf and Stock Publishers
199 West 8th Avenue, Suite 3
Eugene, Oregon 97401

The History of the Translation of the Holy Scriptures into the English Tongue
With Specimens of the Old English Versions
By Conant, H. C. and Conant, Thomas J.
ISBN: 1-59244-343-5
Publication date 9/12/2003
Previously published by I. K. Funk & Co., Publishers, 1881

EDITOR'S PREFACE.

THE following history of the English Bible was first published in the year 1856. It was received with general favor, and was republished without change in 1859. It was popular in its spirit and form; and for the first time it brought before the reader, in moderate compass, the whole subject of English Bible translation. Its materials were drawn from all that had been written directly on the subject, and from every other source from which light could be obtained. A list of the authorities consulted, in the preparation of the work, is added at the end of the author's preface.

In preparing this revised edition, the history has been compared throughout with works bearing on the subject that have appeared since its first publication; and such changes have been made as were found necessary to conform it to the present state of knowledge. The editor is specially indebted to the new and accurate researches of Mr. Westcott, in his History of the English Bible, and to Dr. Philip Schaff's Introduction to the American reprint of the Treatises of Trench, Lightfoot, and Ellicott, and to the Revision of the English version of the New Testament.

A closing chapter is added by the editor, bringing the history down to the present time; showing the steps by which the way has been gradually prepared for renewing the work of revision, under circumstances more favorable, and with materials far more ample, than at any former period in English history.

While these lines are going to the press, the Anglo-American revision of the English New Testament is made public, and received here with general interest, and with a sale of the book unprecedented in the publication of any other work, so far as is known to the writer. That such is the case augurs well for the interest felt in the Divine Word, and in all that may contribute to the purity of its text, and render its teachings more clear and intelligible.   T. J. C.

AUTHOR'S PREFACE.

This volume was undertaken from the wish to meet a widely extended and increasing desire for information, in a popular form and within moderate limits, respecting the history of our English Bible. How came we by this Bible? What were its antecedents? In what religious, social, political condition of England had it its birth? What influences determined its primitive character and form? To what modifying agencies has it been subjected in the progress of its history? These and similar questions are now, in the present awakened state of public interest on the subject of Bible translation, asked by multitudes of intelligent and thoughtful persons, who have neither the time nor the means for searching out the answers for themselves. The valuable works on the subject, already before the public, are not adapted to the wants of general readers, being chiefly useful as works of reference for bibliographical students. That of Anderson (Annals of the English Bible), though rich in valuable and interesting information for certain portions of the history, is deficient in others; and it is, moreover, too voluminous, as well as too immethodical, to attract such as do not enjoy a superfluity of leisure and of patience. It has been my object in this volume simply to furnish such an account of the early English versions and revisions as may give a clear idea of their origin and leading characteristics, and of the general influence of each in moulding the religious history of the English race. This design admitted of greater conciseness, without abridging those historical and personal details which best exhibit the subject in its connection with actual human life.*

Brief as the work is, however, the labor bestowed on its preparation has not been trifling. Indeed its very brevity is the result of no little labor. The length of time embraced in the history, and the variety of subjects and of characters necessarily introduced for its illustration, required not only much diligent investigation for the collection of materials, but much labor in sifting them, in order to keep the work within limits suited to common readers. But the task, though

---

* From these remarks it will be seen that a critical description of editions and copies does not come within the design of this volume.

toilsome, has been full of pleasantness; and I shall count myself happy if it shall become the means of communicating to other minds a more lively and more intelligent interest in the subject of which it treats. No other Christian people can show a vernacular Bible with such a history as ours; so consecrated by high purpose and noble sacrifice, so baptized in the tears and blood of faithful souls, so linked with the inmost life and history of the people. At what cost the Divine Word has been placed in the possession of the English race, and what it has done for that race, are matters which every Christian and every lover of his country has an interest in knowing. Without such knowledge, we can neither rightly estimate its value nor labor intelligently for the perpetuation of its influence.

The principal works consulted in the preparation of this volume are the following:

LIFE AND OPINIONS OF JOHN DE WYCLIFFE; by Robert Vaughan, D.D. 2 vols. 8vo. London, 1828.

JOHN DE WYCLIFFE, A MONOGRAPH; by Robert Vaughan, D.D. 1853.

The first of these works is not superseded by the second, which omits many interesting details of the earlier memoir. To the two I am chiefly indebted for the facts of Wickliffe's history, and for the extracts from his writings.

THE HISTORY OF THE LIFE AND SUFFERINGS OF THE REVEREND AND LEARNED JOHN WICLIFFE, D.D. By John Lewis. London, 1720.

PREFACE TO WICLIFFE'S BIBLE; edited by Forshall & Madden, Oxford, 1850.

HENRY'S HISTORY OF GREAT BRITAIN; 4th ed. London, 1805.

Of this writer the Halle Encyclopædia (Ersch u. Gruber's) says: "The affairs of the church, the inner history of the people, government, manners, commerce, the arts and sciences, engaged his attention to a greater degree than they did that of Hume; and all these he combines in a series of graphic and instructive delineations, the result of his own careful and impartial researches." For the character of the Romish priesthood, and the condition of England under their sway, this author has been chiefly relied on in the present work.

HENR. KNYGHTON, CHRONICA ANGLIÆ, (in Twysden's *Scriptores decem*, Vol. II.).

HALLAM'S MIDDLE AGES.

ANNALS OF THE ENGLISH BIBLE; by Christopher Anderson. 8vo. London, 1845. 2 vols.

The materials for the personal history of Tyndale have been chiefly furnished by this work.

MEMOIR OF WILLIAM TYNDALE, by George Offor (prefixed to Bagster's reprint of Tyndale's New Testament, London, 1836).

INTRODUCTION TO BAGSTER'S HEXAPLAR NEW TESTAMENT.

WRITINGS OF TYNDALE AND FRITH. (Works of the Eng. Reformers, ed. by Thomas Russel, London, 1831.)

RUDHART'S THOMAS MORUS, aus den Quellen bearbeitet; 2te Ausg. Augsburg, 1852.

FOXE'S ACTS AND MONUMENTS; folio, London, 1641.

BURNET'S HISTORY OF THE REFORMATION; 2 vols., 4to, London, 1850.

THE WORKS OF SIR THOMAS MORE, KNYGHTE, sometime Lorde Chancellour of England, wrytten by him in the Englysh tonge; 4to, pp. 1458. London, 1557.

The only edition of his English writings. It was published by Rastell in the last year of Queen Mary's reign; and was dedicated to her majesty, as an important aid to her efforts for the re-establishment of Romanism.

ARCHBISHOP PARKER, DE ANTIQUIT. BRIT. ECCLESIÆ; London, 1729.

MEMORIALS OF MILES COVERDALE; London, Samuel Bagster, 1838.

MEMOIR OF MILES COVERDALE; prefixed to Bagster's reprint of Coverdale's translation of the Bible.

LEWIS' HISTORY OF THE TRANSLATIONS OF THE HOLY BIBLE INTO ENGLISH; London, 1818.

PREFACE TO THE GENEVAN NEW TESTAMENT, 1557; Bagster's fac-simile reprint, London.

PREFACE TO THE GENEVAN BIBLE, AND DEDICATION TO QUEEN ELIZABETH, 1560 (from the Edition of 1583).

STRYPE'S MEMORIALS OF ARCHBISHOP CRANMER; 2 vols., 8vo. Oxford, 1840.

STRYPE'S LIFE AND ACTS OF ARCHBISHOP PARKER, 1 vol. fol. London, 1740.

STRYPE'S HISTORY OF THE LIFE AND ACTS OF ARCHBISHOP GRINDAL; 1 vol. fol. London, 1710.

STRYPE'S LIFE AND ACTS OF ARCHBISHOP WHITGIFT; 1 vol. fol. London, 1718.

These Memoirs of the English Protestant Primates in the sixteenth century were written by their ardent admirer and apologist, himself a zealous High-Churchman. From his representations of the growth of Puritanism in the English Church, and the measures used for its suppression, has been drawn the account given of them in this volume.

FULLER'S CHURCH HISTORY; 3 vols. 8vo. London, 1842.

STRYPE'S ANNALS OF THE REFORMATION; Oxford, 1824.

ARCHBISHOP PARKER'S PREFACE TO THE BISHOPS' BIBLE.

HEFELE, DER CARDINAL XIMENES; Tübingen, 1851.

BISHOP BARLOW'S ACCOUNT OF THE HAMPTON COURT CONFERENCE; London, 1604.

WILKINS, CONCILIA MAGNÆ BRIT. ET HIB. London, 1737.

GELL'S ESSAY TOWARDS THE AMENDMENT OF THE LAST ENGLISH TRANSLATION OF THE BIBLE; 1 vol. fol. 1659.

FULKE'S DEFENCE OF THE ENGLISH BIBLE (ed. for the Parker Society, Cambridge, 1843).

WHITELOCKE'S MEMORIALS OF THE ENGLISH AFFAIRS; London, 1732.

JOURNALS OF THE HOUSE OF COMMONS, published by order of the House.

TISCHENDORF'S REISE IN DEN ORIENT; Leipzig, 1846.

TRANSLATORS' PREFACE TO KING JAMES' REVISION (Field's Edition, 2 vols. fol. London, 1659), and DEDICATION TO THE KING.

TABLE OF CONTENTS.

CHAPTER I.
THE BIBLE THE PEOPLE'S CHARTER. Relation of Wickliffe to his Age......... 1-4

CHAPTER II.
THE PAPAL ARMY IN ENGLAND. The Secular Clergy. The Monks. The Mendicant Friars... 5-18

CHAPTER III.
COUNTER-INFLUENCES; THEIR INEFFICIENCY. Edward III. The Barons. Magna Charta. The Universities. House of Commons............................. 19-24

CHAPTER IV.
THE BIBLE-APOSTLE. Opposes the Mendicant Friars, on the Ground of Scripture. Summoned to Parliament. Argues against the Papal Claim to Tribute. Advocates the Exclusion of Churchmen from Civil Office. Becomes Theological Professor at Oxford. His Teachings Anticipate those of the Reformation............................. 25-32

CHAPTER V.
THE POPE AND BISHOPS IN THE FIELD. Wickliffe sent as Ambassador to the Papal Court. Cited before the Convocation as a Heretic. Scene at St. Paul's. Five Papal Bulls for his Apprehension. His Advice to Parliament. Trial at Lambeth. Vindicates the Civil and the Ecclesiastical Rights of the Laity. Rescued by the Londoners.. 33-38

CHAPTER VI.
THE NEW-TESTAMENT MINISTRY REVIVED. Wickliffe's Views of the Clerical Office. Labors of his "Poore Priestes." Alarm of the Romish Clergy. Fraudulent Legislation. True Apostolic Succession... 39-43

CHAPTER VII.
WICKLIFFE ATTACKS THE CITADEL OF PAPAL INFLUENCE. The Catholic Theory of Communion. Wickliffe's Protestant stand-point. Silenced at Oxford. Retires to Lutterworth... 44-48

CHAPTER VIII.
WICKLIFFE'S WRITINGS FOR THE PEOPLE. Originates Religious Tracts. Influence of his Popular Writings 49-51

CHAPTER IX.
THE FIRST ENGLISH BIBLE. Wickliffe's previous Labors in Bible-translation. Right of the Laity to the Scriptures. His Version made from the Vulgate. Wickliffe's Death.. 52-55

CHAPTER X.

INFLUENCE OF WICKLIFFE'S VERSION. England's only Bible for a hundred and thirty years. Its Wide Diffusion. Rapid Growth of the Spirit of Religious Freedom. Checked by Henry IV. The Lollards. Statutes against Wickliffe's Bible. Its Character and Claims.. 56-61

CHAPTER XI.

WICKLIFFE'S INFLUENCE ABROAD. Effect of his Writings in Bohemia. Huss, and Jerome of Prague. Council of Constance. Sentence against Wickliffe's Writings. His Body condemned to be Disinterred and Burned. Execution of the Decree. Increased Spread of his Views in Bohemia. Bohemian Bibles. Influence of Bohemia on the Reformation. Wickliffe's Relation to Modern Christianity.................. 62-65

CHAPTER XII.

RELIGIOUS ASPECTS OF ENGLAND. Wickliffe's Bible, and the Lollards. Revival of Learning in the Schools. Spread of the Reformation in England.............. 66-71

CHAPTER XIII.

TYNDALE'S NEW TESTAMENT. Tyndale's early History. His Youthful Attempts at Bible-translation. Seeks the Patronage of Tunstal, Bishop of London. Finds that the Bible cannot be Translated in England. Humphrey Monmouth his Friend and Patron. Translates his New Testament in Hamburg. Goes to Cologne to Print it. Aided by English Merchants. THE BIBLE HATER. Councillor Rincke. Tyndale Obliged to Flee from Cologne to Worms. Change of Plans. The New Testament in England. THE SECRET SEARCH. Fyshe's "Supplication of Beggars." Thomas Garrett. Scenes at Oxford and Cambridge. Dr. Barnes' Trial. Burning of New Testaments. THE KING ENLISTED. Luther's Blunder. Royal Prohibition of Tyndale's Translation. Efforts for its Suppression on the Continent. THE BISHOPS ON THE ALERT. Archbishop Warham buys up New Testaments. Wolsey as Vicar-General. Trial of Arthur and Bilney. Constant Multiplication and Spread of the New Testament... 72-89

CHAPTER XIV.

TYNDALE'S REFORMATORY WRITINGS. "Parable of the Wicked Mammon." "The Obedience of a Christian Man." Light Thrown by these Writings on the State of the Times, and the Extortions of the Clergy. Tyndale's View of Church-offices and Sacraments. Defends the Right of the Laity to the Bible. Theological Training in the Universities. The Bible the only Safe Guide....................................... 90-101

CHAPTER XV.

CARDINAL WOLSEY'S MEASURES TO SILENCE TYNDALE. Application to the Princess-Regent of Brabant for his Arrest. Imprisonment of his Friend Harman. The British Merchant takes Reprisals. Councillor Rincke Overreached. Tyndale Safe in Marburg.. 102-106

CHAPTER XVI.

THE NEW ANTAGONIST. Character of Sir Thomas More. His Early Connection with Erasmus and the Cause of Church-Reform. Spirit and Sentiments of his Utopia.. 107-111

CHAPTER XVII.

THE REFORMER TRANSFORMED. Alarmed for the Ancient Faith. Distrusts the Reformation as Revolutionary. More's Inward Religious History. Characteristics of his Controversial Writings for the People. His Fundamental Principle—the Infallibility of the Church. The Church the Authoritative Interpreter of Scripture.......... 113-121

TABLE OF CONTENTS. ix

CHAPTER XVIII.

SHALL THE PEOPLE HAVE THE BIBLE? More Concedes the Principle of Vernacular Translation. Advises Postponement to a more Favorable Period. Grounds of his Opposition to Tyndale's Translation. Contrast with Tyndale's Views. Persecuting Spirit of the Anti-Bible Principle. Tyndale's Challenge Unanswered, ... 122-134

CHAPTER XIX.

SIR THOMAS MORE AS LORD CHANCELLOR. The Civil Power now takes the Lead in Persecution. Royal Manifesto against Heretics. Grand movement against Heretical Books. The Scripture in the Vernacular declared Injurious. Royal Proclamation against Tyndale's Writings. Tunstal's Bible-burning. How he Obtained the Bibles. More Avows himself a Persecutor. Defends the oath *ex-officio*. His Opinion of Juries. Advocates the Violation of Safe-conducts Granted to Heretics. More's Reverse. Cannot Violate his Conscience. His Bitterness toward Heretics Unchanged...... 135-144

CHAPTER XX.

THE ROYAL PATRONESS. Counter Influences. Anne Boleyn's connection with the Reformation. Richard Harman. Tyndale's Gift. Anne's Influence in favor of the Bible... 145-149

CHAPTER XXI.

THE MARTYRDOM OF TYNDALE. Efforts to Entrap Tyndale. The English Envoy, Stephen Vaughan. Interviews with Tyndale. Sir Thomas More, the Instigator of these Measures. Vaughan's Plea for Religious Liberty. The New Envoy; his Efforts to seize Tyndale. The Reformer's Life at Antwerp. The Bishops' Plot. Tyndale's Apprehension. Thomas Pointz. The Decree of Augsburg. Tyndale's Condemnation and Death... 150-162

CHAPTER XXII.

TRIUMPH OF THE PRINCIPLE. Truth not Dependent on its Champions. Review of the Progress of the Bible up to Tyndale's Death. Thomas Crumwell; grounds of his interest in the People's Bible. Matthew's Bible. Its Singular Introduction into England. Authorized by the King for use in Churches. Allowed to all Classes. Henry's zeal; stringent requisitions in Favor of the Bible; copies placed in Churches for the Use of the People. Its Welcome by the Commonalty. Prelates obliged to Countenance it. Romish Dogmas in Bad Repute. Henry's Alarm at the Influence of the Bible. Restrictions on its use. The Six Articles. Character of Edward's Reign. The Principle Triumphant. The Protestant Principle, as Applied to Bible-Translation. Permanence of Tyndale's New Testament.................................... 163-177

CHAPTER XXIII.

THREE LATER VERSIONS. Coverdale's Bible. Reasons for the Undertaking. Utility of Various Translations. Character of the Version. Hindrances. Coverdale, the Overseer of the Great Bible (Tyndale's). His nonconformity and sufferings. TAVERNER'S BIBLE. CRANMER'S BIBLE. Early Life of Cranmer. Veneration for the Scriptures. Influence as Primate in Favor of Vernacular Translation. Revision of Tyndale's Version. Preface. Counter-plot of the Bishops. The Anglican Church. Cranmer's Intolerance. Treatment of Gardiner; of Hooper; of Sectaries and Heretics. Essential Vice of a State Church. Vital Distinction between the Anglican and the Romish Church. Progress of the Bible under Edward VI..... 178-191

CHAPTER XXIV.

THE REIGN OF TERROR. Character of Queen Mary. Her Early Misfortunes. **First Steps on Her Accession.** Obscurantism Inaugurated. Protestant Exiles. Romanism Re-established. Unparalleled Cruelties. The Congregations. Evidences of the Progressive Influence of the Bible.. 192–199

CHAPTER XXV.

THE GENEVAN BIBLE. English Exiles. Spirit of the Age in Respect to Bible-Translation. Proposal of a New Version. Zeal of the Lay-exiles. John Bodleigh. Peculiar Advantages at Geneva. Calvin's Preface to the New Testament. Scholarship of the Genevan Bible. Division into Verses. Becomes the Family Bible of England. Causes of its Success. Its Agency in the Development of Puritanism. Its Influence not wholly Beneficial.. 200–206

CHAPTER XXVI.

THE BISHOPS' BIBLE. Preliminary View. Liberal Spirit of the Returned Exiles. Counter-policy of Elizabeth. Action of Her First Parliament. The Court of High Commission. The Star Chamber. The Reformed Clergy Succumb to the Queen; Establishment of Uniformity. Nonconformity the Nurse of Civil Freedom. List of Dangerous Innovations. Grounds of Puritan Dissent. Measures of Archbishop Parker. Trial of Sampson and Humphrey; Citation of the London Ministers; Oppressive Injunction Coverdale and Fox. Leading Traits of the Conflicting Parties.. 207–220

CHAPTER XXVII.

THE BISHOPS' BIBLE.—Continued. Archbishop Parker the Projector and Overseer of the Work. His Motives. Continued Influence of the Genevan Version. Anti-Episcopal Feature of the Church-Bible. Parker's Preface. Scholarship of the Bishops' Bible. Its Sectarian Character. Subsequent Restoration of Readings from the Vulgate.. 221–228.

CHAPTER XXVIII.

THE RHEMISH OR DOUAY BIBLE. Translators' Views of Vernacular Bibles. Policy of the Romish Church. Cardinal Ximenes. Reasons for this Translation. Its Characteristics. Influence of the Douay Bible...................... .... 229 232

CHAPTER XXIX.

THE COMMON VERSION. State of Parties at the Death of Elizabeth. Reactionary Influence of Persecution. Prospect of a Puritan Sovereign. James' non committal Policy. Summons the Hampton Court Conference. Triumph of the Prelatical Party. Royal Epistle. New Translation Proposed by the Puritans. Motives of James' Concurrence. State of Public Opinion. Hugh Broughton's efforts for a Revision of the Church-Bible. The Puritanic Influence of the Genevan Version. The King's plan.. 233–244

CHAPTER XXX.

THE COMMON VERSION—Continued. The King's liberal arrangements for Securing and Rewarding Competent Revisors. Rules of Translation prescribed by the King. Principles involved in these Rules. Their Influence on the Character of the Version. Its Scholarship. Contemporaneous Criticism. Obstacles to its Reception, within and without the Church. Measures for a New Translation. The Just Claims of the Common Version. Leading Characteristics and Influences of English Bible-Translation.. 245–258

CHAPTER XXXI.

DEMAND FOR A MORE THOROUGH REVISION. Early movements for Revision. Action of the Long Parliament. Robert Gell's Essay. Bishop Lowth's Translation of Isaiah. Gilbert Wakefield's Version. Dr. George Campbell's Work. Archbishop Newcome's Critical Versions and Historical View. The Advance in Learning. Modern Era of Textual Criticism. Discovery of Ancient MSS. Labors of Mill, Griesbach, Tischendorf, and others. What Modern Scholarship has Accomplished. Discoveries in Archæology, etc. American Bible Union. Versions of the Five Clergymen. The Anglo-American Revision. Rules for the Guidance of Translators. The New Testament Published 259–266

APPENDIX.

I. SPECIMENS OF THE EARLY ENGLISH VERSIONS......................... 268–281
II. THE IMMACULATE CONCEPTION.. 282
III. THE SOLDIER'S BIBLE.. 282–284

CHAPTER I.

THE BIBLE THE PEOPLE'S CHARTER. RELATION OF WICKLIFFE TO HIS AGE.

IT was a great day for England, when John Wickliffe first conceived the idea of giving to his countrymen the WHOLE BIBLE in the common tongue. The execution of that idea is the leading event of the fourteenth century. It would not be too much, perhaps, to call it the leading event in Anglo-Saxon history.

To Wickliffe belongs the peculiar honor of having rekindled, from the ashes of the past, the doctrine of the essential worth and equal rights of men. His claim that, in regard to the highest interest of humanity, all men are equal; namely, in the right of each to know for himself, and to obey the will of God; that here the king can claim nothing above the serf, the priest nothing above the layman; the absolute supremacy of the individual conscience in matters of religion; this involved the ultimate recognition of all inferior rights.

This idea, which breathes through the whole spirit of primitive Christianity, had been long lost to the world. It was indeed alien to the spirit of the world. The most enlightened nations of antiquity knew it not. The wisest and purest of pagan philosophers, who searched deepest into the character of God and the destiny of men, never attained to this glorious and ennobling truth. Even when they come so near it as to discern a special providence guiding the affairs of individuals, it is still only the great men, the patriots and philosophers, whom they deem worthy of such care. "Great men," say they, "enjoy the peculiar oversight and influence of the gods; inferior persons they disregard." The highest truths, those especially which respect the nature of God, must be veiled in mysteries and sealed by oaths from the vulgar rabble, who are to be held in subjection by scarecrows and mummeries, which the wise ones laugh at. Even their Elysium was peopled only by the spirits of sages and heroes. Thus were the masses of the human race abandoned, to live and die like the brutes which perish.

When Christ appeared, there dawned a new day for the poor and down-trodden. He made it the distinguishing glory of his ministry to preach the Gospel to the poor. The Christian communities, which owed their existence to the immediate effusion of his Spirit after his ascension, were strictly companies of brethren, with one Head and Lawgiver, their risen and glorified Lord. Men from the most diverse conditions of society here met on terms of perfect equality; united by a noble and endearing relationship, whose ties were stronger than those of caste, or blood, or nation. What a foundation was here laid for the protection and elevation of the weak and defenceless classes of society!

With the decline of the apostolic spirit in other respects, this idea also faded from the Christian consciousness. A splendid hierarchy, appointed to rule God's heritage, was an institution utterly at variance with the conception of the Church as a community of brethren. With the growth and consolidation of this mighty spiritual power, the lay element in the Church continually declined in importance, till at length the people became the mere tools and bond-slaves of the priesthood.

The aim of the Romish prelacy was no less than the entire monopoly of all ecclesiastical and all secular rule. The vital element of power, knowledge, it had gradually withdrawn wholly into its own hands. It has frequently been made the subject of praise to the papal clergy, that they alone were the depositaries of learning, at a period when all other classes of society were sunk in ignorance and barbarism. Should it not rather be accounted their shame? Who can doubt, that if the hosts of the Romish priesthood had encouraged the general diffusion of knowledge, the dark ages would have been ages of light? Could not the parish priest have awakened, in the humble portion of his flock, that spirit of improvement which is everywhere, even in the most debased heathen countries, the fruit of Protestant missions? Could not the monastery have become a fountain of intelligence to all the adjacent community? Boast not of the light thus hid within the cloister, for the use and delight of its few holy inmates, while thousands of their fellow-creatures groped, under their very walls, in the blindness of the deepest midnight!

But a general diffusion of knowledge, and the monopoly of power in the hands of a few, are ideas entirely incompatible with each other. The power of the hierarchy demanded the ignorance of the masses. The policy by which it reached its end was masterly. When the Holy Scriptures were taken from the common people, they lost the charter of their rights as men; in time, the very consciousness of their manhood. Thus the great body of all the nations of Christendom sunk from one degree of debasement to another, till they became the prey of every spoiler; till the people, the cultivators of the soil, the industrious artisans, the actual producers of the national wealth, had no power, no rights. They were the rabble, the vulgar herd, the mob, to be used or abused without limit or mercy, for the benefit of their masters.

Nothing could more significantly indicate their social position, than the scantiness of contemporaneous information in regard to it. History relates the doings of Popes and Councils, of Kings and Nobles. But it seems rarely to have occurred to the learned chronicler of the times, that the condition of the people constitutes any part of history. Now and then some social earthquake rends the veil, and we catch a glimpse which makes the heart ache ; for we see there, spite of ignorance, superstition, and all the vices of their degraded state, living human souls, burning and writhing under the keen sense of outrage and oppression ; capable, therefore, of sweet affections, of generous and noble deeds, of goodness and piety. At some new or more galling wrong, outraged humanity has overburst the bounds of discreet submission. The rude mass, for a moment, heaves convulsively ; agonizing cries for redress, fierce threats of vengeance, disturb the air ; and then it is crushed down again by the iron hand of power, to weep, and bleed, and curse in silence.

Such was the condition of a majority of the inhabitants of England in the fourteenth century. Where now was help and redemption to be looked for ? The barons had already, a hundred years before, wrested from the monarch the recognition of their own rights, the famous MAGNA CHARTA. But on their side was wealth and power. With his immense landed possessions, his castle-fortress, his thousands of retainers, each baron was a petty king. Combination among these powerful lords was equivalent to success. But the poor, unlettered, unarmed populace gained nothing by this triumph of their masters. Their only hope, though they knew it not, was in the restoration of what will ever be the only Magna Charta of the weak—THE HOLY SCRIPTURES.

Then arose the Man of the Age. Among the brilliant and imposing forms that crowd the arena of that stirring time—the magnificent Edward III., and his chivalrous son, the martial barons, the gorgeous array of ecclesiastical dignitaries—stands alone and preëminent the apostolic form of John Wickliffe, Rector of Lutterworth.

We call him the man of the age, who into a dead Past drops the seed of a living Future ; who infuses into the social mass leavening ideas, which, sooner or later, by their inherent quickening energy, work essential changes in the inner and outer life of society. This John Wickliffe did. The supreme and binding authority of the Holy

Scriptures as the guide of Christian faith and life ; the right of all men, without distinction, to the possession of the Scriptures ; these are the living thoughts which Wickliffe cast into the soil of the fourteenth century. They inspired the labors of his active years ; they culminated in that great gift to the Anglo-Saxon race, the Holy Bible in the common tongue.

To us, in this later age, these ideas may seem too obvious to merit the place here assigned them. Not so when first announced. Then, they startled like an earthquake. And well they might ; for they struck at the root of that vast system of spiritual fraud, by which merchandise had so long been made of the souls of men.

It may seem, also, that too wide and lasting an influence is ascribed to Wickliffe's version of the Scriptures. A work circulated only in manuscript, and at a period when so few of the laity acquired even the first rudiments of learning, cannot, it may be thought, have made a very deep impression on the national character. But when we take into account Wickliffe's preparatory labors, for more than thirty years, it will be seen that no book, before the invention of printing, ever enjoyed such advantages for becoming generally known. His conflicts with the Papacy at home and abroad, involving political and social questions of vital interest to the nation, his preaching and his writings in the despised vernacular, and the labors of his " poore priestes" (those pious itinerants whom he had sent forth over the length and breadth of England), had awakened a mental activity, a spirit of inquiry, before unknown : and in numerous instances an earnest religious life. The attention of all classes had thus been turned to the Holy Scriptures. Among high and low, there was that hunger for the word of God, whose power to conquer difficulties we, in this day of intellectual and spiritual fullness, can but imperfectly appreciate.

The details of the following chapters will enable us to estimate more perfectly the labors and influence of this great man, the Father of English Bible-Translation.

CHAPTER II.

THE PAPAL ARMY IN ENGLAND.

WE first find Wickliffe in active conflict with the errors and abuses of the age, about the middle of the fourteenth century. Let us briefly survey the religious circumstances of England at that time.

At the first glance, we observe three leading forces, which, from the date of the Conquest, had been contending for supremacy in England, viz. : the Crown, the Barons, and the Papacy. The monarchs strove continually to stretch the royal prerogative into absolutism ; the barons to maintain and increase their feudal rights at the expense of the crown ; while the Pope aimed at nothing less than to make England a mere appanage of Rome. In this great game, the Papacy had proved itself by far the shrewder hand. Siding now with the king, now with the nobles, it had improved every internal division in the kingdom, every appeal to itself as supreme arbiter, for securing new advantages and a firmer hold. It had now an ecclesiastical army in England, countless in numbers, so thoroughly organized and so bound by self-interest to its will, as to render the Pontiff of Rome the controlling power in the English realm. This army was arranged in three grand divisions. First,

THE SECULAR CLERGY.

This body, including bishops with their subordinate dignitaries, and the various ranks of parish priests under their control, were charged with the spiritual oversight and instruction of the community. To the office of the prelates were attached immense landed estates, princely revenues and high civil, as well as ecclesiastical powers ; the lower clergy, residing on livings among the people, were supported chiefly by tithes levied on their respective parishes.

The corruption of this body throughout Christendom had given rise, even so early as the fourth century, to monachism. Their frightful profligacy in the time of Wickliffe was mainly due to three causes, all of which originated directly from their connection with the See of Rome.

1st. Their exemption, in common with all other orders of the clergy, from civil jurisdiction. A clergyman, of whatever offence against the laws of the land he might be guilty, could not be tried by any civil court of the realm. All such offenders were claimed by the Church, whose tribunals, subject only to appeals to Rome, dealt so tenderly with her beloved sons, that the land groaned under the crimes of its religious teachers. It was publicly stated to Henry II. by his judges, that during the first ten years of his reign, more than a hundred murders had been committed by clergymen, besides thefts, robberies, and other crimes, for which they could not punish them.* Successive English sovereigns strove with all their might to wrest from them so dangerous an immunity. But this independence of secular government being essential to the Pontiff's absolute control over his vassals, their morals, and the welfare of the country, were of no weight in the balance. Thus, early in this century, an effort having been made by Edward II. to bring the clergy under some subjection to the laws, Pope Clement directed a bull to the Archbishop of Canterbury, complaining "that clerks invested with the sacerdotal character, and shining with the splendor of pontifical dignity, were tried by laymen, condemned, and hanged, when found guilty of robbery or murder, to the great provocation of the Supreme King, who hath forbidden the secular power to touch his anointed." He requires, therefore, that the grievance be redressed, on the penalty of excommunication to the offending monarch and his kingdom.

2d. Their enforced celibacy. The native English clergy long resisted the imposition of this part of the Romish policy; but were at length compelled to bow to the iron system, which sought to bind them to the central power by the obliteration of every tie of family and country. The name of Anselm, shine as it may in the history of systematic theology, should be forever infamous to the friend of humanity, for the pitiless rigor with which he enforced this measure. In 1102, he held an ecclesiastical council at London, where no fewer than ten canons were made for this single object. All priests, even the very lowest, were commanded to put away their wives immediately, not to suffer them to live on any lands belonging to the Church, never to see or speak to them, except in cases of the greatest necessity and in the presence of two or three witnesses. "Those unhallowed wretches who refused, were instantly to be deposed and excommunicated, and all their goods, as well as the goods and persons of their wives, as in the case of adulteresses, were to be forfeited to the bishop of the diocese."† Succeeding prelates followed the lead of Anselm, and episcopal and legantine councils urged the measure, till the long

---

* Henry's Hist., vol. vi. p. 59.   † Henry, vol. v. p. 307.

struggle ended in the final establishment of celibacy, and the secular clergy were sealed to utter and irreclaimable profligacy.

3d. The sale of clerical offices. The claim of the Papacy to the control of the English benefices, asserted centuries before, but long withstood by the secular power, was at this time fully established in practice. The Pope of Rome was now farmer-general of the English Church. He who could pay highest was sure of the place in market, whether it were a country parish, or the Primacy of England; and the buyer must in turn, farm it out in the way which would bring the largest percentage on the cost. The richest prizes fell to Italians, parasites of the Pope, some of whom, though unable to speak a word of English, and who had never set foot on English soil, held twenty, thirty, nay, some of them fifty and sixty valuable benefices in the English Church. On the revenues thus obtained they lived in magnificence at Rome, and laid up enormous fortunes, notwithstanding the large yearly sums paid out of them into the papal treasury. The resident clergy who held of such masters must, of necessity, be like their masters. An honest, merciful, conscientious priest stood no chance of promotion under such a system. Hence, as we learn from Wickliffe, men who were too poor or too conscientious to pay the required bribes, were virtually excluded from the sacred office, whatever might be their piety and talents. Thus the professed ministers of salvation were converted into an army of Romish bailiffs, whose great business it was to enrich their masters and themselves out of the plunder of the people, and whose anathemas were launched from the pulpit against those who withheld tithes, as worse than adulterers, murderers, and blasphemers.*

* " General excommunications," as they were called, which came into use about the middle of the thirteenth century, " were," says Henry, " at first denounced chiefly against such as injured the clergy by detaining their tithes, defrauding them of any of their dues, or stealing anything belonging to the Church. They were to be published by every parish priest in his holy vestments, with bells tolling and candles lighted, before the whole congregation, in the mother tongue, on Christmas, Easter, Pentecost, and All-Hallows-day. That these excommunications might make the greater impression on tender consciences or timorous natures, they contained the most horrible infernal curse that could be devised: ' Let them be accursed eating and drinking; walking and sitting; speaking and holding their peace; waking and sleeping; rowing and riding; laughing and weeping; in house and in field; on water and on land, in all places. Cursed be their head and their thoughts; their eyes and their ears; their tongues and their lips; their teeth and their throats; their shoulders and their breasts; their feet and their legs; their thighs and their inwards. Let them remain accursed from the bottom of the foot to the crown of the head, unless they bethink themselves

THE MONKS.

The Monks, known also as the Regular Clergy, and the Religious Orders, lived in small communities by themselves, having taken the vows of perpetual chastity, poverty and seclusion.

We have no right to doubt that monachism was, in its origin, a sincere attempt to revive the piety of the primitive Church; or that it did for a time check the progress of corruption, and by the cultivation of learning, shed an ameliorating influence into the darkness and barbarism of the times. But it had an inherent vice in its constitution—a want of adaptation to the nature of man. It was a morbid, not a healthy, offshoot of Christianity. For a while, the spirit infused into it by its austere founders maintained supremacy. But with the growth of worldly power and wealth, this artificial life gradually died out, and the latent evils of the system developed themselves in loathsome luxuriance. Ambition, avarice, and the grossest forms of vice took the place of ascetic virtue. An overwrought spiritualism reacted into a swinish sensualism. Monasteries became the lazar-houses of Christendom. Such do we find them in England in the fourteenth century.

The wealth of the English monks at this period almost passes belief. During the eleventh and twelfth centuries, the endowment of monasteries was a mania in Christendom. Lands, buildings, precious stones, gold and silver, were lavished upon them with unsparing prodigality. Rich men, disgusted with the world, or conscience-stricken for their sins, not unfrequently entered the cloister and made over to it their whole property. During the crusading epidemic, many mortgaged their estates to the religious houses for ready money, who never returned, or were too much impoverished to redeem them. In this way vast riches accrued to their establishments. They understood, to perfection, all the traditional machinery of the Church for extracting money from high and low. The exhibition of relics, the performance of miracles, and above all the sale of indulgences, and of masses for the dead,* formed an open sluice through which a steady golden stream poured into the monastic treasury.

---

and come to satisfaction. And just as this candle is deprived of its present light, so let them be deprived of their souls in hell.'"

* The will of Lord Hastings, made long before his death, and indicating, therefore, a common usage of the time, (and this so late as the reign of Richard III.) gives some idea of the wealth realized from the source last named. After other specifications, he bequeaths to ten conventual establishments, property of various kinds, amounting in value to not less than fifty thousand dollars of our time,

Of the extent and magnificence of their establishments, and their sumptuous style of living, we have a sufficient index in the fact, that they often entertained the sovereign with his whole retinue when on a royal progress, and that Parliaments and State Councils were sometimes held in their spacious halls. We must not fancy the English monastery as a gloomy, isolated residence, where emaciated anchorites wept and fasted, and prayed their lives away in holy conflict with sin and Satan. No more cheerful and imposing sight could meet the traveler's eye than the stately Abbey, with its church of costliest architecture, its abbatial palace, its cloisters, dormitories, stables, and numerous offices, its bowling-alleys, fish-ponds, walks and gardens, all enclosed by the embattled wall with its grand, sculptured gates; while outside clustered the humble dwellings of the dependent tenantry, and the broad Abbey lands with their beautiful variety of grain-fields, orchards, vineyards, pastures stocked with well-fed herds and forests swarming with game, stretching beyond the limit of the eye.* Within these little territories the Abbots reigned as sovereign princes, coined their own money, decided at their tribunals all civil and criminal as well as ecclesiastical cases, and exercised the power of life and death.

The Abbey kitchen, cellars, and refectory bore witness to the care bestowed on the well-being of its holy inmates. They did full justice to the bountiful provision thus made for their growth and edification. The Abbey cook was in great odor of sanctity among his brethren. The historian of Croyland Abbey gratefully records the pious disposition of Brother Lawrence Chateres, cook of that monastery, who, "animated by the love of God and zeal for religion," had given forty pounds for the recreation of the convent with the milk of almonds on fish-days. By the help of this nourishing little delicacy, "served," by direction of the authorities, "with the finest bread and best honey," the brethren might hope to sustain those trying Fridays when the bill of fare only numbered from ten to twenty dishes. Well might the old ballad sing:

on condition of a perpetual yearly service "for the sowles of me and my wife, myn ancestors, and all Christian sowles," to be performed "solemnly with note, Placebo and Dirige, and on the morrow mass of requiem with note." To ensure a handsome start on the ascent to bliss, he further directs that, as soon as notice of his death is received," a thousand priests shall say a thousand Placebo and Dirige with a thousand masses for my sowle, in oon day, if reasonably possible." Alas for the poor who must begin at the foot of the ladder, aided only by the stray provision "for all Christian sowles"! How hardly shall they that have *not* riches enter the kingdom of heaven!—so reads this Romish gospel.

* The lands of Fountains' Abbey extended thirty miles without interruption.

> "O the monks o' Melrose made gude kale
> On Friday, when they fasted!"

Truly, it was something of a chasm which separated these monks from those which Anthony, ten centuries before, gathered around him in the deserts of Upper Egypt.

Their profligacy was equal to their luxury. Those hells of vice, uncovered in the monasteries by the commissioners of Henry VHI. in the sixteenth century, were not the growth of that age alone. Such as they were then they were two centuries before, and the cry that went up from them to the ear of heaven was like that of Sodom and Gomorrah.

These establishments, with all their accumulations of property and influence, were subject to no jurisdiction within the realm. Formerly, they had been amenable to the bishops of the diocese in which they were located. But this did not suit the policy of the Romish Pontiff, whose power and gains were best promoted by keeping the different divisions of his army quite distinct from each other, united in nothing but their common opposition to the civil government and their common dependence on himself. He had, therefore, exempted the monasteries, one by one, from subjection to episcopal authority, and made them directly answerable to himself. The monks at first rejoiced at their escape from the bishops; but soon found that they had exchanged their tyranny for that of a harder master. Their interior affairs were now under the Pontiff's immediate cognizance and direction; and neither service nor money could be denied to a superior from whom so much was to be hoped and feared.

In some respects the Monks were, without doubt, public benefactors. The Abbey lands were the best cultivated in England; and furnished an example of good husbandry which, in the course of time, imparted a stimulus to the agricultural interests of the whole country. But it takes free and hopeful men to be benefited by such an example; and at this period, the burden of political and clerical oppression lay like an incubus on the capacities of the people. Father Oberlin, the good Swiss pastor, could change his rocky Alpine valley into a paradise as if by miracle. It was indeed by a miracle, such as Monk never wrought—the transformation of the dull boors of the valley into beings who had something to love, and something to live for.

The hospitality and charity of the Monks has also been celebrated. Let full justice be done them in these respects. Yet at a time when travelers were as scarce as diamonds, the tax on their hospitality could not have been very heavy; and the jovial brethren no doubt regarded the news brought by the visitor from distant parts, as payment in full for his three days' food and lodging. Their charity to the poor was precisely such as has always been witnessed in connection with the Romish Church ; a charity often liberal to prodigality, but founded on the degradation of the masses, and the foster-mother of mendicancy with its train of vices ; a charity which encourages the vicious, insolent and idle, but neglects the modest and virtuous ; which feeds men as it feeds brutes, in total disregard of their improvement as human beings.

The higher dignitaries in both these classes of the clergy, by virtue of their great temporalities held in feudal tenure from the crown, were barons of the realm, and sat in parliament under the title of "lords spiritual," taking precedence in rank of the lay nobles. In the summons to the barons of the realm for a parliament, archbishops, bishops, and abbots already headed the list. They too had their fortified castles and bands of armed retainers, by whose aid they alternately defied the monarch, chastised the insolence of the secular barons, silenced those "shoeless villains," the people, in their disgusting clamors for bread and freedom ; or, in foreign lands, pushed the triumphs of the cross or the quarrels of the Pope at the point of the sword.* By prescriptive right, derived from times when the superior intelligence of the clergy gave them some claim to the distinction, all the high offices of state, all places of trust and honor about the court, were in the hands of the clergy. In 1371, the offices of Lord Chancellor, Lord Treasurer, Keeper and Clerk of the Privy Seal, Master of the Rolls, Master in Chancery, Chancellor and Chamberlain of the Exchequer, and a multitude of inferior offices, were all held by churchmen.

These relations enabled them to resist successfully every attempt to bring them to a political level with the other subjects of the realm.

---

* Henry Spencer, Bishop of Norwich, was a notable specimen of the martial prelate. When, in 1381, the men of Norfolk rose against their masters with the demand, too far in advance of their age to be successful, for "life, liberty and the pursuit of happiness," this zealous man of God fell upon the insurgents at the head of his armed followers, slew many, and carried a great number prisoners to his episcopal castle. Then doffing his armor for the priestly vestments, he hastily administered to them "the last consolations of religion," and sent them straight to the gibbet and the block. Two years after, he was military leader in a crusade sent from England to support the claims of Urban VI. Being obliged to forego his plan of attacking the French territory, he turned in a tempest of fury upon the friendly Flemish town of Gravelines, and butchered its defenceless inhabitants, leaving not so much as one infant alive ; then marching on to Dunkirk he left four thousand Flemings dead on the field.

Parliament could not so much as lay a tax for the support of government upon this privileged class, nor try a member of it even for high treason. Grants to the crown, and all the questions relating to the clergy, were settled in their own Convocations or Ecclesiastical Parliaments, which rivaled the royal assembly in state and splendor. Their episcopal and abbatial courts claimed cognizance of all civil and criminal cases, in which "clerks," that is churchmen of whatever grade, were concerned, even though the other party were a layman; of tithes, marriages, wills; in short, of everything which it could be pretended was in the remotest way connected with religion.

As if this were not enough, they maintained in full force the ancient *right of sanctuary*, that is, of harboring fugitives from justice. Once within the sacred precincts of church or abbey, they could defy the law and all its ministers. This usage, first intended as a shield to the oppressed, had now become the refuge of the vilest criminals. Debtors, able but unwilling to pay, thieves, assassins, felons of every sort, looked out securely from under the wing of the Church and laughed at justice. Thus protected through the day, they often issued from the holy portals under cover of night to pursue their trade of burglary, arson, or highway robbery, not always unattended by such as had a more permanent residence in that secure abode.

Learning had, of course, declined under these influences. A clergy who were the mere mercenaries of a foreign power, their revenues entirely independent of the will of the people, and whose very relations as ministers of the Church furnished incentives to pride, worldliness, and the grossest sensual indulgence, could have no motives to seek a generous intellectual culture.

But to this was added another element. One of the essential conditions of their power was the ignorance and moral debasement of the laity. For this reason, not a word of the public services of religion was allowed to be given in a tongue which the people could understand. Why then should they weary themselves in those liberal and sacred studies for which their office made no demands, and which would be a hindrance rather than a help in the path of clerical promotion? In some departments of knowledge, they were indeed adepts. The clergy furnished the sharpest lawyers and the most adroit medical quacks, of any class in the kingdom. But of all that properly pertained to the spiritual office, they were profoundly ignorant. Multitudes of the parish priests could only mumble over the prescribed sentences in their Latin Missal and Breviary, like the formula of a charm or incantation, without the remotest idea of its meaning. The Monks, once foremost in learning, were in a still worse condition. Not only had they lost the ability to read those precious manuscripts, which lay entombed in the worm-eaten chests of the convent libraries, but the very tradition that such languages as the Hebrew and Greek, or such a book as the Bible, ever had existence. If a brother, animated by an extraordinary zeal for letters, was found copying in the *Scriptorium*, most likely it was at the sacrifice of some priceless relic of antiquity, which had been *sponged out* to furnish the Vandal scholar parchment for the absurd Saint-Legend he was ambitious of transcribing.

THE MENDICANT FRIARS.

It cannot be supposed that a clergy, such as has been described, much as they might be feared, could be generally popular. The common people, especially, were prepared by their neglect of the duties of their office, their insolence and merciless rapacity, to welcome that new fraternity which came into existence early in the thirteenth century, and which now formed the most efficient corps of the Papal army in England. The followers of St. Francis had made their first appearance in the kingdom about one hundred years before the time of Wickliffe. They were now to be found in every lane and by-way, conspicuous by the close-shaven crown, unshod feet, coarse brown frock and rope girdle, by which they sought a visible contrast with the luxurious Monks and Priests of the old regime.

The conception of the Mendicant Orders bears upon it the unmistakable stamp of genius. It sprang up in the bosom of an indurated system, with all the force and freshness of a new vitality. Amid the worldly luxury, pomp, and indolence, which for ages had characterized the Romish clergy, there was now to reappear the affecting spectacle of poverty, humility, and active benevolence exhibited by Christ and his apostles. Priest and Monk had alike despised, neglected and oppressed the people. The Friars were to devote themselves to the people. Instead of idly withdrawing into monasteries, under pretence of greater sanctity, they were to spread themselves, an army of evangelists, among all classes; to seek out the poor in the highways and hedges, and offer them the Gospel on such terms that the humblest might share its blessings. The parish priests had almost abandoned preaching as a part of their vocation, confining their services to Mass and the Confessional. The Friars seized on the neglected instrument of popular influence, and by it made themselves masters of the common mind. The priests had rendered themselves odious by the compulsory exaction of tithes. The Friars, in return for their self-denying and laborious services, asked only such alms as the charity and gratitude of the faithful should bestow freely ; while, by the vows of their order, they were forever precluded from holding property in the soil.

It is not strange that they should soon have won the entire confidence and affection of the people. Even the best and most enlightened men, who had long groaned over the vices and indolence of the clergy, hailed their advent as the dawn of a radical reformation in the Church. They found, too late, that it was but sending the locust to root out the canker-worm. What could be expected of a body of men, armed by the infallible Head of the Church with an unlimited commission to trade in sin, and responsible for their lives and teachings to neither secular nor spiritual power in the country where they lived ? The pitiable ignorance and credulity of the masses invited imposition. When the barefoot Friar, clad in his serge gown, and weary with toiling over the rough and miry ways, announced in some neglected hamlet that he had come to offer pardons, indulgences, the redemption of their deceased friends from purgatory, and all the precious wares of the Church, at a price within the reach of the poorest laborer or beggar, it seemed to the deluded people like good tidings of great joy. He could, moreover, by certain old rags, pigs' bones, rusty nails, bits of rotten wood, and similar rubbish which he carried about with him under the name of relics, ensure them good crops, and fruitful herds, and faithful wives, all for a very reasonable consideration. His animated harangues, seasoned with marvellous stories, all to the honor and glory of his Order, took their ears captive. Then he was so affable, so condescending ! He was not too proud to sit down under the thatched roof and eat with his rustic hosts, washing down the plain fare with draughts from the pewter tankard, while his merry joke and tale were the best sauce of the feast. He could expatiate, too, with great edification, on the pride and wealth and extortion of the Monks and Priests, who were lords of such vast domains, and rioted in palaces on the hard earnings of the poor. As for him, he demanded nothing. But should the worthy friends see fit to replenish his empty wallet with such needfuls as they could spare for the poor brethren, the saints would assuredly return the pious gift fourfold into their basket and store. As a farther security that such bounty should not lose its reward, he carefully entered on his tablets the name of every one who contributed fish or bacon, poultry, flax or wool, for the community, with the promise that he should be duly remembered in their prayers ; though, as Chaucer, who drew his pictures from the life, informs us, the list was wiped out without ceremony as soon as his back was turned on the simple donors.

> "When folk in church had gave him what they list,
> He went his way, no longer would he rest—
> With scrip and tipped staff, ytucked high,
> In every house he 'gan to pore and pry,
> And begged meal and cheese, or else corn.
> His fellow had a staff ytipped with horn,
> A pair of tables, all of ivory,
> A pointell ypolished fetously,
> And wrote always the names as he stood,
> Of all the folk that gave them any good,
> Askance that he would for them pray :
> 'Give us a bushel of wheat, malt, or rye,
> A God's Kichell,* or a triffle of cheese,
> Or else what ye list, I may not choose,
> A God's halfpenny or a mass penny,
> Or give us of your brawn, if ye have any ;
> A dagon of your blanket, deare dame—
> Our sister deare, lo, here I write your name—
> Bacon or beef, or such thing as ye find.'
> A sturdy harlot went hard aye behind,
> That was their host's man, and bare a sack
> And what men gave him, laid it on his back.
> And when he was out at the door, anon
> He plained away the names, every one
> That he before had written in his tables ;
> He served them with niffles and with fables."

This was the most successful blow which had ever yet been struck for the Papacy. Hitherto, the relation between the clergy and people had been such as to allow of a wholesome dislike of the priesthood. The faults of superiors and oppressors are easily discerned by those on whom they trample ; and it might be hoped that in time the common mind would rise above the delusions of a system whose temporal bondage was so hard to bear. But under this new form, it wormed itself into the very heart of the people. It fell in with all their prejudices, flattered their vanity, vulgarized religion to their tastes, cheapened it to their means, and bound them, heart and soul, to their spiritual teachers.

Their special commission, held directly from the Pope, rendering them amenable to himself alone, gave the Friars a great advantage. Under this all-powerful sanction they ranged from parish to parish, from diocese to diocese, regardless of all prescriptive rights, literally underselling all competitors, and crowding them out of market. Crime of every sort, secure of absolution in the most private manner and at the cheapest rate, increased with fearful rapidity. One bishop

---

* A little cake.

complained that he had in his diocese some two thousand malefactors, of whom not fourteen had received absolution from the parish priests, who yet defied punishment, and claimed their right to the sacraments on the pretence of having been absolved by the Friars.

But they were not confined to the poor. Like the Apostle, but with a very different object, they became all things to all men. They neglected no class of society ; they had an eye to every source of influence. Many of them took high rank as men of learning, according to the standard of the age. Even in the universities, whose prime object was the education of the secular clergy, the Friars gained an ascendency which threatened to convert them into nurseries of their own Order. They increased in numbers with unparalleled rapidity, and by their holy beggary and traffic soon became enormously rich. Being prohibited the ownership of land, they invested their funds in magnificent churches and convents, in gold and silver plate, rich vestments and precious stones ; while the interior of their sacred dwellings witnessed excesses not surpassed by those of the monastery.

> " Round many a convent's blazing fire
> Unhallowed threads of revelry are spun ;
> There Venus sits disguised like a Nun,—
> While Bacchus, clothed in semblance of a **Friar**,
> Pours out his choicest beverage.
> * * * * * *
> The arched roof, with resolute abuse
> Of its grave echoes, swells a choral cheer
> Whose votive burden is—OUR KINGDOM'S HERE !"

But they never forgot that drops make the ocean ; never became too proud to beg from the poor. Wickliffe found the land swarming with them, a gross and sordid pack, still maintaining by their low arts all their power over a debased and cheated people.

The song of jolly Friar Tuck, in Ivanhoe, gives a lively picture both of the popularity and the grossness of the Order, though the darkest shades are of course omitted in the portrait :

> " The Friar has walked out, and where'er he has gone,
> The land and its fatness is marked for his own ;
> He can roam where he lists, he can stop when he tires,
> For every man's house is the Barefooted Friar's.
>
> He's expected at noon, and no wight till he comes
> May profane the great chair and the porridge of plums;
> For the best of the fare, and the seat by the fire,
> Is the undenied right of the Barefooted Friar.

THE PAPAL ARMY IN ENGLAND.

> He's expected at night, and the pastry's made hot,
> They broach the brown ale, and they fill the black pot ;
> And the good wife would wish her good man in the mire,
> Ere he lacked a soft pillow, the Barefooted Friar.
>
> Long flourish the sandal, the cord, and the cope,
> The dread of the devil and trust of the Pope ;
> For to gather life's roses, unscathed by the briar,
> Is granted alone to the Barefooted Friar."

All the resources, whether of property or influence, thus accumulated by these immediate protégés and vassals of the Pope, was so much capital to the Papacy itself. How rich a vein of material wealth had been opened to his Holiness may be judged of by the fact, that in 1299 the Franciscans were able to offer him fifty thousand ducats in gold for permission to own land—a petition which he refused, however, after quietly pocketing the money. He would allow them to form no ties with the country in which they lived, which might interfere with unconditional subserviency to himself. The increase of his direct influence on all the internal affairs of the kingdom, and over the mind of the nation through their means, was still more important. The secular clergy, as we have seen, had become his creatures ; the monasteries, by successive strokes of policy, had been withdrawn from episcopal jurisdiction, and made immediately accountable to himself. But as large land proprietors, it was possible for exigencies to arise when these orders of the clergy might prefer the interests of the country to his own. The system was made complete by the addition of a corps, exceeding them both in number, who had no dependence but his favor, no ties which could interfere with unconditional subserviency to himself ; and whose revenues must be the fruit of incessant activity in imbuing the popular mind with attachment to the Papacy.

The stimulus imparted by their success to the whole body of the clergy was, moreover, highly satisfactory. All eyes were turned with increasing eagerness toward the great dispenser of patronage. Rome became more and more the central point of interest, the grand mart of office, the final court of appeal to all parties, and the papal treasury overflowed with the bribes of rival suitors. Such being the result, the quarrels among his vassals over the division of the spoils at home did not disturb the serenity of the Head of the Church.

Nor even yet had he exhausted his devices for governing and draining England. His special officers, located at all important points in the kingdom, held the double office of papal spies and tax-gatherers ; while his legates and nuncios, armed with plenipotentiary powers, held their courts over the heads of both kings and bishops, and decided momentous ecclesiastical questions, vitally affecting the interests of the State, by the simple authority of the successor of St. Peter.

By these various methods, the Pontiff drew yearly from England five times the amount of the whole royal revenue ;* and this was the smallest injury sustained by the enslaved country from the unnatural connection.

* So stated in the petition of the " Good Parliament," 1376. *Vaughan.*

CHAPTER III.

COUNTER-INFLUENCES; THEIR INEFFICIENCY.

IF now we inquire for any counter-influences at work in England in the fourteenth century, we shall find, at several points, a decided hostility to the encroachments of the Papacy. Edward III. was too spirited and ambitious a monarch to look on patiently, while so large and influential a body of his nominal subjects disowned his authority, and the Pope of Rome exercised more power in his realm, and drew from it far more money than himself. But his quarrel was not with the religion of the Papacy. He was jealous, as well he might be, of the political power and the wealth of the clergy. It chafed him sorely to see papal legates and provisors running through his kingdom, draining it of money, interfering with his own government, and acting as spies to his enemies.* But there is little indication of any enlightened, generous concern for the moral condition of his people, or even for their temporal welfare. He was always ready to grind them down to the last point of endurance, sparing neither their property nor their blood, in furtherance of his own ambitious and selfish projects. His efforts had for their object no real reformation within the Church, nor would a living, spiritual Christianity have been welcomed by him more cordially than by the Pope himself. His resistance was, moreover, too fitful and capricious to effect a permanent change even in the outward relations of England to the Papacy, being ever the first man to violate his own laws when tempted by some present advantage. Thus the odious system of papal provisions,† against which such spirited laws were enacted by his authority, remained nevertheless in full practical force, because the king himself would still appeal to the Pope whenever he could not otherwise secure the appointment of his favorite candidate.

The same was true of the Secular Barons; though, having less to gain from the Papacy, these were, in general, more consistent in their

---

* During his reign the Papal court was fixed at Avignon, in France, and seven successive Pontiffs were Frenchmen.

† Reversionary grants by the Pope to benefices not yet vacant, without reference to the rights of the native legal patrons. The sale of these provisionary grants was a source of large income to the Papal Court.

opposition to its encroachments. There is frequently something very imposing in the tone and bearing with which these martial nobles meet the pretensions both of the sovereign pontiff, and of their own despotic monarchs. Seen through the magnifying haze of time, they rise before us as the representatives, in an age of lawless tyranny, of the great principles of human freedom. A closer view greatly diminishes our admiration. No king was ever more ready than they to defer to the Pope as the vicegerent of God, when it suited their own purposes. No king ever ruled his subjects with a more iron hand, than did these liberty-loving nobles their dependents and vassals. Magna Charta itself was the fruit of a coalition, formed under the sanction of Innocent III., between the nobles and the clergy, for the twofold purpose of protecting themselves against the despotism of King John, and of chastising his attempt to throw off the Papal yoke.* Small would have been the gain to liberty, had not other influences come in to extend its provisions somewhat beyond the interests of these "upper classes." Happily, John was not yet brought so low, but that he could claim the insertion of certain articles as distasteful to the Barons as theirs were to him. Happily, they were not so strong, but that the rich though despised tradesmen of London could demand certain provisions for their class as the price of their aid. Even then, it brought to the great body of the people no hope of freedom or improvement. The laboring classes, i.e., the majority of the English people, are but twice mentioned in this famous instrument, and then it is, as Henry remarks, "for the benefit of their masters."† Even then Magna Charta, interpreted by the circumstances of the times, was a guarantee for the perpetual domination of the Romish clergy in England. In the nobles of the fourteenth century, we discover no essential advancement in moral character or breadth of views, beyond those of a hundred years before. Their remonstrances against Papal oppression take no higher or bolder tone, nor would they have made any greater figure in the history of English freedom, had they not been immediately followed by the labors of a genuine reformer.

If we turn to the Universities, the sacred schools of those times, in the hope of finding some dawning of a better day, the same disap-

* See an admirable analysis of the Great Charter in Henry's History, vol. vi. p. 65.

† The 4th article provides against "the waste of *men and goods*" on the estates of minors to the detriment of the heir when he shall come of age ; the 6th secures to a "villain" his implements of husbandry against seizure as payment of fines —a practice very inconvenient to those who lived by his labor.

pointment meets us here. True, they were marked by a strong feeling of nationality, and an active jealousy of that papal influence which was exerted so injuriously to the interests of the native clergy. Their members hated the Friars as the emissaries of the Pope, and their own chief rivals. But for liberal ideas, sound learning, or devoted piety, the academic halls of this period are searched in vain. It would indeed be strange, if the nurseries of the clergy should have surpassed in these respects the demands of the Church. The speediest road, both to wealth and clerical preferment, was then found in the practice of the civil, and especially the canon law ;* and accordingly, many young candidates for the ministry spent their entire term of University study in fitting themselves to become, in a sense not altogether evangelical, "fishers of men." The profession of medicine being also very lucrative, and almost monopolized by churchmen, large numbers of the young clergy became deeply skilled in the mystery of healing as then understood—for instance, curing small-pox without scars, by wrapping the patient in "red scarlet cloth"; or stopping epileptic fits, by saying Mass over the patient and causing his parents to fast. For those of a speculative turn, there was the scholastic philosophy, with its abstruse discussions of entities and non-entities, substances and accidents, substantial forms and occult qualities. The Universities could boast their *subtle, sublime, profound, angelic, and seraphic* doctors of theology, who could discuss through endless folios the questions : "Does the glorified body of Christ stand or sit in Heaven ? Is the body of Christ, which is eaten in the sacrament, dressed or undressed ? Were the clothes in which Christ appeared to his disciples after his resurrection, real or only apparent ? Was Christ the same between his death and resurrection, as before his death and after his resurrection ?" Subjects even more frivolous and absurd engaged the attention of the sharpest intellects of the times. Thus, the question : "Whether a hog, taken to market with a rope tied round its neck which is held at the other end by a man, is carried by the rope or by the man ?" was gravely argued by the logicians, and declared insoluble, the reasons on both sides being perfectly balanced. But their disquisitions were not all so innocent. The obscene and blasphemous character of some of their speculations proves too clearly, that the foulest moral impurity is quite compatible with childish folly.

Such had been the general character of these "theological semina-

---

* The system of Papal jurisprudence drawn from the decisions of Popes and Councils.

ries," ever since the Bible had been cast aside in the spiritual instruction of the people. The decline of all liberal and comprehensive culture had kept pace with the decline of the study of the Holy Scriptures. The great Roger Bacon declared, in the preceding century, that among the scholars of his time, there were but three or four who had any knowledge of Greek or Hebrew. There was, however, then to be found occasionally in the Universities a *Bible doctor* (so-called in contempt of the antiquated and unprofitable direction of his studies), though it was difficult for a teacher so far behind the age to obtain the use of a lecture-room, or the command of a regular hour, or to persuade a handful of young men to listen to his instructions. But it was now long, since one of these fossil-specimens of the past had appeared among scholars. Even a copy of the Latin Vulgate was scarcely to be found at the Universities. In 1353, three or four young Irish priests came over to England to study divinity; but were obliged to return home "because not a copy of the Bible was to be found at Oxford." The morals of these schools, frequented yearly by many thousands of English youths, were not a whit superior to their learning. Frequent allusions occur, in the records of the time, to the fearful prevalence of the most debasing vices, among both teachers and students.

In glancing along the course of English history, from the Conquest to the middle of the fourteenth century, one fact strikes the attentive reader with peculiar force. During that whole period, we do not perceive the development, in the life of society, of a single radically new idea. Several truly great men had sat on the English throne; the English Church had given birth to scholars, theologians, and statesmen of no mean rank. Nor was it destitute of yet nobler names, shining with the lustre of personal piety and zeal for religion, amid the thick moral darkness. But they all drift with the powerful current, which set in with William I. and his Anglo-Norman church. Their attempts to remedy existing evils are superficial and fragmentary, utterly ineffectual to arrest the mighty onward tide of priestly domination and corruption. Much is vaguely asserted respecting the progress of civil liberty during this period. The courts of law attained, it is said, a theoretical perfection in the time of Edward III. which has scarcely been surpassed. But if we look at the actual condition of the people in the fourteenth century, we see little that deserves the name of progress. Violence and bribery everywhere overawed or corrupted justice. "There was not," we are told, "so much as one of the king's ministers and judges who did not receive bribes, and very few who did not extort them."* Perjury was a vice so universal, that the words of scripture might have found an almost literal application to the English people, from the king to the serf—"All men are liars." Life and property were kept in perpetual insecurity, by the numerous and ferocious bands of robbers which roamed over the country, under the protection of powerful barons, who sheltered them in their castles, and shared with them their booty. Englishmen and Englishwomen were still sold like cattle at the great fairs. Grossness of manners characterized all ranks, and exhibited itself in the most revolting forms of licentiousness among the leading classes. "Like priest, like people," was never more fully verified than in this portion of English history.†

The recognition of the right of burgher representation, in the establishment of the House of Commons, has been appealed to, as the beginning of the England that now is. But what was this, in reality, but a mere extension of the old idea that "might makes right," the recognition of a new potency, in addition to that of the stronger arm, viz., the potency of PROPERTY? A great and glorious advance it indeed was, over the reign of brute force! But it did not spring from the root of true liberty. The idea of MAN, with his inborn inalienable rights—now the characteristic idea of the Anglo-Saxon race—had never then dawned on the English mind. When, in 1381, a hundred thousand English laborers came up to London, with the humble request that they might become men, they met in no class with less sympathy than among the free commoners.—When Richard II. announced to parliament, at its next session, that he had revoked the charters of freedom with which he had deluded his poor subjects, the House of Commons expressed its cordial approbation of the cruel fraud, and declared that they would never give their assent to the abolition of serfdom, "though it were to save themselves from all perishing in a day." It was the House of Commons too, who petitioned at a still later period, that serfs might not be permitted to send their children to school—" and this for the honor and glory of all the freemen of the realm!" And the majority of Englishmen, be it remembered, were then serfs, or in a state of civil disability scarcely above that of absolute slaves of the soil.

* Henry, vol. viii., 384.
† This picture may seem too dark for truth; but the reader will find it fully borne out by the histories of the time. See, particularly, Henry's History, vols. v., vi., viii., and x. The showy virtues of chivalry, the portraiture of which, by novelists and poets, has made this period so dear to the fancy, are by no means inconsistent with the vices here depicted.

Allowing, then, the utmost that can reasonably be claimed for the progress of freedom, there was as yet no sign presaging England's glorious future ; nothing to which we can look back and say : Here was the earnest of her great destiny ! . In the nature of the case, there could not be. Of civil liberty in its true and noblest sense— that which embraces in its protecting arms the whole people, and allows full scope to the development of the individual as a moral and social being—of this the world has seen no example, where a State religion holds the consciences of men in blind subjection to the priesthood, and denies the Bible to the common people.

CHAPTER IV.

THE BIBLE-APOSTLE.

Such was the gloomy and almost hopeless scene presented by England, when there appeared on the stage a teacher of religion, whose whole life and opinions had their source in the teachings of the Bible.

How Wickliffe had come into possession of the Bible, at a time when it was an unknown book to the great body of the clergy as well as laity, and was wholly ignored in "the course of theological study" at Oxford, history does not inform us. His first discovery of the treasure might reveal a religious experience no less affecting, a providential guidance no less striking, than in the case of Luther. Perchance the earnest student, urged by an inward want which found little satisfaction in the dry and frivolous discussions of the lecture-room, was rummaging those old chests in the crypt of St. Mary's,[*] when the beautifully written and illuminated BIBLIA SACRA caught his eye. With the first glance at the strange words of life and truth, how would the monkish legends and the musty disquisitions of the sententiaries be forgotten ; and hour after hour glide away unnoted amid those dim old vaults, while the enchained reader bent, torch in hand, over the page of inspiration ! This indeed is but fancy. But it is no mere fancy that Wickliffe found a Bible ; and that he pored over it so long and earnestly, and with such fervent prayer to God, that it became to him the source of a new spiritual existence, and the guiding star of his destiny.

Those beautiful words uttered in one of his sermons at Lutterworth, might fitly serve as the motto of his whole subsequent career : " Oh Christ ! thy law is hidden in the sepulchre ; when wilt thou send thy angel to remove the stone, and show thy truth unto thy flock !"

It is not within the scope of this sketch, to portray in detail Wickliffe's successive labors as a Reformer. These will only be briefly mentioned, as indicating the path by which he was conducted to his last and crowning work ; that work, without which all his previous efforts would have proved like inscriptions on the sand—THE RESTORATION OF THE BIBLE TO THE COMMON PEOPLE.

---

[*] At this time the library of Oxford was kept in a few chests under St. Mary's Church.

OPPOSES THE MENDICANTS.

His first conflict was with the Friars, about the year 1360 ; who. having succeeded by the help of the Pope in thrusting themselves into important offices in the University, were exerting a most baneful influence on its students, inducing great numbers of them to take the vows of their Order. He had also had ample opportunities of observing their abominable lives, and the arts by which they practised on the credulity of the lower classes. No doubt they had many times before provoked his stern rebuke. But the long-felt indignation now kindles into the Reformer's zeal. He feels in himself the summons to come forth and do battle for the truth.

It is interesting to note the standpoint of Wickliffe in this, the initiative step of his career as a reformer. We have indeed nothing from his pen which can be assigned to the exact date of this controversy ; but his writings on the same subject, which have been preserved, sufficiently indicate his position. Grostete, Armichanus, and other great and good men of the English Church, had severely censured the immoralities of the Friars. Wickliffe depicts their atrocious practices with a still more fearless hand.—But he goes much farther than this. He strikes at the root of the evil. In his view, their system, from the foundation upward, is a lie ; their very existence, high treason to Him who has revealed in the Scriptures the most perfect law of faith and life. The Friars had put forth the bold claim, that their religion took precedence, in dignity and merit, of the religion of Christ. According to them, there had been three dispensations ; the first, contained in the Old Testament, proceeding from the Father ; the second, that of the New, proceeding from the Son ; and finally, " the everlasting gospel," proclaimed by the angel in the Apocalypse (who was no other than St. Francis, the founder of their Order), which was, of course, to supersede every other.

The reasoning by which Wickliffe meets this assumption shows how firmly he had anchored himself on the revealed word. The religion of Christ, he argues, must be most perfect, inasmuch as its founder is most perfect. To charge him with not teaching the best religion, is to charge him with want, either of the highest wisdom or the highest love. It is also most perfect in its rule of life, being purely divine, without mixture of human error. It is most perfect in the example which it furnishes, since Christ and his apostles " be chief knights thereof." It is most perfect in the freedom of its service, as it " standeth in all love and freedom of heart, bidding nothing but what is reasonable and profitable, and Christ himself declares :

' My yoke is easy and my burden is light.' " But the Friars pretended that their works of merit far exceeded the demands of Christ. "Can any man," asks Wickliffe, "more than fulfill that first and great command, to love God with all the heart, all the mind and all the strength, and his neighbor as himself?" Then cannot any man exceed the demands of Christ's religion. He, therefore, who pretends to amend Christ's religion in fact denies it, and is an apostate from the faith. But the point of most significance, for its reference to his future career, is found in his contrast between the Friar's religion and that of Christ, in respect to the sanction under which they respectively claim belief. "Christ's religion," he says, "is most true, because confirmed of God and not of sinful men ; and because by it the Pope and every other man must be confirmed, or else he shall be damned ; while the new Orders, being confirmed only by the Pope, may turn out to have been confirmed by a devil."

Thus, in this first attack on the errors of the age, Wickliffe struck the key-note of all his future labors.

SUMMONED TO PARLIAMENT.

So bold an assault on this powerful body could not fail to provoke their mortal enmity. But it also fixed on him the favorable attention of those who were jealous of the political power of the Pope and clergy. In 1365 he was present at the parliament to which Edward III. submitted the demand of Urban V. for the renewal of King John's tribute ; * and, from the circumstances, there can be no doubt that he had been invited to London to aid the resisting party by his counsels. That he was one of its acknowledged leaders, is seen in the fact, that soon after Parliament's indignant repudiation of the papal claim, he was challenged by name, in a violent anonymous tract on the subject ; and that he responded to the call, as one whose right and duty it was to speak in the case. From his reply, we learn the considerations which had influenced the decision of Parliament ; and from their general correspondence to his own views, expressed elsewhere, it can hardly be doubted that they were, for the most part, first borrowed from his own mind. Here, also, we observe the same reference to the teachings and authority of the Scriptures. The Pope, he argues, cannot claim, as the representative of Christ, anything beyond what Christ claimed for himself. But Christ's office was

---

* Urban required, not only the thousand marks yearly, as promised by John, but the payment of all arrearages, principal and interest, for the previous thirty years ; in default of which, the king was cited to appear before the pontiff, and answer for his conduct as to his feudal lord.

purely spiritual; he refused all secular dominion; nay, so far was he from exercising temporal lordship, that he subsisted on charity, and had not where to lay his head. He concludes, therefore, that England owes no civil allegiance to the Pope, and may properly repel his aggressions upon her temporal sovereignty. On the same general ground he maintained also, that the secular possessions of the clergy are held on the same tenure with that of the other subjects of the realm, and are liable to control, or if abused, to forfeiture by the secular powers which first bestowed them; and in all civil cases, the persons of ecclesiastics should, as in the case of the laity, be subject to the civil courts. In this, he struck at that grand prerogative of the clergy, for which Lanfranc, Anselm, Becket, and a long line of popish heroes had waged deadly warfare with their sovereigns.

In 1371, we find his name connected with a parliamentary movement for an additional reform in respect to the clergy, viz.: their exclusion from secular offices. Their monopoly of all places of honor and profit in the State, joined to their ecclesiastical power, had given them a most dangerous preponderance in the government; and yet, strange to say, Wickliffe seems to have been the first who questioned their perfect right to it. He indeed opposed this admixture of the spiritual and temporal on purely religious grounds. Such a coalition was, in his view, incompatible with the New Testament conception of the sanctity and high responsibility of the sacred office. "He that warreth, entangleth not himself with this life," was his favorite axiom on that subject. He complains that "prelates and great religious possessioners, are so occupied in heart about worldly lordships and pleas of business, that no habit of devotion, of praying, of thoughtfulness on heavenly things, on the sins of their own hearts or those of other men, may be preserved; neither are they found studying and preaching the Gospel, nor visiting and comforting of poor men." These are the reasons for which he concludes, that "neither prelates nor doctors, priests nor deacons, should hold secular offices." But the doctrine thus first suggested from a religious point of view, was eagerly caught up by the laity for its political application, and was made the subject of one of the most important memorials submitted to Parliament during this eventful reign.

PROFESSOR AT OXFORD.

The following year he received his degree of Doctor in Theology, and commenced a course of divinity lectures at Oxford. The strong impression immediately created in the University is not surprising. By the testimony of Knyghton, a man well qualified to judge in such matters, and withal a bitter opponent of Wickliffe's doctrines, he was "as a theologian, the most eminent of his time ; in philosophy, second to none ; as a schoolman, incomparable." And again : "No man excelled him in the strength and number of his arguments ; and he excelled all men in the irresistible power of his eloquence." Walden, another of his inveterate enemies, confessed in a letter to Pope Martin V., that he had often stood amazed beyond measure at the excellence of his learning, the boldness of his assertions, the exactness of his authorities, and the strength of his arguments." But his mastery of scholastic lore was not the secret of his power. It was the living influence of a spirit, which, having drunk deeply at the fountain of Eternal Truth, yearned to lead others thither also. Casting aside the absurd speculations and sophistries which they had been wont to hear from the Professor's chair, he reasoned with his pupils on such themes as the being, nature, and attributes of God ; the immortality of the soul, its faculties and affections ; the essential nature of sin and of holiness. Nor did he content himself with abstract truth. In the lecture-room he was still the practical reformer. Thus from the consideration of the nature of sin, he proceeds to the conclusion, that the distinction between mortal and venial sin, "about which the prelates babble so much," is a mere priestly contrivance for making gain ; that the doctrine of priestly absolution and indulgence is an impious invasion of the prerogatives of God, who is alone able to forgive sin. The great churchmen who were so free with their dispensations, were, in his bold language, " blasphemers of the wisdom of God, pretending in their avarice and folly, to understand what they know not ; sensual simonists, who chatter on the subject of grace as if it were something to be bought and sold like an ox or an ass." Saint-worship had at this time almost supplanted the worship of God, and had substituted, for the one Mediator, a countless army of intercessors in the Saints of the Romish Calendar.* The following extract shows

* A striking exemplification of this tendency is seen in the case of Thomas Becket, that bold, bad man, who had been canonized by the Romish Church as a martyr, and thereafter reigned for centuries as the chief English Saint. His shrine in Canterbury Cathedral was enriched with offerings of astonishing magnificence and value, and every fifty years a jubilee in his honor drew together an innumerable company of pilgrims. At the fifth jubilee, in 1420, the concourse is said to have amounted to 100,000 persons. "The devotion towards him had quite effaced in that place the adoration of the Deity : nay, even that of the Virgin. At God's altar, for instance, there were offered in one year three pounds, two shillings and sixpence ; at the Virgin's, sixty-three pounds, five shillings and sixpence ; at St. Thomas', eight hundred and thirty-two pounds, twelve shillings and threepence. But the next year the disproportion was still

how Wickliffe, even thus early in his public career, had risen above the superstitions of his age : " Whoever entreats a saint, should direct his prayer to Christ as God, not to the special Saint, but to Christ. Nor doth the celebration or festival of a saint avail anything, except in so far as it may tend to magnify Christ, inciting us to honor him, and increasing our love to him. If there be any celebration in honor of the saints, which is not kept within these limits, it is to be ascribed, without doubt, to cupidity, or some other evil motive. Hence, not a few think it would be well for the Church, if all festivals of that nature were abolished, and those only retained which had respect immediately to Christ. For then, they say, the memory of Christ would be kept more freshly in the mind, and the devotions of the common people would not be unduly distributed among the members of Christ. . . . . For the Scriptures assure us that Christ is the Mediator between God and man." Freedom of religious opinion, and the right of private judgment, are distinctly vindicated in these lectures. " Christ," says he, " wished his law to be observed willingly, freely, that in such obedience men might find happiness. Hence *he appointed no civil punishment to be inflicted on transgressors of his commandments*, but left them to a punishment more severe, that would come after the day of judgment." Human tradition he set aside as of no account in matters of religion. " If there be any truth," he says, " it is in the Scripture ; and there is no truth to be found in the schools, that may not be found in more excellence in the Bible."

Even those who were attached to the person and opinions of Wickliffe were alarmed at his boldness. They begged him to remember, when thus exposing himself to the wrath of the great " satraps of the Church," that his appeal to the Scriptures for the truth of his views would be of little avail, in a time when the Scriptures themselves were of no authority. " Without doubt," he replied, " what you say is true. The chief cause of the existing state of things is our want of faith in the Holy Scriptures. We do not sincerely believe in the Lord Jesus Christ, or we should abide by the authority of his word, especially of the Evangelists, as of infinitely greater weight than every other. It is the will of the Holy Spirit, that the books of the Old and New Law should be read and studied, as the one sufficient source of instruction ; and that men should not be taken up with other books, which, true as they may be, and even containing scripture truth, are

greater : there was not a penny offered at God's altar ; the Virgin's gained only four pounds, one shilling and eightpence ; but St. Thomas had got for his share nine hundred and fifty-four pounds, six shillings and threepence." Hume's England, quoted from ed. 1796, in *Eng. Reformers*, vol. i., p. 52.

not to be confided in without caution and limitation. Hence Augustine often enjoins it on his readers, not to place any faith in his word or writings, except so far as they have their foundation in Scripture. Of course we should judge thus of the writings of other holy doctors ; much more of the writings of the Roman Church and her doctors, in these later times. If we follow this rule, the Scriptures will be held in becoming reverence. The papal bulls will be superseded, as they ought to be. The veneration of men for the laws of the papacy, as well as for the opinions of our modern doctors, which, since the loosing of Satan, they have been so free to promulgate, will be restrained within due limits. What concern have the faithful with writings of this sort, except as they are honestly deduced from the fountain of Scripture ? By such a course, we can not only reduce the mandates of popes and prelates to their proper place, but the errors of these new religions might be corrected, and the worship of Christ well purified and exalted."

Such were the doctrines—and what other than these were " the glorious doctrines of the Reformation" ?—which Wickliffe, two centuries before Luther, taught openly in the halls of Oxford. Here he strove to raise up, from the flower of the rising clergy, a corps of devoted spirits who should be prepared, in the conflict which he foresaw as inevitable, to do battle for the truth. The high moral enthusiasm which inspired words like the following, must have been like an enkindling flame to their young hearts : " All Christians," thus he addresses them, " should be the soldiers of Christ. But it is plain that many are chargeable with great neglect of this duty ; being prevented by fear of the loss of temporal goods and worldly friendships, and apprehensive about life and fortune, from faithfully setting forth the cause of God, from standing manfully in its defence, and if need be, from suffering death in its behalf. From the like source comes that subterfuge of Satan, argued by some of our modern hypocrites, that it cannot be a duty now, as in the primitive Church, to suffer martyrdom, since in our time the great majority of men being believers, there are none to persecute Christ to the death in his members. But this is, without doubt, a device of Satan to shield sin. For the believer, in maintaining the law of Christ, should be prepared, as his soldier, to endure all things at the hands of the satraps of this world ; declaring boldly to Pope and Cardinals, to Bishops and Prelates, how unjustly, according to the teaching of the Gospel, they serve God in their offices, subjecting those committed to their care to great injury and peril, such as must bring on them speedy destruction. All this applies, indeed, to temporal lords, but not in so great a degree as to the clergy ; for as the abomination of desolation begins with a perverted clergy, so the consolation begins with a converted clergy. Hence we Christians need not visit pagans to convert them, by enduring martyrdom in their behalf ; we have only to declare with constancy the word of God before Cæsarean Prelates, and *straightway the flower of martyrdom will be ready to our hand!*"

Wickliffe did not think it sufficient to sow the good seed among the clergy alone. While engaged in his duties as Professor, he preached on the Sabbath to promiscuous auditories, in the mother tongue, the same great truths which he taught to his students during the week ; and in the intervals of academic duty, he gave himself to the work which he loved above all others—that of Christian preacher and pastor, in the rectory of Fyllingham. More than three hundred of his pastoral sermons, more or less complete, remain as witnesses of his zeal and fidelity as a religious teacher of the common people, and not less of the evangelical purity of his doctrines.

Thus passed two laborious, but peaceful, years of Wickliffe's life. In favor with the court, for the stand which he had taken against the Pope, and with the university, for his zeal against the Friars ; honored for his genius, his learning, and his virtuous life, he was at this time regarded as the chief light and ornament of Oxford. Thus, in the providence of God, time was afforded for his principles to become known and to take root in many minds. We now turn a new leaf in his history.

CHAPTER V.

THE POPE AND BISHOPS IN THE FIELD.

In 1372, a royal commission had been sent to Avignon, to remonstrate with the Pope against the sale of English benefices, which was still prosecuted on the largest scale. When the embassy returned without having accomplished anything, and Parliament resolved to repeat the attempt more vigorously, Wickliffe was summoned by royal authority from Oxford, to join the new commission. That he should have been selected for such a purpose, is a striking proof of the weight attached to his opinions and personal character. But this second effort resulted no better than the first. After two years spent in wearisome and fruitless negotiations, Wickliffe returned to England, thoroughly disgusted with the duplicity and corruption of the Papal court,* and fully convinced that no reformation was to be hoped for from this quarter; that if England wished to save her civil and religious liberties from swift and utter destruction, she must look for rescue elsewhere than to the Head of the Church. His bold exposures and appeals were, without doubt, the moving spring of those energetic measures of reform in the House of Commons, which followed his return from Bruges.

But they had other results. A few months after his return (early in February, 1377), the ecclesiastical parliament held its session in London; and one of its first matters of business was to receive accusa-

---

* Wickliffe and his associates were not allowed to proceed to Avignon, but were met by the papal commissioners at Bruges. In the following letter of Petrarch, written from Avignon while it was the seat of the papal court, we may find a sufficient reason why the sturdy assailant of the vices of the clergy should not have been allowed a nearer approach to his Holiness.—"You imagine," says he, "that the city of Avignon is the same now as when you resided in it. No! it is quite different. True, it was then the worst and vilest place on earth; but it is now a terrestrial hell, a residence of fiends and devils, a receptacle of all that is most wicked and abominable. What I tell you is not from hearsay, but from my own knowledge and experience. In this city there is no piety, no reverence or fear of God, no faith or charity, nothing that is holy, just, equitable, or humane. Why should I speak of truth, when not only the houses, palaces, courts, churches, and the thrones of Popes and Cardinals, but the very earth and air, seem to teem with lies? A future state, heaven, hell, and judgment, are openly turned into ridicule, as childish fables."—*Henry's History.*

tions against John Wickliffe, " as a person holding and promulgating many erroneous and heretical opinions." The nineteenth of the same month was fixed on for his trial, and a summons dispatched to Oxford requiring his presence at the time and place appointed. To us, who look back upon this movement through the subsequent developments of history, it seems an event of no little interest and importance. It was the first war-cry of the enemy ; the signal for that battle which was to bathe the soil of England with the blood of her noblest sons and daughters, and was never to cease till the Bible and its principles should become triumphant over the hosts of darkness and error.

Wickliffe did not shrink from the conflict, which he must have long foreseen. He immediately came down to London, prepared to meet the charges of his enemies with the weapons of scripture truth. But it was well understood, that these were of little account in the " holy convocation" before which he was to answer ; and two of his powerful court friends—John, Duke of Lancaster, fourth son of Edward III., and Percy, Earl Marshal of England—determined to accompany him, and see that he had fair play. When we remember the unlimited power of this high court in matters of religion, the unscrupulous character of its members, and that Wickliffe had assailed them in interests vital to their very existence, this will not seem an unnecessary or injudicious kindness.

The nineteenth of February came. At an early hour, the immense interior of old St. Paul's was densely filled with prelates, priests and citizens ; while a noisy, heaving, struggling crowd blackened the surrounding area. Courtney, Bishop of London, seated on the magnificent episcopal throne, and surrounded by robed and mitred dignitaries, smiled in conscious power and anticipated triumph. Would Wickliffe venture to appear ? Or would he flee, and hide himself from the vengeance he had provoked ? In either case, he was a doomed man. What then must have been the prelate's surprise and rage, when the opening crowd disclosed the apostolic figure of Wickliffe, robed in his simple college gown, and leaning on his peaceful white staff, between the martial forms of Lancaster and Percy ! Forgetting all prudence and propriety, he started angrily from his seat, and addressed the two noblemen in a tone of insolent rebuke, such as peers and soldiers are not wont to endure patiently. Their reply was in a spirit no less haughty ; and the fierce colloquy ended in a tumult which broke up the meeting, and the innocent occasion of the uproar quietly withdrew, without having been asked a question, or having uttered a word.

But his enemies were not to be thus baffled. They now determined to invest their proceedings with an authority to which all must bow, viz., that of the Pope himself.—His Holiness gave ready ear to their application. In the June following the abortive meeting at St. Paul's, no less than five bulls were sent from Avignon to England, all having for their object the apprehension of Wickliffe, and his delivery to the ecclesiastical power. One was addressed to the King, three to the Archbishop of Canterbury and the Bishop of London, and one to the University of Oxford. The purport of all was the same. The Head of the Church deplores the defection of England from the true way, made known to him by persons of credit, so that she who was once the defender of the faith has become the nurse of heresy. This sad change is ascribed chiefly to " the labors of John Wickliffe, Master in Divinity, more properly Master in Error, who had proceeded to a degree of madness so detestable, as not to fear to assert, dogmatize, and publicly teach opinions the most false and erroneous, contrary to the faith, and tending to the entire subversion of the Church." It is enjoined, therefore, that if, on inquiry, these charges prove to be well founded, said Wickliffe be committed to prison, and kept in sure custody till he shall have answered to the accusation, and judgment be received thereon from the Holy See. The Bishops are exhorted to use all diligence to guard the King, the Prince of Wales, the nobility, and royal councillors from the infection of these pestilent errors. The King is called on to sustain the authority of the clergy, in doing their duty in the execution of these bulls. The University is summoned, by virtue of the obedience due to the apostolic letters, and on pain of losing all graces, indulgences, and privileges granted to it by the Holy See, to deliver up the person of John Wickliffe, and of all others embracing his errors, into the custody of the prelates commissioned by the Pontiff for that purpose.

Thus terrible to the kingdom of darkness, is a man who gives fearless utterance to the truth !

The death of Edward III., the same month in which these formidable instruments were prepared at Avignon, and the reëstablishment of Lancaster's power on the accession of the youthful Richard II., induced the prelates to suspend their vengeance for a time ; so that the existence of these bulls was known to none but themselves, until the following January. Meantime Wickliffe did not fail to give them abundant occasion to " nurse their wrath and keep it warm," against the favorable hour. The first parliament under the new king, held in October, resumed with great spirit the subject of papal encroachment. In the course of the discussion, a question came up on which Wickliffe's opinion was demanded, it is said, in the name of the king, viz.:

"Whether the kingdom of England may lawfully, in case of necessity, detain and keep back the treasure of the kingdom for its own defence, that it be not carried away to foreign and strange nations, the Pope himself demanding and requiring the same under pain of censure and by virtue of obedience?" This was not a question of abstract right, but one of imminent practical import at the very moment—England being then at war with France, and the French Pope, by virtue of his spiritual office, draining her of money to furnish weapons to her enemy.

In his reply, Wickliffe, as usual, goes to the root of the matter, by an appeal to the nature and tenure of the apostolic office, as exhibited in the New Testament. "Christ saith to the Apostles: 'The kings of the nations rule over them, but ye shall not do so.' Here lordship and rule is forbidden to the Apostles, and darest thou [their successor] usurp the same? If thou wilt be a lord, then shalt lose thy apostleship; or, if thou wilt be an apostle, thou shalt lose thy lordship; for truly thou must depart from one of them. If thou wilt have both, thou shalt lose both, or be of that number of whom God complains: 'They have reigned, but not through me; they have become princes, and I have not known it.' Now, if it doth suffice thee to rule with the Lord, thou hast thy glory. But if we will keep what is forbidden us, let us hear what he saith: 'He that is greatest among you, shall be made as the least; and he which is highest shall be as the servant;' and for an example, he set a child in the midst of them. So then, this is the true form and institution of the Apostle's trade; LORDSHIP AND RULE IS FORBIDDEN; MINISTRATION AND SERVICE COMMANDED." Therefore, concludes the Reformer, the temporal goods heretofore bestowed on the Pope were not his by the right apostolical, but simply as alms, given at the pleasure of the donor. And as the duty of alms-giving is measured by the necessity of the recipient and the ability of the donor, it cannot be the duty of England, in her present impoverished condition, to bestow charity on the Pope, who is already overloaded with riches. Wherefore, England may detain her treasure for her own defence, even against the direct command of the Pope. With such simplicity and ease did Wickliffe, with the New Testament for his guide, loose a knot which had been tightening for centuries, and was now puzzling the wisest heads of the age.

But it was now his enemies' turn to strike a blow. Three months after this, a special messenger conveyed the papal bull, so long concealed, to Oxford, and delivered it in due form to the Chancellor of the University. In an accompanying letter, the prelate demanded that Wickliffe be sent to St. Paul's, there to make answer to the charges against him. The University authorities, displeased with this papal and episcopal interference in their affairs, showed no haste to comply. But a synod being assembled at Lambeth in April, Wickliffe promptly obeyed a summons to be present.

This time, he faced his enemies alone. A written statement of his imputed errors and heresies being furnished him, he, in turn, replied to the charges in writing, improving the occasion to give a still more full and distinct exposition of his views. Exceptions have been taken to this document as, in some portions, seemingly vague and evasive in its character. But in his perfect clearness in the statement of views most hazardous to express before such an assembly, and in the manner in which the paper was received by his opponents, we have sufficient evidence that all the weapons used by the Reformer on this occasion were worthy of his character, and well chosen for the time and place. The assertion that political dominion, or civil secular government, inheres in the laity, not in Peter or his successors ; and that it is lawful for the secular power to take away temporalities from churchmen who habitually abuse them, "*notwithstanding excommunication, or any other church censure,*" could not have been misunderstood by the tribunal before which he was arraigned. But he took a yet higher and bolder tone. It had come to be understood, that all legislative and judicial competency in religious matters was vested in the clergy; that they, in fact, constituted THE CHURCH ; while the part of the laity was simply that of implicit, blind submission. In opposition to this, Wickliffe maintains that ecclesiastics, nay, even the Pope of Rome himself may, in some cases, be corrected by their subjects, and " for the benefit of the Church, be impleaded by both clergy and laity." For the Pope, he argues, being our peccable brother and liable to sin as well as we, is, like us, subject to the law of brotherly reproof. "When, therefore," he proceeds, " the whole college of cardinals is remiss in correcting him for the necessary welfare of the Church, it is evident that the *rest of the body*, which, as it may chance, *may chiefly be made up of the laity*, may medicinally reprove and implead him, and reduce him to lead a better life."

What would have been the issue of this trial, it is not difficult to conjecture, had it not been averted as unexpectedly as before at St. Paul's. Deliverance came, however, in this case, from a very different source, and in a manner which testified the spread of Wickliffe's opinions among the common people. A general alarm for his safety prevailed among his friends, increased, no doubt, by the fact that the trial was conducted before a secret tribunal. This feeling burst forth at last into act. The populace began to stream from various quarters toward the place of meeting, and were there joined by many of the first citizens of London. Pressing their way into the building, the excited crowd burst open the door of the council-room, and rushing in, loudly demanded Wickliffe. And when, in the midst of the tumult, Sir Lewis Clifford entered the assembly, and in the name of the King's mother (widow of the Black Prince) forbade any definitive sentence by the Court, a panic fear seized on the bold churchmen. In the indignant words of one of their own historians,[*] they became " as a reed shaken by the wind, and grew soft as oil in their speech, to the manifest forfeiture of their dignity and the injury of the whole Church. With such fear were they struck, that one would have thought them as a man who hears not, or in whose mouth there are no reproofs." So far from being detained " in custody and sure prison," while awaiting the decision of the Holy See, Wickliffe returned peaceably to Oxford, to lecture, preach, and write against the sins of Popery with more zeal and effect than ever. The expected sentence from Avignon never arrived. The death of Gregory XI. while the matter was still pending, and the distractions incident on the " Schism of the Popes"[†] which followed, turned the attention of the clergy in another direction, and the Reformer was left for some three years longer, to pursue his career unmolested.

[*] Walsingham.
[†] During the next fifty years, the Papal Church was blessed with two and sometimes three infallible heads, who mutually accused each other as heretics, Simonists, impostors, and everything else that is vile and impious—" not the worst proof," as Henry quaintly remarks, " of their infallibility."

CHAPTER VI.

THE NEW-TESTAMENT MINISTRY REVIVED.

NOT far from this time, Wickliffe started a movement which, for its vital bearings on the interests of religion and for the perpetuity of its influence, stands second only to his great work of giving the Bible to the people.

From the study of the New Testament, he had arrived at certain conclusions very much at variance with the opinions of the time. Some of these have already been noted in the foregoing narrative; but, for the sake of clearness, the principal points will here be mentioned, in connection with others. He believed—

1st. *That the primitive Church recognized no hierarchy*, with its ascending ranks and orders of spiritual princes. "By the ordinance of Christ," says he, "priests and bishops were all one. But afterward, the Emperor divided them, and made bishops to be lords, and priests their servants." "I boldly assert one thing, viz.: that in the primitive Church or in the time of Paul, two orders of the clergy were sufficient, that is, a priest and a deacon. In like manner, I maintain that in the time of Paul, presbyter and bishops were names of the same office. —All other degrees and orders have their origin in the pride of Cæsar. If indeed they were necessary to the Church, Christ would not have been silent respecting them. Every Christian should judge of the office of the clergy from what is taught in Scripture, especially in the Epistles of Timothy and Titus, and should not admit the new inventions of Cæsar."

2d. *That the priest's office is simply that of the ministry of the word.* The legislative right claimed by Popes, prelates and councils, and the power of excommunication and absolution attributed to every member of the clerical order, were, in his view, impious invasions of the prerogatives of Christ.

3d. *That it is the right and duty of all priests, by virtue of their office, to preach the gospel:* and this, without waiting for any special license from bishops; nay—so stringent is the obligation—even in the face of their prohibition. "*The highest service to which man may attain on earth*"—such are his noble words—"*is to preach the word of God.* This service falls peculiarly to priests, and therefore God more straitly demands it of them. Hereby should they produce children to God, and this is the end for which God wedded the Church. It might indeed be good to have a son that were lord of this world; but better far to have a son in God, who, as member of Holy Church, shall ascend to heaven. And for this reason, Christ left other works, and occupied himself mostly in preaching, and thus did his apostles, and for this God loved them." —" Jesus Christ, when he ascended to heaven, commanded it especially to all his disciples, to go and preach the gospel freely to all men. So also when Christ spoke last with Peter, he bade him thrice, as he loved him, to feed his sheep; and this a wise shepherd would not have done, if he had not himself loved it well. In this stands the office of the spiritual shepherd. And as the bishops of the temple hindered Christ, so is he hindered now by the hindering of this deed. Therefore Christ told them that at the day of doom, Sodom and Gomorrah should fare better than they. And thus, if our bishops preach not themselves, and hinder true priests from preaching, they are in the sin of the bishops who killed the Lord Jesus Christ."

4th. *That the ministry is to be supported by the voluntary contributions of the people.* As we have seen, Wickliffe had long maintained, that ecclesiastical endowments were opposed to the spirit of the New Testament, and were one of the main sources of the corruption of the clergy. But he goes farther than this. In his view, the system of tithes had no better foundation. "Men wonder highly," says he in a treatise entitled '*The Curse Expounded*,' "why curates are so severe in exacting tithes, since Christ and his apostles took no tithes, as men do now; neither paid them, nor even spoke of them, either in the Gospel or the Epistles, which are the perfect law of freedom and grace. But Christ lived on the alms of holy women, as the Gospel telleth; and the apostles lived sometimes by the labor of their hands, and sometimes took a poor livelihood and clothing, given of free will and devotion by the people, without asking or constraining." "Paul proved that priests, preaching truly the gospel, should live by the gospel, and said naught of tithes. Certainly tithes were due to priests in the Old Law—but it is not so now, in the law of grace." "Lord! why should our worldly priests charge Christian people with tithes, offerings, and customs, more than did Christ and his apostles? Would to God, that all wise and true men would inquire, whether it were not better to find good priests, by free alms of the people, with a reasonable and poor livelihood, to teach the gospel in word and deed as did Christ and his apostles, than thus to pay tithes to a worldly priest, ignorant and negligent, as men are now compelled to do by bulls and new ordinances of priests!"* In connection with this, he maintains that ordination by a bishop confers no fitness for the sacred office; it is merely the outward recognition of a fitness which can come from God alone, and when this is proved to be wanting, becomes in the nature of the case, null and void. The people should themselves decide in this matter, by comparing the life of the teacher thus placed over them with the infallible standard of Scripture.

The revival of the New Testament principle, in a body of pious, self-denying working ministers, depending for their maintenance on the voluntary contributions of those for whom they labored, became now one of Wickliffe's prime objects. His wonderful success in this undertaking attests how strong, and how deeply spiritual, was his influence among the youth of Oxford. Christ himself was the model on which he sought to form them for this self-denying work.

"Jesus himself," says he, "did indeed the lessons he taught. The Gospel relates how he went about, in places of the country both great and small, in cities and castles, or in small towns, and this that he might teach us to become profitable to men everywhere, and not to forbear to preach to a people because they are few, and our name may not in consequence be great. For we should labor for God, and from Him hope for our reward. There is no doubt that Christ went into small uplandish towns, as to Bethphage and Cana in Galilee, for Christ went to all those places where he wished to do good. He labored not for gain, he was not smitten with pride or covetousness." "It was ever the manner of Jesus, to speak the words of God wherever he knew they might be profitable to those who heard them.

---

* In these views we find an easy solution of the disrepute in which Wickliffe has been held by writers of the Church of England. The pious Milner (Church History) is filled with horror at the Reformer's radical notions of clerical emolument. It is no wonder, he thinks, that a man who entertained such views of tithes, should have been suspected of abetting Wat Tyler and other incendiaries of the time of Richard II. His illustration of the inconvenient results of Wickliffe's doctrine is a specimen of *naiveté* hardly to be excelled. "He disliked," says he, "all church endowments, and wished to have the clergy reduced to a state of poverty. He insists that parishioners have a right to withhold tithes from pastors who are guilty of fornication. Now, if, in such cases, he would have allowed every individual to judge for himself, who does not see what a door might be opened to confusion, fraud, and the encouragement of avarice!"— Luther's and Melancthon's prejudice against Wickliffe is explicable on the same ground. They could hardly believe that a man holding such heterodox views of clerical property, could understand the doctrine of justification by faith. Surely "the best of men are but men at best!" But the wincing proves how vital a point of State religions had been touched by the uncourteous Reformer.

Hence Christ often preached, now at meat, now at supper, and indeed at whatever time it was convenient for others to hear him." " Christ sought man's soul, lost through sin, thirty years and more, with great travail and weariness, and many thousand miles upon his feet, in cold, and storm, and tempest." As the result of these efforts a band of young missionaries, fully imbued with their instructor's views and glowing with a kindred zeal, dispersed themselves through the remote villages and hamlets of England, preaching to all who would listen, the glad tidings of a free salvation. Like the seventy sent out by our Lord, they went on foot, clad in coarse garments, the pilgrim's staff in their hands—and, if so happy as to own such a treasure—with a Latin Bible hid in the bosom of their gowns. Wherever they found an audience—whether in a church or a church-yard, in the busy market-place, amid the noisy chaffering and boisterous amusements of the fair—there they proclaimed to the people " all the words of this life." To the venal sale of indulgences and priestly absolution, they opposed the unbought grace of the gospel ; to the invocation of saints, the one Mediator between God and man ; to the worship of pictures and images, the worship of the one living and true God ; to the traditions of men and the authority of priests, the pure revelation of God's will in the Holy Scriptures. Their own blameless lives enforced their teachings. Asking nothing, they received thankfully what was required for their simple wants ; and even from this were ever ready to spare something for the needy. The contrast thus furnished with the gross lives and insatiable beggary of the Friars, was too striking to be overlooked. The apostolic motto, " Not yours, but you," which was written on all their labors, sunk with the power of demonstration into the people's heart. Such was their zeal, and such the eagerness with which they were received, that whole shires became pervaded with their doctrines. John Ashton, it is said, was personally known over half of England. So rapid was their increase in numbers and influence within four years, that in 1382 a great Convocation was assembled in London, for the special purpose of concerting measures to arrest their progress. The archbishop of Canterbury, the bishops and other prelates, masters of divinity, doctors of civil and canon law, and a great part of the clergy of the realm being there present, united in an appeal to the king for the suppression of these preachers, as a body of men who were perverting the whole nation with their heretical and seditious doctrines. A decree, framed for this purpose by the assembled prelates, received the *secret* concurrence of the king and lords, and was surreptitiously inserted in the statute-book as a regular Act of Parliament. After a statement of the imminent danger to the Church and realm, the document thus concludes : " It is therefore ordained and assented in this present Parliament, that the king's commission be made and directed to the sheriffs and other ministers of our sovereign lord the king, or other sufficient persons, and, according to the certifications of the prelates thereof, to be made in the chancery from time to time, to arrest all such preachers, and also their fautors, maintainers and abettors, and hold them in arrest and strong prison, till they shall purify themselves according to the law and reason of Holy Church. And the king willeth and commandeth, that the Chancellor make such commission at all times that he, by the prelates or any of them, shall be certified and thereof required, as aforesaid."

When this fraud was discovered by the lower House, they insisted that the act should be repealed ; but the prelates so managed that it kept its place in the statute-book, and through many succeeding years formed the basis of prosecutions for heresy.

The measures thus resolved on were followed up with energy, but with little effect. The love of the people was as a wall of fire round about their faithful teachers. Many country baronets of wealth and influence likewise espoused their cause ; and sometimes, when danger was apprehended, a body-guard of gentlemen was seen around the pulpit, ready, if necessary, to defend with their good swords the right of Englishmen to speak and to hear, according to the dictates of their own consciences. The intimidated sheriff, having served on the preacher a citation to appear before the bishop, would retire ; and before adequate forces could be raised to execute the writ, the evangelist was proclaiming in some far-off hamlet the glad tidings of salvation to its neglected poor. The devices of prelates, and the decrees of kings, were not able to break again " the apostolic succession" thus revived by Wickliffe ; nor has it been interrupted from that day to the present. From that day, the Bible-conception of the Christian ministry, evolved in such beautiful completeness by this master-spirit five hundred years ago, has been slowly leavening the English mind ; and from the conflicts for religious liberty to which it has given birth, civil freedom likewise has caught its noblest impulses. To estimate its full import, we must trace its influence through English history till its full development, on these western shores, gave to the world the spectacle of a Christian nation, without a State Church ; where government is maintained, and religion flourishes, without a Bishop or a King.

CHAPTER VII.

WICKLIFFE ATTACKS THE CITADEL OF PAPAL INFLUENCE.

We must now briefly contemplate Wickliffe in yet one more conflict, deeply interesting in itself, and still more interesting as forming the transition to the greatest, and closing labor of his life.

In the years 1379-80, the subject of the Eucharist assumed a very prominent place in his lectures at Oxford. In this doctrine, as held in the papal Church, the Reformer grappled with no mere airy metaphysical dogma. The welcome it received from the Romish clergy when first promulgated, in the ninth century, and the tenacity with which they have clung to it even down to the present day, attests their appreciation of its practical importance. "The sacrament of communion," says a recent Catholic writer,[*] "is the highest of our mysteries, and is the central point of all the institutions of the Catholic Church." And again: "The Catholic view of communion pervades the whole Catholic religious and ecclesiastical system." "By the reformation of the sixteenth century, the whole Catholic system was attacked; as the reformers, rejecting the traditions of the Church, took the Bible alone for their guide in matters of belief, and departed, at the same time, from the Catholic theory of communion. If they had left the Catholic doctrine on communion, the priesthood and Mass would necessarily have remained too." A consideration of a few leading points involved in the doctrine fully justifies these assertions; and shows that it forms the dividing line between Romanism, with its traditions, its mystic sense, and its blind submission to the priesthood, on the one side, and on the other, Protestantism, with its respect for the human understanding, and its acceptance of the Bible as supreme authority.

Its very starting-point was the repudiation of the bodily senses, of the reason, and of Scripture, as reliable sources of evidence. The *dictum* of the Church was here all and in all. Sight, smell, taste, touch, though obstinately reporting the bread to be still bread; the plainest conclusions of reason, and the obvious import of Scripture;

---

[*] See the article *Lord's Supper*, in the Encyc. Americana, where the Romish view is presented by one of its adherents with great clearness, and will be seen to differ in no respect from that combated by Wickliffe in the fourteenth century.

all weighed nothing in opposition to that " mystic sense," which the Church had seen fit to impose on the ordinance of the Supper. So interpreted, it presented a strange combination of Jewish and Pagan ideas under Christian names. It was Jewish, in its notion of a perpetually repeated sacrifice for sin ; for, at each performance of Mass, the living Christ, " body and blood, soul and divinity," was offered anew as a propitiation to the Father ! It was Pagan, in its worship of an inanimate, created object as God, and in its multiplication of gods. For not only did the wafer become, by the consecrating words, a proper object of adoration, but each separate fragment into which it was broken contained the whole Christ, and was to be worshipped as such. Of the spiritual worship of the one invisible, uncreated God, and of the atonement made by Christ, once for all, nothing was left but these monstrous, distorted shadows.

From this view of the Lord's Supper, necessarily proceeded that of the mysterious sanctity and prerogatives of the clerical office. Who could set limits to the spiritual power of one who could thus " make his Maker"? By what arguments could the credulous believer be persuaded, that anathemas and absolutions from lips that pronounced the awful " Hoc corpus meum," were of no effect ? The simple minister of the word thus rose into the dignity of a sacrificing priest, whose consecrated hands offered the atonement, without which there was no remission of sins. Nay, he could reach even to the place of departed spirits, and there reverse the decisions of God himself on those who had died in sin. It was chiefly through this doctrine, that the Romish clergy had obtained their strange sway over the minds of men ; for having, in regard to this vital point, given up the Scriptures, reason, and their very senses, into the keeping of their spiritual guides, there was nothing to save them from being blind victims of every other imposition. Body and soul were both sealed for bondage. The outer light of Scripture was taken away ; the light that was in them became darkness.

There has been much controversy as to the precise views entertained by Wickliffe himself in regard to the Eucharist, originating probably in a misapprehension of the obscure scholastic language of his learned discussions. Nothing can be the more explicit, or satisfactory, than the views expressed in his English writings on the subject, intended for the common people. Thus in his " Wyckett," an English treatise in defence of the scripture doctrine of the Supper, he asks, " May the thing made turn again and make him that made it ? Thou then that art an earthly man, by what reason mayst thou say that thou makest thy Maker ? Were this doctrine true, it would follow that the thing which is not God to-day shall be God to-morrow ; yea, the thing that is without spirit of life, but groweth in the field by nature, shall another time be God. And yet we ought to believe that God is without beginning or ending." "Christ saith, I am a very vine. Wherefore do ye not worship the vine for God, as ye do the bread ? Wherein was Christ a very vine ? Or wherein was the bread Christ's body ? It was in *figurative* speech, which is hidden to the understanding of sinners. And thus, as Christ became not a material or earthly vine, nor a material vine the body of Christ, so neither is material bread changed for its substance into the flesh and blood of Christ."

But whether, in that dark age, he attained to perfect light on this or other doctrines, is to us of little moment, compared with his noble vindication of the two great Protestant principles—the word of God the sole guide in matters of religion ; individual inquiry and conviction the right and duty of all men.

It was from this purely Protestant stand-point, that Wickliffe assailed the vital dogma of the Papacy. He resented the indignity it offered, both to the reason which God had kindled as a light in the soul of man, and to the revelation of his own will in the Scriptures. "Of all the heresies that have ever sprung up in the Church," thus he writes in the Trialogus, "I think there is not one more artfully introduced by hypocrites, or one imposing such manifold fraud on the people. It repudiates the Scriptures ; it wrongs the people ; it causes them to commit idolatry. It is not reasonable to suppose that God can have designed to put confusion on that intelligence which he has himself implanted in our nature. Of all the external senses that God has bestowed on man, touch and taste are the least liable to err in the judgment they give. But this heresy would overturn the evidence of these senses, and without cause ; surely the sacrament which does that must be a sacrament of Antichrist." "Let the knowledge obtained by our external senses deceive us, and the internal senses will, of necessity, fall under the same delusion. But what," he exclaims, "can have moved the Lord Jesus Christ thus to confound and destroy all power of natural discernment, in the senses and minds of his worshippers ?" "It is," he says in his Trialogus, "as if the Devil had been scheming to this effect, saying—'If I can, by my vicar Antichrist, so far seduce believers as to bring them to deny that this sacrament is bread, and to believe in it as a contemptible quality without a substance, I may after that, and in the same manner, lead them to believe whatever I may wish ; inasmuch as the opposite is plainly taught, both by the language of Scripture, and by the very senses of mankind.' Doubtless, after a while, these simple-hearted believers may be brought to say, that however a prelate may live—be he effeminate, a homicide, a simonist, or stained with any other vice—this must never be believed concerning him by a people who would be regarded as duly obedient. But by the grace of Christ, I will keep clear of the heresy which teaches that if the Pope and Cardinals assert a certain thing to be the sense of Scripture, therefore so it is ; for that were to set them above the Apostles."

But though he would not allow the witness of the human senses and reason to be set aside by mere Church authority, the Scriptures were, on this as on every other doctrine, the only infallible guide. " Let every man," he says in the conclusion of his ' Wyckett,' " wisely, with much care and great study, and also with charity, read the words of God in the Holy Scriptures." " Now, therefore, pray we heartily to God that this evil time may be made short, for the sake of the chosen men, as he hath promised in his holy Gospel ; and that the large and broad way to perdition may be stopped, and that the straight and narrow way which leadeth to bliss may be made open by the Holy Scriptures, that we may know what is the will of God, to serve him with truth and holiness, in the dread of God, that we may find by him a way of bliss everlasting. So be it !"

For two or three years, Wickliffe was zealously engaged in disseminating these views in the lecture-room, in the pulpit, and by his ever active pen. That he was permitted to do it so long unquestioned, he owed chiefly to the distractions in the Papacy, which, for a long period, furnished the prelates of Christendom with full occupation. But from the sequel, it is clear that his course was watched by eager foes, who were merely " biding their time." Such he had even at Oxford, and by various changes, they at length came to have the ascendency in the University administration. In the spring of 1381, Wickliffe challenged the University to a public disputation on the subject of the Eucharist. In the twelve theses which he published as the basis of the discussion, he declared that " the bread we see on the altar is not Christ, nor any part of him, but simply an effectual sign of him ; and that the doctrines of transubstantiation, identification, and impanation, have no basis in Scripture." This brought on the crisis. Berton, their chancellor, being a partizan of the Religious Orders, and, of course, hostile to Wickliffe, resolved that he should not have the éclat of a victory at Oxford. Instead, therefore, of responding to his challenge, he assembled a secret council of twelve theological doctors, eight being from the Orders, who unanimously pronounced Wickliffe's doctrine to be erroneous, and contrary to the determinations of the Church. They decreed, furthermore, that "if any person, of whatever degree, state, or condition, shall in future publicly teach such doctrine in the University, or shall listen to one so teaching, he shall be suspended from all scholastic exercises, shall be liable to the greater excommunication, and shall be committed to prison." Truly, a compendious method for purging Oxford of heresy!

Wickliffe was seated in his lecture-room, discussing this very subject before his class, when the University officers entered, and announced the above decrees. It has been asserted by his enemies, that he betrayed some confusion while listening to the proclamation. It surely would argue no remarkable weakness, had so sudden and rude an assault—and in that place of all others—shaken his firm spirit for the moment. Wickliffe was not a man of iron nerves, but, as we see from his portrait, and from the reflection of his life and writings, of the most quick and lively sensibility. The emotion was but for an instant. Rising with dignity, as soon as the reading of the official document was finished, he protested against this arbitrary suppression of opinions, which could not be confuted in a free discussion, and declared his intention to appeal to the King for the protection of his rights.

The Chancellor's power could not reach beyond Oxford. Wickliffe therefore retired to Lutterworth, and devoted himself to writing and preaching, while awaiting a reversal of Berton's unjust decision. But this never came. The rude dismissal, thus described, proved to be the close of his connection with a school of sacred learning of which he had been so long the most illustrious ornament. No doubt it was an event in many ways painful to himself, and exulted in by his enemies as a signal, if not final victory over the bold Reformer. Could they have foreseen the result, they would have left him unmolested in the Professor's chair. Their short-sighted hatred served but to introduce that crowning period of his labors, which gave to priestcraft in England its deadly wound, and made his influence and name imperishable.

CHAPTER VIII.

WICKLIFFE'S WRITINGS FOR THE PEOPLE.

From the period of Wickliffe's retirement to Lutterworth, a marked change appears in the direction of his labors. The plans of reform on which he had spent so large a portion of his best years, seemed now farther from realization than ever. All hope of improvement proceeding from the " Head of the Church," from the clergy, or from the enlightened action of the secular power, was now seen to be vain. Even Oxford, the last refuge of intellectual and religious freedom, had barred her doors against him. It all served but to ripen in his mind the great idea, by which his labors were to be separated from the decaying Past, and to receive a living, organic connection with the whole future of his country and his race. He turns from king and noble, from Pope, and priest and scholar, with the determination to place the light of divine truth, freed from all veil or covering, in the honest keeping of the common people.

Under the inspiration of this idea, Wickliffe entered with redoubled vigor on the final stage of his activity. He was now in his fifty-seventh year ; and though disease, and the excitements of his stormy life had shaken his bodily frame, the eagle spirit seemed gifted with more than youthful fire. Never before had he exhibited such productive energy. His English writings for the people budded under his pen like leaves in spring. It is evident, from various passages in his works, that he looked upon this golden opportunity as very brief ; that persecution, to close perhaps in martyrdom, was among the anticipations of each to-morrow. He labored, therefore, as one who has a message of life and death to deliver, and fears he may not have time to utter it. " I should be worse than an infidel"—thus he writes in one of his works on the Eucharist—" were I not to defend unto the death the law of Christ ; and certain I am, that it is not in the power of the heretics, and disciples of antichrist, to impugn this evangelical doctrine. On the contrary, I trust through our Lord's mercy to be superabundantly rewarded, after this short and miserable life, for the lawful contention which I wage. I know from the Gospel, that antichrist, with all his devices, can only kill the body ; but Christ, in whose cause I contend, can cast both body and soul into hell-fire. Sure I am, that he will not suffer his servants to want what is needful for them, since he freely exposed himself to a dreadful death for their sakes, and has ordained that all his most beloved disciples should pass through severe suffering with a view to their good."

It is a matter of regret, that the limits of this sketch allow only of a few brief extracts from these writings, so characteristic of the genius and spirit of the man. The whole range of subjects which had formed the groundwork of his life-labors, was here presented in a form admirably adapted to the common mind. In his own noble, homely, expressive English, the true language of the people, he unmasks the character, the false pretensions and corrupt doctrines of the priesthood ; and encourages the humble reader, in the exercise of the understanding which God has given him, enlightened by the Scriptures, to meet them like a free Christian man. They are not, however, mainly of a controversial nature, though most of them must, of necessity, contain pointed allusions to the specific sins and errors of the clergy. But his chief object, in the exposure of error, is to gain for the great saving truths of the Gospel, an immediate, life-imparting contact with the souls of his readers. He seeks to detach them from their false guides, only that he may lead them to the one Saviour from sin and misery.

Among the most interesting of his offerings to the poor and humble in society, are those little treatises, designed strictly as helps to a devout and holy life. His English writings, in general, are characterized by a brevity singular in that day of interminable folios. But these mark still more strikingly, the practical genius of the Reformer. Our modern religious tracts, that mighty agency for the diffusion of truth, are but the reproduction of the device struck from his prophetic brain five hundred years ago. " *The Poor Caitiff* " * is a collection of such little detached pieces, none of them extending beyond a few pages, some only over a leaf or two, and others but a single page. From their extreme brevity, they could be multiplied and scattered almost without limit, even in an age when printing was unknown. It has been well said of Dr. Watts, that the true greatness of his character nowhere appears so clearly as in his " Divine Songs for Children." With yet deeper reverence do we sit at the feet of Wickliffe, the royal ambassador, the friend of princes, the most eminent scholar of his time, as with sublime simplicity, humility, and

---

* Published in the " British Reformers" of the London Religious Tract Society. *Caitiff* was the common appellation of a person in the lower ranks.

sweetness, he speaks to the neglected and degraded poor, these heavenly words of instruction and consolation. They are the best refutation of the malevolent charge that his influence tended to popular disorder. Two or three passages must suffice here.

"To any degree of true love to Jesus, no soul can attain unless he be truly meek. For a proud soul seeks to have his own will, and so he shall never come to any degree of God's love. Even the lower that a soul sitteth in the valley of meekness, so many the more streams of grace and love come thereto. And if the soul be high in the hills of pride, the wind of the fiend bloweth away all manner of goodness therefrom." "Singular love is, when all solace and comfort is closed out of the heart but the love of Jesus alone. Other delight or other joy pleases not; for the sweetness of him is so comforting and lasting, his love is so burning and gladdening, that he who is in this degree may well feel the fire of love burning in his soul. That fire is so pleasant that no man can tell but he that feeleth it, and not fully he. Then the soul is Jesus loving, on Jesus thinking, and Jesus desiring, only burning in coveting of him; singing in him, resting on him. Then the thought turns to song and melody." "God playeth with his child when he suffereth him to be tempted; as a mother rises from her much beloved child, and hides herself and leaves him alone, and suffers him to cry, Mother, Mother, so that he looks about, cries and weeps for a time; and at last, when the child is ready to be overset with troubles and weeping, she comes again, clasps him in her arms, kisses him and wipes away the tears. So our Lord suffereth his loved child to be tempted and troubled for a time, and withdraweth some of his solace and full protection, to see what his child will do; and when he is about to be overcome by temptations, then he defendeth him and comforteth him by his grace."

These writings were the text-books of piety to the persecuted Church of Christ, for more than a hundred years; and next to the English Bible, were the most efficient agency in molding its opinions and character, and in making ready, against the happier times to come, a people for the Lord. They often had the honor of being cast with the inspired word into the flames, or of mingling their ashes with those of the martyr, convicted of having read and believed their words, on whose faithful bosom they had been hung as a mark of shame. So largely were they multiplied, and so sacredly treasured by the people, that after a century and a half of rigid proscription and destruction, it was found no very difficult matter to make entire collections of these writings.

CHAPTER IX.

THE FIRST ENGLISH BIBLE.

But Wickliffe's great work for the people was not yet done. The labors just narrated, though in themselves inestimable, were but the pioneers of one infinitely more important ; but voices, crying through the waste places of England, " Prepare ye the way of the Lord !" This crowning work, even now progressing amid the hurry and pressure of his other toils, was the TRANSLATION OF THE ENTIRE SCRIPTURES OF THE OLD AND NEW TESTAMENTS INTO THE ENGLISH TONGUE.

There is no reason to suppose that this was a new idea to Wickliffe's mind. In the nature of the case it could hardly be so. From the very beginning of his career, we have seen him vindicating the supreme authority of the Scriptures against that of the self-styled Church. His appeal was ever to " the Law and the Testimony." " Whoever spoke not according to this word," though it were the infallible Head of Christendom, " there was no light in him." In his efforts to enlighten the laity, the need of the inspired standard of truth, in their own language, must have pressed itself upon him with increasing weight. We find, accordingly, that even during the hurry of his public life, he had found leisure to prepare, from time to time, translations of single portions of the New Testament, in connection with expositions, for the use of the people. In the prologues to these works, the propriety and duty of giving the Scriptures to the laity, in their mother tongue, is claimed in the most explicit manner. Thus, in the prologue to Luke, he says :* " Therefore a poor caitiff, let from preaching for a time for causes known of God, writeth the Gospel of Luke in English, with a short exposition of old and holy doctors, to the poor men of his nation, which know little Latin or none, and be poor of wit and worldly chattel and, natheless, rich of good will to please God.—Thus, with God's grace, poor Christian men may somedeal know the text of the Gospel, with the common sentence of old, holy doctors, and therein know the meek and poor and charitable living of Christ and his apostles, to sue them in virtues and in bliss ; and also know the proud and covetous and veniable living of Anti-

---

* Preface to Wickliffe's Bible.

christ and his followers, to flee them and their cursed deeds, and pains of hell. For, no doubt, as our Lord Jesus Christ and his apostles profess plainly, Antichrist and his cursed disciples should come, and deceive many men by hypocrisy and tyranny ; and the best armor of christian men against this cursed chieftain with his host, *is the text of holy writ.* Christ Jesus, for thine endless power, mercy, and charity, make thy blessed law known and kept of thy people. . . . . Amen, good Lord Jesus !" So in his prologue to John's Gospel : " Our Lord Jesus Christ, very God and very man, came to serve poor, meek men, and to teach them the Gospel ; and for this cause St. Paul saith that he and other apostles of Christ be servants of christian men by our Lord Jesus Christ. And he saith also, I am debtor to wise men and unwise ; and, Bear ye the charges of one another, and so ye shall fill the law of Christ. Therefore a simple creature of God, willing to bear, in part, the charges of simple poor men well willing in God's cause, writeth a short gloss in English on the Gospel of John."

These earlier translations mark a tendency in Wickliffe's mind, which could hardly fail to expand, under favorable circumstances, into the purpose to give the whole Bible to his countrymen. Accordingly, from the period of his retirement from Oxford, the right of the laity to the Scriptures forms a prominent subject in his writings ; and is vindicated with a noble confidence in divine truth, and in the intelligence and honesty of the common mind, which some modern Protestants would do well to study. The following paragraph is worthy of being written in letters of gold : " As the faith of the Church is contained in the Scriptures, *the more these are known in their true meaning the better ;* and inasmuch as secular men should assuredly understand the faith they profess, that faith should be taught them in whatever language may be best known to them. Forasmuch, also, as the doctrines of our faith are more clearly and exactly expressed in the Scriptures, than they may probably be by priests—seeing, if I may so speak, that many prelates are but too ignorant of Holy Scripture, while others conceal many parts of it ; and as the verbal instructions of priests have many other defects—the conclusion is abundantly manifest, that believers should ascertain for themselves what are the true matters of their faith, by having the Scriptures in a language which they fully understand. For the laws made by prelates are not to be received as matters of faith, nor are we to confide in their public instructions, nor in any of their words, but as they are founded on Holy Writ—since the Scriptures contain the whole truth. And this translation of them into English should therefore do at least this good, viz.: placing bishops and priests above suspicion as to the parts of it which they profess to explain. Other means, such as the friars, prelates, the pope, may all prove defective ; and to provide against this, Christ and his Apostles evangelized the greater portion of the world, by making known the Scriptures to the people in their own language. To this end, indeed, did the Holy Spirit endow them with the knowledge of tongues. Why, then, should not the living disciples of Christ do in this respect as they did ?"

The realization, for his own countrymen, of this manifest purpose of God in respect to all nations, now became the leading object of Wickliffe's efforts. Calling in the assistance of the ripest scholars among his followers, he prosecuted the task with such vigor, that, in the year 1384, the entire translation was completed. The forge in the old rectory study must have glowed day and night during this period ; and yet, in such consummate silence did the hallowed labor proceed, that it was doing its work among the people before its existence was suspected by the clergy. The yell of rage with which they greeted its appearance, betrayed their consciousness that the ancient foundations of their power were shaken.

This ancient version was not, indeed, made from the original sources—the Hebrew and Greek Scriptures. No copies of these existed at that time in all western Europe. Through converted Jewish scholars, a slight interest in the study of Hebrew had already been awakened on the continent ; but this had not yet extended to England. It had fared even worse with the Greek language, which was now as unknown on the island as though it had never had an existence.

In making his version from the Latin Vulgate, Wickliffe, therefore, only submitted to a necessity. It is matter of thankfulness that, in the absence of the original Scriptures, so good a representative of them* should have been within his reach. Jerome, who was the first Biblical scholar of his age, was thoroughly acquainted with both Greek and Hebrew ; and his version, being executed in the fourth century, was based on manuscripts older, by several centuries, than those to which later English translators had access. Hence, in not a few instances, Wickliffe's translation gives the true meaning of a passage, where its successors failed to do so. But, on the other hand,

---

* "The Vulgate," says the learned and judicious Dr. George Campbell, " is, in the main, a good and faithful version." In reference to the accusation that it favors Popery, he adds : " Could this point be evinced in a satisfactory manner, it would allow more to Popery, on the score of antiquity, than, in my opinion, she is entitled to."

the disadvantages of translating from a translation, especially in the case of a book so ancient and so peculiar as the Bible, are of a very serious character. The copy follows the model in its errors as well as its excellencies. Some portions of the Vulgate were executed with unpardonable haste ; and in many points, Jerome was deterred from doing justice to his own scholarship, by the storm of calumny and abuse brought upon him by his deviations from the defective versions then in popular use. In such cases there was no help for Wickliffe, except where Jerome was courageous enough to protest against his own translation in his notes. In the course of ten centuries, moreover, the text of the Vulgate itself had suffered much from the carelessness or the arbitrary alterations of its monkish transcribers ; and though repeated attempts had been made for restoring it, the Latin Bibles of the fourteenth century were far from being a perfect representation of the original work. It is plain that a version executed under these circumstances could only serve a temporary purpose, and must give place to another when the advance of learning should restore the sacred originals to the hands of Christian scholars.

But Wickliffe's Bible has a glory which cannot be affected by its critical deficiencies. Its appearance was the virtual settlement of the great question of Christendom : " Shall the people have the Scriptures ?" It was the prophecy and the earnest of Protestantism.

Soon after the completion of this great work, Wickliffe was summoned from the toils and conflicts of life. On the 29th of December, 1384, as he was performing divine service in the church at Lutterworth, he was seized with paralysis ; and after lingering two or three days in a state of unconsciousness, the great soul which had struggled so long and so bravely against the hosts of darkness, awoke in the joy of its Lord.

Within four years from his death, a revision of his translation was given to the public by his most intimate pupil and friend, John Purvey, being executed, no doubt, in obedience to his own injunctions. The alterations are confined mainly to those portions of the Old Testament ascribed to Wickliffe's chief coadjutor, Dr. Nicholas Hereford —a good scholar according to his age, but too literal and stiff in his renderings. The remaining books of the Old Testament, and the whole of the New, were touched with caution, and retained almost unchanged the first impress of the master-hand.

CHAPTER X.

INFLUENCE OF WICKLIFFE'S VERSION.

From the nations speaking the English tongue, Wickliffe's version has claims to grateful reverence, which have never yet been fully appreciated. England's first Bible, it was, for a hundred and thirty years, her only one. Not only so, but it constituted her earliest popular literature. For, with the exception of Wickliffe's own writings, it was the first book of any magnitude ever written in the English language. The noble Saxon of our forefathers, displaced at the Conquest, by Latin as the language of books, and by Norman-French as that of polite life, became the badge of degradation and servitude. The English into which it gradually changed, by a mixture with Latin and French, had, in process of time, so far regained the ancient rights of the vernacular, as to be, at this period, the spoken language of the great body of the people. Yet in such contempt was it still held, that scarcely an attempt had been made to use it in composition, till Wickliffe, with his great heart of love for the people, laid hold of it as the vehicle of religious instruction. He took the rude elements directly from the lips of the despised ploughmen, mechanics, and tradesmen. He gave it back to them in all its unadorned, picturesque simplicity, but fused by the action of his powerful mind into a fitting instrument of thought, and enriched with the noblest literature which the world has produced; the utterances of inspired poets, prophets, and apostles, the inimitable histories, narratives, and portraitures, through which divine wisdom has told the sublime story of providence and redemption.

What seeds were those then sown in the virgin soil of the common English mind! What must have been the quickening of intellectual life, in a community where the Book of books furnished almost the only aliment of the hungry soul! Were not the children eager to read for themselves those wondrous stories? Did not the ear of age forget its deafness, to hear the glad tidings of a Saviour and a future rest? Would not a new consciousness of worth steal into the soul of the rude clown, when he learned what God had done to redeem him? The more deeply we enter into the circumstances and spirit of the times, the stronger will grow the conviction that this first English Bible must have been like an awakening breath from heaven, the beginning of days to the common people of England.

As has been remarked before, no book before the invention of printing ever had such advantages for becoming widely known. Wickliffe, the great practical reformer, with his thorough knowledge of all classes of English society, had not urged through this gigantic task as a mere experiment. He had his eye on a definite, practicable result, the means for accomplishing which were in his own hands. Aside from the demand for the Scriptures, excited by his general influence during a long public career, he had at command one of the most effective agencies of modern publication. The active, hardy, itinerant preachers whom he had sent out to proclaim, by word of mouth, glad tidings to the poor, who had threaded every part of England, and become intimately acquainted with the character and wants of its population, now formed a band of COLPORTEURS for the written word. They knew in what far-off hamlets pious souls were counting the days to the return of their missionary, and pining for the bread of life ; what thinking merchants and tradesmen in the great towns, what honorable men and women among the country gentry were eager to search the Scriptures, whether these things were so. Several copyists, no doubt, had kept pace with the progress of the translation ; and as fast as a few chapters, or a book was completed, these faithful agents would make known the priceless treasure in the homes of the people. Many a touching scene might be imagined, of rustic groups by the wayside, in the church-yard, or around the peat fire at evening, listening for the first time to the words of the Bible in their mother tongue. Then, how would the beautifully written manuscript be passed round, from hand to hand, to be admired and wondered at ; and not seldom to be wet with tears from eyes that beheld for the first time, in English characters, the name of Jesus ! Nor would the missionary be suffered to depart, before a copy, of at least some portion, had been obtained. If no professional copyist was to be found, hands all unused to the labor of the pen would scrawl painfully a rude transcript of a Psalm, of the Ten Commandments, a few chapters of the Gospels, or of Paul's epistles, to remain as a lamp of heavenly light, when the living preacher had departed. It is a fact of intensest interest and significance, that numerous fragments of this kind were subsequently found among the Lollards. True, a large majority of the middle and lower ranks must have depended for their knowledge of the holy oracles on the ear alone. But when the memory is little occupied, and the heart writes the lesson on its tablets, much of the very language of Scripture may even thus be handed down, unimpaired, through successive generations. The truth of this is abundantly verified in the history of Wickliffe's later followers, as sketched in the second part of this work.

When first sent abroad, moreover, the version enjoyed the sunshine of royal favor, in the person of Anne of Bohemia, the accomplished wife of Richard II., who was herself a devoted student and advocate of the Scriptures. Though she was soon withdrawn by death, yet in the providence of God, nearly twenty years elapsed before its progress was materially checked by persecution. It needs no documents to assure us that during this period, copies must have been rapidly multiplied and diffused far and wide over England. The hundred and seventy copies, more or less complete, which have come down to our own time, are the index of many times that number which perished by use, by accident, or by the flames of Romish bonfires.

But we have more direct evidence ; the testimony of contemporaneous opposers of vernacular translations. The language of Knyghton, a distinguished writer of the Romish Church, recognizes the firm hold it had secured of the public mind, but a short time after the death of the translator. "The Gospel," says he, " which Christ committed to the clergy and doctors of the Church, *that they might sweetly dispense it to the laity*, according to the exigency of the times and the wants of men, this Master John Wickliffe has translated into the Anglic (not Angelic) * tongue ; thereby making it more open and common to the laity, and to women who can read, than formerly it was to the best instructed among the clergy. And thus the Gospel pearl is cast forth, and is trodden under foot of swine ; and what was once reverenced by clergy and laity is become, as it were, the common jest of both ; and the jewel of the clergy, their peculiar treasure, is made forever common to the laity."

The rapid spread among all classes of the laity, of Wickliffe's sentiments in regard to the Papacy, fully justified the apprehensions of the clergy. The House of Commons was so infected with the dangerous principles of religious liberty, as to render it a very uncomfortable instrument to manage ; and even among the nobles a considerable number took decided ground on the same side. The dreaded weapon of ridicule came freely into play in the conflict, and did its usual execution. Pasquinades, satirizing the ignorance and vices of the clergy, were posted up at St. Paul's, and other public places, and were soon in the mouths of the whole populace.

---

* A taunt upon the despised vernacular, as too rude and uncouth for such a purpose.

Had the tide of popular feeling received no check, the emancipation of England from the Papal yoke might have been anticipated by more than a century. But the Reformation would probably have been to a fatal degree unsound and superficial. There was first a work to be done in the nation's heart.

In 1395, during Richard's absence for the conquest of Ireland, the aspect of public opinion became so alarming that the prelates dispatched messengers entreating his return without delay. "As soon," says a contemporary popish historian, "as he heard the report of the commissioners, being inspired by the Divine Spirit, he hastened back, thinking it more necessary to defend the Church than to conquer kingdoms." His stringent measures toward the offending nobles soon reduced them to submission; many others, of course, followed in their wake, and the cause exchanged the prestige of success and distinguished patronage for the humiliation of defeat. When, in 1399, Henry IV., son of the Duke of Lancaster, Wickliffe's former friend, succeeded to the throne, the hopes of the party revived. But Henry's title needed the support of the clergy, and the price of their aid was the sacrifice of the cause of which both his father and himself had once been advocates. His first act. was to send a messenger to an ecclesiastical assembly, then in session at St. Paul's, "begging the prayers of the Church for the King and kingdom, and promising that he would protect the clergy in all their liberties and immunities, and assist them with all his power in exterminating heretics." He kept his word but too faithfully.

It was a bitter but wholesome disappointment. The political enthusiasm, that mere transient reflection of the true light from worldly minds, soon died out under the cruel persecutions which followed; but the religious principle grew strong in the good and honest hearts who loved the truth because it was of God. During the next quarter of a century, "the flower of martyrdom," of which Wickliffe had spoken, was won by a noble line of Christian heroes, representing widely separated classes of society. Thomas Badby, the tailor; John Claydon, the farrier; Thorpe and Sawtree, the learned clergymen; Cobham, the mirror of chivalry and manly piety, stand side by side, as equal champions for the faith of Christ; while a multitude endured trials of cruel mockings, and scourgings, and imprisonment in loathsome dungeons, whose names are lost on earth.

Throughout this period, the books of Wickliffe, and especially his translation of the Bible, are recognized as the grand source of heresy. The statute of 1401, procured by Archbishop Arundel, made the possession of any of his writings punishable by death at the stake. In

1408, it was decreed by the clergy in convocation assembled, "that no schoolmaster should hereafter mix religious instruction with the teaching of youth, nor permit discussion about the sacraments, nor *the reading of the Scriptures in English;* that books of this sort, written by John Wickliffe, and others of his time, should be banished from schools, halls, and all places whatsoever ; that no man hereafter should translate any part of Scripture into English on his own authority ; and that all persons convicted of making or using such translations should be punished as favorers of error and heresy." In 1417, the right of sanctuary allowed to the highway robber and murderer, was denied by a formal act of parliament, to men whose only crime was that of reading the Scriptures in English. What better proof than these measures could be asked, of the wide diffusion and influence of Wickliffe's Bible ? Under the action of the statute last mentioned, so many were implicated in London and elsewhere, and so serious were the confiscations of property, that the King himself (Henry V.) was obliged to interpose, and hold the officers of the law in check by royal authority.

During the political agitations of the reign of Henry VI , public attention was effectually diverted from religious controversy, and the Lollards gradually disappear from the page of history. A night of ignorance, priestly tyranny, superstition and social disorder, a night whose gross darkness was hardly equalled by any that had preceded it, settled down on England. But the followers of Wickliffe were not extinct, nor had the Book perished whence they drew their life. Driven from the higher classes, truth had taken refuge among the unnoticed poor, and in silence and obscurity was nurturing the influences which were to ensure her triumph in the happier times to come. The light which Wickliffe had kindled, often smothered, then hidden from public view, but never for a moment extinguished, at length mingled its beams with the full day of the Reformation.

But this ancient version has yet another claim on our regard. It furnished, for all time, the type and pattern of THE ENGLISH BIBLE. In the century and a half during which it was the well-spring of the religious life of England—that long, dark day, when persecution kept the flock of Christ fast by the source of strength and consolation—its homely, child-like, expressive phraseology had become too deeply hallowed in the English mind as the medium of inspiration, ever again to be dissevered from it. A comparison with the subsequent versions which have found favor with the common people, will show them to be, in this respect, all offsprings of this parent-stock. Improved in many important particulars, so as to reflect with greater exactness the sense of the inspired originals, they are yet substantially, in form and manner, but reproductions of that in which our unlettered forefathers first read the revelation of God. Nay, I think it will be the feeling of many readers, that, while they are thus superior in correctness and in adaptation to more cultivated periods ; yet, in graphic, nervous force, in a certain untamed vigor, and a raciness of flavor which belongs to the youth of language, the patriarchal version has never been quite equalled. It was, to use Lord Bacon's beautiful illustration of a kindred point, "*the first crush of the grape.*" When, moreover, we remark how intelligible it remains to the present day, how much more near is its phraseology to our own language of common life than that even of Chaucer, we can hardly avoid the conclusion that it was this book, pre-eminently, which gave shape and fashion to our mother tongue, and by its continually increasing spread, gradually molded into permanent uniformity the language of the people.

Thus, in a threefold sense, did England's first Bible become the central point of English history. The tree which Wickliffe planted has clasped with its ever-lengthening roots the life of five centuries.

CHAPTER XI.

WICKLIFFE'S INFLUENCE ABROAD.

But it was not in England alone that Wickliffe's influence was felt, on the errors of the age. The religious interests of Bohemia lay near the heart of the enlightened and pious Queen Anne; and under her auspices the Reformer's writings had early been carried, in great numbers, into her native country. His opinions were received with favor by the reigning king and queen, became the subject of free discussion in the University of Prague, and spread widely among the common people. In the year 1400, in accordance with his great principle, the Scriptures were translated into Bohemian, making the second vernacular translation of modern Europe.* In 1404, the celebrated John Huss became a convert to these views; and from his ardent spirit the movement received an impulse which, within twenty-five years after the death of Wickliffe, had moved all Bohemia with his sentiments, and threatened an entire subversion of the Romish power. The importance of these events can only be rightly estimated, by taking into the account the mental activity and force of character which distinguished the Bohemians as a people, and the high intelligence and liberality of the nobles. Prague was not only the most populous, wealthy, and splendid city in Germany, but the acknowledged centre of the arts and sciences. Defection from the Papacy, at this point, involved far more than the loss of Bohemia. A light kindled on this eminence must shine far and wide over the surrounding nations.

In 1408 the Archbishop of Prague seized and committed to the flames some two hundred volumes of the English Reformer's writings. These belonged mostly to members of the University, and were, of course, but a small part of the number in the country.† In 1409, Pope Alexander V. issued a bull to the government of Bohemia, requiring the suppression, by the most stringent methods, of all teaching of Wickliffe's doctrines. His successor, John XXIII., cited Huss to appear before him at Rome; and this being declined, excommunicated him, and laid the city of Prague under an interdict.

---

* This, though not noticed by Vaughan in his Life of Wickliffe, is one of the most interesting events connected with his labors and influence.

† Vaughan.

At this crisis, Jerome of Prague came forward to defend the persecuted reformer, and to sustain the cause for which he suffered. Jerome had studied at Oxford, where, probably, he first imbibed Wickliffe's sentiments ; and in Paris he became known as their advocate, in a public controversy with the celebrated Romish theologian, Gerson. On his return to Bohemia he was imprisoned in Vienna, as a favorer of Wickliffe's doctrines ; but was released at the intercession of the University of Prague, where he was held in the highest esteem for his genius and learning. He now stood forth boldly, as the leader in the conflict, and took even higher ground against the doctrines and government of the Papal church than Huss himself. Opposition only fanned the rising flame ; and the continual conflict of opinion led all classes, more and more, to a study of the Holy Scriptures, as the only reliable standard of truth.

Things were in this condition when the famous Council of Constance was assembled, in the city from which it takes its name. Its object was, in part, the termination of the scandalous quarrel of the three rival popes, which was fast undermining the credit of St. Peter's chair ; in part, the suppression, by some adequate measures, of the alarming growth of Wickliffe's sentiments in Christendom. This Council was one of the most imposing ever convoked by the Romish Church. It numbered among its members and attendants, a German Emperor, twenty princes, one hundred and forty counts, a pope, more than twenty cardinals, seven patriarchs, twenty archbishops, ninety-one bishops, six hundred other prelates, and about four thousand priests. Its deliberations extended from the year 1414 to 1418.

The acts by which this great assembly is chiefly known to posterity are the deposition of three infallible popes, followed by the election of a fourth ; the burning of John Huss and Jerome at the stake, and the decrees against the writings of Wickliffe. Huss had been decoyed to Constance, by the promise of being allowed to defend his opinions before the assembled clergy of Christendom ; but, in violation of a safe-conduct from the hand of the Emperor Sigismund, he was put to death. In July, 1415, Jerome having ventured into the vicinity in hope of aiding his beloved and revered brother, was likewise seized, and after a long imprisonment, followed him to the stake. But the truth had taken too deep root in Bohemia to perish by such means. The assembled dignitaries of the Romish Church had beheld, with amazement, Bohemian nobles and citizens reasoning before them, with no less learning than boldness, from the word of God. A cause thus advocated has ceased to depend on leaders.

John Wickliffe had the honor of being recognized by this august assembly as the source of all the influences which had thus turned the world upside down. Among its earliest acts, fifty-five articles from his writings, which had already been condemned in England, Rome, and Prague, now received the solemn ban of the Council; and subsequently, it is said, two hundred and sixty more were condemned in like manner. His works of every kind, and wherever found, were adjudged to the flames.

Not satisfied with these measures, the Council, before closing, passed a sentence on his dead body, directing that it should be disinterred, and burned to ashes, as an expression of the abhorrence in which his doctrines and his memory were held by Holy Church. The decree was executed in 1428, when Archbishop Chichely, Primate of England, himself went down to Lutterworth, attended by a large train of the English clergy, to superintend the ceremony. From beneath the humble chancel, where they had slept in peace more than forty years, the bones of the Reformer were dragged rudely forth to the light of day; and being carried down the hill on which the church stood, to a little stream called the Swift, were there consumed by fire, and the ashes thrown into the river.

The enemies of truth took this as a presage of the speedy and final destruction of Wickliffe's influence. But they were false seers. "The Swift," says quaint old Fuller, "conveyed his ashes into the Avon, Avon into the Severn, Severn into the narrow seas, they to the main ocean. And thus they are the emblem of his doctrine, which now is dispersed all the world over." In Bohemia, the progress of his opinions was only accelerated by the cruel and treacherous dealing of the Council; and during the entire fifteenth and sixteenth centuries, this favored country exhibited a shining example of the power of Bible Christianity to call forth the energies, as well as to exalt the morals of a nation. Fourteen translations of the whole Bible, besides ten of the New Testament, which have come down to this day, bear witness to the zeal of her Christian scholars. She had her printed Bible fifty years before England. Education was common to her whole population, and the arts and sciences were brought to a remarkable perfection. When in 1620, during the progress of the thirty years' war, Bohemia lost her nationality, three-fourths of her population were Protestant; and seventy thousand men, with nearly the whole nobility, the entire body of the Protestant clergy, scholars, and artists, and in general, the most cultivated part of the nation, went forth as voluntary exiles, preferring rather to renounce their country than their religion. The monks from Spain, Italy, and Southern Germany, who poured into the subjugated country, found it a toilsome labor to restore the ancient reign of darkness. Every Bohemian book was condemned as presumptively heretical. There were individuals who boasted of having burned sixty thousand manuscripts, the precious relics of her early popular and sacred literature. Such works as were saved from the flames were shut up in monasteries, in secure rooms guarded by iron grates, doors, locks, bolts, and chains, and often inscribed with the warning title, *Hell*. A clearer exemplification of the influence and aim of the two religions could hardly be found in history.

It is easy to see what must have been the influence of this people, during their long period of prosperity, and how essentially it must have contributed toward preparing the way for the great work of the sixteenth century. The Reformation of Huss flowed into that of Luther; and when the latter reached England, its waters mingled with that earlier stream whose sources we have traced in the personal labors of Wickliffe.

The mind stands amazed over the view thus opened, of the mighty consequences to mankind flowing from the life of a single individual. If anything could surprise us more, it would be that party spirit could have caused such services to humanity to be forgotten, and the very existence of the apostle of modern Christianity to become almost a myth in the land of his birth. But as certainly as truth is to triumph, and the last vestige of priestcraft to disappear before the light of the pure word of God, the name of John Wickliffe will brighten as the ages pass, and the beautiful eulogy of the martyrologist be accepted as no more than justice to his character and labors : " This is out of all doubt, that at what time all the world was in most desperate and vile estate, and that the lamentable ignorance and darkness of God's truth had overshadowed the whole earth, this man stepped out like a valiant champion ; unto whom may justly be applied, that is spoken in the book of Ecclesiasticus, of one Simon, the son of Onias : ' Even as the morning star being in the midst of a cloud, and as the moon being full in her course, and as the bright beams of the sun, so doth he shine and glister in the temple and Church of God.' "

CHAPTER XII.

RELIGIOUS ASPECTS OF ENGLAND.

A CENTURY and a half had now elapsed since Wickliffe gave England her first Bible. During this whole period the Church, backed by the State, had made it a steady aim to root out the tendencies which he had implanted in the common English mind. Yet, at the beginning of the sixteenth century, we find them still existing in all their living energy among the Lollards. The " voluntary system" had proved adequate to the perpetuation of an order of devoted, working ministers, " willing to endure all things for the elect's sake ;" men, who from pure love for souls, made a joyful sacrifice of worldly gain and ease, and went forth, at the hazard of their lives, to preach the Gospel to the poor. Many shires of England were acquainted with the toil-worn, weather-beaten forms of these humble apostles of Bible piety, and about the time of Henry VIII.'s accession, numerous little congregations of " *Brethren in Christ*," (so they called themselves), were existing in different parts of the kingdom as the fruit of their labors. Being almost wholly from the lower classes, and taught by former persecutions to observe the greatest caution and secrecy, the timid flock had grown and multiplied undetected by their powerful foes.

At this period they seem to have enjoyed a fresh access of spiritual life. Thomas Mann, one of their preachers, who died for heresy in 1518, is reported in the bishop's record of his trial as " confessing that he hath turned seven hundred people to his religion ; for which he thanketh God." Such was their increase in zeal and numbers, that they could no longer escape observation. They were tracked to the lonely, unfrequented spots where they met under cover of night to worship God ; neighbor was made spy on neighbor ; husbands and wives, parents and children, brothers and sisters, were beguiled or forced to bear witness against each other. The Lollards Tower again echoed with the clanking of chains ; the rack and the stake once more claimed their victims. But those dark days of tears and blood have left a precious memorial for after times, furnished by the very hands which were striving to blot ' this pestilent sect ' from the face of the earth. From the registers of the bishops, before whom those accused of heresy were tried, has been gathered a long list of lowly martyrs and confessors who, but for these cruel persecutors, would never have been heard of out of the plebeian sphere in which they were born. Nor do we need any better testimony than is furnished by these records, to the purity both of their doctrines and their lives. A simple, blameless people, full of love and good works, there was nothing to be found against them " save in the matter of the law of their God."

What strikes one with most surprise, in these humble Christians, is the identity of their views at once with those of Wickliffe and his immediate followers, and with those afterward known as the distinguishing traits of Protestantism. But the solution is easy. It was because they all drew from one and the same source, THE INSPIRED WORD OF GOD. Through their whole history, the living preacher and the written Scripture had gone hand in hand. There is abundant evidence, not only that Wickliffe's version was still preserved among them, but that they had numerous copies of it in whole or in part, which were diligently read by the families of common laborers and mechanics.

One of the most common charges against the Lollards of this period, was the possession of some portion of Wickliffe's Bible, and the ability to read it, or to repeat from it by heart. Among those "troubled" as suspected heretics, between the years 1509 and 1517, five persons were charged with having met together secretly to read " certain chapters of the Evangelists in English, containing in them,"—such was the sentence of the learned bishops—" divers *erroneous and damnable opinions and conclusions of heresy.*" One Christopher Shoomaker, burned at Newbury, was accused of having gone to the house of John Say, and " read to him out of a book, the words which Christ spake to his disciples." In 1519 seven martyrs were burned in one fire at Coventry, " for having taught their children and servants the Lord's Prayer and Ten Commandments in English." The register of Longland, Bishop of Lincoln, for the single year 1521, contains a list of *some hundred names*, most of whom were accused for reading or repeating portions of the Scriptures in the English language. Jenkin Butler accused his own brother of reading to him a certain book of Scripture, and persuading him to hearken to the same. John Barrett, goldsmith of London, was "troubled" for having recited to his wife and maid the Epistle of James without book. John Thatcher was accused of teaching Alice Brown this saying of Jesus : ' Blessed are they that hear the word of God and keep it.' Thomas Philip and Lawrence Taylor were cited for reading the Epistle to the Romans and the first chapter of Luke in English. " Cuthbert, Bishop of London, sitting judicially in the chapel within his palace, at London, ministered in word against John Pykas," who confessed " that about five years last past, at a certain time his mother, then dwelling at Bury, sent for him, and moved him that he should not believe in the sacraments of the Church, for that was not the right way. And then she delivered to him one book of Paul's Epistles, in English (manuscript) ; and bid him live after the manner and way of said Epistles and Gospels, and not after the way the Church doth teach.' John Tyball was accused before this same bishop, of having had 'certain of Paul's Epistles after the old translation.' In 1529, John Tukesbury, a respectable citizen and leather merchant, of the city of London, confessed to having in his possession ' a manuscript copy of the Bible, and that he had been studying in the Holy Scriptures from the year 1512.'

Their supply of Bibles was indeed scanty, compared with that enjoyed since the introduction of the press ; but the lack was made up by an earnestness which could overcome all obstacles. We must not judge of these awakened minds and hearts by the general standard of their class at the time. Was only a single copy owned in a neighborhood, these hard-working laborers and mechanics would be found together, after a weary day of toil, alternately reading and listening to the words of life ; and so sweet was the refreshment to their spirits, that sometimes the morning light surprised them with its call to a new day of labor, ere they had thought of sleep. Their highest aim was to become possessors of some portion of the sacred volume. One man among them is mentioned, as having given a load of hay for a few chapters of one of Paul's Epistles. Some devoted the savings of years to this object. They have even been known to give a sum equal to eight or ten pounds of our time, for one of those little tracts which Wickliffe wrote so long before, for the instruction and comfort of the pious poor.

But they were not merely superior to their class. In the intelligence of their belief, in their sense of the true worth and destiny of man, in their thirst for knowledge, as well as in purity of manners and ardor of piety, they were, as a body, in advance of the highest ranks both of clergy and laity. "To see," says their faithful and affectionate historian Fox, " their travails, their earnest seeking, their ardent zeal, their reading, their watching, their sweet assemblies, their love and concord, their godly living, their faithfully marrying with the faithful, may make us now, in these our days of free profession, to blush for shame." That many, who bore the name of Lollards, failed in the hour of fiery trial and abjured their faith, merely proves that the influence of their views extended far beyond the bounds of the true believers. As a people, they were the recognized advocates, in a period of unsurpassed darkness and slavery to priestcraft, of the freedom of the human mind, of the rights of conscience, and of the supreme authority of the Holy Scriptures. To their influence is doubtless to be assigned the first place, among the causes which led to the English Reformation.

Let us turn now for a moment to the preparation going on in other classes, for the new epoch which was soon to dawn.

In all her external relations, England was still the most obedient vassal of Rome. Henry VIII. ,by training a bigoted adherent of the Church, vied with the " most Christian monarchs" of former times, in humbling his kingdom before the papal footstool. A golden rose, touched by the apostolic finger with holy chrism, was, in his esteem, a full equivalent for the rich English benefices which his Holiness disposed of unquestioned among his insatiable Italians. At no time had the clergy, as a body, been more ignorant, more corrupt, or more powerful, or the great mass of the people more abject slaves of superstition.

Still the new day which had dawned on continental Europe could not be wholly shut out. Even before Luther had commenced his reformatory labors, a more liberal style of learning had been introduced into the English Universities, through the labors of Erasmus and a few native scholars of like spirit. Greek professorships had been established, the New Testament in the original was studied by a considerable number, and public lectures were read on some portions of it. Hebrew, also, received some attention. These innovations were received by the great body of the clergy with anything but favor. With the quick instinct of birds of night, they discerned, far off, the hated approach of day. Dr. John Collet, who nobly led the way in the new path, by his lectures on Paul's Epistles (delivered at Oxford so early as 1497, " without fee or reward"), was interrupted by a prosecution for heresy, instituted by the Bishop of London, and escaped only through the personal kindness of Archbishop Warham, who dismissed the case without trial. When, in 1516, the Greek Testament of Erasmus made its appearance, a terrible hue and cry arose among the clergy. Priests used their influence at the confessional to warn young students against it, and one college at Cambridge was found so conservative as to forbid the dangerous book to be brought within its walls. Standish, afterward Bishop of Asaph,* conjured the king, on his knees, to put down Erasmus. The monks made them-

---

* Abbreviated, *Ep. a St. As.* (*Episcopus a Sancto Asino*, as put by Erasmus in his Epistles).

selves especially conspicuous by the zeal of their opposition, declaring from the pulpit that " there was now a new language invented, called Greek, of which people should beware as the source of all heresies : that in this language had come forth a book, called the New Testament, which was now in everybody's hands, and was full of thorns and briars ; that there was also another language started up which they called Hebrew, and that they who learned it were turned Jews."

"Remember ye not," says Tyndale in 1531 ; "how within this thirty years, and far less, and yet dureth to this day, the old barking curs, Dun's disciples, and the like draff, called Scottists, the children of darkness, raged in every pulpit against Greek, Latin, and Hebrew : and what sorrow the schoolmasters that taught the true Latin tongue had with them ? Some beating the pulpit with their fists for madness, and roaring out with open and foaming mouth, that if there were but one Terence and Virgil in the world, and that same in their sleeves, and a fire before them, they would burn them therein, though it should cost their lives."

But the spirit of the age was too strong to be thus repressed. Henry VIII. was himself ambitious to be known as a scholar and patron of learning ; and he not only encouraged classical study, but, in 1519, commanded by a royal mandate, that the study of the Scriptures in the original languages should henceforth constitute a regular branch of academic instruction at Oxford. His minister, Cardinal Wolsey, whose far-sighted intellect perceived in the new agencies at work in the age, a power which might perhaps be controlled, but could never be destroyed, threw himself into the vanguard of the cause of liberal learning. Cardinal's College, established by him at Oxford, was a magnificent project for converting progress itself into a barrier against progress ; for raising up a clergy qualified by rigid intellectual discipline and eminent scholarship, to snatch from the reformers the leadership of the awakening age. That college, he resolved, should be " the most glorious in the universe." To furnish it with adequate endowments he ejected, by his authority as Papal Legate, the inmates of forty-one priories and nunneries, and devoted their riches to this object, sending forth their inmates to seek a home in other establishments. The most distinguished teachers were called in to add lustre to the new foundation, and its Fellows were the picked men of both universities. It was wisely planned. But the Cardinal, with all his sagacity, had not taken into the reckoning that the men thus trained might be the first to desert the cause he sought to uphold. Cardinal College rose into sudden eminence as a school of liberal learning, and in the same proportion became a nursery of the new opinions. Its accomplished youth, their minds emancipated by enlarged enquiry, and their hearts instructed by the Scriptures in that liberty wherewith Christ makes free, devoted themselves with generous ardor to the cause of truth and spiritual freedom.

Meanwhile, the multiplication of books through the press, by promoting general intelligence, had increased the disaffection of all classes toward the Romish clergy. Voices were heard to and from the people, in numerous little treatises, exposing the errors and vices of the Church. The thunder of Luther's tones then came reverberating over the water ; and, in spite of the vigilance of the clergy, translations of his writings were extensively circulated in England.

Thus, long before the quarrel of Henry with the Pope led to an external separation from Rome, the way had been preparing for a reform far more thorough and comprehensive ; a reform based on radical changes in the opinions and convictions of his subjects. To that true reform he was no less an enemy than the Pope himself ; and it worked its way against the whole force of his iron will. Its first marked development, the event which inaugurated the AGE OF BIBLE TRANSLATION in England, will form the subject of the next chapter.

CHAPTER XIII.

TYNDALE'S NEW TESTAMENT.

AFTER the view just given of the influences at work in England, it can be no matter of surprise, to find the design of a new translation of the Scriptures already ripened in the bosom of an English scholar, years before Luther began the publication of the Bible in German. That scholar was WILLIAM TYNDALE.

Tyndale was born about the year 1484, and at a very early age was sent to Oxford, which was one of the most celebrated schools of learning then existing. Here he soon attained high rank, and was particularly distinguished for his knowledge of the tongues. But though a proficient in classical literature, his most diligent study was given to the Greek New Testament, in which, also, he was accustomed to read to his fellow students. There is even strong reason for believing that, while still at the University and before he had reached his twentieth year, the purpose of translating the Scriptures was already working in his mind. An autograph collection in the hands of one of his biographers,* of translations made by him of select portions of the New Testament, shows in its ornamental, missal-like headings and borders, the initials W. T., and the date 1502, several times repeated. To the latter are prefixed, in one instance, the significant words "TIME TRIETH"; as if the youthful translator even then had it in view to submit his labors to the test of publication. It is a fact no less remarkable than interesting, that these early attempts were transferred, for the most part verbatim, into his complete New Testament; and that many passages have come down through the successive revisions, unaltered, into our common version! Thus the bent of his mind, from its first known development, marks him out as a man of earnest purpose, who already comprehends what is his work and calling in the age.

Still, however, he was a member of the Romish Church, and had probably thought of nothing beyond a reformation in the existing ecclesiastical institutions. In 1502, the date already mentioned, he

---

* Offor's Memoir prefixed to Tyndale's New Testament. London, 1836.

was ordained a priest, and in 1508 became a friar in the monastery at Greenwich. We are not informed of the circumstances which induced him to withdraw from this relation ; but in 1522 he had returned to his native Gloucestershire, and was filling the office of private tutor and chaplain in a family of rank. While here, he made no secret of his reformatory sentiments, which soon became well known in the surrounding region. The hospitable mansion of his patron was a favorite resort of the prelates and clergy of the neighborhood, and frequent discussions arose at table in respect to the doctrines and measures of Luther, which were now making much noise in England. The dogmatism and deplorable ignorance exhibited by the clerical visitors on these occasions, often drew from the modest tutor a spirited defence of the Reformer, and an earnest recommendation to test his views by the New Testament. "He spared not," says Foxe, "to show them simply and plainly his judgment ; and when they at any time did vary from his opinions, *he would show them in the book, and lay before them the manifest places of Scripture*, to confute their errors and confirm his sayings." In these controversies the dignitaries were so uniformly mortified by defeat, that they gradually ceased their visits ; " preferring," as Fuller remarks, "the loss of Squire Welch's good cheer, to the sour sauce of Master Tyndale's company."

But if they could not reason, they could persecute ; and their ill will soon exhibited itself in the citation of Tyndale before the chancellor of the diocese, on a charge of heresy. There was quite a rally of the clergy to witness his humiliation. In his own words, "All the priests of the country were present the same day." But under some influence not now apparent, the Chancellor, after "threatening him grievously, and reviling and rating him as though he had been a dog," allowed him to depart without punishment. Some of his friends counselled a prudent concealment of his views in future ; but "the fire in his bones" refused to be shut up. A Popish clergyman soon after remarked to Tyndale, in reply to an earnest plea for a vernacular Bible : "We had better be without God's laws than the Pope's !" "I defy the Pope and all his laws," cried the indignant reformer ; "*and if God spare my life, ere many years I will cause a boy that driveth the plough to know more of the Scriptures than you do !*" A pledge which he nobly redeemed at the price of exile, poverty, a life of toil and persecution, and finally of a martyr's death.

It is interesting to remark how firmly, at this period, the thought had fixed itself in Tyndale's mind, that the translation of the Scriptures out of the original tongues was emphatically the work demanded by the wants of the age. He thus explains the motives which moved him to put his hand to the task :

"A thousand books had they lever to be put forth against their abominable doings and doctrines, than that the SCRIPTURE should come to light. For as long as they may keep *that* down, they will so darken the right way with their mist of sophistry, and so tangle them that either rebuke or despise their abominations, with arguments of philosophy, and with worldly similitudes and apparent reasons of natural wisdom ; and with wresting the Scriptures unto their own purpose, clean contrary unto the process, order and meaning of the text ; and so delude them, expounding it in many senses before the unlearned lay people (when it hath but one plain, literal sense, whose light the owls cannot abide), that though thou feel in thine heart, and art sure, how that all is false that they say, yet couldst thou not solve their subtle riddles.

"Which thing only moved me to translate the New Testament. Because I perceived by experience, how that it was impossible to establish the lay people in any truth, *except the Scriptures were plainly laid before their eyes in their mother tongue.*"

Convinced that the prosecution of his design was impracticable where he then was, and fearing, moreover, to jeopardize the family of his kind patrons by remaining under their roof, Tyndale now resolved to seek another home. The plan he formed in this exigency strikingly illustrates his simplicity of character, and his ignorance of the state of things in " high places." The opposition from which he had suffered he ascribed to the peculiar ignorance and stupidity of the Gloucestershire clergy.

"When," says he, " I was so turmoiled in the country where I was, that I could no longer dwell there, ... I thiswise thought in myself : this I suffer, because the priests of the country be unlearned, as God knoweth they are a full ignorant sort, which have seen no more Latin than they read in their Portesses, and Missals,* which yet many of them can scarcely read. And therefore, because they are thus unlearned, thought I, when they come together to the ale-house, which is their preaching place, they affirm that my sayings are heresy."

From the enlightened clergy of the metropolis he expected very different treatment. He fixed his eyes on Tunstal, Bishop of London, whom Erasmus, in his Annotations on the New Testament, had proclaimed a paragon of learning and liberality, as the man under whose countenance he was to execute, in safety and quiet, and with all such aids as he might need, the beneficent task of giving the

Bible to England. "I thought," says he, "if I might come into this man's service, I were happy. For even in the Bishop of London's house, I intended to have done it."

Bidding farewell to his pleasant home in Little Sodbury Manor, Tyndale now turned his steps toward London, provided with a letter from his patron to Sir Harry Guildford, the King's Comptroller. The story of his disappointment must be given in his own words:

"And so," he says, "I gat me to London, and through the acquaintance of my master, came to Sir Harry Guildford, the King's Grace's Comptroller, and brought him an oration of Isocrates, which I had translated out of Greek into English, to speak unto my Lord of London for me. This he also did, as he showed me, and willed me to write an epistle to my lord, and to go to him myself, which I also did, and delivered my epistle to a servant of his own, one William Hebilthwayte, a man of mine old acquaintance. But God, which knoweth that which is within hypocrites, saw that I was beguiled, and that *that* counsel was not the next way to my purpose. And therefore he gat me no favor in my lord's sight. Whereupon my lord answered me—'his house was full, he had more than he could well find, and advised me to seek in London, where,' he said, 'I could not lack a service.'"

The historical novelist might go far, without finding richer materials for character-painting than are furnished by this little narrative. The guileless country scholar, his head teeming with classical and sacred lore, and his heart burning with a great thought of beneficence to his country—with his letter from the country baronet, and his oration of Isocrates for credentials—and the proud, worldly church dignitary, whose friendship and protection he came to solicit, would make an exquisite contrast. To the Bishop of London the poor, unknown clerk is a very different personage from the celebrated Erasmus, the protégé of popes and princes; and Tyndale is shown out of the stately episcopal palace, with the kind advice to seek his fortune elsewhere. "Truly," thus muses the disappointed scholar, "it was all in the tongue of Erasmus, which maketh of little gnats great elephants, and lifteth up above the stars whoever giveth him a little exhibition!"—There came a time, and not long after, when Bishop Tunstal found this same William Tyndale a man of far more account, so far as the interests of the Romish hierarchy were concerned, than the great Erasmus.

Nearly a year was consumed in vain efforts to secure a situation favorable to the accomplishment of his design. Evidently there was something in his deportment and conversation which did not commend him to the church dignitaries of the capital. The last six months, he found a home in the hospitable abode of Humphrey Monmouth, a wealthy citizen, afterward an Alderman of London. It was, however, far from being an idle or unprofitable year. He preached, it would seem, regularly at St. Dunstan's church, Fleet Street, on the Sabbath, and was as indefatigable a student as ever. But the most valuable lessons of the year were obtained from the study, for which the metropolis furnished such rich advantages, of the working of the existing Church system, its influence on the character of the clergy, and through them, upon the moral condition of the kingdom, and the general interests of Christendom. He now saw that a plan for enlightening the people, like that which he had formed, was in contravention of the first principle of their policy, that the power of the clergy rests on the ignorance of the masses. Before the close of the year he had relinquished all idea of attempting its execution in England.

"And so," he says, "I abode in London almost a year, and marked the course of the world, and heard our preachers, how they boasted themselves and their high authority; and beheld the pomp of our prelates, and how busy they were, as they yet use, to set peace and unity in the world; though it be not possible for them that walk in darkness to continue long in peace (for they cannot but either stumble, or dash themselves at one thing or another, that shall clean disquiet them altogether), and saw things of which I defer to speak at this time; and understood at the last, not only that there was no room in my Lord of London's palace to translate the New Testament, but also that there was no place to do it in all England, as experience doth now openly declare."

Accordingly, late in the year 1523,* being furnished by his noble friend, Monmouth, with the sum of ten pounds (equal to one hundred and fifty of the present time, or nearly seven hundred dollars), Tyndale bade a final adieu to his native land, and embarked for Hamburgh. In this city he remained between one and two years, diligently improving the quiet and security here afforded for the prosecution of his translation.

Having nearly or quite completed it, he drew on Monmouth for an additional ten pounds, contributed by other English friends, which he had left with him for safe-keeping, and repaired to Cologne for the

---

* In the statement of dates and places, the authority of Anderson (Annals of the English Bible, London, 1845) is, for the most part, followed in this division of the work.

purpose of printing his manuscript at one of its celebrated presses. His arrangements were made with the greatest secrecy, for Cologne was far from being favorable to the sentiments of the Reformation.

One interesting fact should not be omitted in this connection. The English merchants, residing for purposes of trade in the commercial cities of Germany, seem, as a general thing, to have been deeply imbued with Protestant principles. Many of them became the steady friends and protectors of Tyndale, and entered with warm zeal into his design of giving the Bible to their common country. They aided him with money; their ships were at his service for the conveyance of his precious offering into England, concealed in boxes and bales of merchandise. Of like spirit must have been their partners in the English ports, to whom it was consigned. Thus we have a glimpse into a state of opinion and feeling, in a most influential class of English society, which might well excite the utmost jealousy and vigilance on the part of the churchmen. Such friends Tyndale found at Cologne; and his work was passing through the press under happy auspices, when an exigency arose, beyond their power to meet, which drove Tyndale hastily from the city.

THE BIBLE-HATER

Just at this critical moment, when the salvation of England seemed to hang on the successful completion of the undertaking, there arrived in Cologne one of the most busy and malignant enemies of the truth that the world has seen. The especial distinction of John Cochlæus was his intense hatred to vernacular translations of the Bible, in which he is said to have surpassed all his contemporaries. The rancor which characterized his numerous writings against German reformers and his unceasing efforts, by word and deed, to counteract their influence, had so offended the Protestant feeling of Frankfort, where he formerly resided, that he was obliged to flee from that city. The same thing having been repeated at Mentz, he took refuge at Cologne at the very time when his presence was, seemingly, most disastrous to the cause of truth. Just then he was exceedingly anxious to bring out the works of Rupert, an ancient abbot of Deutz, who was claimed by both parties in the great controversy; but he found it difficult to convince any of the Cologne printers that the enterprise would pay. After many unsuccessful attempts, Peter Quintel, the very printer employed by Tyndale, was persuaded to make the trial; and thus the best of opportunities for ferreting out the important secret was furnished to the man who, of all others, would be likely to make the worst use of it.

For a person of his rank, and an ecclesiastic, Cochlæus seems to have been on terms of very jovial fellowship with the printers. The manner in which he improved the intimacy is most fitly related in his own words.

" Having thus become more intimate and familiar with the Cologne printers, he sometimes heard them boast, confidently, when in their cups, that, whether the King and Cardinal of England would or would not, all England would, in a short time, be Lutheran. He heard, also, that there were two Englishmen lurking there, learned, skillful in languages, and fluent, whom, however, he could never see or converse with. Calling, therefore, certain printers into his lodging, *after they were heated with wine*, one of them in more private discourse, discovered to him the secret by which England was to be drawn over to the side of Luther, namely, 'That three thousand copies of the Lutheran New Testament, translated into the English language, were in press, and already were advanced as far as the letter K, *in ordine quaternionum*. That the expenses were fully supplied by English merchants, who were secretly to convey the work when printed, and disperse it widely through all England, before the King or the Cardinal would discover or prevent it.' "

Having considered with himself " the magnitude of the grievous danger," Cochlæus repaired, next day, to the house of Hermann Rincke, a distinguished patrician of Cologne, who had held many high offices at court, was familiar both with the Emperor and with the King of England, and had great influence in the city government, and to him disclosed the whole affair. Herr Rincke was not the man to let slip an opportunity for laying a king under obligation. Accordingly, after satisfying himself by personal investigation at the printing house that Cochlæus was not mistaken, he laid the matter before the city Senate, and made such a representation of the case, that they issued an order interdicting the printer from proceeding farther in that work. Tyndale did not wait for the second blow. Hastily gathering up his manuscripts, and the sheets as far as printed, he fled with his assistant, George Roye, up the Rhine to Worms. This place, being fully pervaded by the doctrines of Luther, offered a far more secure retreat than Cologne, and here, accordingly, he remained till the year 1527.

Arrived at Worms, he was personally safe, and might hope to complete his work without interruption. But a new difficulty lay in his way. The New Testament which he had commenced printing was in quarto form, with explanatory notes and glosses, and a long Prologue at the beginning. All this had become known to his enemies, who would, of course, furnish such a description of the volume to the authorities in England as would enable them to seize all copies the instant they arrived. Tyndale decided at once upon his course. Laying aside his quarto for the present, he had an edition of the text merely struck off in octavo form, in which, for the Prologue, he substituted an Epistle to the Reader, at the end, thus effacing, so far as possible, every feature by which the book might be identified. This he probably intended should precede the quarto, by an interval sufficiently long to allow the alarm excited by Cochlæus to die away. But, through some circumstances, now unknown, its transmission to England was delayed till the quarto also had been completed, and both editions arrived very nearly at the same time, toward the close of December, 1525. The labor was not, indeed, fruitless; for the little octavo had been quietly making its way through the country, nearly three quarters of a year before its existence was suspected. The quarto, on the contrary, was discovered scarcely a month after its arrival. The circumstances of its detection furnish a lively picture of the state of the times.

THE SECRET SEARCH.

In the year 1523, Symon Fyshe, a lawyer of Gray's Inn, London, having taken part in a privately acted play which reflected severely on Cardinal Wolsey, was that same night betrayed, and obliged to flee from his own house, and at length from England. While still in exile, probably in the year 1524, he composed a tract addressed 'to the King our Sovereign Lord,' entitled 'The Supplication of Beggars,' which set forth, in a bold and spirited manner, the danger to the nation and the throne from the grasping avarice of the clergy. In this, he averred, was the true ground of their opposition to the Bible for the people. "This is the great scab *why they will not let the New Testament go abroad in your mother-tongue*, lest men should espy that they, by their cloaked hypocrisy, do translate, thus fast, your kingdom into their hands."—Copies of this stirring appeal were soon secretly circulating in England, and produced wherever read a deep impression. On Candlemas day, February 2, 1526, advantage was taken of a royal procession to Westminster, to scatter large numbers in the streets, thus distributing it far and wide, among all classes of people.

How slight a cause will alarm the abettor of error! The great Cardinal, clothed with almost regal and pontifical power, the man who had been truly called the 'king of his king,' trembled at these few pages of a friendless, banished man. It was not without reason; for they had in them the omnipotence of truth! So imminent seemed to him the danger, that on the very next day, orders were issued by his authority for a "*secret search*" after Lutheran books,* to be made simultaneously in London, and both the Universities. Three years before, a similar measure had been resolved on, as a check to the progress of reform, and had then obtained the king's full concurrence. Without waiting for any further expression of the royal will, Wolsey now proceeded to carry out this act into instant execution. Such were the circumstances which led to the discovery, thus early, of the English New Testament.

Suspicion having fastened particularly on one Thomas Garrett, curate of All-Hallows Church, as a receiver and distributor of prohibited books, he was searched for through all London. It was found, however, that he had gone to Oxford, with a quantity of such books, for the purpose of there making sale of them " to such as he knew to be lovers of the Gospel." Thither he was pursued, in the determination, says Foxe, " to apprehend and imprison him, and to burn all and every his foresaid books, and himself too, if they could, so burning hot was their zeal." But having received a friendly warning of his danger, he fled on the morning of the 7th, and concealed himself. The impression of that day of terror is affectingly given in the words of Anthony Dalaber, one of the pious Oxford students, who was a devoted friend, and, soon after, a fellow-sufferer, of Garrett.

" When he was gone down from my chamber, I straightway did shut my chamber door, and went into my study, and took the New Testament in my hands, kneeled down on my knees, and with many a deep sigh and salt tear, I did with much deliberation read over the tenth chapter of Matthew's Gospel ; and when I had so done, with fervent prayers I did commit unto God our dearly beloved brother Garrett, earnestly beseeching him in and for Jesus Christ's sake, his only begotten Son, our Lord, that he would vouchsafe not only safely to conduct and keep our said dear brother from the hands of all his enemies, but also that he would endue his tender and lately born little flock in Oxford with heavenly strength by his Holy Spirit, that they might be able thereby valiantly to withstand, to his glory, all their fierce enemies, and might also quietly, to their own salvation, with all godly patience, bear Christ's heavy cross ; which I now saw was presently to be laid on their young and tender backs, unable to bear so

---

* *Lutheran* was now the term of reproach, as *Lollard* had been during the preceding century. Under this name were included not only the translated works of the German reformers, but all English books, both old and recent, which contained sentiments similar to theirs, Tyndale's original writings and his New Testament among the number.

great a burden without the great help of his Holy Spirit. This done I laid aside my book safe."

Many such scenes, no doubt, passed that night in solitary rooms at Oxford, when the English New Testament of Tyndale was consecrated to its holy work by the tears and prayers of humble and trembling hearts. On the following Friday, poor Garrett fell into the hands of his enemies. After being compelled, in company with Dalaber and several other convicted students, to march in procession from St. Mary's to Cardinal College, where each of them cast one of the condemned books into a large bonfire kindled for the purpose, the two friends were imprisoned at Osney Isle till near the close of the year, when Garrett was brought before Tunstal for the trial which resulted in his martyrdom.

But these were not the only victims at Oxford. Cardinal College, that darling of Wolsey's heart, was found to be deeply infected with the dreaded poison. The books detected under the flooring of its rooms and in other secret places, too plainly betrayed the humiliating fact. The Cardinal's anger was in proportion to his disappointment. Of the suspected, some escaped to their friends; but ten or more members of this model college, with about an equal number from the others, were apprehended, and immured in a deep cellar under Cardinal College, used as a repository of salt fish. Three of them sunk within a week under the effects of a putrid atmosphere and unwholesome food, and a fourth soon followed. The rest, after lying from March to August in this loathsome dungeon, with nothing to subsist on but the fish with which it was stored, were made prisoners at large by Wolsey. He probably thought that by this time the lads were well cured of heresy.

Among the number thus released was John Frith, then about twenty-two years of age, a young man of rare genius and acquirements, and of fervent piety. He soon escaped to the continent; and having joined his spiritual father and best beloved friend, Tyndale, became his assistant in translating the Bible.

We must now turn to the sister university. Cambridge lay under still stronger suspicion of heresy than Oxford, and with good reason. Here, several years before, Thomas Bilney had been converted by the study of Erasmus' Greek Testament; and, through his labors, Hugh Latimer, and Robert Barnes, Prior of the Monastery of Augustin Friars at Cambridge, had also learned the way of life. From them a powerful evangelical influence had spread into the various colleges of the university, so that even as early as 1523 certain bishops had urged the importance of a visitation, for the purpose of trying those who were infected with heresy. Wolsey, who always resented the interference of inferior prelates in matters which he had taken under his special supervision, and who probably thought he could arrest the epidemic whenever he might please to speak the word, silenced the movement. Perhaps, moreover, he could not prevail on himself to extinguish, at once, the only light amid the stupid conservatism of Cambridge ; for the suspected parties were the sole promoters and examples of liberal learning in the university. Whatever were the cause, the truth was permitted to spread three years longer, unobstructed by any authoritative interference.

But a crisis gradually approached. Growing bolder and more earnest in the truth, Latimer openly inveighed against the crime of *locking up the Scriptures from the people in an unknown tongue*. Upon this he was cited for heresy before West, Bishop of Ely, and forbidden to preach either in the churches of the university, or anywhere within his diocese. But the monasteries were exempt from episcopal jurisdiction, and Barnes opened his chapel to the silenced preacher. Such were the crowds who rushed to hear him that the place could not contain them. Barnes himself was now invited by the parish of St. Edwards to preach in their church ; and, though constitutionally timid, and hitherto, it would seem, cautious in his policy, he now resolved to give free and full utterance to his convictions. The rising tide of popular favor, an influence to which he was very susceptible, may have caused something of human vanity and presumption to mingle with his better feelings ; for, not contenting himself with a clear exhibition of Christian truth, he launched into a bold tirade, full of wit and sarcasm, against the worldly pomp and magnificence of the Lord Cardinal himself, then in the height and plenitude of power. A rebuke well merited, indeed, but which could hardly fail to lead to consequences for which, alas ! poor Barnes was but ill-prepared. This was on the 24th of December, 1525. A storm immediately arose in the university, one party siding most zealously with the preacher, as a champion of the faith, the other firmly resolved on his humiliation or his ruin. Public disputations on the contested points were kept up through the whole of January, and the first week of February, in which learned men from at least seven different colleges took part. Meanwhile a full account of the transaction had been sent to the Cardinal.

Things were thus progressing at Cambridge, and Wolsey's proud spirit had been stung to madness, by the report of Barnes's attack upon those peculiarly tender points in his character, when the distribution of Fyshe's tract, on the second of February, completed his chagrin and irritation. The emissaries of the "*secret search*," at Cambridge, had a double commission ; first, the apprehension of Dr. Barnes, and secondly, the seizure of heretical books, and of those in whose possession they were found. Of these, not fewer than thirty names were on their list, and the rooms of each had been exactly designated and described. But at the first instant of the officers' arrival, Dr. Forman, of Queen's College, himself an adherent of " the new learning," had given the warning word ; and by the time the sergeant-at-arms, attended by the Vice-Chancellor and the Proctors, was ready to go the rounds, Cambridge was, to all appearance, purified of heresy. Not a " seditious" book was to be found ; and the officer, with only Dr. Barnes in charge, returned to London, no wiser than he came.

The next day after his apprehension, Barnes stood before Wolsey, whose bitter taunts and hard demeanor betrayed how deeply his pride had been wounded. " What ! Master Doctor," he asked, " had you not scope enough in the Scriptures to teach the people, that my golden shoes, my pole-axes, my pillars, my golden cushions, my crosses did so offend you, that you must make me *ridiculum caput* before the people ? We were jollily that day laughed to scorn. Verily, it was a sermon fitter to be preached on a stage than in a pulpit." Poor Barnes for a time held out bravely, alike against threats and persuasions. But when the final alternative was put to him—" *Abjure or burn*"—his faith proved insufficient for the trial. Having, in great agony of mind, at length yielded to the demands of his judges, the next Sunday was appointed for the public expiation of his offence, at St. Paul's. On that day, the triumphant cardinal, attired in purple, surrounded by six and thirty abbots, mitred priors and bishops, in damask and satin, sat enthroned in all his pomp—the highest representative of the Church of Rome in England—and beheld at his feet the leading champion of evangelical truth—an abjuring heretic ! Beside him stood—each like him with a faggot, the mark of shame, on his shoulder—five honorable merchants, convicted of the crime of aiding to bring the Bible into England. Within the rails were displayed the evidences of their guilt—"*great baskets full of books*," in part the New Testaments of Tyndale—the precious booty gathered by the previous week's " search" in Oxford and London. After a sermon against Luther and Barnes, by Fisher, Bishop of Rochester, these baskets were emptied into a large bonfire, kindled before the great crucifix at the north gate of St. Paul's, wherein also the heretics, after making three times the circuit of the fire, cast their faggots. Wolsey then retired under a canopy, in great pomp, and Fisher proclaimed to the assembly certain days of pardon and indulgence, for being present on this occasion ; though by his own statement, when he afterward published his sermon, they had made such a tumult as to drown his voice during its delivery. At the close of the ceremony the unhappy Barnes, in accordance with the good faith and tenderness usually shown by the Romish Mother to those who have returned to her bosom, was sent back to prison.

Such was the greeting which the New Testament received at the hands of the priesthood, on its first arrival in England, in the sixteenth century. It was just as they had treated Wickliffe's Bible a hundred and forty years before. The spirit of the Romish Church had remained unchanged.

THE KING ENLISTED.

Thus far, however, these measures had received no direct countenance from the King. In the "secret search" just described, the cardinal had acted simply on his own ecclesiastical authority. But a few weeks only had elapsed, when Luther's imprudence, and Henry's vanity, furnished the means of enlisting him as a persecutor, with a zeal no less violent than theirs.

Henry VIII.'s book against Luther, by which he gained from the Pope the title in which he so much gloried—"Defender of the Faith" —and Luther's uncourteous, not to say virulent reply, are matters familiar to my readers. In 1525, Luther—urged, as he afterward professed, by Christian, King of Denmark—made a most blundering attempt at reconciliation with Henry, by a letter, in which he begged pardon for his former one, as foolish, precipitate, and offensive ; but, at the same time, explaining that he now understood the real author of the King's book to have been Wolsey, whom he denounced as "a monster, the abhorrence of God and man, and the plague of the realm of England." It so happened, moreover, that the original letter never reached Henry, but only a printed copy, and that not till six months after its date, or about one month after the degradation of Barnes, and the burning of the New Testaments at St. Paul's.

The wily cardinal well knew how to turn Luther's *faux pas* to his own ends. Incensed beyond measure at the Reformer's depreciation of his precious book, and of his own claim to be its author, and justly angry that the letter should have been given to the public months before he saw it, Henry was easily persuaded that the New Testaments secretly conveyed in such numbers into the country, were from the same source, being part and parcel of Luther's plot to turn all England to his heresy. The fact that the translator's name was withheld, gave color to the assertion. The King was now quite willing to aid in their suppression ; and, accordingly, the first royal manifesto in defence of the burning the English Bible, and the severe punishment of those who should read it, soon appeared. To his Latin reply to Luther, was prefixed an English address to his own subjects, in which, after an account of Luther's unfortunate letter, and his " device" of translating the New Testament into English, " with corruptions in the holy text, as well as with certain prefaces and glosses, for the advancement and setting forth of his abominable heresies," he proceeds in the following paternal style : " In the avoiding whereof We, of our special tender zeal toward you, have, with the deliberate advice of the most reverend Father in God, Thomas Lord Cardinal, Legate *a latere* of the See Apostolic, Archbishop of York, Chancellor and our Primate of this realm, and other reverend fathers of the spirituality, determined the said and untrue translations to be burned, with further sharp correction and punishment against the keepers and readers of the same, reckoning of your wisdom very sure, that ye will well and thankfully receive our tender and loving mind to you therein, and that ye will never be so greedy of any sweet wine, be the grape never so pleasant, that ye will desire to taste it, being well advertised that your enemy before hath poisoned it."

The King's dutiful subjects, however, were neither disposed to take his word, nor submit to his authority in this matter. The idea, so long nourished in the humble congregations of the Lollards, that no power in Church or State can lawfully shut up the word of God from the people, had now spread far and wide in England. While, therefore, unremitted inquisition was made for the sacred book, and great numbers were discovered and destroyed, so that, we are informed, " during this year Bibles were burned daily ;" yet, so far did the demand and supply outstrip the activity of the clergy, that the country was filled with copies. Tunstal, Bishop of London, who had been absent during this excitement, as Ambassador to Spain, returning in the autumn, found his diocese plentifully sown with both the quarto and the octavo editions. On the 24th of October the following decree was issued under his episcopal seal :

" By the duty of our pastoral office we are bound diligently, with all our power, to foresee, provide for, root out, and put away, all those things which seem to tend to the peril and danger of our subjects, and specially the destruction of their souls ! Wherefore, we having understanding, by the report of divers credible persons, and also by the evident appearance of the matter, that many children of iniquity, maintainers of Luther's sect, blinded through extreme wickedness, wandering from the way of truth and the Catholic faith, craftily have translated the New Testament into our English tongue, intermingling therewith many heretical articles and erroneous opinions, pernicious and offensive, seducing the simple people, attempting, by their wicked and perverse interpretations, to profanate the majesty of Scripture, which hitherto hath remained undefiled, and craftily to abuse the most Holy Word of God, and the true sense of the same ; of the which translation there are many books imprinted, some with glosses, and some without ; containing, in the English tongue, that pestiferous and most pernicious poison, dispersed throughout all our diocese, in great number—which truly, without it be speedily foreseen, without doubt will contaminate and infect the flock committed unto us, with most deadly poison and heresy, to the grievous peril and danger of the souls committed to our charge, and the offence of God's Divine Majesty : Wherefore we, Cuthbert, the Bishop aforesaid, grievously sorrowing for the premises, willing to withstand the craft and subtlety of the ancient enemy and his ministers, which seek the destruction of my flock, and with a diligent care to take heed unto the flock committed to my charge, desiring to find speedy remedies for the premises, Do charge you, jointly and severally (the Archdeacons), and by virtue of your obedience, straightly enjoin and command you, that, by our authority, you warn, or cause to be warned, all and singular, as well exempt as not exempt, dwelling within your archdeaconries, that within thirty days' space, whereof ten days shall be for the first, ten for the second, and ten for the third peremptory term, under pain of excommunication, and incurring the suspicion of heresy, they do bring in, and really deliver unto our Vicar-General, (Geoffrey Wharton), all and singular such books as contain the translation of the New Testament in the English Tongue : and that you do certify us, or our said Commissary, within two months after the day of the date of these presents, duly, personally, or by your letters, together with these presents under your seals, what you have done in the premises, under pain of contempt ! Given under our seal, the four and twentieth day of October, A.D. 1526, in the fifth year of our consecration."

The Archbishop of Canterbury had already called an assembly of bishops, to consult on the alarming state of his province ; and a few days after the publication of Tunstal's decree, an archiepiscopal " Mandate," couched in nearly the same terms, directed a search of the entire province, for the single object of seizing copies of the English New Testament.

Aware, however, that all this would avail little, so long as the offensive volume continued to pour in from abroad, they resolved on an energetic effort to cut off the source of supply. Such an eager craving for the Scriptures had been created among the English people, that a printer of Antwerp, Christopher Endhoven by name, had taken it up as a profitable business investment ; and, without consulting Tyndale, had already brought out a third edition of his translation. This, with the former editions, was now coming into England, through members of the English House of Merchant Adventurers established in that great commercial emporium.

The office of confidential agent of the Crown to the Imperial City at this time (the King's Merchant, as he was called) was Sir John

Hackett, who held also the high office of Envoy to the Court of Brabant, of which the Princess Margaret, aunt of the Emperor Charles V., was then Regent. Directly after the issuing of Tunstal's decree, Henry addressed a letter to the Princess, and another to the Governor of the English House, both of which had for their object the seizure and burning of English New Testaments found in that country, and the punishment, by banishment and confiscation, of all engaged in printing and circulating it. Chancellor Wolsey also wrote two letters to Hackett, to the same effect. The zeal and pertinacity with which the Envoy pushed the matter, though, as appears from his own letters, highly offensive to the Lords of Antwerp, and not over-welcome to the Princess Margaret, shows the urgency of his directions from home. But there were laws in Antwerp ; and its citizens could not be touched, "in life or goods," for offences merely charged, and not proved against them, even though the accuser were a king. Some three or four hundred volumes were seized in various cities and burned, and Endhoven was temporarily imprisoned. But he was neither banished nor his property confiscated ; and while Hackett was picking up a few hundred stray copies, thousands, as they all knew too well, were making their way toward England, or were already there.

THE BISHOPS ON THE ALERT.

Finding it out of the question to put a forcible stop to the circulation of the TERRIBLE BOOK—to them the book of doom—the prelates now fell upon a new expedient. They resolved to clear the market by wholesale purchase from the printers and dealers ! This Warham, the Primate of England, effected so far as it was possible, through Hackett the Envoy, at an expense to his archiepiscopal province, of about five thousand dollars of our money. This was in the spring of 1527.

Tunstal, meanwhile, was equally busy in searching for copies already in the country, but not with the same success. He was just proceeding to more stringent measures in his diocese, which should utterly root out the obnoxious influence, when his appointment, in conjunction with Wolsey and Sir Thomas More, to a political embassy to France, obliged him to leave the matter in charge with his Vicar. He, either through disinclination or fear, did nothing about it, and the persecution was stayed till his superior's return, in October.

Wolsey came back from France with the new dignity of Vicar-general of the Pope through the king's dominions, that is, with authority to exercise all the functions of the Pope in England. Its ecclesiastical affairs were placed under his absolute control ; its clergy, from highest to lowest, became subject to him as their supreme Head. His entrance on the high office was signalized by a general council which met in obedience to his summons, at Westminster, in November. Having pompously announced that "now all the abusions of the Church should be amended," he opened the court by an examination of two distinguished advocates of the truth, Arthur and Bilney, on the charge of heresy. After thus giving his countenance to the proceeding, and by his arrogant and contemptuous bearing toward men infinitely better than himself, setting a worthy example to his bishops, he left the trial in their hands, being himself occupied with "the affairs of the realm."

The sad result of the trial must be told. On the 2d of December Arthur abjured, nor is he ever again heard from in the ranks of the faithful. On the 7th, Bilney, after enduring for four days every species of mental torture, from the threats, the persecutions, and sophistical casuistry of Tunstal, West, and Fisher, followed his example. The next day, his head bowed with shame, and his heart even then racked with remorse, he bore a faggot at St. Paul's, and was then remanded to prison during the Cardinal's pleasure. Being at length released, he returned to Cambridge in a state of agony, scarcely short of despair; so that for some two years his friends dared not leave him alone, day or night. "They comforted him," says Latimer, "as they could, but no comfort would serve. And as for the comfortable places of Scripture, to bring them to him was as though a man should run him through the heart with a sword." But at length, He who forgave the denial of Peter, spoke peace to the troubled conscience of his servant, and filled his soul with more than its early joy in believing. Saying that he must "*go up to Jerusalem*," he now took leave of his friends, and passing through the shires of Norfolk and Essex, he spent many weeks preaching the gospel from house to house, and distributing copies of Tyndale's New Testament. Being at length seized near London, the timid, but most loving and sincere disciple, received strength to confess his Master boldly before men, and went up to heaven in the fiery chariot of martyrdom.

Thus determined and thorough were the measures of the high powers in Church and State, for the suppression of the word of God. Royal and priestly prohibitions, decrees, mandates, secret inquisition, foreign diplomacy, and persecution, had all been tried in turn. And what had they effected? So mightily grew and prevailed the demand for the Scriptures, that even while Endhoven lay in prison at Antwerp and the issue of his case was still doubtful, another Antwerp printer, if not indeed more than one, had judged the prospect of pecuniary profit worth the risk of embarking in the same enterprise. On the 23d of May, 1527, Hackett writes to Wolsey, that in spite of all his efforts, " some *new* printers of the town of Antwerp were offering in the market divers English books, called ' The New Testament,' " and that he had heard of " more than two thousand such like English books" having been offered for sale at the late Frankfort fair. Hundreds of these were already on English ground. One John Raimund, or Ruremonde, an Antwerp printer, was convicted of having caused fifteen hundred of Tyndale's New Testaments to be printed at Antwerp, and of bringing five hundred copies into England at one time. To such an extent had the city of London, especially, been pervaded by the influence, within the space of two years, that it was deemed unsafe, for one who had been at all " inclined to the new learning," even to breathe its air. Thus, as recorded in Tunstal's Register of the trials in his diocese, Sebastian Herris, curate of the Parish Church of Kensington, being charged with possessing a copy of Tyndale's New Testament, is forbidden, at his dismissal, to tarry or abide within the city of London, (*being so dangerous a place to be infected with heresy*) above a day and a night ; but to go thence elsewhere, and not approach near the city anywhere, four miles in circuit, for the space of two years.

The enemies of light could not yet perceive the futility of their warfare ; and while the divine seed sown, as it were, by the winds of heaven, was taking root in every direction, they were still erecting their clumsy bulwarks to prevent its entrance into England.

CHAPTER XIV.

TYNDALE'S REFORMATORY WRITINGS.

WICKLIFFE had closed his labors as reformer by giving the Bible to his countrymen. In his case, this was the natural order of things; for the mind of his age needed to be awakened by a long preparatory process to a consciousness of the want which the Scriptures only could supply. With Tyndale the process was just the reverse. The voice of his age cried out for the word of God; and it was his first object, by meeting this demand, to lay a broad and sure foundation for the great work of reform, which he saw to be accomplished. The New Testament being completed and sent forth on its mission, he now appears as the practical reformer, and applies its teachings in a direct assault upon the doctrines and practices of the Romish clergy.

Well worthy does he show himself, in this respect also, to be the Elisha of the elder prophet. In his exposures of time-honored abuses, and his stern rebukes of those " Cesarean Prelates" who sought to perpetuate them for their own selfish ends, we see the same fearless moral energy, the same reference to the supreme authority of God's word, and heartfelt love and respect for the common people, which distinguished Wickliffe. With this deep earnestness was mingled, moreover, a vein of homely, racy humor, not unlike that of Luther, which imparts often a vivacity and quaint force to his indignant remonstrances and appeals, well adapted to influence the popular mind.

In these writings we find abundant confirmation of one important fact, before alluded to; that from the days of Wickliffe there had been little progress, in any respect, connected with the essential well-being of the nation, *except so far as the influence of the Bible had extended*. In the character of the clergy, the state of learning in the universities, the moral condition of the people, and the recognition of their rights, either civil or religious, on the part of government, the main current had flowed steadily toward a lower deep of darkness, degradation, and oppression. The counter current which was now beginning to make itself felt in every sphere, owed all its springs, and for the most part can be directly traced, to the reviving influence of the Scriptures. A century and a half nearly, during which the vernacular Bible had been thrust out of the reach of the mass of the community, had developed in the character of the English race no inherent forces for retrieving its condition, and forming itself into a free, intelligent and virtuous people.

The two treatises with which he immediately followed his New Testament, marked him out before all Christendom as a standard bearer in the cause of the Bible and the people, against that of the Pope and priesthood. He had sent forth the New Testament without his name; "following," as he says, "the counsel of Christ, which exhorteth men to do their good works secretly, and to be content with the conscience of well-doing." The consequence was, however, that certain anonymous works against the prelacy by other hands, written in a spirit of bitterness and railing with which Tyndale had no fellowship, were confidently ascribed to him. In the preface to the first of these treatises, therefore, he disavows the books falsely charged to him, and henceforth appears under his own name. From this time onward it was a name of power among both the friends and enemies of the truth in England.

The "Parable of the Wicked Mammon," is a development rich with Scripture knowledge and Christian experience, of the connection between faith and works in our salvation, and strikes at the root of the popish trust in mere outward observances and ceremonies. Two or three brief quotations must suffice from this work, as a sample of its manner, and an illustration of the pure morality and universal benevolence resulting from the doctrine of justification by faith, rightly understood and truly received into the heart.

"The Spirit of God accompanieth faith, and bringeth with her light, wherewith a man beholdeth himself in the law of God, and seeth his miserable bondage and captivity, and humbleth himself, and abhorreth himself; she bringeth God's promises of all good things in Christ. God worketh with his word and in his word. And as his word is preached, faith rooteth herself in the heart of the elect, and as faith entereth and the word of God is believed, the power of God looseth the heart from the captivity and bondage under sin, and knitteth and coupleth him unto God, and to the will of God; altereth him, changeth him clean, fashioneth and forgeth him anew, giveth him power to love and to do that which before it was impossible for him either to love or do, and turneth him unto a new nature, so that he loveth that which before he hated, and hateth that which before he loved; and is clean altered and changed, and contrary disposed; and is knit and coupled fast to God's will, and naturally bringeth forth good works . . . And that doth he of his own accord, as a tree bringeth forth fruit of her own accord. And as thou needest not to bid a tree bring forth fruit, so there is no law to put unto him that believeth and is justified by faith. . . . And as a whole man when he is athirst tarrieth but for drink, and when he is hungry abideth but for meat, and then drinketh and eateth naturally, even so is the faithful ever athirst and an hungered after the will of God, and tarrieth but for occasion. Where faith is mighty and strong, there is love fervent and deeds plenteous, and done with exceeding meekness ; where faith is weak, there love is cold, and the deeds few, and seldom bears flowers and blossoms in winter.

"The order of love and charity which some dream, the Gospel of Christ knoweth not of ; that a man should begin at himself, and serve himself first, and then descend, I wot not by what steps. Love seeketh not her own profit, but maketh a man to forget himself, and to turn his profit to another man, as Christ sought not himself or his own profit, but ours. The term, 'myself,' is not in the Gospel ; neither yet father, mother, brother, kinsman, that one should be preferred in love above another. But Christ is all in all things. Every Christian man to another is Christ himself, and thy neighbor's need hath as good a right to thy goods as hath Christ himself, which is heir and lord over all. And look, what thou owest to Christ, that thou owest to thy neighbor's need ; to thy neighbor owest thou thine heart, thyself, and all that thou hast and canst do. . . . In Christ we are all of one degree, without respect of persons. Notwithstanding, though a Christian man's heart be open to all men, and receiveth all men, yet, because that his ability of goods extendeth not so far, this provision is made, that every man shall care for his own household, as father and mother, and thine elders that have holpen thee, wife, children and servants. When thou hast done thy duty to thy household, and yet hast farther abundance of the blessing of God, that thou owest to the poor that cannot labor, or would labor and can get no work, and are destitute of friends. . . . If thy neighbors which thou knowest be served, and thou yet have superfluity, and hearest necessity to be among the brethren a thousand miles off, to them thou art debtor. Yea, to the very infidels we be debtors if they need, so far forth as we maintain them not against Christ, or to blaspheme Christ. Thus is every man that needeth help thy father, mother, sister, and brother in Christ ; even as every man that doth the will of the Father is father, mother, brother, and sister unto Christ."

The work which followed this—"The Obedience of a Christian Man"—is an exposition of the teachings of Scripture on the social duties of men, in all the relations of life. It was intended as a defence of the Bible against the charge brought by the clergy, that its circulation among the laity tends to confusion and insubordination in society. It proves that it is they, on the contrary, who, by substituting for the true light of God's word their own false doctrines and traditions, have subverted all social order and virtue ; and that their zeal against the Bible is but hatred of that which, if permitted to go freely among the people, would strip them of their ill-gotten power.

In the first part of the treatise, husbands and wives, parents and children, masters and servants, sellers and buyers, rulers and ruled, are taught their mutual duties, as set forth by direct Scripture precept, or as plainly deducible from its great law of love. He is no less faithful to the king than to the subject, warning him of the dangers to which monarchs are especially liable, and of the final account to be rendered by him of all he has done in his high office, both good and bad. It is a strong proof that the tyrannical course of Henry VIII. was due less to his natural disposition, than to the evil influence of his spiritual guides, that he was deeply impressed by this treatise when he first read it, and remarked : "This is a book for me, and for all kings."

The second part is a searching exposure of the abuses practised on the people by the priesthood, their corruption of Christian doctrines and ordinances ; the "feigned ordinances," by which they rule so cruelly over the consciences of men, and wring from them their worldly goods ; their usurpation of the civil power, and the consequent impoverishment, internal confusion, and foreign wars, into which their insatiable ambition and avarice has plunged the realm.

" ' Curse them [so he represents the Pope as saying to his vassals, the clergy] four times in the year. Make them afraid of everything, and namely [especially] to touch mine anointed ; and make them to fear the sentence of the Church, suspensions, excommunications, and curses. Be they right or wrong, bear them in hand that they are to be feared yet. Preach me and mine authority, and how terrible a thing my curse is, and how black it makes their souls. On the holidays, which were ordained to preach God's word, set up long ceremonies, long matins, long Masses, and long even-songs, and all in Latin, that they understand not ; and roll them in darkness, that ye may lead them wherever ye will. And lest such things should be too tedious, sing some, pipe some, ring the bells, and lull them and rock them asleep.' And yet Paul (2 Cor. xiv.) forbiddeth to speak in the church or congregation, save in the tongue that all understand. For the layman thereby is not edified or taught. How shall the layman say Amen (saith Paul) to thy blessing or thanksgiving, when he wotteth not what thou sayest? He wotteth not whether thou bless or curse.

"'What then saith the Pope?' 'What care I for Paul? I command, by virtue of obedience, to read the Gospel in Latin; let them not pray but in Latin; no, not their Pater Noster. If any be sick, go also and say them a Gospel, and all in Latin; yea, to the very corn and fruits of the field, in the procession week, preach the Gospel in Latin. Make the people believe that it shall grow the better.' It is as good to preach it to swine as to men, if thou preach it in a tongue which they understand not.—How shall I prepare myself to God's commandments? How shall I be thankful to Christ for his kindness? How shall I believe the truths and promises which God hath sworn, while thou tellest them unto me in a tongue which I understand not?

"'What then,' saith my Lord of Canterbury, to a priest that would have had the New Testament gone forth in English; 'what,' saith he, 'wouldst thou that the lay people should wete what we do?'"

"Mark well how many parsonages or vicarages are there in the realm, which, at the least, have a plough-land* apiece. Then note the land of bishops, abbots, priors, nuns, knights of St. John, cathedral churches, colleges, chauntries, and free chapels. For though the house fall in decay, and the ordinance of the founder be lost, yet will they not lose their lands. What cometh once in, may never more out. They make a free chapel of it, so that he which enjoyeth it shall do nought therefore. Beside all this, how many chaplains do gentlemen find at their own cost, in their own houses? How many sing for souls by testaments? Then the proving of testaments, the prizing of goods, the Bishop of Canterbury's prerogative. Is that not much through the realm in a year? Four offering days, and privy tithes. There is no servant, but that he shall pay somewhat of his wages. None shall receive the body of Christ at Easter, be he never so poor a beggar, or never so young a lad or maid, but they must pay somewhat for it. Then mortuaries for forgotten tithes (say they). And yet what parson or vicar is there, that will forget to have a pigeon-house, to peck up somewhat both at sowing-time and harvest, when corn is ripe? They will forget nothing. No man shall die in their debt; or if any man do, he shall pay it when he is dead. They

---

* "The measurement of the *plough-land* varied in different counties, and in the same counties at different times. In general, it designated as much arable land as could be managed and tilled by one plough, and its team of horses or oxen, in the year; having meadow, pasture, and houses and cattle attached to it."—Note to Works of the Eng. Reformers, vol. i., p. 544.

will lose nothing. Why? It is God's; it is not theirs. It is St. Hubert's rents, St. Alban's lands, St. Edmond's right, St. Peter's patrimony.—Item—if a man die in another man's parish, besides that he must pay at home a mortuary for forgotten tithes, he must there, also, pay the best he there hath. Whether it be a horse of twenty pound, or how good soever he be; either a chain of gold of an hundred marks, or five hundred pounds, if it so chance. Then beadrolls. Item—christenings, churchings, banns, weddings, offering at weddings, offering of wax and lights, which come to their damage; beside the superstitious waste of wax, in torches and tapers, throughout the land. Then brothers and pardoners.—What get they also by confessions? . . . . Soul-masses, dirges, month-minds, peace-minds, All-souls day, and trentals. The mother Church and the high altar must have somewhat in every testament. Offerings at priest's first masses. Item—no man is professed, of whatsoever religion it be [i.e. of whatever clerical order], but he must bring somewhat. Then hallowing or rather conjuring of churches, chapels, altars, super-altars, chalice, vestment, bells. Then book, bell, candlestick, organs, vestments, copes, altar-cloths, surplices; then towels, basins, ewers, censer, and all manner of ornaments, must be found them freely, they will not give a mite thereunto. Last of all, what swarms of begging friars are there! The parson sheareth, the vicar shaveth, the parish priest polleth, the friar scrapeth, and the pardoner pareth; we lack but a butcher to pull off the skin.

"What get they in their spiritual law (as they call it) in a year, at the arches, and in every diocese? What get the commissioners, and officials, with their somners and apparitors, by bawdry in a year? Shall ye not find curates enough, which to flatter the commissioners and officials withal, that they may go quit themselves, shall open to them the confessions of the richest of their parishes, whom they cite privately, and lay to their charges secretly. If they desire to know their accusers, 'Nay,' say they, 'the matter is known well enough, and to more than ye are ware of. Come, lay your hand on the book; if ye forswear yourself, we shall bring proofs; we will handle you, we will make an ensample of you.' Oh, how terrible are they! 'Come and swear,' say they, 'that thou will be obedient to our injunctions!' And by that craft, wring they their purses, and make them drop as long as there is a penny in them."

"'Not given to filthy lucre, but abhorring covetousness;' and as Peter saith, 'Taking the oversight of them, not as though ye were compelled thereunto, but willingly. Not of desire of filthy lucre, but of a good mind ; not as though ye were lords over the parishes. Over the parishes, quoth he ! O Peter, Peter, thou wast too long a fisher ; thou wast never brought up at the Arches, neither wast Master of the Rolls, nor yet Chancellor of England. They are not content to reign over king and emperor, and the whole earth ; but challenge authority also in heaven and in hell. It is not enough for them to reign over all that are quick, but have created them a purgatory, to reign also over the dead, and to have one kingdom more than God himself hath."

" They take away first God's word, with faith, hope, peace, unity, love, and concord ; then house and land, rent and fee, tower and town, goods and cattle, and the very meat out of men's mouths. All these live by purgatory. When others weep for their friends, they sing merrily ; when others lose their friends, they get friends. The Pope, with all his pardons, is grounded on purgatory. Priests, monks, canons, friars, with all other swarms of heretics, do but employ purgatory, and fill hell. Every Mass, say they, delivereth one soul out of purgatory. If that were true—yea, if ten Masses were enough for one soul—yet were the parish priests and curates of every parish sufficient to scour purgatory. All the other costly work of men might be well spared."

In the course of the treatise he explains his view of what the Scriptures teach respecting the Sacraments, the offices in the Church, the support of the clergy, and their relation to the civil power. In regard to all these, his views coincide in all essential points with those of Wickliffe. There are but two Sacraments, Baptism and the Lord's Supper ; and their efficacy depends on the spirit in which they are received.—There are but two offices in the Church of Christ, Bishop, or Elder, and Deacon. The duty of the first is to serve the Church in spiritual things, being "nothing but an officer to teach, and to minister the Sacraments ordained, and not to be a mediator between God and us." "According as every man believeth God's promises, longeth for them, and is diligent to pray unto God to fulfill them, so is his prayer heard, as good the prayer of a cobbler, as of a cardinal ; and of a butcher, as of a bishop ; and the blessing of a baker that knoweth the truth is as good as the blessing of our most holy father the pope." " Christ, when he had fulfilled his course, anointed his apostles and disciples with the same spirit, and sent them forth, without all manner of disguising, like other men also, to preach the atonement and peace which Christ had made between God and man. The apostles, likewise, disguised no man, but chose men anointed with the same spirit ; one to preach the word of God, whom we call, after the Greek tongue, a bishop or priest ; that, is, in English, an overseer and an elder." " This overseer, because he was taken from his own business and labor to preach God's word unto the parish, hath right, by the authority of his office, to challenge an honest living of the parish, as thou mayst see in the Evangelists, and also in Paul. For who will have a servant, and will not give him meat, drink, and raiment, and all things necessary? How they would pay him, whether in money, or assign him so much rent, or in tithes, as the guise now is in many countries, was at their liberty." " Likewise in every congregation chose they another after the same example, and even so anointed, as it is to see in the said chapter of Paul, and Acts vi. Whom after the Greek word we call deacon ; that is to say, in English, a servant, or a minister, whose office it was to help and assist the priest, and gather up his duty, and gather for the poor of the parish, which were destitute of friends, and could not work. . . . . . . Every man gave according to his ability, and as God put into his heart, to the maintenance of the priest, deacon, and other common ministers, and of the poor, and to find learned men to teach, and so forth." " ' We,' will they say, ' are the pope, cardinal, and bishops ; all authority is ours. The Scripture pertaineth unto us, and is our possession. And we have a law, that whosoever presumes to preach without the authority of the bishops, is excommunicate in the deed-doing. Whence, therefore, hast thou thine authority ?' will they say. ' The old Pharisees had the Scripture in captivity, likewise, and asked Christ : By what authority doest thou these things ? . . . . Christ asked them another question, and so will I do our hypocrites. Who sent you ? God ? Nay, he that is sent of God, speaketh God's word. Now speak ye not God's word, nor anything, save your own laws, made clean contrary unto God's word. . . . And as for mine authority, or who sent me, I report me unto my works, as Christ. If God's word bear record that I say truth, why should any man doubt but that God, the father of truth and of light, hath sent me ? . . . ' By this means, thou wilt that every man be a preacher,' will they say. ' Nay, verily. For God will that not, and therefore, will I it not ; no more than I would that every man were mayor of London or every man of the realm King thereof. God is not the God of dissension and strife, but of unity and peace, and of good order. I will, therefore, that where a congregation is gathered together in Christ, one be chosen after the rule of Paul, and that he only preach, and else no man openly : but that every man teach his household after the same doctrine. But if the preacher preach false, then whosoever's heart God moveth, to the same it shall be lawful to rebuke and improve the false teacher, with the clear and manifest Scripture, and that same is, no doubt, a true prophet sent of God. For the Scripture is God's, and their's that believe, and not the false prophets'."

The law of spiritual life and growth, as contained within each congregation of believers, being derived continually from Christ, the ever present head, is beautifully developed in the following passage :

"Here [within the congregations of Christ] all thing is free and willingly ; and the Holy Ghost bringeth them together, which maketh their wills free, and ready to bestow themselves on their neighbor's profit : and they that come offer themselves, and all that they have, or can do to serve the Lord and their brethren ; and every man, as he is found apt and meet to serve his neighbor, is put into office. And of the Holy Ghost are they sent, with the consent of their brethren, and with their own consent also : and God's word ruleth in that congregation, into which word every man confirmeth [conformeth] his will ; and Christ, which is always present, is the head."

He is equally explicit in regard to the clerical claim, still as perfectly intact as in the days of Wickliffe, of exemption from civil jurisdiction. In the summary, at the close of the book, of its contents, he says :

"I proved also that all men, without exception, are under the temporal sword, whatsoever names they give themselves. Because the priest is chosen out of the laymen to teach this obedience, is that a lawful cause for him to disobey ? Because he preacheth that the laymen may not steal, is it therefore lawful for him to steal unpunished ? Because thou teachest me that I may not kill, or if I do, the King must kill me again, is it therefore lawful for thee to kill and go free ? . . . . The priests of the old law, with their high bishop, Aaron, and all his successors, though they were anointed by God's commandment and appointed to serve God in his temple, and exempt from all offices and ministering of worldly matters, were yet under the temporal sword, if they brake the laws. . . . I proved, also, that no king hath power to grant them such liberties."

The clergy still held the monopoly of all the high secular offices of the kingdom. Thus speaks the reformer on this point :

"Let kings take their duty of their subjects, and that is necessary to the defence of the realm. Let them rule their realms themselves, with the help of laymen that are sage, wise, learned, and expert. Is it not a shame above all shames, and a monstrous thing, that no man should be found able to govern a worldly kingdom, save by bishop and prelates, that have forsaken the world, and are taken out of the world, and appointed to preach the Kingdom of God? . . . To preach God's word is too much for half a man; and to minister a temporal kingdom is too much for half a man; either other requireth an whole man; one, therefore, cannot well do both. . . . Paul saith in the ninth chapter of the first Corinthians, ' Woe is me if I preach not.' A terrible saying, verily, for popes, cardinals, and bishops. If he had said, ' Woe be unto me if I fight not, and move princes to war, or if I increase not St. Peter's patrimony ' (as they call it), it had been a more easy saying for them."

The Preface to this book, itself about thirty pages in length, is properly a tract in defence of the translation of the Scriptures into the mother tongue, and their unrestricted use by the laity. He argues this from the fact, that Moses gave the people of Israel the law in their mother tongue; that the Prophets wrote, and David uttered his psalms in the mother tongue; that the sermons recorded in the Acts were preached to the people in the mother tongue; that the Bible was translated by Jerome into his mother tongue.—" What should be the cause," he asks, " that we, which walk in the broad day, should not see as well as they that walked in the night, or that we should not see as well at noon as they did in the twilight? Came Christ to make the world more blind? By this means, Christ is the darkness of the world, and not the light, as he saith himself." He pleads for it, also, because God in the Old Testament, required in all the people a knowledge of the law, and Christ, in the New, commanded to search the Scriptures; because, as Christ foretold, there are false Christs and false prophets, whose deeds and doctrines must be judged by Scripture; because the spiritual guides of the people teach doctrines contrary to, and subversive of each other, and it cannot be known which is right but by Scripture.

"' Nay,' say they, ' the Scripture is so hard, that thou couldst never understand it, but by the doctors.' That is, I must measure the meteyard by the cloth. Here be twenty cloths of divers lengths, and divers breadths; how shall I be sure of the length of the meteyard by them? I suppose, rather must I be sure of the length of the meteyard, and thereby measure and judge the cloths. If I must first believe the doctor, then is the doctor first true, and the truth of the Scripture dependeth of his truth; and so the truth of God springeth of the truth of man. Thus, antichrist turneth the roots of the trees upward." It was pretended, moreover, that no man could understand Scripture, till he had made himself master of philosophy, by the study of Aristotle and the doctors. This leads Tyndale to notice the character of the so-called philosophy taught in the universities, which we find to be no other than those same solemn frivolities of Duns Scotus, and the other scholastics which had driven all true learning out of Oxford in the fourteenth century. As then, it was connected with the bitterest hostility to revelation. No one could speak with more authority on this point than Tyndale, who had resided there so many years, and had partaken in the struggle consequent on the attempt of Christian scholars to introduce the Greek and Roman classics, and the original Scriptures into the course of academic study. He maintains that, so far from this philosophy being necessary to prepare one for a knowledge of the Scriptures, these are needed to protect him from the contaminating influence of the philosophy. "And then, if they go abroad, and walk by the fields and meadows of all manner of doctors and philosophers, they should catch no harm. They should discern the poison from the honey, and bring home nothing but that which is wholesome."

"But now," he proceeds, "do ye clean contrary, ye drive them from God's word, and will let no man come thereto until he have been two years master of art. First they nosel them in sophistry, and in *benefundatum*. And there corrupt they their judgments with apparent arguments and with alleging unto them texts of logic, of natural *philautia*, of metaphysic and moral philosophy, and of all manner of books of Aristotle, and of all manner of doctors, which yet they never saw. Moreover, one holdeth this, another that; one is a real, another a nominal. What wonderful dreams they have of their predicaments, universals, second intentions, *qui dities, haec scities*, and relatives. And whether *species fundata in chimera* be *vera species*. And whether this proposition be true *non ens est aliquid*, whether *ens* be *æquivocum*, or *univocum*.—*Ens* is a voice only, say some. *Ens* is *univocum*, saith another, and descendeth into *ens creatum*, and into *ens increatum, per modos intrinsecos*. When they have this way brawled eight, ten, or twelve years, or more, and after that their judgments are utterly corrupt, then they begin their divinity; not at the Scripture, but every man taketh a sundry doctor, which doctors are as sundry, and as divers, the one contrary unto the other, as there are divers fashions and monstrous shapes, none like another, among our sects of religion. Every religion, every university, almost every man, hath a sundry divinity. Now whatsoever every man findeth with his doctor, that is his Gospel, and that only is true with him, and that holdeth he all his life long; and every man to maintain his doctor withal, corrupteth the Scripture, and fashioneth it after his own imagination, as a potter doth his clay. Of what text thou provest hell, will another prove purgatory, another *limbo patrum*, another the assumption of our lady, and another shall prove of the same text that an ape hath a tail. And of what text the grave [gray] friar proveth that our lady was without original sin, will the black friar prove that she was conceived in original sin."

How finely, after this exposure of the folly of human wisdom, does Tyndale say : " God is not man's imagination, but only that which he saith of himself. God is nothing but his law and his promises ; that is to say, that which he biddeth thee to do, and that which he biddeth thee believe and hope. God is but his word, as Christ saith (John viii.), I am that I say unto you ; that is to say, That which I preach I am, my words are spirit and life. God is that only which he testifieth of himself ; and to imagine any other thing than that, is damnable idolatry. Therefore saith the 118th Psalm, Happy are they which search the testimonies of the Lord ; that is to say, that which God testifieth and witnesseth unto us. But how shall I that do, when ye will not let me have his testimonies or witnesses in a tongue which I understand ? Will ye resist God ? Will ye forbid him to give his Spirit unto the lay, as well as unto you ? Hath he not made the English tongue ? Why forbid ye him to speak in the English tongue, then, as well as in Latin ?"

CHAPTER XV.

CARDINAL WOLSEY'S MEASURES TO SILENCE TYNDALE.

It is not strange that a voice like this should sorely have disturbed those whose treachery and oppression were thus laid open, in plain English, for all classes of the laity to read and comment on. No wonder that Cardinal Wolsey and his bishops thought it necessary to silence this terrible censor, who, from his obscure retreat in a foreign land, could stretch forth his hand and shake the very pillars of the hierarchy. From this time it became one of their leading objects, by force or fraud, to compass his apprehension and death.

In June, 1528, the Lord Cardinal instructed Sir John Hackett, still envoy at the Court of Brabant, to procure from the Princess Regent his arrest, on the charge of heresy, and that of two other men, viz., Roye, erroneously supposed to be still engaged with him in translating the Bible, and Harman, a wealthy and honorable English merchant residing in Antwerp, who was known to have been zealously engaged in bringing the New Testament into England. But Hackett was obliged to reply that the Privy Council, after debating the case with him, had decided that it was unlawful, even for the Emperor himself, to deliver up a heretic, except after examination first held where he was; and not then, except by advice of Inquisitors of the faith there present. They promised, however, to apprehend the obnoxious persons if they could be found, together with their books; and if, on being confronted with learned men from England—who it was requested might be sent over for the purpose—their guilt should appear, they were to be delivered to Wolsey, or punished there, " according to their deeds."

After fourteen days' search, Harman and his wife—" *as greatly suspected of such like faction as her husband is*"—were taken and committed to prison, and an inventory of their goods delivered to the Emperor. Still, Hackett saw so little prospect of success in this case, that he suggests to Wolsey to drop the charge of heresy, and demand Harman as a traitor to the King of England.

" I would," writes this honorable ambassador, " that your Grace had this Richard Harman there in England; for, as I hear, he is a *Roethe* of great mischief. And to get him out of these countries, I know no better means at this time, than, if the King's Highness have any action of *treason* at him, that his Highness, or your Grace, write a good letter to my Lady, that she should send you the aforesaid Harman, as traitor to the King—leaving the heresy beside, to the correction of these countries, if your Grace think so good ; and in this manner we may have *two strings to our bow :* for I doubt greatly, after the statutes of these countries, that, revoking his heresies, for the first time he will escape with a slender punishment ; but for treason to the King they cannot pardon him in these parts, after the Statutes of our Intercourse, dated the year 1505. I certify your Grace, that it were a good deed, and very convenient, to chastise these Lutherans that be accused of heresy, that they were as well comprehended in the 'Intercourse' as traitors be ; for as soon as they be past the seas they know no more God, neither King."

Wolsey seized on this hint, and obtained a letter from the King, requesting that Harman should be given up as a traitor. But the Princess required, in turn, specifications of his crime ; and finally, Hackett informs his Grace that, "notwithstanding the King's patent letters, the Lady Margaret would not deliver up the heretics." Mr. Harman was released, after an imprisonment of more than seven months—the term for which he could be detained having expired, without any proof having been brought by Hackett of the charges made against him. But the envoy soon found that he had been meddling with a game at which two could play. Having gone to Antwerp a few weeks after, on some business for the King, he found himself arrested at Harman's suit for all the costs and charges of his imprisonment ; since "the law of Antwerp [a free, imperial city], had aforetime declared him, by their sentence, absolute, free and frank, of all such actions as the Margrave, or the Scout of Antwerp, as officers of the Prince, by my information laid to his charge." Next day he was obliged to answer for himself before the city Senate ; and after a mortifying detention, was only permitted to depart on condition that he should appear in person, or by his procurator, whenever summoned for the farther prosecution of the cause. On arriving at Brussels he made his complaint to the Princess and her Council, who professed themselves much displeased with the treatment he had received ; but except a severe rebuke to the Lords of Antwerp, and requisition that their *Amant* (the officer who had caused his arrest) should ask his pardon, no amend was made for the affront, and Hackett did not again find it expedient to be much in Antwerp. The British merchant had read him a lesson which he long had cause to remember.

All efforts to discover Tyndale and Roye had been thus far unsuccessful, but Wolsey was not disheartened. It had been ascertained that the Testaments with which Harman had been concerned " were sent to him out of *Germany*"—a vexatious proof that Warham's expensive purchase had not exhausted the supply. But it might also furnish a clue to the translators. He therefore took into his confidence two friars of Greenwich—West and Flegg by name—and dispatched them secretly to Cologne, with a letter to counsellor Rincke (the same who lent his influence to Cochlæus in 1525) soliciting his aid for the apprehension of these two men, as well as in buying up " all books printed in the English language." They were authorized by the Cardinal to draw on Hackett for whatever money was necessary to effect these objects.

The honorable councillor was prompt to meet the wishes of his great friend at the Court of England. He informs him that he had himself been to Frankfort on the business, and, " *by gifts and presents*," had so conciliated the Frankfort consuls, as well as some of the senators and judges, as to secure, through their aid, possession of " all the books from every quarter," which, but for his labors, would soon have been brought over to England and Scotland, " inclosed in packages, artfully covered over with and concealed in flax. "I have," he adds, " lately brought the printer himself, John Schott [of Strasburg], before the consuls, judges, and senators of Frankfort. I put him upon oath, that he should confess whatever books he had printed in the English language, the German, French, or any other idiom. Then, upon his said oath, he confessed that he had as yet printed only one thousand books (*sex quaternionum*) and one thousand (*novem quaternionum*) and this by the order of Roye and Hutchyn [Tyndale], who, wanting money, were not able to pay for the books printed. . . . Wherefore, *I have purchased them almost all, and now have them in my house at Cologne.*" He then desires instructions how he shall dispose of them, and closes with the suggestion : " As to myself and mine, by the favor of God, *possibly there may be an opportunity for his Royal Highness and your Grace to recompense us.* May your Grace, therefore, prosper many happy years !"

Of Tyndale, Roye, or their accomplices, he could as yet find no trace ; but he promises, with his " utmost diligence" to ferret out their haunts, and get them into custody. For further consultation with his Grace on this important mission, he sent back West, together with his own son and a confidential servant, " who," he says, " will conceal and keep quiet the whole matter, whatsoever your Grace may commit to them—whom I specially send over into the presence of the King and your Grace, for the more convenient dispatch of this very business, that I may explain and execute the matter in a way which may be acceptable to the King's grace and yours."

He seems, however, to have spent his labor, and the money of his employers, to but little profit. The two thousand books referred to in his letter as purchased from Schott, were, no doubt, those anonymous productions before alluded to, written by Roye and others against the Cardinal. Schott, who was of course anxious to rid himself of his dead stock, may have baited Rincke, by pretending that it consisted, in part, of works by Tyndale; but it does not appear that he ever printed anything at Strasburg.

As to the reformer himself, the councillor was entirely off the track. Tyndale was, at this time, at Marburg in Hesse Cassel, where the new and flourishing Protestant University, the first ever established, had called together men whose eminent scholarship and congeniality of views with his own must have rendered it a residence equally delightful and advantageous. During this year and part of the next (1528-9), the only press then existing at Marburg was kept in busy occupation by Tyndale and his beloved associate Frith, with new works in English, for the instruction of their countrymen. Here is dated the short treatise on the Scripture Doctrine of Marriage, and the exposition of 1 Cor. vii.; both of which were intended to counteract those lax and corrupting views of the conjugal relation which had gained currency through the influence of a clergy without principle and above law.

Meanwhile, Tyndale's writings and his New Testament were making steady progress in England, in spite of all vigilance and opposition. It is a deeply interesting fact, that it was among the humble believers whom, under the name of Lollards, we have seen enduring persecution for their attachment to Wickliffe's Bible, that the most eager interest was manifested in the improved translation. They had still their secret meetings for the reading and exposition of the Scriptures and other devout exercises, in London, as also in Colchester, Witham, Braintree, and various other places in Essex, and in the Friary of Clare in Suffolk; and it was chiefly from their ranks that the bishops were furnished with the victims, through whose punishment they sought to check in the community the growing desire to become acquainted with the Scriptures. Yet we have the most satisfactory evidence that they continued to increase in numbers, as well as in the depth and ardor of their piety, and that their influence was felt as a powerful leaven through the humbler classes of the community. These "Congregations"—so they were now called—seem to have been strictly assemblies of believers, organized on the model of the apostolic Churches, for the stated worship of God, and the enjoyment of the sacraments. They will come again before our notice, in the history of the persecutions during the reign of Mary.

But alarming as was the aspect of affairs in England, when Rincke made his report to the Lord Cardinal, that dignitary seems to have given no farther attention to the matter. Before the end of the year, he was too busy in negotiating the King's divorce, and in otherwise propping up his own falling fortunes, to concern himself either with apprehending heretics, or rewarding the services of such friends as the disinterested patrician of Cologne. Henceforth, he appears only as a subordinate character, and a man of higher mark takes the lead in this great conflict.

CHAPTER XVI.

THE NEW ANTAGONIST.

THE steady progress of light, during the two years following the introduction of Tyndale's New Testament into England, had convinced the prelacy that it could not be arrested by authority and force alone. The public mind was deeply infected with the new opinions, and the more they strove against the influence by outward violence, the more it grew. They were at length compelled to yield so much to truth, as to come down from their proud position and meet it in its own way ; to submit to what they most abhorred—the discussion of the case before the people, in plain English. They felt too, little as they would have been willing to confess it, that no common opponent would answer, to measure lances with William Tyndale. They selected for the purpose one who, in natural genius, accomplished scholarship, and power as a writer was, by common consent, the choicest man in England. His readiness and felicity as an extempore orator had gained him the name of "the English Demosthenes," while his literary productions had placed him among the most elegant Latinists, and the most admired philosophers and wits of Europe. He had held conspicuous public stations already more than twenty years ; and as Advocate, Under-Sheriff and Justice of the Peace for the city of London, had won the highest general estimation, as a man of profound legal knowledge and almost unequalled sagacity and skill in the management of public business. In 1517, in compliance with the imperative command of Henry VIII., though much against his own wishes, he entered the immediate service of the crown, and from that time exercised a leading influence on the affairs of the realm. But his power was not merely that of talent and station. His unspotted domestic virtue, true old-Roman contempt of luxury and show, and his unimpeachable integrity in every public relation, in a time of unsurpassed extravagance and corruption—when even cardinals and bishops hardly made a secret of their profligacy, and bribery was the rule in courts of justice—had given him a moral weight in the nation, such as was possessed by no other man.

It is not strange, then, that when SIR THOMAS MORE consented, at the solicitation of the bishops, to undertake the refutation of the growing heresy, its opponents should have indulged the most confident anticipations that its influence with the popular mind was about to suffer a complete overthrow. There were strong reasons, too, why the friends of truth should be satisfied with the choice. In addition to Sir Thomas More's reputation for candor and uprightness, he had shown leanings, in his previous life, which might naturally lead them to expect from him greater liberality toward their views, than could be looked for from the clergy. He had been early linked, by the most intimate literary and religious friendships, with the cause of progress. From his youth he had been a passionate lover of classic learning, then so closely associated with the study of the Scriptures. The enlightened and pious Dean Colet, before mentioned as the first lecturer on Paul's Epistles at Oxford, was his spiritual confidant and adviser, and was regarded by him with the reverence and affection due to a father. While still at the university, his acquaintance with Erasmus, who had already commenced his splendid career as the champion of liberal culture, gave a powerful impulse and direction to his mental development. It could hardly fail that while drinking with Erasmus at the fountain of the Muses—experiencing in himself the solid benefits and the exquisite pleasures of communion with the great masters of thought and style—young More should come to look, with his friend's eyes, on the obstacles then opposed to the progress of true learning, in the character and influence of the clergy. He became, heart and soul, one of the noble corps who, with Erasmus at its head, broke the ranks of OBSCURANTISM in the sixteenth century. The weapons of his leader, those light arrows feathered with wit, but tipped with the fatal poison for the darklings—truth—were those also which More excelled in handling. Indeed, in the opinion of Dean Colet, he was the only real wit of his time in England; and he used his power unsparingly against the owls and bats who had so long held undisturbed reign in the schools.

The friendship, cemented by so many kindred qualities, grew with years. On Erasmus' second visit to England, enriched with wider knowledge, and laden with laurels, More's house was his home; and it was here that he wrote his famous satire on the Monks—"MORIA, or *The Praise of Folly*." In 1515, being sent by the King on a commercial embassy to the Netherlands, Sir Thomas had the pleasure of doing his friend a very good service in reference to this book, as well as in another respect, of still more importance to the interests of religion. Through Erasmus, whom he met at Bruges, and other distinguished literati of the Low Countries, he was made acquainted, more fully than he could be in England, with the hostility which all of them

—but especially Erasmus—had to encounter from the enemies of liberal learning. At this time the contest raged mainly round two points—his *Moria*, whose biting satire had deeply wounded the self-love of the lower clergy, against whom it was particularly directed; and his projected publication of the Greek New Testament from manuscripts, with a new Latin translation.

The Theological Faculty of the University of Louvain,[*] took it upon themselves, in a special manner, to frown on these irreverent and sacrilegious proceedings; even decrying, with the utmost fury, the study of the Greek language, as not only useless, but in the highest degree pernicious to theologians. One of their number, Martin Dorpius by name, a respectable Latin scholar, and a well-disposed man—but with conservative tendencies, which led him to take alarm at everything new—had assailed the labors of Erasmus in a published letter, severely censuring the *Moria*, but, above all, the proposed New Testament. This, as an innovation tending to weaken the authority of tradition, he deprecated as full of peril to the interests of religion. The temperate reply of Erasmus was followed by another letter from Dorpius, reiterating his previous charges. By this time Erasmus was at Basle, fully occupied with printing his New Testament, and More felt himself called on to take up the pen in his defence. He addressed a letter to Dorpius, in which he vindicated the propriety of thus exposing the faults of the clergy, and fully justified the efforts of his friend to promote the study of the Scriptures. Dorpius had said, that the theologian has more important and more difficult things on his hands than *the explanation of the Bible !* More wishes him joy, that a book in which Jerome and Augustine found so much which was difficult, should all be so plain and easy to him : yet wonders much that he could place the hair-splitting questions, arbitrary distinctions, and stupid repetitions of Peter Lombard's Sentences, and similar works, in a higher rank than the study of the Bible. So convincingly, yet in so kind a spirit, did he combat the alleged necessity and obligation of adhering to the Vulgate, as sole and supreme authority, and plead for a thorough knowledge of Greek, as the only reliable basis of New Testament interpretation, that Dorpius was wholly brought over to his views. He immediately devoted himself with such ardor to the study of Greek, and took part so decidedly with the friends of liberal learning, that his colleagues turned all their vengeance on him as an apostate from their ranks, and never rested till they drove him from the Professor's chair.

[*] Founded in 1426 ; in the 16th century it had 6000 students.

Two years after, 1517, Sir Thomas More surprised the literary world by his philosophical romance, UTOPIA; a splendid blossom of genius and culture, but deriving its chief interest to us from its views of various matters connected with religion, especially of religious toleration and the rights of conscience. A few of the most noticeable points only can be mentioned.

The citizens of THE HAPPY REPUBLIC, with few exceptions, believe in an infinite, incomprehensible, everywhere present Being, whom they call Father; but from this centre they diverge into many varieties of religious belief. It is one of their fundamental laws that "*each man can live according to his own religion, and that no violence be used to convert him to another faith.*" For they think it unseemly and arrogant to attempt to force on all what one may happen to esteem as true; and if there is but one true religion, it must, in due time, by the aid of reason and gentleness in its advocates, win the victory by its own inherent power. Christianity found easy access among this people; and the adherents of the old faith neither sought to deter any from becoming its converts, or persecuted them afterward. Only when a new proselyte was so excessive and denunciatory in his zeal as to endanger the public peace, he was exiled, without farther punishment, from Utopia. Disbelievers in the immortality of the soul, and in a future state of rewards and punishments, were alone disfranchised on account of their opinions, being counted as brutes, incapable of being influenced by the motives necessary to constitute a useful or safe citizen. Yet even these were not punished with death, nor terrified by threats into hypocrisy; and the priests and fathers of the community sought, by argument and reason, to cure them of their folly.

The organization of the priesthood in the republic furnishes opportunity for many significant hints at abuses in the Romish Church. The priests of Utopia are few in number, only thirteen in each city; they are chosen by the people from the worthiest in the land—of the good, the best—and that there may be no constraint in the matter, by secret vote. Public opinion demands of them the greatest sanctity of character, which, however, is not deemed incompatible with marriage. They conduct the public worship and exercise the office of censors of morals, with no power, however, except to counsel and admonish. They hold no civil office. In case of war a deputation of priests accompanies the army, their business being *to pray*—first, for peace, second, for a bloodless victory to their countrymen. They have the charge of education, and the result of their capacity and fidelity is universal intelligence and mental activity. The youth of

Utopia are thoroughly grounded by them, first in good morals and religion, then in the principles of their government, in music, logic, mathematical science, astronomy, and in the Greek language and literature. *All instruction is given in the mother tongue.*

A recent Catholic biographer of Sir Thomas More,* anxious for the consistency of this great champion of the Church, maintains that the Utopia is to be regarded as simply a work of pleasantry and fancy, not intended as an exposition of his real views, either on government or religion. But it is not usual to write even a work of fancy for the express purpose of commending principles exactly the opposite of those which the author approves; especially when the application to the circumstances of the time is so unavoidable as in the Utopia. Taken, moreover, in connection with his previous relations, no room is left to doubt that, at this period, he recognized the need at many points of a reform in the existing Church, and that he was the advocate of universal religious toleration.

Such had been the general character and course of this distinguished man till past his fortieth year.† On what grounds he could appear as the antagonist of Tyndale, why he did not rather welcome the honest efforts of the reformer, and join hand in hand with him to promote the progress of intelligence and religion, must have been a matter of query to many at that day. But however that was to be explained, at least candor, justice, and philosophic liberality in the treatment of his opponents, might be confidently expected of Sir Thomas More.

* Rudhart, *Thomas Morus*, Augsburg, 1852. To this interesting work I am indebted for the materials of the foregoing chapter.

† The year of his birth cannot be exactly ascertained; but from the manner in which both he and Tyndale refer to his age in their controversy, it is evident that he must have been considerably the senior, and that the statement in the text is within bounds.

CHAPTER XVII.

THE REFORMER TRANSFORMED.

There are many examples of the theoretical reformer, converted by the practical experience of life into the most rigid of conservatives. Seldom, indeed, is so strange a transformation witnessed, as that now to be presented in the case of Sir Thomas More. But his own writings furnish a sufficient solution of the problem, and show that the process was perfectly natural, by which the advocate of freedom and progress became the champion of a Church which repudiates progress, and denies even the right to think; the opposer of faithful translations of the Bible, and of their free use among the people; and the intolerant, bloody persecutor. The case is one full of instruction to those in every age, who think to secure the peace of society, and the permanence of existing institutions, by shutting out the light of truth from the common mind. It is a service perilous alike to principles and to reputation.

During the eleven years which had elapsed since the Utopia saw the light, great changes had been witnessed in Europe, which threatened in their onward progress to subvert the ancient religious institutions of all Christendom. Before 1517, the name of Luther had scarcely been heard of out of Wittenberg. Now, some of the most important states of Europe had renounced their connection with Rome and openly embraced his doctrines; nor was the utmost vigilance of the still Catholic governments sufficient to exclude the influence. Under the name of PROTESTANTISM, a vast religious and political organization, full of youthful energy and sustained by the convictions of the people, disputed with the Papacy for the control of Christendom.

It cannot be doubted that Sir Thomas More had desired reforms in the Church. He may even have regretted that the social and religious system of Christendom had not been originally constructed on more equitable principles. He was willing, we may believe, that various faiths should be tolerated, under strict subordinacy to the state religion. But a Reformation like that which he now saw sweeping over Europe and invading England was not what he had wished. Like Erasmus, he was terrified at the storm which he had himself helped to raise, and would fain unsay the spell and exorcise the unruly elements into their ancient peace.

To this was added another consideration. The popular agitations which followed the establishment of Protestantism in Germany were ascribed by Catholics, no doubt by many very sincerely, to the influence of the new religion ; which, by removing the old restraints, and inculcating freedom of conscience and freedom of thought among all classes, had implanted in the lower orders the spirit of misrule and discontent, to end in tumult, insurrection and revolution.

It was under the lively apprehension of similar results in England, that the cautious statesman entered the lists as the champion of the ancient faith. He could not, or would not, understand that Tyndale and his fellow reformers had no connection with Luther, and sought no political ends. Nor was this, in truth, a matter of much consequence. He saw in their fundamental principles causes which must work out, substantially, the same effects, and which, while undermining the old fabric of religion, could not but endanger the secular government with which it was so vitally connected. He fancied England already in a blaze with the incendiary fires of Lutherans, lawlessness and riot everywhere in the ascendant, and all the goodly framework of society which it had taken centuries to build up, involved in general ruin. Much in the existing institutions might be unjust and oppressive, but no settled order of things could, in his view, be so bad as a revolution.

But the mainspring of his zeal, the motive which furnished its most powerful impulse, and dipped his pen in gall and wormwood, is to be found in something more personal to himself, namely, in his own inward religious history. The distinguishing doctrine of the Reformation, *justification by faith alone*, was the object of his deepest aversion. With all his intelligence, Sir Thomas More could not rise above the belief that the hair shirt which he wore next his skin, the frequent fastings, vigils, and flagellations with which he afflicted his body, were offerings acceptable to the God of love. The strong religious tendencies which early in life had inspired the wish to become a monk,* and the deep conviction of his own infirmities which had led him to relinquish it as a matter of conscience, had only strengthened with years. To stand well in the sight of God, and, as the necessary means thereto, to train his sinful nature into entire subjection to the divine law, was undoubtedly the first object of his life. But the unconscious pride which led him to reject the unbought

---

* Rudhart, ch. ix.

righteousness of Christ as the full expiation for sin, made him the bond slave of superstition. He clung to the Church which promised him heaven as the reward for his deeds, with all the tenacity of the Pharisee to his ancient ritual. The faith which took its starting-point from the opposite principle, he hated with an intensity proportioned to the violence of the conflict in his own bosom. A more striking parallel to the early history of Paul can scarcely be found, than is furnished in the religious career of this great man. Both, striving with all the earnestness of high and powerful natures, to win heaven by fulfilling "every jot and tittle of the law," became, through that very aim, the bitterest persecutors of those who brought glad tidings of grace and truth to man. Among all those who pursued, to prison and to death, the flock of Christ in England in the 16th century, Sir Thomas More must be allowed the first place in cruel and unrelenting intolerance ; and the cause is, in part at least, that in him as in Saul of Tarsus, a nobler character was perverted, by false doctrine and party zeal, into a tool of bigotry and despotism. Certainly it would be hard to find a more lamentable exhibition of their corrupting influence than this controversy with Tyndale. We cannot but believe, many times, that his furious exasperation of manner is due as much to the convictions on which he is obliged to trample as to a sincere zeal for the cause he advocates ; while ever and anon, in the midst of serious argument, there gleams out a reckless, mocking spirit, between profanity and jest, which makes us doubt whether he has not, in the process, undermined his own confidence in all religion ; and if his faith has survived, whether he has not lost his honesty. To such a height of absurdity does he sometimes rise, that it is impossible not to feel that he is laughing at the arguments with which he is seeking to convince the undiscerning rabble. Worse than all is the debased moral tone of these writings, the ridiculous tales, indecent jests, and Billingsgate abuse which deform his pages, indicating far more the design to win the people to his party by catering to their degraded tastes, than to infuse into them the elevating influences of truth and virtue. Well did he deserve the rebuke of Tyndale, who, in his reply to the "Dyaloge," makes the single remark on one chapter of unmitigated grossness : "*This chapter is worthy of the author and of his worshipful doctrine.*" In noble contrast stand Tyndale's own writings for the people ; whose pure, honest, earnest pages are sufficient witness that their author sought to gain his readers for no party, but to restore the reign of God, the dominion of holiness and of the love of Christ in their hearts.

License to read the books of Tyndale, for the purpose of refuting them, was granted to Sir Thomas More by the Bishop of London,* in March, 1528; but the first division of his work did not appear till the summer of the following year, though he had, as he informs the reader, labored at it "night and day." It was a folio of two hundred and fifty pages, the title of which was set forth, with all due pomp and circumstance, as follows : " A Dyaloge of Syr Thomas More, Knyghte : One of the Counsaill of our Sovereign Lord the Kinge, and Chancelloure of his Duchy of Lancaster. Wherein be treated divers matters, as of the veneracyon and worship of images and reliques, praying to sayntes and goyinge on pilgrimage. Wyth many other thynges touching the pestylente secte of Luther and Tyndale, by the tone begun in Saxony, and by the tother labored to be brought into England." The controversy extended through the years 1529-1533. Sir Thomas More's part filled several folio volumes. A considerable portion of it appeared under the imposing name of the " Chancelloure of England "; to the remainder he dedicated the year which followed his resignation of the Great Seal. Besides the works directed against Tyndale by name, the " Supplication of Soules," in reply to Fyshe's Supplication of Beggars ; the " Confutation of Frere Barnes' Church," and others which likewise came from his busy pen during this period, belong to the same general subject, and together form a very complete view of the doctrines and policy of the Romish Church, by one of its ablest defenders.

These English writings, it should be borne in mind, were for the people, and were intended to counteract those of Tyndale and his fellow-reformers. What then was the process by which the end was sought ? and what, if successful, must have been the influence on the condition and prospects of the English people ?

The fundamental principle of the new advocate, with which his whole theory stood or fell, was the infallibility of the Church of Rome —THE MOST HOLY CATHOLIC CHURCH CANNOT ERR. How is this proved ? Primarily, by Scripture, which, in this point is supreme and absolute authority. Christ promised Peter that his faith should not fail. But Peter's faith did fail ; therefore, this must have been addressed to him, not as an individual, but as the representative Head of the Church ; since otherwise, Christ is made untrue to his word. Likewise to all his Apostles, as the representatives of the Church, he promised that the Holy Ghost should be with them and in them ; " the Comforter shall teach you all things ;" " he that heareth you,

---

* What a picture of the mental bondage in which England was then held, is disclosed by this single fact. A man like Sir Thomas More, obliged to ask leave of the bishop to read the works of Tyndale !

heareth me, and he that despiseth you, despiseth me ; and lo ! I am with you alway, even to the end of the world." And Christ also directed, that if any would not hear the Church, he should be accounted a heathen man and a publican.—But what Church is this, and how is it to be known? "It is," says More, "the common known body of all Christian realms remaining in the faith of Christ, not fallen off, nor cut off with heresies." "The very Church of Christ here in earth, which hath the right faith, and which we be bounden to believe and obey, is this universal known people of all Christian nations, that be neither put out, nor openly departed out, by their willful schisms and plainly professed heresies." "The Catholic Church is God's perpetual apostle, however nations soever fall therefrom, and how little and small soever it be left." "I said, and yet say, that these words of our Saviour Christ, ' Whoso heareth you, heareth me,' were no more proper commandment to bind any man to believe the apostles, than to believe the whole Catholic Church, and general councils that represent that whole body of the Catholic Church ; and that they were not spoken to the apostles only, no more than the Holy Ghost was promised to be sent to the apostles only."*—That this is the apostolic, and therefore infallible Church, is proved by miracles which God has wrought through her, from the time of Christ down to the present. "And this is, therefore, the way that God hath taken from the beginning ; that is, to wit, he hath joined his word with wonderful works, to make his word perceived for his own. Thus did he in every age before the coming of Christ. Thus did he in Christ himself, whose words he proved by his wonderful works. . . . Thus did he also by his blessed apostles, whose doctrines he confirmed by miracles. And thus hath he done ever since."† "And now, in such things as God seeth most need, and the hereticks most busy to assault, there doth he most specially fence in his Church with miracles. . . . . He hath wrought, and daily doth many wonderful miracles, and the like of those that he wrought in the time of his apostles, to show and make proof that his Catholic Church is his perpetual apostle, how many nations soever fall therefrom, and how small soever it be left,"‡—" Our Saviour saith that his own miracles passed all that had been before, and that yet his apostles and disciples and faithful-believing folk should do as great and greater. And we see in the Catholic Church God hath done, and daily doth for his saints. . . as great miracles in confirmation of our faith in that behalf, as ever he did in the time of the apostles. The false

---

* Confutation of Tyndale, p. 504.   † Ibid.   ‡ Ibid., p. 449.

churches of heretics do no miracle. . . . But God worketh his miracles in his true Church, to shew his true Church, that is to wit, his true apostle."*—The genuineness of these modern miracles, on which so much is made to depend, is argued through several chapters of the Dialogue, in a manner which, for the credit of the distinguished author's sincerity, we trust was more satisfactory to him than it is to his readers at the present day. The instances which he adduces make a heavy draught on our faith in his honesty. One of these, to which he professes to have been an eye-witness, must suffice as a specimen.

"And myself saw, at the Abbey of Barking, beside London, to my remembrance about thirty years past, in the setting an old image in a new tabernacle, the back of which image being painted over, and of long time before laid with beaten gold, happened to crack in one place, and out there fell a pretty little door, at which fell out, also, many relics, that had lien unknown in that image God wot how long. And as long had been likely to be again, if God by that chance had not brought them to light. The Bishop of London then came thither to see there were no deceit therein. And I, among others, was present there while he looked thereon and examined the matter. And in good faith, it was a marvel to me to behold the manner of it. I have forgotten much thereof, but I remember a little piece of wood there was, rudely shaped in cross, with thread wrapped about it. Writing had it none, and what it was we could not tell; but *it seemed as newly cut as if it had been done within one day before!* And divers relics had old writings on them, and some had none. But among other, were certain small kerchiefs which were named there Our Lady's, and of her own working. Coarse were they not, nor were they not large, but served as it seemed, to cast in a plain and simple manner on her head. But surely they were as clean seams to my seeming as ever I saw in my life, and were therewith as white, for all the long lying, *as if they had been washed and laid up within one hour!* And how long that image had stood in that old tabernacle, that could no man tell; but there had, in all the church, none as they thought stood longer untouched. And they guessed, that four or five hundred years ago, the image was hidden when the abbey was burned by infidels, and those relics hidden therein; afterward, the image was found and set up many years after, when they were gone that hid it. And so the relics remained unknown therein, till now that God gave that chance that opened it."†

That this is the true Church is attested also by the common con-

* Confutation, p. 449.   † Dialogue, p. 192.

sent of the "old holy doctors," who, having proved their saintship by indubitable miracles, testify in their writings that this is the very true Church. "The miracles and consent of these holy doctors, do prove that this must needs be the very true Church in which they have written, and their miracles have been done."

The essential point being satisfactorily established—that the Catholic Church is the true Church, which being continually pervaded by the fullness of divine influence, cannot err—the way is prepared for exalting her teachings above those of the written Word. Provision is thus made for all those doctrines and usages in the Church, which are not commanded by Scripture ; or are, by all ordinary rules of interpretation, even in direct contrariety to it. By establishing the authority of the Church, it has made itself superfluous. The unwritten word—that is, the traditions taught by the apostles, and handed down from age to age, and the new teachings of the Church itself in successive periods, through her general councils—are of equal authority with the written word. Several of these he enumerates, in a passage of the "Confutation," as follows :

"By these traditions have we the praying to saints, and the knowledge that they pray for us. By these traditions have we the holy Lenten fast. . . . By these have we also the Saturday changed into Sunday. . . . By these have we the hallowing of chalices, vestments, paschal taper, and holy water, with divers other things. By these traditions of that Holy Spirit, hath the Church also the knowledge how to consecrate, how to say Mass, and what thing to pray for and to desire therein. By this have we also the knowledge to do reverence to the images of holy saints, and of our Saviour, and to creep to his cross, and to do divine honor unto the blessed sacrament of the altar." And these are things not merely true in themselves ; the belief of them is necessary to salvation. For if the Church, in teaching the worship of saints, of images, relics, and the host, teaches what is false, she teaches damnable idolatry ; to disbelieve it, therefore, if true, is damnable error and heresy. To judge from the earnestness with which he contends for these "unwritten verities," they were of far more moment in his eyes than those revealed in Scripture. Such frantic zeal in defence of the worship of saints and relics can hardly be accounted for in such a man, except on the supposition that he saw in these the stronghold of the Church with the populace. So anxious was he to present the holy fabric without a flaw to the common eye, as to defend the superstition of praying to St. Loy for sick horses, and St. Appoline in the toothache, and St. Sythe for lost keys ; and of the offering by discontented wives of pecks of oats to St. Wilgefort, to rid them of their husbands—hence, called by them St. Uncumber. He gravely accounts also for the fact, that the head of John the Baptist is enshrined in more than one place, and in general, that the bones of the saints are so singularly multiplied in Christendom ; and proves that under the inspired guardianship of the Church there can be no serious mistake. Nay, so meritorious and so necessary is the reverence of relics, that if, by chance, a pig's bones were worshipped as those of a saint, the service would be far more acceptable to God than the profane rejection of the whole doctrine by heretics.*

But how if these teachings seem to contradict the plain language of the Scriptures ? The remedy is easy. The Church which cannot err is the constituted expounder of the written word. " She has the assistance of God and the Holy Ghost. For else might the Church be most easily beguiled in the very receiving of Scripture, wherein they take outwardly but the testimony of men from mouth to mouth, and hand to hand, without other examination. But that secret means that inclineth their credulity to consent in the believing all in one point, *which is the secret instinct of God*, this is the sure mean that never can, in any necessary point, fail in Christ's Church." " Worst of all wretches shall he walk, who cometh to the Scripture of God to try whether the Church believe right or not. For either doubteth he whether Christ teach his Church true, or whether Christ teacheth it at all or not. And then he doubteth whether Christ in his words said true, when he said he would be with his Church to the end of the world."

He particularly cautions theological students against the dangerous practice, to which so many of them were then inclined, of " giving themselves to the study of Scripture alone, with contempt of logic and other secular sciences, and little regard to the old interpreters" ; and tells a sad story of some who had thus come to a very bad end. " For the sure avoiding whereof," he continues, " my poor advice were, in the study thereof, to have a special regard to the writings and comments of the old holy fathers. And yet, or he fall in hand with the one or the other, next to grace and help of God to be got with abstinence and prayer and clean living, afore all things were it necessary to come well and surely instructed in all such points and articles as the Church believeth." " Finally, if all he can find in other men's works, or invent by God's aid of his own study, cannot suffice to satisfy, but that any text yet seem contrary to any point of the Church's

* Dialogue, 2d Book.

faith and belief, let him then, as St. Augustine saith, make himself very sure that there is some fault, either in the translator or in the writer [copyist], or now-a-days in the printer ; or finally, that for some let or other, he understandeth it not aright. And so let him reverently knowledge his ignorance, lean and cleave to the faith of the Church as an undoubted truth, leaving that text to be better perceived when it shall please our Lord, with his light, to reveal and disclose it."

CHAPTER XVIII.

SHALL THE PEOPLE HAVE THE BIBLE?

BUT the central point of interest in this controversy was the subject of vernacular translations of the Bible. Of these the Lord Chancellor professed himself a warm advocate. Nothing, in his view, could so conduce to the growth of piety and good morals among the people, as the Holy Scriptures faithfully translated into their mother tongue. To argue against this was to reflect on " the holy writers that wrote the Scriptures in the Hebrew tongue, and against the blessed evangelists that wrote the Scripture in Greek, and against all those in likewise that translated it out of every of those tongues into Latin" ; for these were all written in what was, at the time, the vulgar tongue. To deny it to the unlearned in English, required also that it should be denied in the Latin to the laity and to the great body of the priesthood also, who were as incompetent to understand " hard and doubtful texts" in the vulgate, as the very women to do so in their own language. Nor did the objection that many would abuse the privilege to their own destruction, seem to him a sufficient reason for withholding it from all. " If any good thing will go forward, somewhat," he says, " must be adventured." " To keep the whole commodity from any whole people, because of harm that by their own folly and fault may come to some part, were as though a lewd surgeon would cut off the leg by the knee, to keep the toe from the gout, or cut off a man's head by the shoulders to keep him from the toothache." " I would not, for my mind, withhold the profit that any one good, devout, unlearned layman might take by the reading, not for the harm that an hundred heretics would fall in by their own willful abusion."*

In regard to *the principle of the thing*, it appears, therefore, that Sir Thomas was entirely one with the reformers. He could illustrate it as forcibly, and plead for it as earnestly, as the most zealous of them all. The only difference between them was on the practical application of the principle in which he and they alike were agreed.

When we come to the practical application, however, this difference is found to be a somewhat serious matter, involving no less than the whole question : " Shall the people HAVE the Bible ?"

* Dialogue, 3d Book.

In the first place, though Sir Thomas More was fully in favor of the Bible for the people, it was not as a matter of necessity, nor as their right. Nor did he plead for the whole Bible to be given to the whole people. Who should receive it, and how much, was at the discretion of their spiritual guides. He proposes the following plan for obviating the mischief apprehended by many learned and pious prelates, from the Scriptures in the mother tongue. "Let a translation be made by some good Catholic and well-learned man, or by divers dividing the labor among them, and the work then allowed and approved by the ordinaries, and by their authority put to print, all the copies then to come whole into the bishop's hands, which he may after his discretion and wisdom deliver to such as he perceiveth honest, sad, and virtuous, with a good monition and fatherly counsel to use it reverently, with humble heart and lowly mind, rather seeking therein occasion of devotion than despicion. And providing as much as may be that the book be, after the decease of the party, brought again and reverently restored unto the ordinary. So that, as near as may be devised, no man have it but of the ordinaries' hands, and by him thought and reputed for such as shall be likely to use it for God's glory and the merit of his own soul. Among whom, if any be proved after to have abused it, the use thereof to be forbidden him either forever, or till he wax wiser." "Though it were not taken to every lewd lad in his own hands, to read a little rudely when he list, and then cast the book at his heels, or among other such as himself to keep a quodlibet or a pot parliament upon, I trow there will no wise man find a fault therein." "Though it may, therefore [on account of the presence of the Holy Spirit in the Church], be the better suffered that no part of Scripture were kept out of honest laymen's hands, yet would I that no part thereof should come into theirs, which, to their own harm, and haply their neighbor's too, would handle it over-homely, and be too bold and busy therewith. And although Holy Scripture be a medicine for the sick and food for him that is whole, yet, since there is many a body sore and soul-sick that taketh himself for whole, and in Holy Scripture is a whole feast of so much divers viand, that after the affection and state of sundry stomachs, one may take harm by that self same that shall do another good, and sick folk often have such a corrupt tallage in their taste that they most like the meat that is most unwholesome for them, it were not therefore, as me thinketh, unreasonable that the ordinary, whom God hath, in the dioceses, appointed for the chief physician to discern between the whole and the sick, and between disease and disease, should after his wisdom and discretion, appoint everybody their part as he should perceive to be good and wholesome for them. And, therefore, as he should not fail to find many a man to whom he might commit all the whole ; so, to say the truth, I can see no harm therein, though he should commit unto some men the Gospel of Matthew, Mark, or Luke, whom he should yet forbid the Gospel of John ; and suffer some to read the Acts of the Apostles whom he would not suffer to meddle with the Apocalypse. Many were there, I think, should take much profit by St. Paul's Epistle *ad Ephesios*, and yet should find little fruit for their understanding in the Epistle *ad Romanos*. And in likewise would it be in divers other parts of the Bible as well in the Old Testament as in the New ; so that I say, though the bishop might, unto some laymen, betake and commit, with good advice and instruction, the whole Bible to read ; yet might he to some man well and with reason restrain the reading of some part, and from some busy-body the meddling with any part at all, more than he shall hear in sermons set out and declared unto him ; and in likewise to take away the Bible from such folk again as be proved by their blind presumption to abuse the occasion of their profit unto their own hurt and harm."

At the conclusion he modestly suggests, with all deference to more wise and learned judges, that he would not himself fear to try the experiment of permitting the Scriptures to go freely among the people. But as the controversy progressed, not so much to his own credit as had been anticipated, he seems to have grown much more dubious on this point. In the " Confutation," written two or three years later, 1532, he argues against having the church service in English, " which," he says, " what it would do here God knoweth ! But as for Allmain (Germany), there as it is so already we see well enough that it doeth no great good there." In the " Apology," written in 1533, he seems quite weaned from the plan which had once been so near his heart. "The people," he asserts, " may have every necessary truth of Scripture, and everything necessary for them to know concerning the salvation of their souls, truly taught and preached unto them ; though the corps and body of the Scripture be not translated unto them in their mother tongue. For else had it been wrong with English people, from the faith first brought into this realm unto our own day, in all which time before, I am sure that every English man and woman that could read it, had not a book by them of the Scripture in English. And yet is there, I doubt not, of those folk many a good soul saved. And secondly, also, if the having of the Scripture in English be a thing so requisite, of precise necessity, that the people's souls should needs perish but if they have it translated into their own tongue; then must the most part perish for all that, except the preacher make farther provision beside, that all the people shall be able to read it when they have it, of which people far more than four parts of all the whole divided into ten could never read English yet, and many now too old to begin to go to school, and shall, with God's grace, though they read never word of Scripture, come to heaven as well. . . . . . Many have thought it a thing very good and profitable that the Scripture, well and truly translated, should be in the English tongue. And albeit that many right wise and well learned both, and very virtuous folk also, both have been and yet are in a far other mind; yet for mine own part, I both have been, and yet am also of the same opinion still, as I have in my Dialogue declared, *if the men were amended and the time meet therefor!*"

In the second place, there seemed to be insuperable difficulties in the way of obtaining such a translation as might safely be trusted in the people's hands. There was a tradition of an ancient orthodox version made known before Wickliffe's;* but where to find it, or how to distinguish it from that seditious and prohibited translation, no man could tell. When moreover, the pious Chancellor reflects, that all through these two hundred years, during which the holy Catholic Church has possessed so many learned and virtuous doctors, not one

---

* In reference to this alleged version, Tyndale replies: "What may not Mr. More say by authority of his poetry? There is a lawful translation that no man knoweth, which is as much as no lawful translation. Why might not the bishops show which were that lawful translation, and let it be printed? Nay if that might have been obtained of them with large money, it had been printed, ye may be sure, long ere this. But, Sir, answer me hereunto; how happeneth that ye defenders translate not one yourselves to cease the murmur of the people, and put to your own glosses, to prevent heretics? You would no doubt have done it, long since, if ye could have made your glosses agree with the text in every place." He adds a serious charge against Sir Thomas More's sincerity. "And what can you say to this, how that besides they have done their best to disannul all translating by parliament, they have disputed before the kings' grace that it is perilous and not meet, and so concluded that it shall not be, under a pretence of deferring it for certain years; where Mr. More was their special orator, to feign lies for their purpose." *Ans. to Sir Thomas More's Dialogue,* vol. ii., p. 175. This is, without doubt, the interview mentioned by More himself (Confutation, p. 422): "The king's highness, and not without the counsel and advice, not of his nobles only with other counsellors attending on his grace's person, [most of them ecclesiastics,] but also of right virtuous and special right well learned men of either university, and other parties of the realm specially called thereunto, hath, after diligent and long consideration had therein, been fain, *for the while,* to prohibit the Scripture of God to be suffered in English tongue among the people's hands."

of them has been moved by the Holy Spirit to undertake this work, he begins to be in doubt whether the wishes he has indulged are in harmony with the will of God. Heretics, alone, seemed to have their minds inclined to Bible translation. A New Testament, translated out of the original Greek into clear and vigorous English, had already appeared, and had commended itself widely to the popular mind. It was the first effort of the kind by an English scholar ; and, as a literary work, might well have been an object of pride to English scholars. But, as the work of a heretic it must be prohibited, and wherever found, burned to ashes by the faithful guardians of the flock. Better far that the people should never have a Bible, than receive it from this poisoned source !

But, unfortunately, the notion had gone abroad among the people that these measures were attributable rather to personal and selfish considerations, than to any concern for their welfare.

"The visible contrariety between that book and the doctrines of those who handled it," was the popular solution of their zeal for its suppression ; an opinion which did not tend to lessen their eagerness to read it, or their prejudices against the clergy. To counteract this impression, and to persuade the people to wait patiently till Providence should send them a Bible, prepared by the right men on the right principles, More put forth all the power of his pen.

He begins * with expressing his surprise, "that any good Christian man having any drop of wit in his head," should complain of the burning of Tyndale's New Testament. Even to call it the New Testament is a misnomer ; since, as he affirms, "Tyndale had, after Luther's counsel, so corrupted and changed it from the good and wholesome doctrine of Christ, to the devilish heresies of their own, that it was clean a contrary thing." "To tell all its faults, were in a manner to rehearse all the whole book, wherein there were found and noted wrong above a thousand texts by tale. To study to find one, were to study where to find water in the sea."

But when he condescends to specify some of these alleged errors, we see that the real gist of the difficulty lies within a nutshell. It was Tyndale's *principles of translation, as applied to certain ecclesiastical terms of the Romish Church*, which formed the true ground of his condemnation with the Lord Chancellor. Out of the multitude of mistranslations, he proposes to mention "two or three, such as every one of the three is more than thrice three in one." "The one is this word, *Priests ;* the other, the *Church ;* the third, *Charity*"—trans-

* Dialogue, 3d Book, 8th chap.

lated by Tyndale, *seniors* (afterward changed to *elders*), *congregation*, *love*. To these he afterward adds several others—as *favor* for *grace ; repentance* for *penance ; knowledging** for *confessing*. This may, at first, seem mere peevish caviling on the part of More ; as Coverdale said, "like a quarrel as to the difference between fourpence and a groat." But this is a mistaken view. These terms were the very pillars of the hierarchical system. In excluding them from his translation, Tyndale had effaced from the English New Testament everything to which the Romish clergy could appeal, in proof of those prerogatives by which they had so long lorded it over the minds and consciences of the laity. The controversy beten More and Tyndale, on these points, shows clearly that they both considered them vital questions. The Lord Chancellor accuses his opponent, over and over, of "going about by this means to *make a change in the faith*." "Because," says he,† "that Luther utterly denieth the very Catholic Church in earth, and saith that the Church of Christ is but an unknown congregation of some folk, here two and there three, no man wot where, having the right faith, which he calleth only his own new forged faith ; therefore Huchyns [Tyndale] in the New Testament, cannot abide the name of the Church, but turneth it into the name of congregation ; willing that it should seem to Englishmen, either *that Christ, in the Gospel, had never spoken of the Church*, or else that the Church were but such a congregation, as they might have occasion to say that a congregation of some such heretics were the Church that God spake of.—Now, as touching the cause why he changed the name of priest into senior, ye must understand that Luther and his adherents hold this heresy, that *holy order is nothing*.‡

---

* This word, as appears from many passages in More's own writings, had the full force of our present form, *acknowledging*.

† Dyaloge, p. 222.

‡ How much importance More attached to this point, is seen from other passages, in which he speaks of the nature and efficacy of the priestly office. " But Tyndale careth not how he set his words, so that he may make us to believe that we need no priest to offer up daily the same sacrifice that our Saviour offered once, and hath ordained to be by priests perpetually offered in his Church."
" Nor would Tyndale have us for his pleasure, in hatred of the order of priesthood, believe that the priest doth at the Mass make none offering of that holy sacrifice for sin. With which heresy he clean taketh away the very fruit of the Mass, in which that blessed sacrament is *most honored of the people*, and is also most profitable unto the people."—Ans. to Tynd. Preface, p. 392. " And be a priest never so nought, . . . yet this advantage take we by the privilege and prerogative of his priesthood, . . . that be he never so vicious, and therewith so impenitent, and so far from all purpose of amendment, that his prayers were afore the face of God rejected and abhorred, yet that sacred sacrifice and sweet

And that a priest is nothing else but a man chosen among the people to preach ; and by that choice to that office, he is priest by and by, without any more ado. . . . But as for saying Mass, and hearing of confession, and absolution thereon to be given ; all this, he saith, that every man, woman, and child may do as well as any priest."
" Ye may perceive that he thus used himself in his translation, to the intent that he would set forth Luther's heresies and his own thereby. For first, he would make the people believe that we should believe nothing but plain Scripture, in which point he teacheth a plain, pestilent heresy. And then would he, with his false translation, make the people ween farther, that such articles of our faith as he laboreth to destroy, and which be well proved by Holy Scripture, were in Holy Scripture nothing spoken of ; but that the preachers have, all this fifteen hundred year, misreported the Gospel, and Englished the Scripture wrong, to lead the people purposely out of the right way."

Nor does Tyndale, in his reply to More, treat the mooted renderings as a matter of indifference. "Wherefore," he says,* " inasmuch *as the clergy* (as the nature of those hard and indurate adamant stones is to draw all to them), *had appropriated unto themselves* the term that of right is common to all the whole congregation of them that believe in Christ,† and with their false and subtle wiles, had

oblation of Christ's holy body, offered up by his office, can take none impairing by the filth of his sin, but highly helpeth to the upholding of this wretched world, from the vengeance and wrath of God, and is to God acceptable, and to us as available for the thing itself, as if it were offered by a better man."—Dialogue, p. 226. And what is the sacrifice which the priest first creates, and then offers ? Let More himself answer. It is " that holy, blessed, glorious flesh and blood of Almighty God himself, with his celestial soul therein, and with the majesty of his eternal godhead."—*Treatise on the Passion*, p. 1264. " It is under the form and likeness of bread, the very self-same body and the very self-same blood, that died and was shed upon the cross for our sin, and the third day gloriously did rise again to life, and with the souls of holy saints fetched out of hell, ascended and styed [rose] up wonderfully into heaven, and there sitteth on the right hand of the Father, and shall visibly descend in great glory to judge the quick and the dead, and reward all men after to their works."—Ib. 1266.

It was no false charge that Tyndale, in refusing to recognize this office in the English Testament, " went about to make a change in the [Romish] faith."

* Tyndale's Works, vol. ii., p. 14.

† More foolishly cavils at this assertion of Tyndale, as if he had said that the laity were in no sense included in the Romish church. But he does not attempt to deny or evade, so patent was the fact, that whenever The Church was spoken of with the idea of power and authority, the clergy alone were included. When the Church was said to have decided on a doctrine, or a course of policy, or to have performed any high judicial act, it was understood of them alone ; the laity having no voice in spiritual matters. Through their courts, synods, and general

beguiled and mocked the people, and brought them into ignorance of the word ; making them understand by the word Church, nothing but the shaven flock of them that shore the whole world ; therefore, in the translation of the New Testament, where I found this word, *ecclesia*, I interpreted it by this word, *congregation.*" " And that I use this word, *knowledge*, and not *confession;* and this word, *repentance*, and not *penance*. In which all, he cannot prove that I gave not the right English unto the Greek word. But it is a far other thing that paineth them, and biteth them by the breasts. There be secret pangs that pinch the very hearts of them, whereof they dare not complain. The sickness that maketh them so impatient is, *that they have lost their juggling terms.*"* " So now the causes why our prelates thus rage, and that moveth them to call Mr. More to help is, not that they find just causes in the translation, but because they have lost their juggling and feigned terms, wherewith Peter prophesied they should make merchandise of the people."†

Now Sir Thomas More did not pretend that Tyndale's translation misrepresented, in these points, the original meaning of the words used in the Greek text. His position was this : The sacred writers did indeed, of necessity, use for the expression of Christian ideas, words taken from common life ; but they used them in a peculiar sense. Thus the Greek word *presbyteros* (translated by Tyndale senior, or elder), meant nothing more than this, until it was employed to designate an office in the Christian Church, to which were attached certain mystical functions and prerogatives. This mystical Christian idea is expressed in English by the word Priest ; and to substitute for it the literal rendering, senior or elder, while it is true to the words of Scripture, falsifies its sense. So *ecclesia*, which meant nothing, originally, but a congregation or assembly, of whatever kind, as by them applied to that mystical body of Christ, wherein he perpetually resides by his Spirit, and which is represented in English by the consecrated word, Church. To translate *ecclesia* by the secular word, congregation, is therefore, to lose the inspired meaning.

There is certainly something plausible in this view at first sight ; but it will not bear the touchstone of the foundation-principle of Protestantism for a single moment. Who was to settle the mystical

councils—subject only to the Pope—they could at pleasure alter or abolish the laws of Christ, and institute (on pain of excommunication, chains and the stake), new articles of faith for the whole body. And this, by virtue of the authority delegated to St. Peter and his successors, was the voice of THE CHURCH.

* Tyndale's Works, vol. ii., p. 22. † Ibid, p. 24.

Christian sense of the words used by the sacred writers? Sir Thomas had a ready answer, The Holy Catholic Church, which cannot err. Once admit that first great tenet, which he had so labored to establish, and all his inferences followed with the force of logical demonstration. Admit that, and it was proved without farther trouble, that a vernacular Bible should conform, in the principles of its translation, to whatever sense the Church, by its doctrines and usages, should have put upon the words of inspiration.

But Tyndale had an altogether different notion of the office of a translator of the Scriptures. No man, and no body of men, might stand between him and the Sacred Oracles, of which he had undertaken to give a faithful reflection to his countrymen. "I call God to record,"—such is his solemn appeal to the Searcher of hearts,— "against the day we shall appear before the Lord Jesus, to give a reckoning of our doings, that 1 never altered one syllable of God's word against my conscience, nor would this day if all that is in the earth, whether it be pleasure, honor, or riches, might be given me." Having diligently labored to ascertain the exact meaning of the sacred original, as it spoke to those whom it first addressed, it was his single aim to reproduce it in those words of his mother tongue which would give that meaning to the minds of his countrymen. He asked not whether the word were holy or profane. Any word was holy to him which conveyed truly and clearly the mind of the Holy Spirit. Sir Thomas More would have welcomed, at least so he professed, a vernacular Bible, if so translated as not to put in question with the common people the faith and practice of his Church. This he deemed a greater evil than to deprive them of the Scriptures. Tyndale believed that, whatever became of that Church or any other, God had a right to speak directly to the common people, and that the people had a right to hear him. It was this belief, and his honest, manly, Christian adherence to it, unmoved by fear or favor, which constituted him God's special messenger to his age, to break the iron rule of priestcraft, and to usher in a new epoch of soul-liberty and pure religion.

The persecuting spirit of the anti-Bible principle is well illustrated in that of its great champion. It being right to forbid the Scriptures to the people, it was right also to use all such means as might be necessary to prevent their obtaining them. It being right to keep the Scriptures out of their reach by laws temporal and spiritual, it was right, also, to affix such penalties to these laws as would insure obedience. It is really appalling, as one turns over these long folios, betokening the author's unwearied interest in his theme, to remark how, from beginning to end, they hiss and sparkle with the fires of remorseless zealotism. The captions to a few chapters of the "Dyalogue" indicate his position in regard to the treatment of those who, in this great matter, ventured to recognize a higher law than that of King Henry, or the Romish Bishops. Chapter thirteenth is headed thus : " The author showeth his opinion concerning the burning of heretics, and that it is lawful, necessary and well done ; and showeth also that the clergy doth not procure it, but only the good and politic provision of the temporality."* Chapter fourteenth : " The author somewhat showeth that the clergy doth no wrong in leaving heretics to secular hands, though their death follow thereon." Chapter fifteenth : " That princes be bound to punish heretics, and that fair handling helpeth but little with many of them." Chapter eighteenth : " The author showeth that in the condemnation of heretics the clergy might lawfully do much more sharply than they do ; and that, in deed and clearness, doth no more now against heretics than the apostle counselleth, and the old holy doctors did." Under the latter heading he instances the case mentioned in the Epistle to the Corinthians, of Hymeneus and Alexander, whom Paul had "delivered unto Satan that they might learn not to blaspheme." " In which words," says More, "we may learn that St. Paul, as apostle and spiritual governor in that country, finding them twain fallen from the faith of Christ, ... did cause the devil to torment and punish their bodies, which every man may well wit was no small pain, and, peradventure, not without death also. . . And this bodily punishment did St. Paul, as it appeareth, upon heretics ; so if the clergy did unto much more blasphemous heretics much more sorrow than St. Paul did to them, they should neither do it without good cause, nor without great authority and evident example of Christ's blessed apostles. And surely when our Saviour himself called such heretics wolves in sheep's clothing, ... the prelates of Christ's Church rather ought temporally to destroy those ravenous wolves, than suffer them to worry and devour everlastingly the flock that Christ hath committed unto their care." He praises also the

* This dishonest evasion was unworthy of Sir Thomas More. "As though," says Tyndale, in his answer, (vol. ii., p. 222), "the Pope had not first found the law, and as though all his preachers babbled not that in every sermon, ' Burn these heretics, burn them, for we have no other argument to convince them ;' and as though they compelled not both king and emperor to swear that they shall do so ere they crown them !" It was customary for the bishop, when delivering over convicted heretics to the secular magistrate bound by his oath of office to burn them at the stake, to intreat *that he would do them no harm !*

foresight and piety of those Christian princes who, like Henry IV., discerning the tendencies of heresy, not only to corrupt the souls of their subjects, but to destroy the realm " with common sedition, insurrection and open war," make provision that "the sparkle be well quenched ere it be grown." Especially is he unwearied in extolling the zeal of that "most faithful, virtuous, and erudite prince," Henry VIII., who by his learned books, and particularly by his determined opposition to heresy within his own realm, has proved himself so eminent a defender of the faith. He is filled with loyal indignation against Tyndale, who, in his "Obedience of a Christian Man," had counselled his readers to suffer any wrong to their persons or property, rather than resist the secular power; a Christian man being, he says, " even bound to obey tyranny if it be not against his faith and the law of God, till God deliver him thereof." Only where the ruler's law conflicts with his conscience and the law of God, then he is bound to obey God rather than man, and patiently abide the penalty.

This was a tender point with the willful and despotic Henry, who claimed to be himself the conscience of his kingdom, and More well knew how to touch it. In that *caveat*, "*if it be not against his faith and the law of God,*" he could discern the germ of all mischief. "They bid the people," he says,* "for a countenance, to be obedient. But they say therewith that the laws and precepts of their sovereign do nothing bind the subjects in their consciences, but [unless] the things by them forbidden or commanded, were before forbidden or commanded in Scripture. . . . . And thus it is sure that, by their false doctrine, they must, if they be believed, bring the people into the secret contempt and spiritual disobedience and inward hatred of the law; whereof must after follow the outward breach, and thereupon outward punishment and peril of rebellion, whereby the princes should be driven to sore effusion of their subjects' blood, as hath already happened in Almain, and of old time in England. Friar Barnes† in his frantic book biddeth the people they should rebel in no wise. But he biddeth them therewith that for all the king's commandment they should not suffer Tyndale's false translation to go out of their hands, but die rather than leave it. . . . And thus ye see how fain he would glory in the people's blood. For he wotteth very well that the king's highness will in no wise, nor in no wise may, if he will save his own soul, suffer that false translation in the hands of unlearned people; which is by an open heretic purposely translated

* Preface to the Confutation, p. 352.   † The same mentioned in Chap. XIII.

false to the destruction of so many souls. Now no man doubteth, that Tyndale himself would no less were done for the maintenance of his false translation of the evangelists, than his evangelical brother Barnes ; but that folk should, against the king's proclamations, keep still his books, and rather than leave them die in the quarrel in defence of his glory. Whereas I did before in my Dialogue say, that Luther's books be seditious, as I now say that Tyndale's be too, and moving people to their own undoing, to be disobedient and rebellious to their sovereigns."

But many a man can persecute in theory, whose heart shrinks from the practical realization of his principles. Not so with Sir Thomas More. It is food for his mirth to recall the sufferings of those godly men, who had perished at the stake for nothing else than their love to God and his truth ; against whom he could himself allege nothing but their rejection of the dogmas of his Church. After a garbled account of the trials of one of them, he exclaims, "And this lo ! is Sir Thomas Hytton, the devil's stinking martyr, of whose burning Tyndale maketh boast."* "I hear also," he continues, "that Tyndale rejoiceth also in the burning of Tewskbury ; but I can see no very great cause why, but if he reckon it for a great glory that the man did abide still by the stake when he was fast bound to it." After stating the proofs of Tewksbury's guilt, namely, that Wickliffe's Wicket,† one of Luther's books, and Tyndale's "Mammon" and "Obedience" were found in his house ; he adds that in his opinion, Tewksbury would never have become a heretic had Tyndale's ungracious books never come into his hands, "for which the poor wretch lieth now in hell and crieth out on him ; and Tyndale, if he do not amend in time, he is like to find him, when they come together, a hot firebrand burning at his back that all the water in the world will not be able to quench."

We shall have occasion to refer again to these writings by and by ; but it is presumed the reader has had a sufficient taste of them for the present. Immediately after the publication of the "Dialogue," in the spring of 1529, Sir Thomas More left England to represent, conjointly with Tunstal and Hackett, the interests of Henry in the royal conference, appointed at Cambray, for adjusting the differences between the Emperor and the King of France. The result was a treaty

---

* Tyndale had alluded in one of his books to the constancy of this good man.

† This treatise of the old reformer, on the Sacrament of the Supper, had recently been printed, and was a favorite manual on the subject with the pious Christians of the time.

between Henry and the Emperor, one article of which secured the continuance of their commercial relations, the other a mutual pledge to prohibit the printing, sale and importation of all *Lutheran books* within their respective dominions.* Under this convenient term were included, as before mentioned, all books in English as well as in other languages, offensive to the Church of Rome ; and of these Tyndale's New Testament stood first on the list.

This important negotiation being happily concluded, the colleagues parted, Tunstal for Antwerp, to repeat the experiment of buying up all the English New Testaments in that market, More for England, to receive full power to put in practice the intolerant principles which he had advocated with his pen.

But the oft-repeated challenge of the reformer, thus expressed in the prologue of his translation of the Pentateuch, remained unanswered : " I submit this work, and all other that I have either made or translated, or shall in time to come (if it be God's will that I further labor in that harvest), unto all them that submit themselves unto the word of God, to be corrected by them ; yea, and moreover, to be disallowed and also burnt, if it seem worthy, *so that they first put forth of their own translating another that is more correct.*"

* Anderson's Annals, vol. i., p. 213.

CHAPTER XIX.

SIR THOMAS MORE AS CHANCELLOR.

SOON after Sir Thomas More's return from France, he was raised to the dignity of Lord Chancellor of England, made vacant by the fall of Wolsey—the highest office in the royal gift. The distinction was the greater, from the fact that this was the first time, during a hundred years, in which it had been bestowed on a layman. This innovation on long-established usages would once have been hailed as an auspicious omen to the cause of religious toleration. When clerical chancellors used the office for the suppression of free inquiry, it was no more than might have been looked for in men whose personal interests were at stake; from a layman a more liberal view of the general interests of the country might naturally be expected.

The result was precisely the reverse. Hitherto the government, as such, had taken no active and avowed part in persecution at home. The decrees, mandates, secret searches, trials of heretics, etc., noticed in the foregoing chapters, had emanated from the direct action of the Church. Now, however, under the administration of the great layman and commoner, we first see the secular power openly linked with the Church in this work, and taking the lead as guardian *ex officio* of the religious opinions of the realm. His position on this subject was significantly indicated in his opening speech as Chancellor; as also in the articles of impeachment against Wolsey, presented by him to Henry in the name of the Lords. In one of these, the Cardinal is accused of having "interfered with the due and direct correction of heresies, highly to the danger and peril of the whole body and good Christian people of this realm." His successor evidently did not intend that his policy should be liable to such a charge; and if we recall the course of Wolsey, we shall feel assured that no half-way measures were in contemplation.

The prognostic was soon verified. On the 24th of December, 1529, just two months after his induction into office, there appeared, "IN THE NAME OF THE KING OUR SOVEREIGN LORD," a manifesto, exceeding in the cruelty of its provisions all that the bishops had hitherto attempted by their own authority. By this "fierce and terrible proclamation," as Foxe calls it, the civil power bound itself to be the right arm of the Church in the extirpation of heresy. "The Chancellor, the Treasurer of England, the Justice of the one bench and of the other, Justices of Peace, Sheriffs, Mayors, Bailies, and other officers," such is its language, " shall make oath, on taking their charge, to give their whole power and diligence to put away, and make utterly to cease and destroy, all errors and heresies commonly called Lollardies.* They shall assist the Bishops and their Commissaries, shall favor and maintain them as often as by them required." " The Justices of the King's Bench, Justices of Peace and of Assize, shall inquire at their sessions of all those that hold errors or heresies, and who be their maintainers, the common writers of books, and also of their schools, sermons, etc." . . . . . . " Offenders to be delivered to the Bishops or Commissaries, by indenture between them, to be made within ten days or sooner, ... to be acquitted or condemned after the laws of Holy Church." If convicted, the secular power was again to receive them, and without farther trial, to carry the sentence of the bishop into execution. The proclamation was especially severe against the writers, venders, and readers of heretical books, of which a list was given, including ninety-four in Latin, and twenty-four in English. At the head stood what More called " the father of them all," the New Testament of Tyndale.

Yet so little effect had these vigorous measures in counteracting the mischief, that in the following spring the aged Bishop of Norwich complains, in a pathetic appeal to the Archbishop, that he is " accumbered by such as keepeth and readeth these erroneous books in English, and believe and give credence to the same, and teach others that they should do so." " My Lord," he adds, " I have done that lyeth in me for the suppression of such persons ; but it passeth my power or of any spiritual man to do it "; and he expresses his apprehension that if not speedily checked, " they will undo us all."

But the high powers of church and state were well aware of the alarming aspect of things, and were already preparing for a movement which they intended should be decisive.

In the library at Lambeth palace is preserved an ancient document, bearing date May 28, 1530, which covers eight skins of parchment, written on both sides in a very fine hand, the record of this combination of the temporal and spiritual powers to prop up the fall-

---

* This name, as Anderson remarks, points to indigenous heresies identical with those of Wickliffe and his followers ; not to those of foreign origin, which were, in distinction, called Lutheran—though the latter term was often applied to both.

ing kingdom of darkness and check the triumphant progress of the word of God.* The Lord Chancellor thus describes the imposing ceremonial of its publication : " For I well know that the King's highness, which as he for his most faithful mind to God, nothing more effectually desireth than the maintenance of the true Catholic faith whereof he is, by his no more honorable than well-deserved title, Defensor ; so nothing more detesteth, than these pestilent books that Tyndale and such other send into the realm, to set forth their abominable heresies withal ; doth of his blessed disposition, of all earthly things abhor the necessity to do punishment ; and for that cause hath not only, by his most famous erudite books, both in English and in Latin, declared his most Catholic purpose and intent, but, also, by his open proclamation divers times iterate and renewed, and finally, in his own most royal person, in the Star Chamber, most eloquently by his own mouth, in great presence of his lords spiritual and temporal, gave monition and warning to all justices of peace in every quarter of his realm, then assembled before his highness, to be by them in all their countries [shires] to all his people declared, and did prohibit and forbid upon great pains, the bringing in, reading, and keeping any of those pernicious, poisoned books, to the intent that every subject of his, by the mean of such manifold effectual warning, with his gracious remission of their former offence in his commandments before broken, should from thenceforth avoid and eschew the peril and danger of punishment, and not drive his highness of necessity to the thing from which the mildness of his benign nature abhorreth."†

The instrument commences with a solemn appeal to God and all true Christian people, and an explanation of the reasons for which it was set forth ; followed by a Bill in English, to be published by the preachers in all the realm ; and closes with the statement, that his Grace's Highness did " then and there, in the presence of all the personages there assembled, require three notaries to make public and authentic instruments, and set thereunto our seal accordingly."

This great movement had not been resolved on without due forethought and preparation. It is stated in the preamble to the instrument itself, that the King, being informed of the alarming spread of heresy in his dominions, through books in the English tongue brought from beyond the sea, had caused a collection of these to be submitted to " his council, prelates, and divers learned men of both universities, and others, for examination ; who, being thus prepared, met for con-

---

* Offor's Memoir of Tyndale, p. 54.
† Preface to the Confutation, p. 351.

sultation at the palace at Westminster, and unanimously resolved that the said books " do swarm full of heresies and detestable opinions." These heresies, some two hundred in number, are engrossed at full length on the deed ; which proceeds to declare, that " the books containing the same, with the translation also of Scripture, corrupted by William Tyndale, as well in the Old Testament as in the New, the King's highness, with the assent of the prelates and universities, has determined utterly to be expelled, rejected, and put away out of the hands of his people. And the King orders all preachers in his realm to publish the commands of his highness in a Bill, in English, to be read in every church and chapel in the kingdom during divine service."

This Bill required all the King's subjects, who had in possession the books specified, or others of like character, henceforth " to detest them, to abhor them, to keep them not in their hands, to deliver them up to the superiors, such as call for them. And if anything of the poison remained in their minds, they were to forget it, or by information of the truth, expel it." " This," it proceeds, " ye ought to do ; and being obstinate, the prelates of the Church ought to compel you ; and your Prince to punish and correct you, not doing the same." Then follows the King's decision in regard to " *the Scripture in the vulgar tongue, and in the common people's hands,*" which is : " that having of the whole Scripture is not necessary to Christian men ; and that the King's highness, having advised with his council and other great learned men, thinketh in his conscience, that the divulging of the Scripture at this time, in the English tongue, to be committed to the people, should rather be to their farther confusion and destruction, than to the edification of their souls. And it was thought there, in that assembly, that the King's highness and the prelates in so doing, not suffering the Scriptures to be divulged and communicated to the people in the English tongue at this time, doth well.'

This action was followed by a royal proclamation, directed expressly and solely against the works of Tyndale. " The King's subjects are commanded to deliver up all such books within fifteen days ; and the judges, justices, constables, and all officers, are ordered to seize all who refuse, or are suspected of possessing them, and bring them before the King and his council, that they may be corrected and punished for their contempt, to the terrible example of other transgressors." It decrees, moreover, that the Scriptures in English " *are books of heresy*, and shall be clearly exterminated and exiled out of this realm of England forever."

These formidable manifestos received an appropriate seal and confirmation at the hands of Bishop Tunstal, the friend and confidant of the Lord Chancellor, in a second great Bible-burning at Paul's Cross. The story of the Bibles used for this purpose has been often repeated, and its truth, in substance, is beyond a doubt.

Bishop Tunstal, it will be recollected, had proceeded from Cambray to Antwerp, for the purpose of getting possession of the English Bibles then in that market. Foxe* thus relates the process by which he accomplished his object :

"Here it is to be remembered, that at this present time one Augustine Packington, a mercer and merchant of London, the same time was in Antwerp, where the Bishop then was ; and this Packington was a man that highly favored Tyndale, but to the Bishop showed the contrary. The Bishop, desirous of having his purpose brought to pass, communed of the New Testaments, and how gladly he would buy them. Packington then hearing him say so, said : ' My Lord, if it be your pleasure, I can in this matter do more, I dare say, than most of the merchants of England that are here, for I know the Dutchmen (i.e., Germans) and strangers that have bought them of Tyndale, and have them here to sell ; so that if it be your Lordship's pleasure to pay for them—for otherwise I cannot come by them, but I must disburse money for them—I will then assure you to have every book of them that is imprinted, and is here unsold.' The Bishop said : ' Gentle Mr. Packington, do your diligence and get them ; and with all my heart I will pay for them, whatever they cost you ; for the books are erroneous and naught, and I intend surely to destroy them all, and to burn them at Paul's Cross.' Augustine Packington then came to Tyndale, and said : ' William, I know thou art a poor man, and hast a heap of New Testaments and books by thee, for which thou hast both endangered thy friends and beggared thyself, and I have now gotten thee a merchant, which, with ready money, shall dispatch thee of all that thou hast, if you think it profitable to yourself.' ' Who is the merchant ?' said Tyndale. ' The Bishop of London,' said Packington. ' O, that is because he will burn them,' said Tyndale. ' Yes,' quoth Packington. ' I am the gladder,' said Tyndale, ' for these two benefits shall come thereof : I shall get money to bring myself out of debt, and the whole world will cry out against the burning of God's word ; and the overplus of the money that shall remain to me, shall make me more studious to correct the said New Testament, and so newly to imprint the same

---

* Anderson, vol. i., p. 214.

again ; and I trust the second will much better like [please] you than ever did the first.' So, forward went the bargain : the Bishop had the books, Packington had the thanks, and Tyndale had the money.'"*

These were the volumes now brought forth to signalize, by a bonfire of Bibles, the recent renewal of the marriage covenant between the State and the Church. In the words of Anderson, " The Clergy and the Star Chamber were now in perfect harmony."

But lest there be any doubt whether he were indeed the leader in these measures, the Lord Chancellor has made a record on the subject with his own pen. In the preface to the Confutation (published in 1532, the third year of his chancellorship), immediately after the passage quoted on p. 137, he adds : " Now seeing the King's gracious purpose in this point, I reckon that, being his unworthy Chancellor, it appertaineth, as I said, unto my part and duty, to follow the example of his noble grace, and after my poor wit and learning, with opening to his people the malice and poison of these pernicious books, to help as much as in me is, that his people, abandoning the contagion of all such pestilent writing, may be far from infection, and thereby from all such punishment, as following thereupon, doth oftentimes rather serve to make other beware that are yet clear, than to cure and heal well those that are already infected ; so hard is that carbuncle catching once a core to be by any man well and surely cured. Howbeit, God so worketh that sometime it is. Toward the help whereof, or if it haply be incurable, then to the clean cutting out that part for infection of the remnant, *am I by mine office in virtue of my oath, and every officer of justice through the realm for his rate, right especially bounden*, not in reason only and good congruence, but also by plain obedience and statute."

During his whole administration the fury of religious persecution never relaxed. On his hands, not less than on the bishops' whose zeal he stimulated, and over whose most execrable acts he cast the shield of his mighty influence and authority, lies the blood of the martyrs who perished during the reign of terror. Some were impris-

---

* Tyndale's conduct, as thus represented by Foxe, has been objected to, as not strictly in accordance with that " simplicity and godly sincerity" which usually characterized him. It is very certain that he could never have originated or managed such a negotiation ; but one can imagine him smiling in grave humor, to see the wily enemy of truth thus circumvent himself. It was a *bona fide* sale ; the Bishop had for his money just what he wanted—only Tyndale turned the bargain from his bad intent to the good one of perfecting and multiplying the English Bible. He attached no such sacredness to a *translation* of the Scriptures, as to flinch from its destruction, when this was to be the means of furnishing one nearer to the inspired original.

oned, loaded with irons, in his own house; some were whipped, some subjected to the torture of the rack, under his personal supervision, while his mocking jests insulted the agony of his victims. He was, moreover, deeply involved in those dastardly intrigues for entrapping Tyndale which ended in the imprisonment and death of this friend of God and man.

It is vain for his eulogists to attempt to wipe out these stains upon his memory, by charging Protestant narrators with misrepresenting facts. Were there not a line of other testimony on record against him, his own writings bear witness to principles so infamous and a heart so cruel, that they would have consigned any other man to the execration of the world. His writings after he retired from office show, if possible, a still more bitter and blood-thirsty spirit than while he was in active life. A great scandal had come upon the clergy in consequence of their tyrannical use of the law *ex officio*, by which persons were arrested on secret information or mere suspicion of heresy, and in secret trial, without being confronted with their accusers, were condemned to the severest punishments, even to death at the stake, on evidence extorted from themselves by cross-examinations, threats and tortures. Even the mere inability to disprove the charge, was ground sufficient for the extremest proceedings of this English Inquisition. Thus might any industrious, peaceable, virtuous citizen, who had incurred the hatred of the clergy, or even of an ill-minded neighbor, be snatched without warning from his dependent family, and after being hurried through a mock trial, be exposed as an abjuring heretic to the derision of the populace; or, as contumacious, be immured in a loathsome dungeon, or be led out to an ignominious and cruel death. Many such cases are related by Foxe, which divide the heart between pity and admiration for the sufferer and burning indignation against those who, under the holy name of religion, could thus oppress their fellow men. Who would not have thought that Sir Thomas More, the enlightened, the just, the humane, as he is represented, would have set himself as a rock against this abuse of irresponsible power? On the contrary, he defends the odious law and its horrible abuses, with all the skill of which he is master. We have no room for his arguments here; but those who feel a curiosity to know with what reasons the most enlightened English statesman of his time could advocate a criminal process for mere opinion, which is now banished from the common law of England in the case of the worst felons, can find them in his *Apology*, and his *Debellacion of Salem and Byzance*,* both written the year after his

* These two works belonged to a controversy between Sir Thomas More and

retirement. It was objected to him at that time, that the felon had at least the benefit of trial by jury : to which he replies, that he never saw the day yet, but that he durst trust as well the truth of one judge as of two juries !"*

But he did something worse, if possible, than to defend the law *ex officio*, viz., advocated the violation, on the ground of heresy, of safe-conducts granted by the King. Such had been furnished to Dr. Barnes, to allow him to come for a limited time into England. More says of him (Pref. to Conf. p. 343), " And yet hath he so demeaned himself since his coming hither, that he hath clearly broken and forfeited his safe conduct, and lawfully might be burned for his heresies if we would lay his heresies and his demeanor since his coming hither both twain unto his charge." To this Frith replies (Eng. Reformers, vol. iii., p. 422) : " This your saying is but a vain gloss ; for I myself did read the safe-conduct that came unto him, which had but only this one condition annexed unto it, that if he came before the feast of Christmas next ensuing, he should have free liberty to depart at his pleasure, and this condition I know was fulfilled. How then should he forfeit his safe-conduct ?" Frith then turns the case very adroitly against the Ex-Chancellor. " But," says he, " Mr. More hath learned of his masters, our prelates (whose proctor he is), to depress our Prince's prerogative, that men ought not to keep any promise with heretics. As though the King's grace might not admit any man to come and go freely into his Grace's realm, but that he must have leave of our prelates ! For else they might lay heresy against the person, and so slay him contrary to the King's safe-conduct ; which things all wise men do know to be prejudicial to his Grace's prerogative royal. . . . . These words had been very extreme, and worthy to have been looked upon, although they had been written by some presumptuous prelate. But that a lay man, so highly promoted

---

an anonymous writer, known, however, to be Christopher Saint Germain, an eminent jurist of the day, who, in two treatises, " *The Pacifier*," and " *Salem and Bizance*," had taken ground, though with great temper and judgment, against the tyrannical course of the clergy in regard to heresy. He was a Catholic, but not a Romanist : and the quotations made from his writings in More's replies, show him to have been a man of equal humanity and justice, far exceeding in breadth and liberality of views his more celebrated contemporary. They are of great value, also, for the light they throw on the prevailing state of opinion in the community. More acknowledged, with a sort of peevish candor, that they had found great favor with the public, and that their brevity and mildness of spirit were held up as models for his own imitation. We cannot see, however, that in either respect he profited by the lesson.

* Debellacion, etc., p. 988.

by his Prince, should speak them, and also cause them openly to be published among his Grace's commons, to reject the estimation of his royal power, doth, in my mind, deserve correction. Notwithstanding, I leave the judgment and determination unto the discretion of his Grace's honorable council."

When the bishops came to offer him several thousand pounds in gold, contributed by the clergy as an expression of their gratitude for the important service rendered them by his pen, he utterly refused it, and said he would rather it were all thrown into the Thames, than that he or his family should be benefited by it to the value of a single groat. He was actuated by a far different, shall we say far better, motive than the love of money. His inspiration was unmixed religious zealotism.

"For albeit they were," he says, "as indeed they were, both good men and honorable, yet look I for my thank of God that is their better, and for whose sake I take the labor, and not for theirs." * He verily thought that he was doing God service.

This inspiration never failed him, nor have we any evidence that the asperity of his zeal was in any degree softened by his own bitter experience of persecution for opinion's sake. There came a time when Sir Thomas More found that he had a law in his own bosom, of more authority than the behest of a king. When Henry requested him to acknowledge, against his conscience, the validity of his marriage with Anne Boleyn, and his supremacy over the Church in England, he felt obliged to refuse, though at the forfeiture of such honors as few men have to lose, of domestic ties peculiarly endearing, and of life itself. Yet even when passing through that bitter conflict of soul, so touchingly described in his letters to his beloved daughter Margaret,† feeling that without the special help of God he should fail in his allegiance to truth—even then, no remorseful memory seems to have crossed his mind of those whom he had racked, body and soul, to compel them to violate their consciences. When it was urged upon him, at an examination before the king's council, that no more was required of him than he had required of heretics, and for the refusal of which they had died at the stake ; he replied that the cases were not parallel, since their consciences were in opposition to the conscience of universal Christendom, i.e., of the holy Catholic Church, as expressed by its constituted authorities ; ‡ but his was in unison

* Apology, p. 876.
† More's English Works, Letter to Margaret Roper, p. 1449.
‡ *Ibid*, p. 1453. An illustration of this principle, interesting for its bearings on a recent decision of the Romish Church, will be found in the Appendix.

with it! Even in those devotional treatises composed in prison, so breathing of self-abasement, of submission to the divine will, of aspiration toward God, the name of heretic revives the same hard, unrelenting tone as he had used in the days of his pride and power. How was it that the shades of the murdered Bilney and Bayfield, of Bainham * and Tewksbury, and of other innocent and holy martyrs, did not crowd his solitary cell, making his heart quake with the horrors of the world to come, or humbling him in dust and ashes as the chief of sinners, because he had persecuted the Church of God! Ah, had it been so, he would have left a fairer name to posterity.

When we contemplate Sir Thomas More in his patriarchal household, the idol of that happy, virtuous, accomplished family, who owed all they were to his wise and affectionate training; as the kind and charitable neighbor; as the incorruptible statesman; as the martyr to conscience, how can we but admire and honor him? Would that the dark pages of his history were not so much more numerous than the bright! Would that the beautiful spectacle of even those last scenes were not clouded by the thought of what he had done, as the fierce religious partizan, to foster in his sovereign those towering notions of royal prerogative, and that tiger thirst for blood, of which he himself was the victim. Surely, it was no more than a just retribution, that he should taste of "*the mildness of that benign nature,*" which he had so extolled when it was directed against heretics. Of no man could it ever be said more truly: "He ate of the fruit of his own doing, and was filled with his own devices."

---

* Bainham, while standing by the stake, spoke as follows: "I came hither, good people, accused and condemned for an heretic, Sir Thomas More being my accuser and my judge. And these be the articles that I die for, which be a very truth and grounded on God's word, and no heresy. They be these: First, I say it is lawful for every man and woman to have God's book in their mother-tongue. The second article is, that the Bishop of Rome is Antichrist, and that I know of no other keys of heaven's gates but only the preaching of the Law and the Gospel; and that there is no other purgatory but the purgatory of Christ's blood." Almost his last words were: "The Lord forgive Sir Thomas More."

CHAPTER XX.

THE ROYAL PATRONESS.

WITH the fall of Sir Thomas More the fury of persecution sensibly abated. Not that his great allies, the bishops, had lost in any degree the persecuting spirit; but they had lost in him the directing mind and will. There was no longer the same thorough inquisition after heretical books; Bibles came more and more freely into England, and were read with far less peril to life. In this result we see indeed the concurrence of other influences which began at this time to affect sensibly the interests of the papal party.

Among these influences none was more potent than the countenance given to the translation and dissemination of the Holy Scriptures by Anne Boleyn, the second wife of Henry VIII.

We need not here recount the steps by which the unfortunate Katherine's beautiful and accomplished maid of honor became the rival and successor of her royal mistress. It is sufficient for our purpose to note the fact that, notwithstanding the earnestness with which Tyndale, like another John the Baptist, had condemned the king's divorce from Katherine, as a wrong not merely to the immediate sufferer, but to that institution which God had ordained as the chief guardian of social order and virtue, the influence of Anne was steadily and courageously given, during the entire period of her reign, to the furtherance of those views, for the sake of which the great reformer had been so long an exile, and the object of relentless persecution from king and clergy. From the date of her marriage, the working of a new and powerful element was felt in the English court. Foxe says of the period immediately preceding: "So great was the trouble of those times that it would overcharge my story to recite the names of all them which, during those bitter days, *before the coming in of Queen Anne*, either were driven out of the realm, or were cast out from their goods and houses, or brought to open shame by abjuration." The "new learning" came gradually into the ascendant; Cranmer, Latimer, and others of like character, men who pleaded openly for the Bible in the vernacular, were promoted to positions of high responsibility; the Scriptures came more and more freely into England, and were read without molestation.

Anne's agency in these changes cannot, in general, be directly traced ; but the unanimous judgment of all parties at the time, indicates her as the main spring of influence in this direction. In one instance of no little interest, we have the direct proof in her own handwriting, of her great power and the use she made of it. Richard Harman will be remembered as the English merchant at Antwerp, who had taken so forward a part in bringing the early editions of Tyndale's New Testament into England. For this, he had not only suffered imprisonment and heavy pecuniary loss, but, what to a man of his character was a far severer calamity, expulsion from the Honorable Company of English Merchant Adventurers,' and this unrighteous action had never been reversed. But the very year after Anne became Queen, Harman ventured into England to seek redress. His application seems to have been made directly to her, as the known friend of the Reformation ; and the result—won from the King, no doubt, by her persuasions—appears in the following letter from her to Crumwell, the State Secretary :

ANNE THE QUEEN.

Trusty and right well beloved, we greet you well. And whereas, we be credibly informed that the bearer hereof—Richard Harman—merchant and citizen of Antwerp, in Brabant, was, in the time of the late Lord Cardinal, put and expelled from his freedom and fellowship, of and in the English house there, for nothing else (as he affirmeth) but only for that he, still like a good Christian man, did both with his goods and policy, to his great hurt and hindrance in this world, help to the setting forth of the New Testament in English. We therefore desire and instantly pray you, that with all speed and favor convenient, ye will cause this good and honest merchant, being my Lord's true, faithful, and loving subject, to be restored to his pristine freedom, liberty, and fellowship aforesaid, and the sooner at this our request, and at your good leisure to hear him in such things as he hath to make further relation unto you in this behalf. Given under our signet, at my Lord's manor of Greenwich, the thirteenth day of May. To our trusty and right well beloved, Thomas Crumwell, Squire, Chief Secretary unto my Lord, the King's Highness.

The tone of this royal epistle—royal in the best sense of the word—cannot but strike the reader with admiration. It is to be remembered, that though Bibles were now allowed to come silently into the kingdom, it was still in violation of express law and statute, and against the opposition of a powerful and embittered party. Yet she takes pains to state precisely the offence for which Harman had suffered, and justifies it as the right and praiseworthy act of " a good Christian man." As Anderson well remarks, " no *man*, either of office or influence, ever so expressed himself while Tyndale lived."

Tyndale had, without doubt, already been made acquainted with the noble stand taken for the truth, by the woman whose elevation he had honestly opposed; and Richard Harman would not now fail, on his return to Antwerp, to inform his friend of the agency through which his errand had reached so happy an issue. Tyndale was then engaged in publishing his revised New Testament. His recognition of the services of Anne to the cause he loved was equally appropriate and delicate—a beautifully printed and illuminated copy of the divine word, on vellum, with the Queen's name, ANNA REGINA ANGLIÆ, arranged in large ornamental letters around the title page.* In the narrative yet to be given of the persecution to which Tyndale was afterward subjected, we shall find traces of her personal interest in the reformer, prompting measures which might have saved him, had she been seconded by hearts as brave and unselfish as her own.

The close of the year 1534 was marked by a strange event; no other than a petition to the King from the clergy in Convocation assembled, for a translation of the Scriptures into English. "This good motion," as we learn from Strype,† was made and warmly advocated by Cranmer. But it was not carried through without violent opposition from the Popish party, headed by Stephen Gardiner, Bishop of Winchester, who declared, that "all the heresies and extravagant opinions then in Germany and thence coming over to England, sprang from the free use of the Scriptures. . . . And to offer the Bible in the English tongue to the whole nation during these distractions, would prove the greatest snare that could be."‡

The next year, Cranmer made a vigorous attempt to consummate this movement, by securing a version of the Scriptures which might be circulated with the advantage of the King's sanction. Unwilling to wait till a new translation from the original could be prepared, and unable to use Tyndale's, which was prohibited by law, he adopted the following plan, as related by Strype in his life :§

"And that it might not be prohibited, as it had been, upon pretence of the ignorance or unfaithfulness of the translators, he proceeded in this method: First, he began with the translation of the New Testament—taking an old English translation thereof,‖ which he divided into nine or ten parts, causing each

---

* Anderson, vol. i., p. 413.
† Memorials of Archbishop Cranmer, vol. i., p. 34.   ‡ Burnet.
§ Strype's Cranmer, vol. i., p. 48.
‖ It is with pleasure that we recognize in this "old English translation," the venerable version of Wickliffe. Of course it could be no other. The awkward device of transcribing one so well known as Tyndale's—which is Anderson's supposition—must immediately have betrayed itself; but a work so rare as Wickliffe's, newly copied, could with difficulty be identified as his, and might therefore well answer Cranmer's purpose.

part to be written at large in a paper book, and then to be sent to the best learned bishops and others, to the intent they should make a perfect correction thereof. And when they had done, he required them to send back their parts so corrected unto him at Lambeth, by a day limited for that purpose ; and the same course, no question, he took with the Old Testament."

How cordial one of the bishops was to this plan is seen in the anecdote told by Strype of Stokesly, Bishop of London, who returned his portion uncorrected, with the answer : " I marvel what my Lord of Canterbury meaneth that thus abuseth the people, in giving them liberty to read the Scriptures, which doth nothing else but infect them with heresy. I have bestowed never an hour on my portion, nor never will. And therefore my Lord shall have his book again, for I will never be guilty of bringing the simple people into error."

Of the secret efforts of Gardiner to frustrate this undertaking, as well as of Anne Boleyn's agency in securing a decision in its favor from the King and of the course of its final failure, we are informed by Archbishop Parker.* Being at this time chaplain to the Queen,† he had the best opportunity for understanding the whole transaction.

"His royal Majesty," says Parker, "was petitioned by the whole Synod, to give commandment that the Holy Scriptures might be translated into the English tongue ; for so it could be more easily discerned by all, what was agreeable to the Divine Law. To this, Stephen Gardiner—the King's most secret counsellor—made resistance as covertly as possible. But through the grace and intercession of our most illustrious and virtuous mistress the Queen, permission was at length obtained from the King, that the Holy Scriptures should be printed and deposited in every church, in a place where the people might read them ; which grant of the King did not go into effect, because this most illustrious Queen soon after suffered death."

Nor was this the only fruit of her zeal for the Scriptures in the language of the people. Before the close of this same year, Coverdale had completed and carried through the press a translation of the whole Bible, which owed much to her patronage, and was dedicated to her, conjointly with the King. Of her connection with it there is sufficient evidence in the fact that her sudden fall arrested it on the eve of publication. Of this version a more particular account will be given in the proper place.

Besides all this there were now pending negotiations for a politico-religious league between Henry and the Protestant princes of Germany, which threatened to establish the Augsburg Confession as the authoritative standard of belief in England. "There were many

---

* De Antiq. Eccl. Brit., p. 385, (Harvard Univ. Library).
† Strype's Life and Acts of Parker, p. 7.

conferences," says Burnet,* "between Foxe, Bishop of Hereford, Doctor Barnes, and some others, with the Lutheran divines, for accommodating the differences between them, and the thing was in a good forwardness. All which was imputed to the Queen."

It is unnecessary to repeat the familiar story of Anne Boleyn's sudden and tragic fate, or to enter into the yet unsettled question of the truth of the charges on which she was tried and condemned. But surely, in the light of the facts above narrated, it is not too much to claim for her the grateful remembrance of all who love the truth as one who fearlessly used her exalted position for the advancement of pure religion and of the translation of the Scriptures into the common tongue, and their free diffusion among the people.

* Hist. Ref. p. 146.

CHAPTER XXI.

MARTYRDOM OF TYNDALE.

FROM the first appearance of Tyndale's work on the king's divorce, the measures already long on foot for his destruction were pursued with fresh energy. Sir John Hackett, as we have seen, had failed in the attempt to procure his apprehension by direct aid from the Court of Brussels. The new scheme was to decoy him into England by the promise of a safe-conduct from the king. Sir Thomas More was then at the height of power; and we have already seen his opinion of the use to be made of a safe-conduct in the case of heretics. Nor were the other high officers of state ashamed to lend their services to the nefarious plot; and royal envoys were charged, in connection with the management of international policy, to be on the watch for William Tyndale. Thomas Crumwell was chief director in the business, and Stephen Vaughan, one of his protégés, now Envoy and King's merchant in place of Hackett, his principal agent. The importance attached to this part of Vaughan's mission may be judged of by the following letter on the subject, addressed by him to the king, January 26th, 1530:

"Most excelent Prince, and my most redoubted Sovereign, mine humble observation due unto your Majesty—My mind continually laboring and thirsting, most dread and redoubtable Sovereign, with exceeding desire to attain the knowledge of such things as your Majesty commanded me to learn and practice in these parts and thereof advertise you, from time to time, as the case should require. And being often dismayed with the regard of so many mischances, as always obviate and meet with my labors and policies, whereby the same (after great hope had, to do something acceptable unto your Highness' pleasure) turn suddenly to become frustrate, and of none effect, bringing me, doubtless, into right great sorrow and inquietude, considering that. Wherefore, lately, I have written three sundry letters unto Willyam Tyndall, and the same sent, for the more surety, to three sundry places—to Frankfort, Hamburg, and Marleborough (i.e. Marburgh); I then not being assured in which of the same he was. I had very good hope, after.I heard say in England, that he would, upon the promise of your Majesty, and of your most gracious safe-conduct, be content to repair and come into England, that I should, partly therewith, and partly with such other persuasions as I then devised in my said letters, and, finally, with a promise which I made him—that whatsoever surety he would reasonably desire, for his safe coming in and going out of your realm, my friends should labor to have the same granted by your Majesty—(but) that now, the bruit and fame of such things (as since my writing to him) hath chanced within your realm, should provoke the man, not only to be minded to the contrary of that whereunto I thought, without difficulty, to have easily brought him, but also to suspect my persuasions to be made to his more peril and danger; than, as I think, if he were verily persuaded and placed before you, (your most gracious benignity, and piteous regard natural, and custom always had, toward your humble subjects considered, and specially to those which, (ac)knowledging their offences, shall humbly require your most gracious pardon), he should ever have need to doubt or fear. Like as your Majesty as well by his letter, written with his own hand, sent to me for answer of my said letters; as also by the copy of another letter of his, answering some other person, whom your Majesty perhaps had commanded to persuade by like means may plain apperceive—which letters, like as together I received from the party, so send I, herewith inclosed to your Highness.

"And whereas I lately apperceived, by certain letters directed to me from Mr. Fitzwilliam, Treasurer of your household, that I should endeavor myself, by all the ways and means I could study and devise, to obtain you a copy of the book, which I wrote was finished, by Tyndall, answering to a book put forth in the English tongue by my Lord Chancellor, and the same should send to your Majesty, with all celerity—I have undoubtedly so done and did, before the receipt thereof. Howbeit, I neither can get any of them, nor, as yet, (is it) come to my knowledge that any of them should be put forth; but being put forth, I shall then not fail, with all celerity, to send one unto your Highness."

In a note to Crumwell, to whom this letter was consigned, he adds: "It is unlikely to get Tyndale into England, when he daily heareth so many things from thence which feareth him. . . . The man is of greater knowledge than the King's highness doth take him for, which well appeareth by his works. Would God he were in England!"

On the 17th of April he had, most unexpectedly, an interview with Tyndale; of which, the very next day, he transmitted the following account in a letter to the King:

"The day before the date hereof, (17th of April,) I spake with Tyndale without the town of Antwerp; and by this means. He sent a certain person to seek me, whom he had advised to say, that a certain friend of mine, unknown to the messenger, was very desirous to speak with me; praying me to take pains to go unto him, to such places as he should bring me. Then I (said) to the messenger —'What is your friend, and where is he?' 'His name I know not,' said he, 'but if it be your pleasure to go where he is, I will be glad thither to bring you.' Thus doubtful what this matter meant, I concluded to go with him, and followed him, till he brought me without the gate, of Antwerp, into a field lying nigh unto the same, where was abiding me this said Tyndale.

"At our meeting—'Do you not know me?' said this Tyndale. 'I do not well remember you,' said I to him. 'My name,' said he, 'is Tyndale.' 'But, Tyndale,' said I, 'fortunate be our meeting.' Then Tyndale—'Sir, I have been exceedingly desirous to speak with you.' 'And I with you; what is your mind?' 'Sir,' said he, 'I am informed that the King's Grace taketh great displeasure with me, for putting forth of certain books, which I lately made in these parts; but specially for the book named "*The Practice of Prelates*,"* whereof I have no little marvel—considering that in it I did but warn his Grace of the subtle demeanor of the clergy of his realm, toward his person; and of the shameful abusions by them practised, not a little threatening the displeasure of his Grace, and weal of his realm: in which doing, I showed and declared the heart of a true subject, which sought the safe guard of his royal person, and weal of his Commons: to the intent that his Grace thereof warned, might, in due time, prepare his remedies against their subtle dreams. If for my pains therein taken —if for my poverty—if for mine exile out of mine natural country and bitter absence from my friends—if for my hunger, my thirst, my cold, the great danger wherewith I am everywhere compassed; and finally, if for innumerable other hard and sharp fightings which I endure, not yet feeling of their asperity, by reason (that) I hoped with my labors to do honor to God, true service to my Prince, and pleasure to his Commons;—how is it that his Grace, this considering, may either by himself think, or by the persuasions of others, be thought to think, that in this doing I should not show a pure mind, a true and incorrupt zeal, and affection to his Grace? Was there in me any such mind, when I warned his Grace to beware of his Cardinal, whose iniquity he shortly after proved, according to my writing? Doth this deserve hatred?

"Again, may his Grace, being a Christian prince, be so unkind to God, which hath commanded his Word to be spread throughout the world, to give more faith to wicked persuasions of men, which presuming above God's wisdom, and contrary to that which Christ expressly commandeth in his Testament, dare say that it is not lawful for the people to have the same in a tongue that they understand; because the purity thereof should open men's eyes to see their wickedness? Is there more danger in the King's subjects, than in the subjects of all other Princes, which, in every of their tongues have the same, under privilege of their sufferance? As I now am, very death were more pleasant to me than life, considering man's nature to be such as can bear no truth.'

"Thus, after a long communication had between us, for my part making answer as my poor wit would serve me, which was too long to write; I assayed him with gentle persuasions, to know whether he would come into England; ascertaining him that means should be made, if he (only) thereto were minded without his peril or danger, that he might do so: And that what surety he would devise for the same purpose, should, by labor of friends, be obtained of your Majesty. But to this he answered—that he neither would, nor durst, come into England, albeit your Grace would promise him never so much surety; fearing lest, as he hath before written, your promise made, should shortly be broken by the persuasion of the clergy; which would affirm that promise made with heretics ought not to be kept.

"After this he told me how he had finished a work against my Lord Chancellor's book, and would not put it in print till such time as your Grace had seen it; because he perceiveth your displeasure towards him for hasty putting forth of his other works, and because it should appear that he is not of so obstinate mind as he thinks he is reported unto your Grace. This is the substance of his communications had with me, which, as he spake, I have written to your Grace word for

---

* The one in which Tyndale condemned Henry's divorce from Queen Katherine.—T. J. C.

MARTYRDOM OF TYNDALE.   153

word, as near as I could by any possible means bring to remembrance. My trust, therefore, is that your Grace will not but take my labors in the best part. I thought necessary to be written to your Grace.

"After these words, he then, being something fearful of me lest I would have pursued him, and drawing also towards night, he took his leave of me, and departed from the town, and I toward the town—saying, 'I should shortly, peradventure, see him again, or if not, hear from him.' Howbeit, I suppose he afterward returned to the town by another way, for there is no likelihood that he should lodge without the town. Hasty to pursue him I was not, because I had some likelihood to speak shortly again with him ; and in pursuing him I might perchance have failed of my purpose, and put myself in danger."

Vaughan, with all his courtier-like subserviency, was evidently quite too good a man for so base an errand. But this cautious attempt to soften the king's feelings was wholly unavailing. A very rough and severe reply from Crumwell, who was extremely vexed at the imprudence of his subordinate, conveyed the expression of the high royal displeasure at the tone of the above letter. Henry was, apparently, much alarmed lest his envoy, while attempting to execute his wishes, should be corrupted by this dangerous man. He strictly forbade, therefore, any further efforts to persuade Tyndale to come into England ; professing that he was "very joyous to have his realm destitute of a person so malicious, perverse, uncharitable, and indurate"; who if once in England, "would, by all likelihood, shortly (which God defend), do as much as in him were to infect and corrupt the whole realm, to the great inquietation and hurt of the commonwealth of the same."

The Secretary then adds his own earnest remonstrance, exhorting Vaughan by all his hopes of court favor and promotion, to show in his future letters to the King, that he bore "no manner of love, favor, or affection to the said Tyndale, nor his works, in any manner of ways, but that he utterly contemned and abhorred the same."

To this, however, was subjoined a postscript, the result, probably, of a subsequent communication from his Majesty, suggesting that heinous as were the offences of Tyndale, if he would but abjure his errors, he might be permitted to return to England with some good hope of the King's mercy. On this hint Vaughan ventured to seek another interview with him, which he reports as follows :

"I have again been in hand to persuade Tyndale ; and to draw him the rather to favor my persuasions, and not to think the same feigned, I showed him a clause contained in Master Crumwell's letter, containing these words following—
'And notwithstanding other the premises in this my letter contained, if it were possible, by good and wholesome exhortation, to reconcile and convert the said Tyndale from the train and affection which he now is in, and to excerpte and take

away the opinions sorely rooted in him, I doubt not but the King's Highness would be much joyous of his conversion and amendment; and so, being converted, if then he would return into his realm, undoubtedly the King's Royal Majesty is so inclined to mercy, pity, and compassion, that he refuseth none which he seeth submit themselves to the obedience and good order of the world.' In these words I thought to be such sweetness and virtue, as were able to pierce the hardest heart of the world; and as I thought so it came to pass. For after sight thereof, I perceived the man to be exceedingly altered, and to take the same very near unto his heart, in such wise that water stood in his eyes; and he answered, 'What gracious words are these!' 'I assure you,' said he, 'if it would stand with the King's most gracious pleasure to grant only a bare text of the Scripture to be put forth among his people, like as is put forth among the subjects of the Emperor in these parts, and of other Christian princes—be it of the translation of what person soever shall please his Majesty, I shall immediately make faithful promise never to write more, nor abide two days in these parts after the same; but immediately repair into his realm, and there most humbly submit myself at the feet of his Royal Majesty, offering my body, to suffer what pain or torture, yea, what death his Grace will, so that this be obtained. And till that time, I will abide the asperity of all chances, whatsoever shall come, and endure my life in as much pains as it is able to bear and suffer. And as concerning my reconciliation, his Grace may be assured—that whatsoever I have said or written, in all my life, against the honor of God's Word, and (if) so proved; the same shall I, before his Majesty and all the world utterly renounce and forsake—and with most humble and meek mind embrace the truth, abhorring all error soever—at the most gracious and benign request of his Royal Majesty, of whose wisdom, prudence, and learning I hear so great praise and commendation than of any creature living! But if those things which I have written be true and stand with God's word, why should his Majesty, having so excellent a gift of knowledge in the Scriptures, move me to do anything against my conscience?'—with many other words, which were too long to write."

For nearly a year nothing more is heard on this topic from Vaughan. But, from a letter to Lord Cromwell in 1531, it appears that what he had already done had effected nothing but to prejudice his own interests at court, and that Sir Thomas More was as busy in the measures against Tyndale, as in the persecutions at home.

A subsequent letter places before us in a vivid light the conflict of opinion then agitating England, the mean and cruel policy employed to bring it to an end, and the triumphant spread of truth against all opposition. The noble sentiments of these extracts place Stephen Vaughan far above the greatest of his employers.

"If Constantyne* have accused me to be of the Lutheran sect, a fautor and setter-forth of erroneous and suspected works, I do not threat marvel, for two

---

* Constantine was accused as a heretic, and as engaged in the transportation of books, in 1528. That year he fled to Brabant, where he supported himself by his profession, having been bred a surgeon. In the year 1531, having ventured

causes specially. One is, for that my Lord Chancellor, in his examination of the said George and of all other men (as I am credibly informed), being brought before him for cases of heresy, doth deeply inquire to know what may be said of me ; and in the examination thereof showeth evident and clear desire in his countenance and behavior, to hear something of me whereby an occasion of evil might be fastened against me ; which, no doubt, shall soon be espied in the patient whom he examineth—who perceiving his desire in that behalf, and trusting, by accusing of me, to escape and avoid his present danger, of pure frailty and weakness, spareth not to accuse the innocent. The other is, for that George, besides the imminent peril and danger in which he was, abiding prisoner in my Lord's house, was vehemently stirred and provoked. What with the remembrance of his poor wife remaining here, desperate, bewashed with continual tears, and pinched with hourly sorrow, sighs, and mourning, and the sharp and bitter threatenings of his poor (state) and condition, likely to be brought unto an extreme danger of poverty ; and more hard than the first, by the excess of his misery, to accuse whom they had longed for, rather than to be tied by the leg with a cold and heavy iron like a beast—as appeared by the shift he made to undo the same and escape such torture and punishments. Will not these perils, fears, punishments, make a son forget the father which begat him ? And the mother that bear him, and fed him with her breasts ? If they will, who should (wonder) though he would accuse me, a thousand times less dear to him than father or mother, to rid him out of the same ?

"Would God it might please the King's Majesty to look into these kinds of punishments ; which in my poor opinion, threateneth more hurt to his realm than those that be his ministers to execute the same tortures and punishments do think or conjecture : and by this reason only—It shall (will) constrain his subjects in great number to forsake his realm, and to inhabit strange regions and countries, where they will practise not a little hurt to the same. Yea, and whereas they (the King's ministers) think that tortures, punishments and death, will be a mean to rid the realm of erroneous opinions, and bring men in such fear that they will not once be so hardy to speak or look, be you assured, and let the King's Grace be therefore advertised at my mouth, that his highness (shall) will duly prove that in the end it will cause the sect to wax greater, and those errors to be more plenteously sowed in his realm than ever afore. For who have so mightily sowed those errors as those persons which, for fear of tortures and death, have fled his realm ? Will they not, by driving men out of his realm, make the rownt (irruption) and company greater in strange countries, and will not many do more than one or two ? Will not four write where one wrote afore ? Counsel you the King's Highness, as his true subject, to look upon this matter, and no more to trust to other men's policies, which threateneth, in mine opinion, the weal of his realm ; and let me no longer be blamed nor suspected for my true saying.

"That I write I know to be true ; and daily do see experience of that I now write, which, between you and me, I have often said and written, though peradventure you have little regarded it. But tarry a while and you will be learned by experience. I see it begun already.

into England, he fell into the hands of Sir Thomas More, who subjected him to a harsh imprisonment in his own mansion ; using his leisure to extract from the poor man, by alternate threats and promises, information against his brethren abroad and all who were suspected of favoring them.

"To some men it will seem, by this my manner of writing, that I being (as they suppose, and as I have been falsely accused to be) one of the sect, do write in this manner because I would that both I and the same sect should be suffered without punishment. Nay truly—But rather I would that an evil doer should be charitably punished, and in such manner as he might thereby be won with other, than lost with a great many. And let his Majesty be further assured, that he will with no policy nor with no threatenings of tortures and punishments take away the opinions of his people till his Grace shall fatherly and lovingly reform the clergy of his realm. For there springeth the opinion. From thence riseth the grudge of his people. Out of that men take and find occasions to complain. If I say truth let it be for such received. If otherwise, I protest, before God and the world, that whatsoever I here write, I mean therein nothing but honor, glory and surety of my only Prince and sovereign, and the public weal of his realm."

The next year discovers a new bailiff in pursuit of Tyndale, Sir Thomas Elyot, Ambassador from Henry to the Emperor. The rancorous hatred of the King and the straits to which the reformer was reduced by his persecution, appear from the following reference to it in a letter addressed March 14th, 1532, to the Duke of Norfolk, then Prime Minister of England:

"My duty remembered, with most humble thanks unto your Grace, that it pleased you so benevolently to remember me unto the King's Highness, concerning my return into England. Albeit the King willeth me, by his Grace's letters, to remain at Brussels some space of time for the apprehension of Tyndale, which somewhat minisheth my hope of soon return; considering that like as he is in wit moveable, semblably so is his person uncertain to come by. And, as far as I can perceive, hearing of the King's diligence in the apprehension of him, he withdraweth him into such places where he thinketh to be farthest out of danger. In me there shall lack none endeavor. Finally, as I am all the King's except my soul, so shall I endure all that shall be his pleasure, employing my poor life gladly in that which may be to his honor or wealth of his realm."

But this attempt was as unsuccessful as the former. The persecuted exile was not without friends to warn him of approaching danger, and to afford him secure refuge in the hour of need. By many members of that honorable and powerful body, the company of English Merchant Adventurers, he was venerated as an apostle. As we have seen in the case of Vaughan, it was impossible for a man of any generosity of soul to come, even briefly, into contact with Tyndale without a deep impression of his exalted moral worth; and we need not wonder that with those who had enjoyed the privilege of daily intercourse with him for years this feeling should rise into an affectionate enthusiasm which would risk everything to save him. A beautiful picture it is which Foxe gives of his course of life in Antwerp and of his relations to his noble countrymen:

"First, he was a man very frugal, and spare of body, a great student and earnest laborer in the setting forth of the Scriptures of God. He reserved or hallowed to himself two days in the week, which he named his pastime, Monday and Saturday. On Monday he visited all such poor men and women as were fled out of England, by reason of persecution, into Antwerp, and these, once well understanding their good exercises and qualities, he did very liberally comfort and relieve; and in like manner provided for the sick and diseased persons. On the Saturday he walked round about the town, seeking every corner and hole where he suspected any poor person to dwell, and where he found any to be well occupied and yet over-burdened with children, or else were aged and weak, those also he plentifully relieved. And thus he spent his two days of pastime, as he called them. And truly his alms were very large, and so they might well be; for his exhibition that he had yearly of the English merchants at Antwerp, when living there, was considerable, and that for the most part he bestowed upon the poor. The rest of the days of the week he gave wholly to his book, wherein he most diligently travailed. When the Sunday came, then went he to some one merchant's chamber or other, whither came many other merchants, and unto them would he read some one parcel of Scripture; the which proceeded so fruitfully, sweetly, and gently from him, much like to the writing of John the Evangelist, that it was a heavenly comfort and joy to the audience to hear him read the Scripture: likewise after dinner, he spent an hour in the same manner. He was a man without any spot or blemish of rancor or malice, full of mercy and compassion, so that no man living was able to reprove him of any sin or crime; although his righteousness and justification depended not thereupon before God; but only upon the blood of Christ and his faith upon the same."

But toward the close of 1534, or the beginning of the following year, a new plot was devised against his life, which ultimately proved successful. It is a noticeable fact that in the two previous attempts, when Sir Thomas More was all powerful in the royal counsels, the King appears as chief mover; whereas his name is not mentioned in connection with the present one. He may not, indeed, have relinquished his own efforts for the same object; but this seems to have been an independent plan, contrived by the leaders of the popish party against their most dreaded opponent. Probably they were deterred from seeking Henry's aid by a fear of the influence of Anne Boleyn. Whatever the cause, the fact is certain, that they attempted to effect their object, not through him, but through his mortal enemy the Emperor, who, as the relative and protector of Katherine, was also the patron of the disaffected English clergy.

The emissaries now despatched on this business were better chosen than those formerly employed by the King; being merely hired villains, with no character to lose and no political duties to divert them from their errand. There were two of them; the one a young man of prepossessing exterior, but a needy and profligate adventurer, named Henry Phillips. He was to play the part of gentleman. The other,

Gabriel Donne, a monk of Stratford Abbey, was to pass as his servant, but was, no doubt, the real director of the enterprise. They were plentifully supplied by their employers with money wherewith to keep up appearances, and to apply bribery wherever needful. Donne first went to Louvain, probably to consult with that enlightened Faculty of Theology which had once been so shocked at the impiety of Erasmus, and had driven Dorpius from the professor's chair. Here he was joined by Philips, and both proceeded to Antwerp.

Tyndale was at that time residing with an English merchant of that city, by the name of POINTZ; a gentleman of ancient Norman family, and of high connections in his native land; but far more honorably distinguished as the lover of the Scriptures and the friend of Tyndale. As Tyndale's company was in great request with the other English merchants, and he was often invited to their tables, where also Henry Phillips, as a rich fellow-countryman, found easy access, the conspirator and his victim soon met. The engaging manners and professed friendship of the young man soon won the confidence of the unsuspecting reformer. Not only did he invite him repeatedly to the mansion of his host, but even induced M. Pointz to receive him as a lodger. The intimate daily intercourse thus established was diligently used by the base man to become acquainted with everything in Tyndale's life and writings which could subserve the purpose of his employers.

Having gained all necessary information, Phillips now began cautiously to take steps for bringing the matter to an end. It was his design at first, as is supposed, to effect the object through the Antwerp city government. In this view he sounded M. Pointz, as he probably did others of his countrymen, to ascertain if he could be bribed into concurrence with such a measure. Such was the interpretation afterward given to mysterious hints from Phillips, which at the time awakened no suspicion. For the idea that any one could dream of bribing Thomas Pointz to betray his friend never entered the thoughts of the noble merchant till events brought their own explanation.

Failing in this plan he made no application to the Antwerp magistracy, but proceeded to the court of Brussels, about thirty miles distant. As King Henry, on account of his quarrel with the Emperor, had no ambassador at Brussels, Phillips had free scope; and by connecting his designs against Tyndale with treasonable propositions against his own sovereign, he succeeded in obtaining a favorable hearing. On his return to Antwerp, the Emperor's attorney accompanied him for the purpose of apprehending Tyndale. Yet even the imperial officials dared not seize an Englishman openly in this free city, where

English influence was so powerful, and several days passed by without action. But at length Pointz left home to be absent a month or six weeks at the great annual fair at Barrow, and the favorable moment was now judged to have come. The remainder of the story is best told in the words of Foxe.

"In the time of his absence Henry Phillips came again to Antwerp, to the house of Pointz, and coming in, spake with his wife, asking her for Master Tyndale, and whether he would dine there with him; saying—'what good meat shall we have?' She answered, 'such as the market will give.' Then went he forth again, as it was thought, to provide, and set the officers whom he brought with him from Brussels, in the street, and about the door. Then about noon he came again, and went to Master Tyndale, and desired him to lend him forty shillings; 'for,' said he, 'I lost my purse this morning, coming over at the passage, between this and Mechlin.' So Tyndale took him forty shillings, which was easy to be had of him, if he had it; for in the wily subtilties of this world he was simple and inexpert.

"Then said Phillips, 'Master Tyndale, you shall be my guest here this day.' 'No,' said Tyndale, 'I go forth this day to dinner, and you shall go with me, and be my guest, where you shall be welcome.' So when it was dinner time, Master Tyndale went forth with Phillips, and at the going forth of Pointz's house was a long, narrow entry, so that two could not go in a front. Tyndale would have put Phillips before him, but Phillips would in no wise, for that he pretended to show great humanity, (courtesy). So Master Tyndale, being a man of no great stature, went before, and Phillips, a tall, comely person, followed behind him; who had set officers on either side of the door on two seats, who being there might see who came in the entry; and coming through the same, Phillips pointed with his finger over Master Tyndale's head down to him, that the officers who sat at the door might see that it was he whom they should take, as the officers afterward told Pointz, and said, when they had laid him in prison, that they pitied to see his simplicity, when they took him. Then they brought him to the Emperor's attorney, where he dined. Then came he, the attorney, to the house of Pointz, and sent away all that was there of Master Tyndale's, as well his books as other things, and from thence Tyndale was had to the castle of VILVORDE, eighteen English miles from Antwerp."

No sooner was this infamous transaction known than Tyndale's friends in Antwerp exerted their utmost in his behalf. By their influence the House of Merchant Adventurers was induced to make a formal application to the court of Brussels for his release. But through the indifference or timidity of their chief officer, to whom the business was entrusted, nothing resulted from the attempt. An effort was also made to secure interest for him at the English Court, but with no decisive effect.* Alarmed for his revered friend, Thomas

---

* Thebald, at this time the confidential agent of Cranmer and Crumwell on the continent, makes report to his employers, in the manner of one who had

Pointz now resolved to try what could be done by his personal energy. He had a brother in England, John Pointz, who had been for twenty years in familiar intercourse with King Henry and his court, and was now a member of the royal household. To him he directed a letter, in which he boldly charges Tyndale's imprisonment upon the Papists, as part of a deep-laid plot for the subversion of his Majesty's government, and of the religious reforms which it supported; and he urges his brother, either in his own person or through others, to bring the matter directly before the King. The honest warmth and fearlessness of this letter, equally free from pretension and servility, is an honorable index not only of the worth of the man, but of the spirit of the class to which he belonged. England, in the sixteenth century, had no such nobles as those princely-hearted merchants of hers, who had dared to search the Scriptures for themselves; none so free in thought, so bold in word, yet none so loyal to their King and country.

This letter seems to have made a decided impression. Before the close of the next month a messenger was dispatched from the English court, less perhaps from the wish to befriend Tyndale, though this was the ostensible object, than to look after those traitorous Englishmen mentioned by Pointz, as so busy at Louvain; one of whom was already known, from Thebald's letter, as engaged in treasonable practices against the King. The relations of the two governments not allowing of direct communication, letters were addressed by Crumwell to two distinguished persons who had great influence at the court of Brussels, requesting their friendly offices in the matter. Having with great difficulty obtained the desired letters, Pointz himself repaired with them to England, and after a month's detention for Crumwell's dispatches in reply, returned with all haste to Brussels. Here he laid his papers before the Council and awaited its decision. This was about the first of November, 1535.

Things now looked very favorable for the venerable prisoner, and Pointz was in daily expectation that he would be delivered into his custody, when he was himself apprehended by the Procurer-General, and placed in strict confinement. This was the work of the infamous Phillips. Perceiving how the case was likely to turn, he could think of no better device than boldly to accuse Pointz as an adherent of Tyndale, and the sole mover, from mere personal and party motives, of the measures for his release. On this charge he had been seized; and

---

been especially directed by them to watch the case.—(Anderson, vol. i., pp. 423-25). To what can the change in Crumwell's policy be ascribed, but the influence of Anne Boleyn? But he was still too selfish, as Cranmer was too timid, to risk the favor of Henry by any direct and earnest efforts in behalf of Tyndale,

thus the good man, instead of welcoming his friend to liberty, found himself a prisoner, and in imminent hazard of his life.

An imprisonment of more than three months followed, during which every obstacle was thrown in the way of his defence; while he was loaded with enormous prison charges, for which immediate payment was demanded without allowing him opportunity to procure the means. Satisfied that his temporal ruin, if not his death, was resolved on, Pointz determined to use his best chance for life and justice by making his escape. This he effected under cover of night; and being well acquainted with the country, he eluded his pursuers, and found his way safely into England.

This is the last attempt on record for the deliverance of Tyndale. Could Pointz have effected anything after his return, it is safe to conclude that he would have done it at every personal risk. Cranmer and Crumwell were still high in power; but she was gone, whose womanly and queenly heart had once infused somewhat of its own generous warmth and courage into theirs, and who had pleaded with the capricious King for truth and its champions. The Reformer was now abandoned to the will of his enemies.

The imprisonment of Tyndale seems not to have been as harsh as that to which heretics had been subjected in England. By his pious efforts the jailor and his family were led to embrace the truth; and in their kind Christian ministry did much, no doubt, to cheer his spirits and soften the hardships of his situation. He was allowed the use of writing materials, and sustained an animated controversy with the Theological Faculty of Louvain. This was permitted, however, for the purpose of drawing from him an avowal of sentiments which might serve as a basis for his trial and condemnation. For under the imperial rule, even heretics could not be dealt with in the summary style so much in vogue with Sir Thomas More and the English bishops.

About a year and three-quarters thus passed away. At length, all things being ripe, his enemies pushed the matter to a conclusion.

In 1530, a very stringent decree against heresy had been issued at Augsburg under the Emperor's authority, directed particularly against the doctrine of *justification by faith*. This still remained in full force. Tyndale had long been known as the chief expositor of the obnoxious doctrine; and his late controversy with the Doctors of Louvain had given occasion to a most explicit statement of his views. Now the Privy Council of Brussels, which had full jurisdiction in all cases—religious as well as political—was completely under the dominion of the priests, having for its president a high dignitary of the Romish Church and a bitter opposer of the truth—the Bishop of Palermo. The reigning Princess herself was a mere tool of the monks. Two years before, Erasmus had said that "those animals were omnipotent at the court of Brussels." Such being the case—to say nothing of the gold with which Phillips was so liberally supplied for enlightening the eyes of the ministers of justice—it would have been marvellous, indeed, had the unfriended prisoner received a favorable sentence. All the forms of justice were allowed him. He declined, however, the offered assistance of an advocate and procurer, saying that he would answer for himself. This he was permitted to do ; and we may be sure that his judges that day listened to an exposition of truth such as they had seldom heard. But they had met to condemn, not to be convinced ; and though unable to confute his arguments, it was easy to prove him guilty under the decree of Augsburg.

On Friday, the sixth of October, 1536, William Tyndale was led forth to die. Having been bound to the stake, he was first strangled and his dead body then burned to ashes. His last words, " uttered with fervent zeal and in a loud voice were these : ' LORD, OPEN THE KING OF ENGLAND'S EYES ! ' "

Thus perished, a victim to priestcraft, the purest of England's patriots and the crown of her martyrs—the best and greatest man of his time !

CHAPTER XXII.

TRIUMPH OF THE PRINCIPLE.

NOTHING is more common with the enemies of truth than to suppose, when the champion of a great principle is struck down, that the principle itself is dead. Especially does the history of Bible translation abound with exemplifications of this remark. Every step of progress in this foundation work of Christian philanthropy—without which all others are but as blossoms without a root, and out of which all others spring by an inevitable law—has been marked with martyrs. Not all martyrs at the stake, like Frith and Tyndale ; but martyrs as to their peace, their reputation, the good will and respect of their fellow-men. And what have the " haters of light" accomplished by such a policy ? Nothing, except to verify that saying of our Lord, in which, just before his own bitter and shameful death, he announced the prime law of growth in his kingdom : " Except a corn of wheat fall into the ground and die, it abideth alone ; but if it die, it bringeth forth much fruit."

For ten years Tyndale had been subjected to a life of extremest privation and suffering. An exile and a fugitive, with no certain home, pinched with poverty, reviled as a traitor, heretic, and blasphemer, hunted like a venomous reptile from one hiding place to another, he confessed, patient and heroic as he was, that " very death were more pleasant to him than life." And now, the purpose of his persecutors was accomplished. The great heart, and busy brain, and hand that never tired in the service of humanity, were turned to ashes, and scattered to the winds. This was their hour, and the power of darkness. That light blotted out, and they fancied that the hated influences it had called into being would perish with it.

At this point let us look back a moment, and see how far their past experience justified such a hope.

It was at the beginning of the year 1526 that the first copies of Tyndale's New Testament appeared in England. From the moment of its discovery in the hands of the young men at Oxford, ecclesiastical proscription, sustained by civil statutes, " dreadful and penal," had been directed against it. Those convicted of the crime of reading, hearing, or circulating it, were fined, whipped, imprisoned, subjected to disgraceful public penance ; and if found unyielding, were burned at the stake. Merchant ships were searched for it ; international laws forbade its importation ; it was bought up wholesale in foreign markets ; great church dignitaries presided over the bonfires in which it was consumed, as at a solemn religious festival. This policy had been pursued with a thoroughness and persistency unsurpassed in the history of religious persecution. And what was the result?

In 1529 a fifth edition of the proscribed book was circulating in England. Such had been the demand for the Word of God awakened within the space of three years! In 1530, the year of Tunstal's great Bible-burning, the people were reading the Pentateuch, as well as the New Testament ; and in the words of Hall, " Bibles came thick and threefold into England." Two years later, Sir Thomas More speaks of them as coming in " by the whole vats-full at once." In 1534 the Convocation itself was compelled, by influences which had become too strong to be overborne, to ask that the King would order a translation of the Scriptures into English. In the Convocation of 1536, the lower House sent to their superiors a " protestation," respecting the alarming spread of heresy in the province of Canterbury. The specifications of false teaching amount to sixty-seven, and afford a most gratifying evidence of the progress of truth. The service of the Mass, worship of saints, auricular confession, penance, absolution, purgatory, are conceded to have become matters of common question. The fifth item declares, that " it is commonly preached, taught, and spoken, that all ceremonies accustomed in the Church, which are not clearly expressed in Scripture, must be taken away, because they are men's inventions." The fifty-sixth complains, that " by preaching, the people have been brought into the opinion and belief that nothing is to be believed except it can be proved expressly from Scripture !" But still more striking, as an index of the times, is the language to which the assembled bishops were obliged to listen from one of their own number—Edward Fox, Bishop of Hereford. Stokesly having offered to confute the new teaching respecting the sacraments—not only by Scripture, but by the old doctors and by the schoolmen also—Fox rose, and after referring to the King's command that they should appeal in this matter to the Holy Scriptures alone, he addressed his brethren in these noble words :

"Think ye not that we can, by any sophistical subtilties, steal out of the world again the light which every man doth see. Christ hath so lightened the world at this time that the light of the Gospel hath put to flight all misty darkness ; and it will shortly have the higher hand of all clouds, though we resist in vain never so much. The lay people do now know the Holy Scripture better than many of us. And the Germans have made the text of the Bible so plain and easy, by the Hebrew and Greek tongue, that now many things may be better understood, without any glosses at all, than by all the commentaries of the doctors. And, moreover, they have so opened these controversies by their writings that women and children may wonder at the blindness and falsehood that hath been hitherto. Wherefore, ye must consider earnestly what ye will determine of these controversies, that ye make not yourselves to be mocked and laughed to scorn of all the world; and that ye bring them not to have this opinion of you, to think evermore hereafter that ye have not one spark of learning nor yet of godliness in you. And thus shall ye lose all your estimation and authority with them which before took you for learned men and profitable members unto the commonwealth of Christendom. For that which you do hope upon, that there was never heresy in the Church so great but that process of time, with the power and authority of the Pope, hath quenched it—it is nothing to the purpose. But ye must turn (change) your opinion, and think this surely, that there is nothing so feeble and weak, so that it be true, but it shall find place, and be able to stand against all falsehood.

" Truth is the daughter of time, and time is the mother of truth. And whatsoever is besieged of truth cannot long continue; and upon whose side truth doth stand that ought not to be thought transitory, or that it will ever fall. All things consist not in painted eloquence, and strength, or authority. For the truth is of so great power, strength and efficacity, that it can neither be defended with words, nor be overcome with any strength; but after she hath hidden herself long, at length she putteth up her head and appeareth."

Stokesly's impatient reply to this and similar speeches, contained in undesigned, but most satisfactory confirmation of what Fox had asserted. " Let us grant," said the incensed prelate, " that the sacraments may be gathered out of the word of God; yet are ye far deceived if ye think that there is none other word of God but that WHICH EVERY SOUTER AND COBBLER DOTH READ IN HIS MOTHER TONGUE !" Before the close of the Convocation, a second petition to the King was agreed on, praying his Majesty, " that he would graciously permit the use of the Scriptures to the laity, and that a new translation of it might be forthwith made for that end and purpose." A wonderful change indeed since the day when it was safe for them to declare all translations into the vernacular unlawful, and when the Scriptures were themselves denounced as heretical and decreed " to be clean forbidden and banished forever out of the realm of England !" Not that the Romish Bishops were any more cordial in their hearts to such a measure than they had ever been; but the advocates of the Bible had now become the stronger party. Their influence was indeed still sufficient to prevent the recognition of either of the existing translations, and they trusted by a " masterly inactivity" in preparing a new one, to put far off the evil day. But they had at least been compelled to concede, by repeated formal acts, the fundamental principle, that it is safe and right to give the laity the Scriptures in their mother tongue. The people, however, did not wait for them. From the year 1530, Tyndale's New Testament had been coming into England at the rate of two editions annually : and at least nine or ten editions crowned the year of his martyrdom.

Such had been the fruit of their opposition while the man still lived, who had been instrumental in giving the chief impulse to this mighty movement. Let us now see what they accomplished by his death.

The events now to be related seem so strange, so far out of the common range of probabilities, that even the most skeptical can hardly fail to discern in them an unseen Power, carrying headlong the counsels of the crafty, and turning to its own beneficent ends the selfish policy of ambitious statesmen and the caprices of a cruel despot. To understand this part of our history a little previous explanation is required.

At the fall of Wolsey, the prospects of Thomas Crumwell, the most attached and distinguished of his adherents, seemed to have received their death blow. From this fate he extricated himself by a single step, equally bold and sagacious, and planted his foot securely on the ladder of political promotion. Two days before the meeting of Parliament he left the residence of his fallen master, saying to one of the household : " I shall make or mar ere I come again !" The very next day he obtained an interview with Henry, and suggested to him that daring line of policy, which in due time added to his royal title that of " Supreme Head of the Church in England," and reduced the proud clergy into the most submissive and most liberal of vassals. Another item of this great plan was the replenishment of the King's coffers by the reduction of monasteries and confiscation of their treasure ; but this had been deferred for prudential reasons to the year 1535, when the King's necessities admitted of no farther delay. As a preliminary step, Crumwell—a layman and commoner, without high connections, or even an education to atone for want of rank—was, by an exercise of royal power, constituted the second man in the kingdom. By his office as the King's " Vicegerent, Vicar-General, Commissary special and general," he not only took rank next to the royal family, and controlled the secular affairs of the realm, but had the right, in the King's absence, to preside in the Convocations of the clergy, and was Superior of all the monasteries. This appointment was followed by the visitation and suppression, in the most summary style, of all monasteries, amounting to three hundred and seventy-six, whose income did not exceed £200 per annum ; thus augmenting the yearly royal revenue by the snug little sum of £75,200—equivalent to more than a million dollars of our time.

This was very gratifying, but there were other consequences not so pleasant. Of course we can find no fault with the dissolution of these haunts of idleness and profligacy. But the wholesome measure was effected in a manner most unjust and inhuman. Talleyrand would have said it was worse than a crime ; it was a blunder ! Thousands of persons suddenly ejected from their comfortable homes, and turned loose upon the world with forty shillings in their hands, to seek living and shelter where they could, were not likely to be preachers of loyalty, or of the religion under whose name they were persecuted. The honest heart of the people, moreover, ever sides with the oppressed. Suffering becomes virtue in their eyes. And they are right ; for cruelty, in whatever form, or upon whomsoever exercised, is the very spirit of the lower regions. The secular clergy had already tasted of the royal mercy ; the higher monasteries might securely count upon their own doom as near at hand. The result was just what might have been expected. In the month of October, 1536, a formidable insurrection burst forth, which threatened the country with all the horrors of a bloody civil war. In Lincolnshire the rising was twenty thousand strong ; in Yorkshire twice that number.

By the firmness and energy of the government the movement was soon quelled ; but it had given formidable evidence that Popery's tough roots still held fast to the English soil, and that it would require more than laws of sequestration, or force of arms, to eradicate it. The keen eye of Crumwell saw what his master's had failed to perceive—that the vicious weed which could not be torn out from the earth of which it had so long held sole occupancy, must be *grown out* by a yet stronger plant. Its hold must be loosened from beneath, or the work on the surface would be done only to be repeated. Behold, then, the unpitying persecutor of Tyndale, the unscrupulous and worldly statesman, whose self-exaltation was the god of his worship, making it one of his chief cares, amid the overwhelming toils of state, and the engrossing schemes of personal ambition, to provide the people with the Word of God ! In this is revealed, more strikingly than in his most brilliant strokes of policy, the penetrating intellect of this great practical genius. His ken went to the bottom of the elemental causes of national life, and discerned that the strength of the new order of things lay not in the external power of government, but in the moral sentiments and convictions of the people.

Crumwell had already given his countenance and aid to the efforts of Cranmer and Coverdale. But henceforward we perceive in his movements in this direction, the unwavering energy of a clear and settled purpose. A BIBLE, to be placed by authority in every church in England, to be read in public as a stated part of the religious instruction of the people, while free access to it should be allowed to rich and poor, who might desire to read it for themselves—such from this time became one of the prime objects of this great politician. From what follows we should judge that he had converted Henry to the same view; and in Archbishop Cranmer he would find an earnest and efficient coadjutor, from purer motives.

But how was this Bible to be obtained? It was hopeless to look for one from the bishops; Cranmer's, which from the very method employed in preparing it was unfit for a standard version, had fallen to the ground; Coverdale's was under a cloud, on account of its connection with the murdered queen. For the version which is to become THE FIRST AUTHORIZED ENGLISH BIBLE, we must look away from England, to the man who had so recently suffered martyrdom for having given it to her people.

We have no direct information in regard to the progress which Tyndale had made in translating the Old Testament, at the time he was imprisoned in the castle of Vilvorde. Only the Pentateuch and Jonah had been given to the world; and it is generally supposed, on the authority of Hall, a contemporary chronicler, that the translation had proceeded no farther than to the close of the historical books. But there are certain indisputable facts which it is difficult to harmonize with this supposition.

Soon after he was thrown into prison, a folio edition of the entire Bible, containing his translations already published, and completed from his manuscripts or some other source, was commenced in Germany by his friend and fellow exile, John Rogers. It was finished within a year after his death, early in the summer of 1537, and published under the assumed name of Thomas Matthew, hence called *Matthew's Bible*. But the editor claimed it for his friend, by inserting his initials, W. T. in conspicuous ornamental letters at the end of the Old Testament.* Why else should he have placed it there; or on what other ground could the act be defended from the charge of fraud? The plea that Tyndale had not had time to complete the work is not sustained by sufficient evidence. Four years had elapsed between the publication of the Pentateuch and his imprisonment; and though his pen was indeed busy in other ways we have no reason to think he had, on this account, laid aside that which he considered pre-

---

* His New Testament was too well known to need any such index to its author

eminently his life-work. His nearly two years' imprisonment would most naturally have been devoted to its completion; and viewed in connection with John Rogers' undertaking, we can hardly doubt it was so. The similarity of this portion of Matthew's Bible to that of Coverdale (published in 1535), has given rise to the belief that the version of the latter had furnished the books which Tyndale had not been able to translate. But, on the other hand, there are striking variations from that version; and since Coverdale had adopted into it Tyndale's well known translation of Jonah, *verbatim*, it is quite as reasonable to suppose that, during the period he was abroad preparing his Bible, he had access to the manuscripts of Tyndale. But, however this question may be decided, the larger and more important part of the newly edited version was, without dispute, the work of the martyred reformer, the very work which for ten years had been proscribed in England.

In the circumstances of its introduction into the kingdom, we see evidences of plan and concert, not to be mistaken. It had been about half carried through the press by private contributions of friends of the Gospel, when two prominent English printers—Grafton and Whitchurch—came forward, and assumed the cost and risk of completing it. As soon as it left the press, Grafton hastened over the sea with a single copy for Archbishop Cranmer. Finding on his arrival that the Primate had just quitted London on account of the plague, he hastened after him to Forde, his country residence, in Kent. This could not have been before the 1st or 2d of August, since Cranmer was still on duty in London the 29th of July.* Yet on the 4th of August he was prepared to endorse the entire translation and in the warmest terms to recommend its adoption as the Bible to be authorized by his Majesty for use in the churches and for universal diffusion among the people. His letter on the subject to Lord Crumwell is as follows:

"My especial good Lord, after most hearty commendations unto your Lordship; these shall be to signify unto the same that you shall receive by the bringer thereof a Bible both of a new translation and a new print, dedicated unto the King's Majesty, as farther appeareth by a pistle unto his Grace in the beginning of the book, which, in mine opinion, is very well done; and therefore I pray your Lordship to read the same. And as for the translation, so far as I have read thereof, I like it better than any other translation heretofore made; yet not doubting that there may and will be found some fault therein, as you know no man ever did or can do so well, but it may from time to time be amended.

"And forasmuch as the book is dedicated unto the King's Grace, and also

* Anderson, vol. i., p. 573.

great pains and labor taken in setting forth of the same, I pray you, my Lord, that you will exhibit the book unto the King's Highness, and obtain of his Grace if you can, a license that the same may be sold and read of every person, without danger of any act, proclamation, or ordinance heretofore granted to the contrary, until such time that we, the bishops, shall set forth a better translation, which I think will not be till the day after doomsday ! And if you continue to take such pains for the setting forth of God's Word as you do, although in the mean season you suffer some snubs and many slanders, lies, and reproaches for the same, yet one day He will requite all together. And the same word, as St. John saith, which shall judge every man at the last day, must needs show favor to them that now do favor it. Thus, my Lord, right heartily fare you well. At Forde, the 4th day of August, [1537.] Your assured ever.—*T. Cantuarien.*"

The Vicar-General was no less prompt. While all the bishops had been dispersed by fear of the plague, he had remained at his post, apparently to see this matter safely through. The absence of all the opposing prelates left the field unobstructed, and he used the opportunity with his usual decision. Within eight days from the date of the above letter, Cranmer acknowledges the receipt of information from his Lordship that he had exhibited the translation to his Majesty, and had obtained his full assent to what had been requested ! Thus in less than a fortnight from the first arrival of Tyndale's whole Bible in England, it is decreed to be " SET FORTH WITH THE KING'S MOST GRACIOUS LICENSE "; and also, that it " be sold and read of every person, without danger of any act, proclamation, or ordinance heretofore granted to the contrary !"

The next year Crumwell, as " Vicegerent unto the King's Highness," issued the following " injunctions" to the clergy, to be observed and kept, on pain of deprivation, sequestration of fruits, or such other coercion as to the King's Highness, or his Vicegerent for the time being, shall seem convenient :

First, " That ye shall provide before the ensuing feast of the Nativity, (December 25,) one book of the whole Bible, of the largest volume in English,* and the same set up in some convenient place within the said church, that ye have care of, where your parishioners may most conveniently resort to the same and read it ; the charges of which book shall be rateably borne between you, the parson and parishioners aforesaid—that is to say, the one half by you, the other half by them.

Secondly, " That ye shall discourage no man, privily or apertly, [openly], from the reading or the hearing of the said Bible ; but shall expressly provoke, stir, and exhort every person to read the same, as that which is the very lively word of God, that every Christian person is bound to embrace, believe, and follow, if they look to be saved ; admonishing them, nevertheless, to avoid all contention

* Thus distinguishing Tyndale's from the two editions of Coverdale now in the market, those being of smaller size.—Anderson, vol. ii., p. 34, Note.

and altercation therein, but to use an honest sobriety in their inquisition of the true sense of the same, and to refer the explication of the obscure places to men of higher judgment in the Scripture."

Nor did Crumwell's efforts stop here. Already the Popish party had begun to rally. For a while the scales fluctuated—now to this side, now to that; but at length settled in favor of Crumwell's enemies. During the three years succeeding the time when he welcomed the vernacular Bible into England, all his powers were tasked to meet the strange and ever-shifting exigencies of the conflict. Through this entire period, he urged on the cause of Bible-translation and circulation, as if that were one of the essential conditions of his political salvation. In 1538, before the first edition of Tyndale's Bible was exhausted, he had persuaded Henry to obtain from Francis I. permission for printing an edition of the English Bible in Paris, where it could be executed in much better style than in England. Thither he sent Coverdale and Bonner—then a loud advocate for vernacular translations—to revise the version and superintend the press, providing on the most liberal scale everything necessary to the fullest success of the undertaking. At the end of six months the interference of the Inquisition stopped the work, and the revisers fled, with what they could save, to England. But Crumwell was not to be thus foiled. He dispatched agents to Paris, who returned not only with the presses and types, but even with the French printers; and in some six weeks the work was again progressing on English soil. This event gave a great impulse to the press and especially to the Bible interest in the kingdom; so that not only the interrupted edition was successfully completed, but it became the parent of many others, published in the heart of England. In the year 1539 no fewer than four editions of the entire Scriptures in English were issued under Crumwell's immediate patronage. During this same period, moreover, he was encouraging and aiding other translators to contribute their versions to the general stock; thus in every way laboring to multiply Bibles among the people.

A beautiful picture is given by Strype, in his Life of Cranmer,* of the influence of this diffusion and free use of the Scriptures. It was a jubilee among the poor of England when, for the first time in the national history, they could listen, from Sabbath to Sabbath, to "the sweet and glad tidings of the Gospel," without the fear of prisons, the scourge, and the stake. "It is wonderful," he says, "to see with what joy this Book of God was received, not only among the

* Page 91.

learneder sort, and those that were noted for lovers of the Reformation, but generally all England over, among all the vulgar and common people ; and with what greediness God's word was read, and what resort to places where the reading of it was. Everybody that could bought the book and busily read it ; or got others to read it to them, if they could not themselves ; and divers more elderly people learned to read on purpose. And even little boys flocked among the rest to hear portions of the Holy Scriptures read." When had such an intellectual awakening of the masses ever been witnessed, in the whole history of the world, as the fruit of Popish policy ! If Crumwell was an unprincipled and ambitious man, he was, nevertheless, a wise legislator, and a true benefactor of the people.

But the star which had shot so rapidly into the zenith, had long since culminated, and now suddenly sunk to rise no more. Henry's popish counsellors had now wholly gained his ear ; and Crumwell, by forwarding the marriage with Anne of Cleves, to whom the King had taken an insuperable disgust, had incurred his master's bitter resentment. On the tenth of June he was arrested on charge of high treason, and being condemned with scarcely the decent show of justice, a fate, alas, too well merited by his own dealings in similar cases, he was beheaded in the Tower, July 28, 1540.

But as the death of Tyndale had not arrested the progress of this glorious cause, so neither did the fall of its illustrious patron. New editions of the English Bible still issued from the press, and Henry again and again repeated his injunctions for its use in the public service of religion. So possessed had he become with the idea of diffusing it among his people, that Bishops Tunstal and Heath, most bitter opposers of vernacular translation, were compelled by his authority to affix their names as editors to two impressions of the great Bible. Immediately after the publication of the injunctions of 1540, the bloody-hearted Bonner set up six large Bibles in St. Paul's for the accommodation of those who wished to read, such a passport was zeal in the cause at that time, to royal favor. The eagerness with which the people embraced this opportunity shows, that with all the Bibles published, little had yet been done toward supplying the demand for the word of God. "They came," it is said, "instantly and generally to hear the Scriptures read. Such as could read with a clear voice often had great numbers round them. Many sent their children to school, and carried them to St. Paul's to hear." Most interesting must have been the groups collected, Sabbath after Sabbath, in the crypt of that ancient cathedral. The great folio Bibles, scattered at convenient distances through the vast, dim interior, each chained to a massive pillar, the lamp above illuminating the reader and the black-letter page over which he bent, and the little congregation gathered close around, formed an apt emblem of the condition of England generally at that time.

This state of things could not long continue. The conflict between light and darkness, now approaching its termination, was not to close without another desperate struggle. Henry, in "graciously" vouchsafing to his subjects the boon of reading the Scriptures, had not properly considered the danger that, while so doing, they might acquire the pernicious habit of thinking for themselves. Against this he had taken every possible precaution by connecting with permission to read and hear the Bible, strict charges to avoid all comment and discussion in respect to its contents; and still more effectually by his Acts " to establish Christian quietness and unity," of which especially the one in 1539, known as the Six Articles, or more appropriately, as *The Whip with six cords*, was regarded as " an end of all controversy." The doctrines enjoined by this statute were, 1. Transubstantiation. 2. Communion under both kinds not necessary to salvation. 3. Priests may not marry, by the law of God. 4. Vows of chastity (celibacy) binding. 5. Private masses to be retained. 6. Auricular confession useful and necessary. Its penalties were: for denial of the first article, death at the stake, without privilege of abjuration; for the five others, death as a felon, or imprisonment during his Majesty's pleasure.*

But it was beyond any human power to join two things so opposed in their natures as the study of the word of God and servile submission to the will of man, in matters of religious faith. It is at the point where these rival influences meet in conflict, above all others, that the " divinity within us" vindicates its heavenly origin, and the soul of the unlettered peasant, or of the timid woman, or even of the little child, rises up in the conscious dignity of a child of God, and claims here full equality with the proudest monarch. It was especially in regard to the first of these prescribed articles, *Transubstantiation*, that the readers of the Bible found it impossible to harmonize their views with those of the King. As from the time of Wickliffe to

---

* The same abject Parliament which authorized this bloody statute, assumed and made it law that Parliament was competent to condemn to death persons accused of high treason, *without any previous trial or confession ;* and then, by another law, passed over this power into the hands of Henry—enacting that " the King, with advice of his Council, might set forth proclamations, with pains and penalties in them, which were to be obeyed as if made by Act of Parliament." He was thus constituted sole proprietor of the lives and property of his subjects.

the separation of England from Rome, the rejection of this doctrine had distinguished those who received the Scriptures as supreme authority, from those who acknowledged the supremacy of the Church with the pope for its head; so had it ever since distinguished them from those who acknowledged the supremacy of the Church with the King for its head. It was the test-point in the trials of the Lollards both in the fifteenth and sixteenth centuries; and the blood of Bilney, Bainham, Frith, and many others, had flowed during this reign, as oblations to this monstrous dogma. So late as 1538, the learned and pious Lambert had perished for the same offence, after enduring a trial of "cruel mocking," at which Henry presided, in awful state, clad all in white—the symbol of the spotless purity of his faith! The passage of The Six Articles was the signal for a fresh onset upon the adherents of the Scriptures. The bishops, who were charged with the office of carrying the statute into effect, sprang like unleashed blood-hounds on the prey. Within fourteen days they had indicted five hundred persons in London alone; and it was clear that the number of offenders would soon exceed the capacity of the city prisons. This was considerably more than Henry had asked of the zeal of his bishops; for he wished to strike a wholesome terror into the community by a few examples, not to make a wholesale massacre of his subjects. By the advice of Crumwell (the year before his death), he repeated the expedient of Henry V. in a similar case; and by a royal pardon, quashed the indictment, so that of the five hundred accused not one was brought to trial, and the fiendish attempt only served to bring out more distinctly the strength of the party it had sought to crush. Still the statute remained in force, and the war with the "Sacramentarians" was waged, if not on so bold a scale with no less malignity, to the close of Henry's reign.

At length the King seems to have been convinced that he could not establish his own will as the standard of faith among his people, while they were allowed the use of the Bible. It was therefore enacted by Parliament in 1543, "that all manner of books of the Old and New Testament in English, of Tyndale's crafty, false, and untrue translation, should by authority of this Act clearly and utterly be abolished and extinguished, and forbidden to be kept and used in this realm, or elsewhere, in any of the King's dominions."

And farther, "that no manner of persons after the first of October, should take upon them to read openly to others, in any church or open assembly, within any of the King's dominions, the Bible or any part of the Scripture in English unless he was so appointed thereunto by the King or by any ordinary, on pain of suffering one month's imprisonment."

And farther, "that no woman, except noble women and gentle women, might read the Bible to themselves alone ; and no artificers, apprentices, journeymen, servingmen, of the degrees of yeomen, husbandmen, or laborers were to read the Bible or New Testament to themselves or any other, privately or openly, on pain of one month's imprisonment."

How vividly do these enactments mirror the times ; revealing the wide-spread and inextricable hold which the Bible had gained upon the English masses ! When "apprentices, journeymen, servingmen, husbandmen, and laborers" had once learned to read the Bible, it was certain that no laws could recall it from the nation's hands. So the imperious monarch found it ; for three years later this statute was followed by another still more sweeping, viz. "that from henceforth, NO man, woman, or person, of what estate, condition, or degree he or they shall be, shall, after the last day of August next ensuing, receive, have, take, or keep in his or their possession, the text of the New Testament of Tyndale's or Coverdale's, nor any other that is permitted by the Act of Parliament, made in the session of Parliament holden at Westminster, in the thirty-fourth and thirty-fifth year of his Majesty's most noble reign."

Eight days after the passage of this Act, July 16, 1546, the heroic Anne Askew perished with three companions at the stake, for refusing to acknowledge Henry's Popish doctrine of the Mass. How entirely the reception of the Scriptures, as supreme authority, was identified with rejection of the special dogmas of his Roman-English church, is seen from the dying words of this intrepid woman : " Finally, I believe all those Scriptures to be true which he hath confirmed with his most precious blood. Yea, and as St. Paul saith, those Scriptures are sufficient for our learning and salvation, that Christ hath left here with us ; so that I believe we need NO UNWRITTEN VERITIES to rule his Church with. Therefore, look, what he hath said unto me with his own mouth in the Holy Gospel, that have I with God's grace closed up in my heart ; and my full trust is, as David saith, that it shall be a lantern to my footsteps." *

On the 28th of January, 1547, Henry VIII. was summoned to meet the victims of his personal resentment and of his murderous religious zeal, a fearful host ! at the bar of the righteous Judge. His son Edward VI., the English Josiah, succeeded to the throne. The stream which had been for a while repressed burst forth with gathered strength ; and this short reign, less than six and a half years,

---

* Anderson, vol. ii., p. 198.

was signalized by at least fourteen editions of the whole Bible, and thirty-six of the New Testament.* A brief interruption succeeded this period of prosperity, during the reign of Mary. But from that time to the present, a period of three hundred years, the Anglo-Saxon race has never seen the day when its rich and its poor might not read in their own tongue wherein they were born, unmolested by Church or State, the wonderful works of God!

THE PRINCIPLE HAD TRIUMPHED.

Wickliffe gave England her first Bible; Tyndale her first Bible translated from the original Hebrew and Greek Scriptures. Thus was fully developed the great Protestant principle, announced by Wickliffe nearly a century and a half before. For the same principle which demands the Inspired Word as the sole standard of religious faith, demands also the most exact representation of it which it is possible to obtain. This is obvious on a moment's thought. Every translation, however able and honest, is but a human reflection of God's revelation of truth, and as such, is liable to the imperfection which attaches to everything human. The philological principles of the translator may sometimes mislead him, or his religious creed may bias his judgment of words; or, in process of time, through the vicissitudes of language, or corruptions in the Church, renderings which were once a just expression of the original may come to convey a false meaning. These considerations apply with double force to a second-hand translation, every remove from the original making the conclusions proportionably unreliable. Hence Wickliffe's version, venerable as the first English Bible, and endeared by the associations of a hundred years of persecution, was at once set aside on the appearance of another drawn directly from the inspired sources.

But to accept any version, to stand for all time in place of the sacred originals, was contrary to the spirit of primitive English Christianity. The glass through which the grand outlines of truth could be discerned was dear for so much of the truth as it revealed; another, which revealed more, was dearer still. We shall observe the influence of this spirit through the whole subsequent history of Bible translation in England. The Christian scholars of that age were fired with a generous, sacred emulation to render THE PEOPLE'S BIBLE a perfect reflection of the inspired Word. In the track of Tyndale's noble version sprang up a long line of revisions and translations, which were gratefully accepted by the Church of Christ as independent witnesses,

† Anderson, vol. ii., p. 237.

of whom one might correct the errors of another, and whose agreeing testimony made the truth doubly certain.

But for the New Testament of Tyndale a peculiar honor was reserved. It furnished not only the basis, but, in great part, the substance of all that followed. To a command of Greek learning surpassed by none of his age, Tyndale added those higher qualities of a translator of the Scriptures so eminently possessed by his great predecessor, Wickliffe, a mind of large grasp and earnest force, illuminated by a heart which knew but the single sublime aim to ascertain the revealed will of God and make it worthily known to man. A mind so qualified for the task could not but express itself with a noble freedom, a simple majesty, in harmony with the inspired utterances of truth. The successors of Tyndale recognized in his translation that impress of the master spirit ; and while they corrected its errors without scruple by the increasing light of sacred scholarship, they transferred the body of it, unchanged, into their own versions. Like a gem repeatedly new cut and polished, it has been handed down from generation to generation, the most precious heirloom of the English race ; and we, at this day, read in large portions of our common version the very words with which Tyndale clothed the Scriptures for the men of his own age, in those times of conflict and of blood.*

* " In the originality of Tyndale is included in a large measure the originality of our English Version. . . . His influence decided that our Bible should be popular and not literary, speaking in a simple dialect, and that so by its simplicity it should be endowed with permanence. He felt by a happy instinct the potential affinity between Hebrew and English ideas, and enriched our language and thought forever with the characteristics of the Semitic mind."—*Westcott's Hist. of the Eng. Bible*, pp. 210-11.—T. J. C.

CHAPTER XXIII.

THREE LATER VERSIONS.

Coverdale's Bible.

THIS version deserves special notice, as one of the most marked indications of the new impulse in favor of vernacular translations effected by Tyndale's early labors. It claims veneration, too, as the first translation of the whole Bible circulated in England. For, though strictly the offspring of the state of public opinion created by his greater contemporary, and commenced several years after the publication of Tyndale's New Testament and Pentateuch, Coverdale's version made its appearance some two years prior to Rogers' edition of Tyndale's Bible.

Miles Coverdale was educated at Cambridge, and was a pupil and intimate friend of Barnes, then the great ornament of the University in liberal learning, and the chief leader at Cambridge of the religious party, stigmatized by the Romanists as " the new learning." When Barnes was arrested by Cardinal Wolsey, Coverdale was one of those who stood faithfully by their teacher, following him to London, and assisted in preparing his defence. It is supposed that the favor of Crumwell, then a protégé of Wolsey, secured him from the immediate consequences of so bold a step. But in 1528, having been accused of preaching against the confessional, the worship of images, and the doctrine of transubstantiation, he was obliged to withdraw from England, and his steps cannot be distinctly traced for several succeeding years. Foxe states that he joined Tyndale on the continent, and assisted him in the translation of the Pentateuch ; but of this there is no reliable proof.

It is not certain at what time he commenced his own translation. He seems to have been moved to the undertaking by a deep feeling of the need of the word of God in English as the only remedy for the moral wretchedness of the nation ; joined to a fear that Tyndale would not be able, under the heavy pressure of persecution, to complete the great work which he had begun. Yet such was his modest estimate of his own qualifications for such a task, that he would not, he avers, have assumed the responsibility, but for the urgent solicitations of those with whose wishes he felt bound to comply. In this, doubtless, he refers to his great friend and patron, Thomas Crumwell.

In his prologue to the Christian reader, prefixed to his translation, he thus explains his feelings and motives :

"Considering how excellent knowledge and learning an interpreter of Scripture ought to have in the tongues, and pondering also mine own insufficiency therein, and how weak I am to perform the office of translator, I was the more loath to meddle with this work. Notwithstanding, when I considered how great pity it was that we should want it so long, and called to remembrance the adversity of them which were not only of ripe knowledge, but would also with all their hearts have performed that they begun, if they had not had impediment ; considering, I say, that by reason of their adversity, it could not so soon have been brought to an end as our most prosperous nation would fain have had it ; these and other reasonable causes considered, I was the more bold to take it in hand. . . . But to say the truth before God, it was neither my labor nor desire to have this work put in my hand ; nevertheless it grieved me that other nations should be more plenteously provided for with the Scriptures in their mother tongue than we ; therefore when I was instantly required, though I could not do it as well as I would, I thought it yet my duty to do my best and that with a good will."

It has been argued that a variety of translations must necessarily endanger the unity of the faith. He meets this objection by an appeal to Christian history :

"Whereas some men think now that many translations make division in the faith and in the people of God, yet it is not so ; for it was never better with the congregation of God than when every church almost had the Bible of a sundry translation. Among the Greeks, had not Origen a special translation ? . . . Beside the seventy interpreters, is there not the translation of Aquila, of Theodotio, of Symachus and of sundry other ? Again, among the Latin men thou findest that every one almost used a special translation ; for insomuch as every bishop had the knowledge of tongues, he gave his diligence to have the Bible of his own translation. . . . Therefore ought it not to be taken as evil, that such men as have understanding now in our time exercise themselves in the tongues, and give their diligence to translate out of one language into another. Yea, we ought rather to give God thanks therefor, which through his spirit stirreth up men's minds so as to exercise themselves therein. Would God it had never been left off after the time of St. Augustine ; then should we never have come into such blindness and ignorance and into such errors and delusions. . . .

Seeing then that this diligent exercise of translating doth so much good, and edifyeth in other languages, why should it do evil in ours? Doubtless like as all nations, in the diversity of speeches, may know one God in the unity of faith, and be one in love, even so may diverse translations understand one another, and that in the head articles and ground of our most blessed faith, though they use sundry words. Wherefore, we think we have great occasion to give thanks unto God that he hath opened unto his Church the gift of interpretation and of printing, and that there are at this time so many which with such diligence and faithfulness interpreteth the Scripture to the honor of God and the edifying of his people."

Coverdale only claimed for his version, according to his title page, that it was translated out of "Douch and Latin." He speaks also of having had by him five several translations, and of having "followed his interpreters." He was a respectable Hebrew scholar, and doubtless had constant reference to the text of the original; but he seems not to have felt sufficient reliance on his own scholarship to venture on a really independent translation. For the same cause his version compares ill with Tyndale's in respect to style; wanting that bold step and that rich expressiveness, which can only come from the actual contact of the translator's mind with the thoughts he is to render in their original forms. Yet his version is, in the main, clear and correct, and in some passages shows a more felicitous rendering than any which came after. Its most serious fault is found in its conformity, in some important particulars, to the Latin Vulgate.

The King's license had been obtained for this Bible; and it was dedicated to him " and his most dearest, just wife, Anne." The decline of the Queen's influence, and her fall soon after its appearance in England, threw a cloud for awhile over the enterprise. But after it had been long delayed in the hands of the bishops to whom Henry had committed it for examination, he at length demanded their opinion. They replied that it had many faults. "But," said he, "are there any heresies maintained thereby?" When they replied that there were none as they had perceived—" Then in God's name," cried the impatient monarch, " let it go abroad among our people." * Subsequently, there is reason to believe, an injunction was issued by Crumwell for its use in churches; but from some cause this never went into effect. The version found, however, considerable circulation, so that a new edition was published the next year; but it never received very general favor.

How far Coverdale was from the arrogance and envy of narrow minds, is seen in the fact that he entered most cordially into Crumwell's plan, in 1538, of republishing Tyndale's version at Paris, and making it the authorized Bible of the kingdom, to be employed in the public service of religion to the exclusion of every other. He himself went to Paris as reviser and corrector of the press; and had well nigh lost his life in the service through the opposition of the French Inquisitors. The work was completed in England under his super-

---

* Bagster's edition of Coverdale's Bible, Memoir, p. 13.

vision, and was known as the GREAT BIBLE, "appointed to be read in churches."

In 1551, under King Edward, Coverdale was made Bishop of Exeter. During Mary's reign he was obliged to seek refuge on the continent ; but on the accession of Elizabeth he returned to England, where he was joyfully received by the friends of the Reformation. He would now have regained his honors but for his conscientious scruples in regard to certain church ceremonies, strenuously insisted on by the ruling powers, but which, in his view, countenanced dangerous popish errors. This subject will be more particularly noticed hereafter.

Even the rectory which had been given to Coverdale as a provision for his old age, was at length taken from him for his steadfast refusal to obey the Act of Uniformity. He continued to preach, however, and the name of Father Coverdale was dear to the common people as that of a faithful, honest and affectionate teacher of the way of salvation. He died in honorable poverty May 26th, 1567, , in the 81st year of his age. "He was buried in the Church of St. Bartholomew, behind the Royal Exchange : and his funeral was attended by multitudes who reverenced his memory and bewailed his loss."

His writings have been collected and published by the Parker Society, and form an interesting monument of his own learning and piety, and of the spirit of the age in which he lived.

Taverner's Bible.

Among the young men of Oxford who in 1526 were immured in Cardinal College cellar for reading Tyndale's New Testament, was one by the name of Richard Taverner. He was especially implicated, as having been engaged in the attempt to conceal the obnoxious books under the floor of a fellow-student's room. On account, however, of his skill in music, he was soon released by Wolsey, who was a lover of all elegant accomplishments, and probably thought it a pity to spoil so fine a voice by the damp air of the cellar. He then devoted himself to the study of law : and was admitted to practice at the Inner Temple.

Though not distinguished during the times of severe persecution which followed, Taverner seems to have remained a faithful adherent of the truth, and particularly of the cause of Bible translation. In 1534 he became attached to the court, under the patronage of Crumwell, and by him was raised to an office of some responsibility and honor. It was while he was still occupying this post that his patron, acting on his now ruling idea that the only security against the revival and triumph of the Popish party in England was to flood the country with Bibles, urged Taverner, who was an expert Greek scholar, to undertake a revision of Matthew's Bible, of which he was so desirous to publish a new edition. The result was the work known as TAVERNER'S BIBLE; which was, according to Bishop Bale, "neither a bare revisal, nor yet strictly a new version, but something between both." His dedication to the King, in which he explains his reasons for undertaking the work, is an interesting indication of the spirit of the time in regard to Bible translation:

"Your Grace never did anything more acceptable unto God, more profitable unto the advancement of true Christianity, more displeasant to the enemies of the same, and also to your Grace's enemies, than when your Majesty licensed and willed the most sacred Bible, containing the unspotted and lively word of God, to be in the English tongue set forth to his Highness' subjects. It cannot be denied, however to the setting forth of it some men have neither undiligently nor yet unlearnedly travailed, that some faults have escaped their hands. But it is a work of so great difficulty so absolutely to translate the whole Bible that it be faultless, I fear it would scarce be done of one or two persons, but rather required both a deeper conferring of many learned wits together, and also a juster time and longer leisure; but forasmuch as the printers hereof were very desirous to have the Bible come forth as faultless and emendently as the shortness of time for the recognizing of the same would require, they desired me, for default of a better learned, diligently to overlook and peruse the whole copy: and in case I should find any notable default that needed correction, to amend the same according to the true exemplars, which thing according to my talent, I have gladly done."

The work was published with King Henry's license, in whose reign it passed through several editions. It continued to be printed occasionally as late as 1551, after which there seems to have been no farther demand for it, and it disappears from the list of versions printed for use among the people.

Cranmer's Bible; The Anglican Church.

The name of Cranmer has already been frequently mentioned in connection with the early history of Bible translation in England. He was educated at Jesus College, Cambridge, and was one of those young men selected by Wolsey for their superior talents and scholarship, to adorn his new college at Oxford. But at the risk of seriously offending the great Cardinal, Cranmer declined the honor and the increased emolument, preferring the greater quiet and independence of his Cambridge home. He afterward became Divinity Lecturer in Magdalen College, and was there held in the highest esteem for his learning and virtue.

While yet a student, Cranmer, like so many other educated young men of that period, was led by his own spiritual wants to an earnest study of the Scriptures ; and from that time the written word of God was the object of his profoundest veneration. Being appointed by his college one of the Examiners of candidates for degrees as Bachelors and Doctors of Divinity, he was accustomed to make their knowledge of the Scriptures a test of admission ; and if this was found unsatisfactory, to turn them back, with the advice to spend some years longer in becoming acquainted with the book "wherein the knowledge of God and the grounds of divinity lay." The Friars were particularly deficient in this respect, their sole training being in the subtleties of the schoolmen ; and Cranmer's strictness subjected him to their mortal enmity. "Yet some of the more ingenuous," says Strype,* "afterward rendered great and public thanks for refusing them ; whereby, being put upon a study of God's word, they attained to more sound knowledge in religion."

From his elevation to the Primacy, in 1533, his influence was steadily directed toward the object of securing to the nation at large the free use of the Bible in English. His earnest but unsuccessful efforts to enlist the bishops in the work have already been noticed ; as well as the generous ardor with which he welcomed Tyndale's Bible in 1537, and his exultation when permission was at length obtained from the capricious Henry that all his subjects, high and low, rich and poor, might read the word of God.

In 1538, the first reprint of Tyndale's whole Bible† was commenced in Paris and finished in London, under the oversight of Coverdale. In 1540, another was published under the immediate superintendence of Cranmer, which, on account of the critical comparison of the translation with the Greek and Hebrew text which it exhibits, takes rank as an important contribution to the work of Bible translation. This is the work known as CRANMER'S BIBLE. In the Old Testament, particularly, the rendering is often an improvement on that of Tyndale ; though elsewhere it shows the influence of unreliable guides in Hebrew philology. Whether the changes were from Cranmer himself, or from scholars employed by him, is not known ; but his learning justifies the supposition that they came from his own hand. Its great blemish is the frequent introduction of readings from the Vulgate ; though these are distinguished by being inclosed in brackets, and printed in a different type. The version of the Psalms given in Cranmer's Bible is the one still retained, with slight

---

* Life of Cranmer. † See pp. 168, 169.

variations, in the Book of Common Prayer in the Church of England. The Church Psalter does not, however, distinguish the additions from the Vulgate; in the fourteenth Psalm, for example, three whole verses are there inserted, with no indication that they do not belong to the Hebrew text.

The prologue to this Bible, written by Cranmer himself, is a most earnest appeal to the laity of all classes to improve their present opportunities of becoming acquainted with the Holy Scriptures, as the great remedy for all the evils of human life. Even among them were still to be found many who retained the prejudices in which they had been trained against the use of the Bible by the laity, and who refused to read or hear the Scripture in the vulgar tongue.

"I would marvel much," he writes, "that any man should be so mad as to refuse, in darkness, light; in hunger, food; in cold, fire : . . . save that I consider how much custom and usage may do. So that if there were a people, as some write, *de cymeriis*, which never saw the sun, by reason that they be situated far toward the north pole, and be inclosed and overshadowed with high mountains; it is credible and like enough, that if, by the power and will of God, the mountains should sink down and give place so that the sun might have entrance to them, at first some of them would be offended therewith. And the old proverb affirmeth that after tillage of corn was first found, many delighted more to feed of mast and acorns, wherewith they had been accustomed, than to eat bread made of good corn."

After quoting at large from St. Chrysostom to prove that the laity, as those who are most exposed to the trials and temptations of life, being "in the midst of the sea of worldly wickedness, standing in the forefront of the host, and nighest to the enemy," need the means of defence and succor ready at hand, far more than those who lead a life of retirement and spiritual meditation, he proceeds :

"Now if I should in like manner bring forth what the self-same doctor speaketh in other places, and what other doctors and writers say concerning the same purpose, I might seem to you to write another Bible, rather than make a Preface to the Bible. Wherefore, in few words to comprehend the largeness and utility of the Scriptures, how it containeth fruitful instruction and erudition for every man ; if anything be necessary to be learned, of the holy Scriptures we may learn it ; if falsehood shall be reproved, thereof we may gather wherewithal ; if anything to be corrected and amended, if there need any exhortation or consolation, of the Scriptures we may well learn it In the Scriptures be the fat pastures of the soul—therein is no venomous meat, no unwholesome thing ; they be the very dainty and pure feeding. . . . Here all manner of persons—men and women, young, old, learned, unlearned, rich, poor, priests, laymen, lords, ladies, officers, tenants, and mean men ; virgins, wives, widows, lawyers, merchants, artificers, husbandmen, and all manner of persons, of what estate or condition soever they be—may in this book learn all things what they ought to believe, what they ought to do, and what they should not do, as well concerning Almighty God, as also concerning themselves, and all other."

These were wonderful words to be heard, in that day, from the highest dignitary of the English Church. The minute specification of various classes and conditions is not without important meaning ; and recognizes a principle far in advance of the opinions then generally current among the great. The good Archbishop seems resolved that no individual shall feel himself excluded or excused from the new-spread feast for lack of a special invitation. This is Cranmer's true glory, his fervent love for the inspired word, and his unwearied efforts to make the divine gift common alike to all. Here he showed himself the true Christian, the true Protestant.

It is, moreover, greatly to his honor that his anxiety to strengthen the newly established order of things was allowed to affect so little his renderings of Scripture. A few ecclesiastical terms, which unfortunately Tyndale had perpetuated, in contrariety to his general principles of translation, were likewise retained by Cranmer. But the word "church" occurs only once in his version, and then merely as the designation of a sacred building, (Acts xix., 37), for which also he had the authority of Tyndale and Coverdale. In all other cases, he uniformly renders *ecclesia* by the noble and intelligible word "congregation."

The year 1542 furnished an index, of a novel character, to the unwearied efforts of the popish prelates to frustrate his efforts in behalf of the Bible ; namely, an order from the King for a revision, *by the bishops*, of the authorized translation of the New Testament. When the people were destitute of a Bible, Cranmer had vainly tried to enlist them in the work of preparing one ; now, when the work had been carried through, against their most strenuous efforts, they were ready to step in and do what they could to mar it. Sorely against his will, the Archbishop was obliged to apportion the task among them ; and then followed meeting after meeting to decide on the plan of execution. At the sixth meeting, Gardiner—who, no doubt, was the contriver of the scheme—brought in a list of above one hundred Latin words,* "which for their genuine and native meaning, and for the majesty of the matter in them contained," he desired might be retained untranslated, or Englished with the least possible alteration, in the new revision. This design, if effected, would have given the people a Bible in name, while it deprived them of much of its substance. "Wanting," says Fuller, "the power to keep the light of the Word

---

* Quoted at length in Fuller's Church History, vol. ii., p. 108.

from shining, he sought, out of policy, to put it in a dark lantern." Thus too, according to the old historian, he sought "to teach the laity their distance; who, though admitted into the outer court of common matter, were yet debarred entrance into the holy of holies of these mysterious expressions, reserved only for the understanding of the high priest to pierce into them. Moreover, this made Gardiner not only tender, but fond to have these words continued in kind without translation, because the profit of the Romish Church was deeply in some of them concerned. Witness the word 'penance,' which, according to the vulgar sound, contrary to the original sense thereof, was a magazine of will-worship, and brought in much gain to the priests, who were desirous to keep that word, because that word kept them." Cranmer, having obtained this evidence of the purpose they had in view, made Henry fully acquainted with it; and as the result, was empowered to inform the Convocation, that "it was the King's will and pleasure" that the examination of the entire translation of the Old and New Testaments should be committed to the Universities. Thus the work was rescued from the hands of its enemies, but it does not appear that the Universities were ever troubled with it.

And yet, with all this zeal for faithful vernacular translations, Cranmer only half understood the principles of Protestantism. With one hand he dispersed Bibles, without stint or restriction, among the people; with the other he laid yokes on their necks, hardly more tolerable than that which their fathers wore, for it equally denied the supremacy of the individual conscience. The Romish bishops had punished dissent from their Church; and this was accounted wrong, because it was the Church of antichrist. Protestant bishops punished dissent from their Church; and this was right, because it was the true Church of Christ! It is amusing, though humiliating, to read the records furnished by the admiring Strype, of the contests between Cranmer and the stout Bishop of Winchester, during the reign of Edward VI. Gardiner had been a sad thorn to the pious Primate in the previous reign; but now the latter had it all his own way, and he resolved to reduce the turbulent prelate to conformity with the true faith. When he could not be convinced by argument, he was sent to the Fleet. Being "somewhat straightly handled," he complained to the Lord Protector that he was allowed no friend or servant, no chaplain, barber, tailor nor physician; "a sign," says the sagacious biographer, "that he gave them high provocation." This was in 1547.

After a three years' imprisonment "it was now thought time," as is quietly remarked, "that he be spoken withal." Accordingly, he was brought up before the King's council, and articles of submission proposed for his subscription, condemning all the essential doctrines and practices of Romanism, and approving whatever had been done during the previous and present reigns for their suppression. We cannot but respect the man who, with liberty and honor on one side,* and disgrace and prison on the other, could maintain with such steadfast spirit his right to what he believed the truth. "After a great deal of pains and patience," on the part of the Archbishop and his fellow-commissioners, maintained unavailingly through two and twenty sessions, the refractory bishop was condemned to a still stricter confinement, in a meaner prison, denied all intercourse with his friends, and the use of books, pen, ink, and paper ; " that he may not write his detestable purposes, but be sequestered from all conferences, and from all means that may serve him to practice in any way." From this imprisonment he was not released till the accession of Mary ; and though we must detest the fiendish cruelty of his spirit, we cannot much wonder that when his turn came to be in power, " he sufficiently wracked his revenge against the good Archbishop, and the true religion."

Nor was such severity confined to Papists. The pious and zealous Hooper, Bishop elect of Gloucester, fully agreed with Cranmer as to doctrine and discipline ; only it went against his conscience to wear the vestments identified with the superstitious and idolatrous rites of Popery. Arguments proved equally fruitless with him as with Gardiner ; and on the report of the Archbishop, " that Hooper could not be brought to any conformity, but rather persevered in his obstinacy, coveted to prescribe orders and necessary laws to his head," the universal panacea was administered by committing him to the Fleet. We wish it could be recorded that conscience proved as unyielding in this instance as in the other. But after a time spent in prison, Hooper learned to appreciate the arguments of his brethren, and exchanged his uncomfortable lodgings in the Fleet for the bishopric and its vestments.

But there were other cases which more nearly touch our sympathies, because infringing, under the sacred name of the Bible, on the religious liberties of the common people. We are told that " now that the liberty of the Gospel began to be allowed, (!) divers false and unsound opinions began to be vented with it." The Archbishop felt it incumbent on him to put a stop to these disorders, by conventing

---

* Nothing but this hypocritical subscription was required as the condition of full restoration to his bishopric and a place in the King's council.

several " heretics" before him, and compelling them to take a public oath of recantation, with such farther penance as seemed to him advisable. One man, for maintaining that the regenerate could not sin, and other notions of like character, was required—besides signing an abjuration, and a promise " never to hold, teach, or *believe* the said errors or damned opinions above rehearsed—to procure two sureties in five hundred pounds (equal at least to twenty thousand dollars) for his attendance the Sunday following at Paul's Cross, and there to stand penitently before the preacher, all the time of sermon, with a faggot on his shoulder." Michael Thombe, a butcher, was convented, for holding " that Christ took not the flesh of the Virgin, and that the baptism of infants is not profitable because it goeth before faith ; but, " by submission and penance, he escaped !"

There was another class of offenders, as described by Strype—" some that took the liberty of meeting together in certain places, and there to propound odd questions, and vent dangerous doctrines and opinions." As a specimen of these disorderly proceedings, it is mentioned that " a number of persons, a sort of Anabaptists, about sixty, met in a house on a Sunday, in the parish of Bocking, in Essex ; where arose among them a great dispute, ' Whether it were necessary to stand or kneel, barehead or covered, at prayers ?' and they concluded the ceremony not to be material ; but that the heart before God was required, and nothing else. Such other like warm disputes there were about Scripture." Similar assemblies were likewise held in Kent. " These," says Strype, " were looked on as dangerous to Church and State." Nine of these from Bocking, " being cowherds, clothiers, and such like mean people," and others from Kent, having been arrested and brought before the council, confessed the cause of their assembly to be " for to talk of the Scriptures." They also admitted that they had refused the communion for two years. Their grounds for so doing being judged erroneous and superstitious, " five of them were committed to prison, and seven bound in recognizance to the King in forty pounds each man."

But " the mild Archbishop," as he is called *par excellence*, could not always satisfy his conscience with fines and prisons. An ignorant young woman, named Joan Bocher, who held the heresy that Christ, being sinless, could not have partaken of the flesh of the Virgin, who was conceived in sin, withstood all the efforts put forth for her conversion. The Archbishop, as well as Ridley and Latimer, labored long and earnestly for this object ; but at length gave over the attempt, and she was condemned to the flames. When the sentence was brought by Cranmer to the young King for signature, he long refused; and when at last he yielded, weeping, to the authority and arguments of his venerated instructor in religion, it was with the solemn declaration, "If there is wrong in this matter it rests wholly on your hands!" In the year 1551, a Dutchman suffered the same death by Cranmer's authority, for denying the divinity of Christ.

Such were the measures to which good men were driven for the support of that State church which has been glorified as the embodiment of the English Reformation. But these measures never grew out of that inward divine life which the Spirit of God, through God's own word, had awakened among the people of England. They were, indeed, the legitimate fruits of the ecclesiastical system which royal despotism had forced upon that noble work; or, in Milton's splendid language, "the verminous and polluted rags, dropt over-worn from the toiling shoulders of Time, deformedly quilted and interlaced with the entire, the spotless, and undecaying robe of truth." The persecuting spirit which so sadly defaces the history of English Protestantism, is due not to Christianity, nor even, primarily, to the men who have been the instruments of oppression. It belonged to the SYSTEM which constituted the civil ruler the controller, *ex officio*, of man's relations to God. When nonconformity to a certain Church is made an offence against the constitution of the State, it must, of necessity, be punished by the civil sword. Nor can any change of organization, nor of men, nor of times, effect any real alteration in the working of this system. Catholic Spain, Protestant England, Calvinistic Geneva, Puritan New England, Lutheran Germany, all bear witness to this assertion. The stake and the gibbet may, indeed, be banished by the advancing light of Christian civilization; but other forms of oppression, suited to the mildness and proprieties of the age, will continue to attest that a State religion, in its very nature, is a denial of the supremacy of conscience, and as such, is and must be an Inquisition and a despotism.

Cranmer, in his efforts to consolidate the Anglican Church, was actuated, no doubt, by pious and patriotic motives. To concentrate ecclesiastical power in the hands of the King of England was his expedient to secure it from reverting to the Pope of Rome; as to make the doctrines of Protestantism the State religion of England, was forever to exclude the teachers of Popery, who were also the sworn enemies of the Bible for the people. To make sure of this end, and that no loophole of access might be left to the abettors of Romanism, required that the lines of orthodoxy should be sharply defined; and especially, that no inward disagreement should cause a weak and broken front to be presented to the enemy. Hence conformity became his one idea ; carried even to the extreme requiring unity in outward forms and ceremonies, and in the cut and color of garments, no less than in the belief of the essential truths of Christianity.

But whatever may be its faults, the Church which recognizes the people's right to the unrestricted use of the Bible in their mother tongue, differs from one which denies this, as light from darkness. If it promulgates error, it also administers the antidote ; if it claims a tyranny over conscience, it deprives no man of the charter wherein he may read his inalienable title to judge for himself how he shall worship God. Accordingly, we find that notwithstanding the indefatigable endeavors of Archbishop Cranmer and his successors to enforce "uniformity and quietness in religion," the spirit of independent thought increased among the people, and Puritanism grew rife in the very bosom of the Church.

While, therefore, we must regret the mistaken policy of Cranmer, which did so much to entail on England the burden under which she has groaned three hundred years, which has cost so much of her best blood, and exiled or disfranchised so many of her most loyal children ; we must still remember him with gratitude as one of the earliest advocates of vernacular translation, and especially as that one who first obtained from the civil power the admission of the Bible into the public service of religion, and liberty for all, without respect to class or condition, to read it for themselves. This was the vital point. This granted, and the enjoyment of that religious liberty and equality which the Bible teaches, was but a question of time and patience.

The reign of Edward VI., during which Cranmer wielded almost unbounded ecclesiastical power, is a period illustrious in the annals of the Bible. With all the Primate's fondness for legislating in matters of religion, he wisely left the word of God to take care of itself, except so far as to give his warmest encouragement to all efforts for multiplying and diffusing it. The fifty editions of Bibles and New Testaments which appeared during this brief reign, in answer to the spontaneous popular demand, are a greater glory to Cranmer than if they had all been issued in obedience to his authority.

In another respect also we see his true liberality in reference to the Scriptures. Four versions, and these in editions varying more or less among themselves, were before the public, and one of these was his own. Yet there is no trace that his vast influence as Primate was used to gain for the latter any preference in the public favor. During these six and a half years there were published, as nearly as can be ascertained, of Coverdale's Bible, two of the whole Bible and two of the New Testament ; of Taverner's two ; of Cranmer's, seven of the whole Bible and eight of the New Testament ; of Tyndale's five of the whole Bible (in eight distinct issues, commonly reckoned as separate editions) and of the New Testament twenty-four. Besides these, were two or three editions of the latter published with Erasmus' Latin New Testament in parallel columns. It is interesting to see from this comparison that Tyndale's New Testament was still the favorite of the common mind ; while the change in the character of the ruling influences is marked by the fact that the long-proscribed name of the translator appeared in full on the title page of at least fifteen editions.

CHAPTER XXIV.

THE REIGN OF TERROR.

AGAIN the scene was changed. A stern adherent of the Church of Rome now sat on the throne of England, in place of the gentle and pious Edward.

It is not strange that the long series of disappointments, mortifications, and sorrows, which had consumed the youth and early womanhood of Mary, should have tinged her spirit with bitterness and gloom. A sadder fate few have experienced. Commencing life with the most brilliant prospects, accustomed almost in infancy to the pomp and adulation of an expectant queen, sought in marriage by the greatest princes of Europe; before the age of twenty-five she saw the marriage of which she was born declared incestuous, her illustrious mother ignominiously supplanted, and herself studiously degraded by her own father. In poverty and neglect, often in jeopardy of her life from her father's jealousy of one he had so deeply injured, she wore away ten weary years. With the sense of personal wrong was mingled indignation and horror at the sacrilegious repudiation of the ancient faith, so intimately connected with it. It required great strength and elasticity of nature, such as Elizabeth possessed, or great Christian magnanimity, to come unharmed out of such a trial. Mary had neither. Narrow in mind, melancholic in temper, the devotee of a faith which nurtures the darker passions, the fearful tempest of life had but withered and chilled her; and she came to the throne yet young, only thirty-six, a blighted woman, a bigoted and morose zealot. The memory of the humiliations and terrors to which she had been subjected, but fed the fierce flame of religious fanaticism, and her power as Queen was valued only as the instrument to avenge herself and her religion.

Mary entered London on the 3d of August, 1553. Her first act was to release and reinstate " her bishops," as she emphatically styled Gardiner, Bonner, and Tunstal, who emerged from their six years' incarceration, unsubdued in spirit, and thirsting for revenge. The former, who possessed in an eminent degree the pride, the talent, and the craft which characterize the higher class of the Romish priesthood, was made Lord Chancellor ; Bonner, a ferocious bully, not above playing the hypocrite when occasion offered, and insatiable in his thirst for blood, became one of Mary's most influential counsellors, and her chief inquisitor. But few days were suffered to elapse after Edward's funeral, when the Queen re-inaugurated the reign of *Obscurantism*, that twin sister of Popery, by an "Inhibition" against reading or teaching any Scriptures in the churches, and printing any books. By the 15th of September, Cranmer, Ridley, Latimer, Hooper, Bradford, and other distinguished reformers, were shut up in the Tower, while John Rogers was made prisoner in his own house, and forbidden to speak to any person out of his own family. In the Parliament which met in October, Cranmer was attainted of high treason; and a bill was passed re-affirming Henry's marriage with Katherine, the preamble to which recognized the late Archbishop as the sole instigator of the divorce. Had this been true, it would be hard to blame Mary for singling him out as a special object of resentment. But both Bonner and Gardiner had been zealous agents in the divorce, long before Cranmer became an actor in it, and the latter was a member with Cranmer of the commission which pronounced the marriage with Katherine unlawful. Both of them had also, with all show of cordiality, acknowledged the King's supremacy. Nay, Mary herself had conceded both points, for the sake of regaining position and influence at court. Her servile letter to her father on the death of Anne Boleyn, and the yet more servile articles which she consented to subscribe, abjuring her religion and with her own hand endorsing the foul stigma which had been cast upon her birth,* should have forever prevented her from making the like acts grounds of accusation against others. But all this shows that her conduct was governed not so much by personal or political, as by religious motives. Gardiner was a true Papist, and this covered all his offences; Cranmer was a zealous Protestant, and this was a crime which cancelled all obligations. For it was Cranmer's intercession which had saved her from the Tower, and from a bloody death at her father's hands; and he had incurred the hatred of the powerful Northumberland by his earnest opposition, only relinquished upon Edward's dying entreaties, to the exclusion of Mary from the succession.

Nor did any execution take place on the charge of treason. A year and a half were the accused reserved in prison, till Cardinal Pole had effected a formal reconciliation between the apostate kingdom and Holy Mother Church, by which the Pope resumed all his

---

* Burnet, vol. i., p. 154.

ancient dominion over England, and the doctrines of Rome became once more the established faith. A stillness, presaging the bursting of the storm, held the nation for a time in suspense and fear.

Meanwhile, all foreigners attached to the reformed principles, great numbers of whom had, during the reign of Edward, fled from persecution in their own countries into England, were warned to depart without delay. In their train, disguised as servants, and by other opportunities, a large body of English Protestants contrived to elude the vigilance of government, and escaped to the continent. Not fewer than eight hundred or a thousand learned men, besides great numbers in other conditions, are estimated to have become exiles during this short reign.

At length, on the 21st of November, 1554, Cardinal Pole arrived in England as Papal Legate, and was received with all the pomp and reverence due to the ambassador plenipotentiary of his Holiness. On the 30th of the same month, he performed the ceremony of reconciling Parliament, as the highest civil assembly of the realm ; on the 6th of December the same was done in the Convocation, the highest assembly of the clergy. This was followed by commissions, issued by the Cardinal to Winchester and other bishops, for trying heretics. It was then that the pent up flames of persecution burst forth with unexampled fury. The alacrity of the commissioned prelates to discharge their bloody office shows with what impatience they had waited for the appointed hour. First, the most eminent of the reformers, those who were regarded as leaders of the host, were condemned and executed ; then attention was turned to humbler victims. The whole country was placed under the most odious system of *espionage*. Justices of the Peace in the several counties were formed into secret vigilance committees, who were directed to lay out their shires into districts, and to employ spies in every parish ; and they were to meet monthly to receive the information thus gathered, to examine such as were accused, and make report to head-quarters. By these thorough measures it was intended utterly to root out and extirpate heresy from the land. The Queen, especially after her marriage with that cold-hearted bigot Philip II., urged on these proceedings against her innocent subjects with unrelenting fury. Even the hope of becoming a mother but added fierceness to her cruelty ; and she declared that unless her mind were quieted by the death of every heretic then in the prisons, "*even to the last one*," she could not hope to pass the approaching crisis with safety.* Bonner himself was then too slow for her impatience.

* Strype's Cranmer, vol. i., p. 528.

It was a terrific period, and, as in all similar trials, "the love of many waxed cold," and multitudes sought to make the impossible compromise between outward assent to what they disbelieved, and inward allegiance to the truth. But there were also many who chose death rather than deny Christ ; and their example did far more to undermine Popery in the hearts of the people, than Cranmer's Church had ever accomplished with its carefully elaborated Articles, and its gentle persuasives of fines and the Fleet. The faith of these steadfast martyrs was an argument which came not in word alone, but in power. It told of an inward life which could overmaster fear and pain, which in the midst of bodily torture could impart a divine joy such as earthly prosperity could never give, and even in the dying agony could inspire a prayer of forgiveness and love for the persecutor.

From February, 1555, to November, 1558, a period of less than four years, there perished in prison by torture, and at the stake, nearly four hundred persons, a large number of whom were in the flower of youth. Of these, two hundred and eighty-eight perished at the stake, many of them under circumstances of peculiar cruelty. As if the spectacle of a single human being shriveling in the flames could not satisfy the cannibal fury of their persecutors, it became the custom to burn them in companies of from three to ten or more. At Colchester five men and five women were burned in one day, six in the morning, and four in the afternoon. At Lewis, in Kent, six men and four women perished together. At Bow, near London, was witnessed, June 27th, 1556, the horrible spectacle of thirteen human beings, eleven men and two women, consumed in one fire. They suffered, not even charged with any offence against morality or the civil law ; but simply because they could not conform their consciences to the doctrines and observances of the Queen's religion.

Such a time was needed, also, to show what the word of God had already done for England. After the first paralyzing shock of terror, the work which had been progressing for thirty years, manifested itself with increasing power ; till at length the demonstrations of popular feeling, though free from every trace of violence or disorder, alarmed the government into comparative moderation. On the occasion last mentioned, twenty thousand persons were estimated to have been present, "whose ends generally in coming there, and to such like executions," says Strype, "were to strengthen themselves in the profession of the Gospel, and to exhort and comfort those who were to die." A single bystander having uttered, in the fullness of his heart, a brief ejaculation in behalf of the sufferers, a responsive Amen burst from the assembled multitude with the sound of thunder.* But the infatuated Queen needed many such lessons before she learned to respect the awful voice of popular conviction.

The persecutions of the year 1558 again brought out to the light those secret societies of believers, or CONGREGATIONS, as they called themselves, which have been already mentioned as the successors of the Lollards. Several of these now existed in London; and from the number of localities specified where they were accustomed to assemble, it appears that they had increased rather than diminished. Whether they had been known during the administration of Cranmer is uncertain; but as they seem to have preserved their separate organization, differing in important respects from the State Church, it is most probable that they had continued to assemble during that period with their wonted silence and secrecy. So far as we can judge, they were simply companies (or, as we should now call them, Churches) of believers, who met statedly for the worship of God and for the celebration of the Lord's Supper, and had no officers but a Pastor and Deacons chosen by themselves. The congregation which assembled in Bow Lane, is known to have existed without interruption twenty-five years, and was probably the parent of all the rest. They had not intermitted their meetings during Mary's bloody reign, and had enjoyed through this period the labors of a succession of godly and able pastors. These had been compelled, one after another, to take refuge in flight; but the members, as a body, had thus far escaped detection.

A tone of piety, beautifully primitive and Scriptural, characterized these quiet, humble companies of Christians. They seem never to have been disturbed by those hair-splitting disputes over free-will and predestination, in which the metaphysical tendencies of some of the leading reformers had embroiled Protestantism; and which, in the earlier days of the Marian persecution, had made even the prisons of the faithful re-echo with the brawls of fiery controversy, and compelled the jailers to secure a decent peace, by separating brother from brother.† Those disciples seem, pre-eminently, to have "kept the unity of the spirit in the bond of peace." Holding fast those grand truths of revelation which pertain to the soul's salvation, it was their simple aim to incorporate them as living energies in their hearts, and to manifest that inward power by lives of holiness and love. Such had been their character from their first beginnings in the days of Wickliffe.

* Anderson, vol. ii., p. 264.
† Strype's Cranmer, Book iii., ch. xiv.

THE REIGN OF TERROR. 197

Bonner's suspicous eye had been for some time directed to the gatherings of these inoffensive people ; and his spies, under the guise of brethren, had been busily engaged in seeking information to be used against them At length, one Sabbath morning—December 12, 1558—as they were about assembling for divine worship at Islington, their pastor, Mr. John Rough, and one of their deacons, Cuthbert Symson, a rich and worthy citizen of London, were there apprehended by the Captain of the Queen's Guard, and taken immediately before the Privy Council. Three days after they were handed over to the tender mercies of Bonner. During his trial before this brutal prelate, Mr. Rough alluded to a visit which he had once made to Rome, and the abominations he had there witnessed. This so infuriated Bonner that he flew upon him like a wild beast, and actually tore out a part of his beard by the roots ! Two days before he suffered, he addressed the bereaved flock of which he had been so faithful a shepherd, in a letter which breathed the spirit of the apostolic age. Like those of Tyndale and Frith, this beautiful epistle tells us, in every sentence, that the BIBLE was the fountain from which his life drew its springs.

Mr. Symson was reserved three months longer in prison, the object being to force from him the names of his fellow-disciples, of which he had the list. Three times in one day was he subjected to torture ; but no agonies could tempt him to betray his brethren. Bonner himself confessed before the Consistory that he was baffled, and that there was something in this man's spirit which he could not understand. "Ye see this man," said he, "what a personable man he is. And furthermore, concerning his patience, I say unto you that if he were not a heretic, he is a man of the greatest patience that ever yet came before me ; for I tell you he hath been thrice racked in one day in the Tower. Also in my house he hath felt some sorrow ; and yet I never saw his patience broken." On the 28th of March this heroic man was burnt at Smithfield, in company with two of his brethren.

The place of their pastor was immediately supplied by the not less holy and intrepid Thomas Bentham. There was need of such a leader, for the persecution now grew hot. Less than a month after the death of Cuthbert Symson, about forty of their number, men and women, had assembled for worship near Islington. With their Bibles in their hands, they were "occupied in the meditation of God's holy word," when they were surprised by a constable and his posse, who succeeded in arresting twenty-two of them. They were immediately imprisoned at Newgate, and there lay seven weeks without being once called up for examination. Two died in prison ; of the remaining twenty, thirteen were condemned on the 24th of June—a month memorable in the history of English martyrdom—to perish at the stake. The rest barely escaped with life.

Seven of the condemned were to be burned at Smithfield. Fearful of the demonstrations which had been witnessed on former occasions of this character, Philip and Mary took the precaution of issuing a proclamation, to be read first at Newgate and afterward at the stake, charging and commanding, that " no man should either pray for, or speak to the condemned, or once say, ' God help them !' " But it needed something more than royal proclamations to repress the mighty emotion now swelling in the great popular heart. At the appointed hour a vast multitude stood awaiting the arrival of the martyrs at Smithfield. Swaying forward at their approach, with a quiet but irresistible movement, they surrounded the prisoners, while the billmen and officers were borne off like chaff on the wave, so that they could not even come near their charge. Then was disclosed the cause of this strange proceeding. In the bosom of that dense crowd were hid the "congregation" and its pastor, who were now seen exchanging with their brethren farewell embraces, and words of encouragement and affection. Then they fell off quietly, and allowed the officers to resume their places. The royal proclamation, enjoining silence, was now read. But on seeing the fire kindled, Mr. Bentham, turning to the multitude, exclaimed : " We know that they are the people of God, and therefore we cannot choose but wish well to them, and say, God strengthen them !" Then in a still louder voice, he added, " *Almighty God, for Christ's sake, strengthen them!*" Again that deep " AMEN ! AMEN !" rose on the air like the sound of many waters, and gave solemn pledge, in the face of earth and heaven, that the heart and conscience of England must and would be free.

But it is time we turn to the direct history of the English Bible during this bloody reign.

It is not a little singular that during these five and a half years there seems to have been no direct legislation against the use of the Scriptures, beyond the proclamation issued by Mary on her accession. That the Queen would gladly have followed, in this respect, in her father's early steps, no one can doubt. That she refrained, is a telling symptom of the state of public opinion. But there were indirect methods of securing the same object ; and there is sufficient evidence that Bibles were seized and burned, and their readers severely punished. In 1555 a second proclamation forbade the importation and use of all or any of the works of certain authors—thirty-five in number—whose names are therein specified. Among the twelve English authors on the list, are Tyndale, Coverdale, and Cranmer ; and though their translations of the Bible are not mentioned by name, we may be sure that they were not only included under the action of this decree, but were the special occasion of it. That it signally failed of the desired end, we learn from the tenor of the third proclamation in 1558, which required all " wicked and seditious books," to be delivered up on pain of *immediate death*, by MARTIAL LAW ! The history now to follow furnishes the key to this last measure, which bears upon its face the evidence of reckless desperation. Not only were the previously existing versions still read in secret in every part of England, but a new one—in some respects more formidable than either of its predecessors—was added to the number several months before the death of the unhappy Queen. It is of this version that a brief account will now be given.

CHAPTER XXV.

THE GENEVAN BIBLE.

A CONSIDERABLE body of the English exiles had established themselves at Geneva in Switzerland, then, as ever since, a city eminent for theological learning. The English Church at Geneva is said to have numbered several hundred members, among whom were many distinguished scholars and preachers. Shut up together in this city of letters, and with few active duties to occupy their time, it is not strange to find them busy in devising plans for benefiting their beloved native land. It was, indeed a time of general intellectual activity among the learned fugitives scattered through various parts of Protestant Europe ; and many excellent works, the fruit of their constrained leisure, were sent over to England to supply in some measure, by the silent labors of the pen, the voice of the living teacher.

In Geneva this activity very naturally directed itself toward an improved translation of the Scriptures. Such an attempt was fully in accordance with the spirit of the age, which had already given birth to independent versions and repeated revisions of the English Scriptures ; and now demanded the perfecting of this great work. In this respect the undertaking presents a wide contrast to that of Tyndale, and exhibits in a striking light the changes effected in little more than a quarter of a century through the labors of that great man. What Anderson well remarks of the version of Coverdale, may with still more propriety be applied to this, and to all subsequent attempts in the same field : " *Their translations were the effect of the times ; the times themselves were the effect of Tyndale's.*" This general tendency could not fail to receive a powerful impulse in Geneva, where, under the leadership of Calvin and Beza, sacred learning was cultivated with an ardor and success far in advance of what was witnessed in any other portion of Christendom. It is not unlikely, from the circumstances, that the first suggestion of the new translation came from Calvin himself. Among these is the fact that his brother-in-law, William Whittingham, as seems to be now conceded, was the translator of the New Testament. But whatever its source, the proposition awoke an instant enthusiasm among the whole body of exiles ; and the lay members of the Church encouraged the projectors not only with their sympathy, but with offers of all the pecuniary assistance needed to carry it through successfully. Among the most forward in this good work was John Bodleigh, father of the founder of the celebrated Bodleian Library, a man of wealth and noble spirit, who, on the completion of the version, took upon himself the chief cost of its publication.*

The New Testament was first translated, and was published in 1557. The ability with which it was executed fully justified the undertaking. Every page exhibited evidences of the advance of Christian scholarship since the appearance of the previous versions. In the Address to the Reader, the translator refers to the peculiar advantages afforded by his residence and relations in Geneva; "being," he says, "moved with zeal, counselled by the godly, and drawn by occasion, both of the place where God hath appointed us to dwell, and also of the store of heavenly learning and judgment which so aboundeth in this city of Geneva that justly it may be called the patron and mirror of true religion and godliness." The utmost thoroughness was aimed at in the work. Not only was the translation made directly from the Greek, aided by comparison with versions in other languages, but the Greek text itself (as published by Erasmus) was revised by manuscripts which had been collected by the scholars of Geneva. When it was completed, Calvin expressed his interest in the work by prefixing to it an introduction, which he calls: "The Epistle declaring that Christ is the end of the Law." It sketches briefly and beautifully the progressive steps by which the need of a Mediator and Redeemer was made known, and the minds of men taught to look forward to him; till at length, in the fullness of time he appeared, and by his miracles, his teachings, his death and ascension, proved himself to be the long expected hope of the world, to which also agreed the witness of inspired men, of angels, and of God himself. The divinely authenticated history of these transactions is contained in the books of the New Testament, which embodies also the teachings of inspired apostles as to the application to be made of them for securing our salvation.

"All these things are published, declared, written, and sealed to us in this Testament, by the which Jesus Christ makes us his heirs in the kingdom of God his Father, and declareth unto us his will, as he that maketh his testament to his heirs to be put in execution. Now we are all called to this inheritance, without putting any manner of difference either between man or woman, small or great, servant or lord, master or scholar, clergy or laity, Hebrew, Greek, French, or Latin, none of them is refused, if that by assured confidence he embraceth that

---

* Anderson, vol. i., p. 322.

which is sent unto him ; briefly, whosoever shall acknowledge Jesus Christ such as he is ordained of the Father. Therefore," he continues, " shall we that bear the name of Christians suffer this Testament to be taken from us, or else to be hid or corrupted, which so justly is ours, and without the which we can pretend to no title to the kingdom of God, without the which we know not the excellent graces and promises which Jesus Christ hath declared towards us, neither the glory and blessedness which he hath prepared for us ?" . . . " O Christians, understand now and learn this point ; for doubtless the ignorant shall perish in his ignorance, and the blind following another blind shall fall with him into the ditch. There is but one way to life and salvation, that is, faith in the assurance of God's promises, which we cannot have without the Gospel." " What thing might there be then that could unacquaint us and drive us back from this Gospel ? Shall injuries, evil sayings, rebukes, loss of worldly honors ? . . . Shall banishment, proclamations of attaint, loss of lands and goods ? . . . Shall afflictions, prisons, rackings, torments, make us shrink from this Gospel ? We learn by Jesus Christ that this is the right path to come to glory. Finally, shall death ? Nay, death cannot take away that life which we wish and wait for."

The tone of the whole epistle is gentle and tender, as if the heart of the writer were melted with sympathy for his persecuted brethren ; and his exposition of the offices of Christ, as the all and in all to the redeemed, of his infinite worth and the fullness of his love, breathe a richness and fervor of piety, which conflicts somewhat with the common notion entertained of the stern reformer.

The New Testament was no sooner completed than the translator, now aided by learned associates, of whom Gilby and Sampson, two of his distinguished fellow-exiles, are supposed to have been the chief, turned his attention to the Hebrew Scriptures. Elizabeth's accession and the consequent happy change of affairs in the autumn of 1558, invited them back to England, whither the great body of English exiles now returned with joyful haste. But so deeply were they impressed with the importance of finishing the great task they had undertaken, that for two years longer they denied themselves the sight of their native land, and labored, as they tell us, " day and night," till it was completed. In 1560 the first edition of the complete Genevan version appeared in England.

As Greek philology was far in advance of Hebrew when the former versions were made, and much had been accomplished in the latter since their time, the Genevan Old Testament exhibited a yet more decided improvement than the New. In both divisions, the style of the translation shows it to have been an entirely independent rendering of the original, neither studiously departing from the former versions, nor trammeled by them where the translator's view of the sense differed from theirs, or where the same sense can be more clearly expressed in another form. As compared with Tyndale's, its manner sometimes appears dry and curt, and we miss in it, or fancy that we miss, the glow with which the heart of the old translator suffused his phraseology ; but the meaning is often brought out with far greater distinctness. The English is in every respect as intelligible as that of our common version, not seldom more so, and the two would still be read with great profit in connection. It is, indeed, much to be regretted that so excellent a version should not be rescued from the dust of past ages, and made accessible to English readers as a help to the better understanding of their Family Bible.

Its usefulness and its popularity were much increased by the brief, pithy notes added by the translators, containing such information in regard to Biblical geography and antiquities, and such doctrinal explanations, as were needed for the clear understanding of the text. Another feature which indicates the liberal spirit of the translators, is the insertion in the margin of various readings, thus placing the unlearned reader, so far as possible, in the position of the scholar, and allowing him to use his own judgment as to which of the readings suits best with the connection. A less commendable novelty is *the division of the text into verses*, a practice till then unknown in English Bibles, but ever since as pertinaciously adhered to as if an integral part of the inspired word. No single thing, probably, had done more toward multiplying sects in the Christian body, and substituting a dry, dogmatic theology in place of the living sap of revealed truth, than this mischievous device, for which there is but one poor plea— the advantage of easy reference.*

To the whole Bible, thus completed, was prefixed an Epistle " to our beloved brethren in England, Scotland, and Ireland," in which they explain their reasons for sending forth a new version.

"Now, forasmuch as this thing [progress in a holy life] is chiefly attained by the knowledge and practising of the word of God, (which is the light to our paths, the key of the kingdom of Heaven, our comfort in affliction, our shield and sword against Satan, the school of all wisdom, the glass wherein we behold God's face, the testimony of his favor, and the only food and nourishment of our souls,) we thought we could bestow our labors and study in nothing which could be more acceptable to God, and comfortable to his Church, than in the translating of the Scriptures into our native tongue ; the which thing, albeit that others heretofore have endeavored to achieve, yet, considering the infancy of those times and imperfect knowledge of the tongues in respect of this ripe age and clear light which God hath now revealed, the translations required greatly to be perused and reformed."

* The Anglo-American revisers of the New Testament have wisely discarded this " mischievous device," and placed the numbers of chapters and verses in the margin.—T. J. C.

The Genevan Bible at once found favor with the people and established itself in a wonderfully brief period as the FAMILY BIBLE OF ENGLAND. Unsustained and even discountenanced by the ruling ecclesiastical powers, it not only supplanted the earlier versions, but maintained its place against two powerful competitors of later date, as the favorite version of the people, for the greater part of a century.

During this time, it passed (including the separate issues of the New Testament) through a hundred and fifty editions. It even made its way to a considerable extent into churches, being preferred by many clergymen even after the publication of the Bishops' Bible. It still continued to be printed for private use long after the appearance of King James' revision, the last ascertained edition bearing date 1644. So pertinaciously, indeed, did the people cling to it, and so injurious was its influence to the interests of the Established Church and of the "authorized version," that in the reign of Charles I., Archbishop Laud made the vending, binding, or importation of it a high-commission crime.* Even so late as 1649, an attempt was made to commend King James' Bible to popular favor, thirty-eight years from its first publication, by printing with it the Genevan Notes! But after that time, the old Family Bible gradually disappeared from the homes and hearths of England, and gave place to that which has been so long known and honored as the Common Version.†

The success of the Genevan version is to be explained chiefly from two causes: First, its intrinsic merits as a faithful and clear transcript of the inspired word, according to the best scholarship of the age. Its character in this respect was so unquestionable as to secure for it universal respect, and to draw even from those who least liked its influence, a frank concession of its excellence.‡ Second, its origin in the stronghold of Presbyterianism, its connection with the name of Calvin, and with the doctrines, the severe simplicity in forms, and the comparative Christian equality prevailing in the Genevan Church, commended it to the warmest sympathy of that large and increasing body, the Puritan party in the Church of England. To them it became the symbol of all they wished to see in their native land, of a church reform which should sweep away everything in Christian worship borrowed from the traditions of the Church of Rome, and which

---

* Anderson, vol. ii., p. 390.

† It is worthy of note, that it is to the Genevan version we owe the fine expression in Dan. vii. 9, "The Ancient of days." All the previous versions had the awkward and unmeaning phrase, "the Old Aged!"—T. J. C.

‡ Strype's Life of Archbishop Parker, p. 207.

should conform it, outwardly as well as inwardly, to the model furnished in the word of God. How much it thus did, directly and indirectly, both for the spread of real piety, and for the development of Puritanism, and of the spirit of religious and civil liberty in England, it is impossible to estimate.

What cause is it for regret that its influence should not have been wholly on the side of truth and freedom ! But the Genevan associations, so intimately linked with its existence, were not all beneficial. Genevan Presbyterianism—far as it had advanced in other respects— had not learned to respect the rights of conscience. While she secured Christian liberty in larger measure and to a greater number than did her Anglican sister, her hand was no less heavy on those outside her consecrated pale ; and the sword of the magistrate was recognized as well by Calvin as by Cranmer, as the proper guardian of the purity and order of the Church of Christ.

This spirit had left its impress, in no questionable characters, on the Genevan Bible. The Old Testament had been completed in the initial period of Elizabeth's reign, when her policy as yet seemed undecided, and the reform party indulged the confident expectation that the English Church, shattered to its foundations by Mary, would be reconstructed in accordance with their views. Under this exhilarating idea the translators in the dedication of their work to that " most vertuous and noble ladie," thus exhorted her to exercise her powers as civil ruler for the suppression of error and establishment of truth :

" Now as he that goeth about to lay a foundation surely, first taketh away such impediments as might justly either hurt, let, or deform the work ; so is it necessary that your Grace's zeal appear herein, that neither the crafty persuasion of man, neither worldly policy nor natural fear dissuade you to root out, cut down, and destroy those weeds and impediments which do not only deface your building, but utterly endeavor—yea, and threaten the ruin thereof. For when the noble Josias enterprised the like kind of work, among other notable and many things, he destroyed not only with utter confuion the idols and their appurtenances, but also burnt (in sign of detestation) the idolatrous priests' bones upon their altars, and put to death the false prophets and sorcerers, to perform the words of the law of God : and therefore God gave him good success, and blessed him wonderfully, so long as he made God's word his line and rule to follow, and enterprised nothing before he had enquired at the mouth of the Lord.

" And if these zealous beginnings seem dangerous, and to breed disquietness in your dominions, yet by the story of King Asa it is manifest that the quietness and peace of kingdoms standeth in the utter abolishing of idolatry, and in advancing of true religion ; for in his days Judah lived in rest and quietness for the space of five and thirty years, till at length he began to be cold in the zeal of the

Lord, feared the power of man, imprisoned the prophet of God, and oppressed the people ; then the Lord sent him wars, and at length took him by death.

"Moreover, the marvellous diligence and zeal of Jehoshaphat, Josiah, and Hezekiah are, by the singular providence of God, left as an example to all godly rulers to reform their countries, and to establish the word of God with all speed, lest the wrath of God fall upon them from the neglecting thereof. For these excellent kings did not only embrace the word promptly and joyfully, but also procured earnestly, and commanded the same to be taught, preached, and maintained through all their countries and dominions—binding them and all their subjects, both great and small, with solemn protestations and covenants before God, to obey the word, and walk after the ways of the Lord. Yea, and in the days of King Asa it was enacted that whosoever would not seek the Lord God of Israel should be slain, whether he were small or great, man or woman."

The shrewd Princess was quite ready to acknowledge the principle thus laid down, but not the application of it intended by its expositors. If conjecture is right in regard to the names of the translators, some of the very men who penned this dangerous counsel and made God's charter of human rights the medium for communicating it to the royal mind, were soon made to drink deeply of the cup which they had mixed for others. Yet even the humiliations so steadfastly endured, and the blood so freely shed by Puritans in this and the succeeding reigns in behalf of religious liberty, could not eradicate from their veins this early taint. Not till they had breathed the free air of the western wilderness two hundred years, did they fully learn the lesson that Christianity can live and flourish unprotected by the State.

Thus the English Bible went forth once more in increased energy, still restricted in its action by human infirmity, but bearing within itself the power gradually to overcome and subdue all that could hinder the perfect fulfillment of its mission.

CHAPTER XXVI.

THE BISHOPS' BIBLE.

IN 1561, the third year of Elizabeth's reign, John Bodleigh, with whom we have already become acquainted in the account of the Genevan Bible, obtained from the Queen's government a patent for the exclusive right to print that version during the seven years next ensuing. In 1566, having a thoroughly revised edition ready for the press, and wishing to print it in England, he applied to Cecil, the Queen's Secretary, for an extension of this license. Before giving him a reply, Cecil consulted with Parker, Archbishop of Canterbury, and Grindal, Bishop of London. Their answer contains three striking points. First, a recognition from these dignitaries of the great merit of the Genevan Bible, on which account they recommended the extension of Bodleigh's privilege to twelve years longer ; secondly, the announcement of their design to set forth a special translation for use in churches ; thirdly, the condition proposed to be annexed to Bodleigh's patent, viz., a promise, " in writing under his hand, that *no impression of the Genevan Bible should pass without their direction, consent, and advice.*"

To elucidate the bearings of this reply requires a brief view of the policy now established in the Elizabethan Church ; a policy which continued to govern it with extended claims and increasing force, till in the hands of Charles I., the overstrung bow broke with its own tension, and State-Church and Church-State fell in common ruin.

At the accession of Elizabeth, there were tokens that the spirit of Christian liberality and union had very considerably increased among English Protestants. Their common sufferings during the preceding bloody reign, and the fraternal sympathy and hospitality which they had received from the reformed churches abroad, had at once exalted in their regard the essential grounds of faith in which they agreed, and lowered their estimate of the external forms in which they differed. In anticipation of the reorganization of the English Church, a general disposition was manifested to lay stress on an exact outward uniformity, and to leave the details of habits and ceremonies to individual conscience and discretion. The letters of the returned exiles to their Presbyterian brethren on the continent not only breathe this spirit of conciliation, but show a decided leaning toward the simpler and more democratic form of Church government which prevailed in the Swiss churches, as being more closely conformed to the New Testament model, and better adapted to the edification of the people.*

But in this they had reckoned without their host. Elizabeth had no intention of being a whit less a monarch than her father. She valued the Reformation not so much for the truth it propagated as for the foundation it offered for her own supremacy. She did not wish the Pope of Rome to rule in her dominions, because she wished to be herself Pope, sole ruler over the actions and the consciences of her subjects. In the preceding reign she had conformed to the dominant faith, probably without much violence to her principles; and her tastes were at least fully in harmony with its aristocratical constitution and its pompous ritual. But under no circumstances could she have become the devotee of any religion. Her clear, masculine intellect, cold heart, and iron will, moved but at the bidding of one passion, and that the least religious of all passions, the love of power. Religion was to her simply the right hand of that power. As such, it was to be cherished; but, as such also, to be held in strict subjection, and to be employed in whatever service would promote her grand design. She was quick to see that only a despotism in the Church could form a sure basis for despotism in the State. Men accustomed in the management of their religious affairs to freedom of opinion and action, would soon begin to enquire whether they were not competent to exercise the same freedom in regard to all things which concerned their interest and happiness. Popular elections in the Church were dangerous precedents to be admitted into an absolute monarchy such as she sought to establish; while the habit of unquestioning subjection to authority in matters of conscience was the surest guarantee of docility to the civil power. Under a government which united in one person the highest ecclesiastical and the highest civil authority, this result was inevitable. So, accordingly, she willed it to be.

The state of the nation at her accession gave free scope to her ambitious plans. Ignorant of their own rights and their own strength, never yet having felt the invigorating thrill of conscious freedom, her subjects had no other idea of security than that of clinging like timid children, to the skirts of royalty. Majesty was then at its highest premium in England. Its frowns were like the artillery of heaven, terrible yet glorious to behold; its smile melted the blessed recipient, as the sun melts wax, into whatever shape it might please the imperial

---

* Burnet, vol. ii.

will to cast him. Protestant Elizabeth, with her large, self-reliant, dauntless nature, seemed to her poor, distracted people like a strong tower into which they might run and be safe; and every prerogative which could be taken from other hands and placed in hers, was supposed to be so much gained toward their well-being. Her first Parliament invested her with powers which, though nominally restricted by the Constitution, rendered her in fact absolute by law.

Two principal enactments, which fixed as in an iron mold the character of her long reign, distinguished this session. The first recognized the royal supremacy in all causes, ecclesiastical and civil; the second established uniformity in religion as the law of the land. A clause in the first of these Acts empowered the Queen and her successors to delegate to such of her subjects as they shall think meet, as often and for as long time as they please, "all manner of jurisdiction, privileges, and preeminences touching any spiritual or ecclesiastical jurisdiction within the realms of England and Ireland, to visit, reform, redress, order, correct, and amend all errors, heresies, schisms, abuses, contempts, offences, and enormities whatsoever." Under this clause originated the HIGH COMMISSION, an ecclesiastical court appointed by the Queen, and accountable to her alone, through which for nearly half a century she and her bishops ruled with an iron rod over the consciences of her subjects. The jurisdiction of this court extended over the whole kingdom, and included alike clergy and laity. Any three members of it were competent to inquire, "on the oath of twelve men, by witnesses, or by any other ways and means they could devise,"* respecting all offences against the Acts of Supremacy and Uniformity, "and also to inquire of all heretical opinions, seditious books, contempts, conspiracies, false rumors or talks, slanderous words and sayings, etc., contrary to the aforesaid laws, or any others ordained for the maintenance of religion in this realm, together with their abettors, counsellors, and coadjutors." Any three of them—the Primate or a bishop being one—were competent to try all cases of willful absence from the divine service, as established by law, and to punish the offenders by Church censures, or by fines levied on their lands, goods, and tenements. Any three of them might try the holder of any ecclesiastical living on matters of faith and doctrine, and eject him at their discretion. Any six of them, whereof some must be bishops, might "examine, alter, review, and amend the statues of colleges, cathedrals, grammar-schools, and

---

* "That is," says Neal, "by the inquisition, by the rack, by torture, or any ways and means that forty-four sovereign judges should devise"; or, it should be added, any three of them.

other public foundations." It was a part of their duty to tender the oath of supremacy to all ministers, and to report the names of such as refused it to the King's Bench. The most odious feature of this odious system, was the power vested in the Commissioners to summon before them any person, merely upon suspicion, and without exhibiting any charge against him, or confronting him with witnesses, to compel him, by the oath *ex officio*, to testify against himself. Many were thus forced not only to convict themselves, but their nearest relatives and friends. But no man was cleared on his own oath. This method of making a man his own accuser in a court of justice was sufficiently detestable in the hands of a Romish Bishop or Chancellor; but in them it was consistent. How Protestant bishops and statesmen could use it, and look a Papist in the face, is a riddle. The mandates of this court, or of any three of its members, were made binding on "all justices of peace, mayors, sheriffs, bailiffs, constables, and all other officers, ministers and subjects, in all and every place, exempt or not exempt, within the realm; neglect of the same to be answered at their utmost perils." * They had their spies in all suspected parishes, to note such as did not come regularly to church; and these being summoned and committed to prison, the keepers were to mark such as came to visit and relieve them, and give information accordingly.†

A powerful ally to the High Commission was furnished by the Star Chamber, a criminal court, likewise appointed by the Queen, and responsible to her alone; whose decisions, though merely expressions of the royal will, were made as binding as Acts of Parliament. The High Commission, being an ecclesiastical court, had some limit in the nature of offences, and was not competent to inflict heavier penalties than fines, deprivation, and imprisonment; though in both these points it stretched its powers beyond all legal bounds. But whatever it could not do, the Star Chamber could; and moreover, nonconformity to the established Church being constituted disobedience to the realm, such ecclesiastical cases as required severer punishments than the former was competent to inflict, could be turned over to the latter, which had the power of life and death. Both bodies being composed in part of the same men, and the monarch supreme in both, they could play unchecked into each others' hands; and they were, in fact, but the mutual complements of that system of despotic rule by which she was able to override constitution and statute, and reduce her subjects

---

* See Strype's Life of Archbishop Grindal, Appendix No. vi.—*The Ecclesiastical commission granted to the High Commission, &c.*

† Neal, vol. i., p. 130.

to mere dependents on her supreme will and pleasure.* It was due to Elizabeth's great personal qualities; her self-control, which could sometimes forbear a present advantage rather than endanger a greater one to come; her wisdom, which could discern in the substantial prosperity of her realm the surest basis of her own supremacy; and to the further fact that, having no standing army to enforce her decrees, her power rested wholly in the affection and confidence of her people, that the nation so long bowed patiently to her heavy yoke, and that even those who suffered most, maintained to the last their loyalty and affection for her person.†

The Queen had not far to look for instruments to carry out her plans. It was, at first, her hope that the Romish prelates who occupied the high positions of the Church at her accession, would, as had been the case with Henry's bishops, acknowledge her supremacy and retain their places. This expectation proving vain, the Queen turned to the reformed clergy. Had they, at this moment, stood firmly united in the views entertained by the great majority, that a certain prescribed cut of the clerical garb must not be made the condition of office in the Christian church, what a glorious epoch might this have proved for the Reformation in England! For at this period of its history there was no disagreement in respect to doctrine, and none that was insurmountable in respect to discipline; and Elizabeth and her counsellors were too wise to have allowed, on such grounds, a breach between herself and the united English clergy. Had but this seemingly little stumbling-block now been removed out of the way, the Church would have been replenished with a learned, godly ministry,

---

* Even that last refuge of liberty, the right of petitioning against existing grievances, was denied by this imperious princess, and that not to private individuals alone, but to Parliament itself. In 1586, the House of Commons, having prayed for a modification in the Church Constitution, were told in reply that "Her Majesty took their petition herein to be against the prerogative of her crown. For by their full consents, it hath been confirmed and enacted, (as the truth herein requireth), that the full power, authority, jurisdiction and supremacy in Church causes, which heretofore the Popes usurped and took unto themselves, should be annexed and united to the imperial crown of this realm."—*Strype's Life of Whitgift, p. 260.*

† This was remarkably exemplified in the case of Mr. Stubbs, a student of Lincoln's Inn, and brother-in-law of that distinguished nonconformist leader, Thomas Cartright. Stubbs had written a tract against the Queen's projected marriage with the Duke of Anjou, who, being a Papist, would, it was feared, be the means of restoring Romanism in England; and for the offence was condemned to lose his right hand. The instant the cruel sentence was executed, by driving a cleaver through his wrist with a mallet, he pulled off his hat with the remaining hand and cried with a loud voice, "God save the Queen!"

mellowed by recent suffering, yet glowing with that active, aggressive zeal for the Gospel which always marks the growth-periods of the Christian body. But it was not so to be. When that which had hitherto been theory became a question of practice, many faltered in their convictions. Might it not be duty, they asked, to sacrifice their feelings on these unessential points, rather than leave the Church wholly unfurnished with a Protestant ministry? Should they not, indeed, by this present small compliance, be securing the power necessary to bring all things right in the end? It was a tempting but a poisoned bait, as might soon be discerned by the change in the spirit of those who yielded. Some of the conforming bishops continued to regard the contested points as really matters of indifference, and sometimes pleaded earnestly for their brethren whom they had left ; but the majority quickly caught the temper of their royal head, and almost outstripped her wishes, at least her views of what was prudent, by the vigor with which they pressed conformity. Thus did a slight compromise with conscience corrupt men whose bearing under poverty, persecution and exile had cast fresh lustre on the faith which they professed.

At this point, the Protestant host of England parted into two hostile bands, never again to reunite. On the one side was the rich and gorgeous Church, linked indissolubly with the State ; an almost absolute sovereign their common head ; the whole legislative and executive power of the kingdom at their command. On the other were a few hundred ministers, confessedly the flower of the English clergy, but in regard to all their temporal interests, their personal freedom and even life, wholly at the mercy of their antagonists. The friends of Protestantism abroad beheld the spectacle with mortification and dismay ; and some of those who had most warmly urged on the adherents of reform, now counselled compliance rather than allow a breach so disastrous to religion, so favorable to the resuscitation of Popery. We who can look back not only upon the conflict but its results, bless that immovable adherence to principle which refused to do evil that good might come. In the decision of those Puritan ministers were involved not only the religious but the civil liberties of the English race. For it may be safely affirmed that at the period now before us no power less strong than conscience, the fear of sinning against God, could have strengthened men to oppose the sweeping tide of absolutism. Under the prevailing influences of the time, with a monarch like Elizabeth, at once despotic and popular, wise to govern and strong to defend her people, civil freedom would have been readily bartered for peace, security, and Protestantism. But conscience was something which these men dared not barter. Resistance to oppression was here not a matter at their option, but a duty to God which they could not evade. Their example became the starting point of free ideas ; and the English people learned at length to question whether they had been made for the sole purpose of being governed.

The contest was at first rather of a negative character, consisting, on the one side, more in a systematic neglect of the nonconforming clergy than in positive persecution ; and on their part in a persevering adherence to their own views of duty. The new Primate, Matthew Parker, had enough to do for a while in securing his own position, and bringing into order that numerous body of the clergy who still adhered to the doctrines of Popery. During this interval, the Act of Uniformity was not rigorously pressed, and a considerable number of ministers who had not subscribed it made their way into inferior places in the Church. These were the preachers of England. Where they were found, there was found also a new religious life among the people, and the errors and superstitions of Popery confessed a power in their zealous labors and holy examples, not acknowledged in parliamentary acts and royal injunctions. Among them was Miles Coverdale, once Bishop of Exeter, more known and honored still as a Translator of the Bible into his mother tongue ; but who was now thankful to be allowed, unpunished, to preach the Gospel here and there as he could find opportunity. Grindal, Bishop of London, a man of kind natural disposition, at length so far compassionated his gray hairs and pitiable state of poverty, as to procure for him in 1562 the little parish of St. Magnus, London, without requiring conformity. Among them was also John Foxe, whose Book of Martyrs had done more than any other work except the Bible to establish the Reformation in the people's hearts ; but who was left unprovided for in the Church which he had laid under so sacred a debt, till Cecil, the Queen's Secretary, obtained for him on his own terms, a prebendary in Salisbury Church.* The universities, moreover, did not join in this wholesale proscription of men for a matter of opinion which affected neither the doctrine nor the life. Sampson † and Humphrey, then the great leaders of the nonconformist party, were both called to Oxford ; the first, who had previously refused the bishopric of Norwich on the stipulated condition, as Dean of Christ church, the

---

* In 1560, he describes himself in a letter to a friend, as a member " of the Order of Mendicants, or of the Friar-Preachers" ; and says that he was " still wearing the clothes that England received him in."

† Sampson, it will be remembered, was one of the translators of the Genevan Bible.

other as President of Magdalen College, and were there held in the highest repute for their learning and virtue. Under these circumstances, the neglect of the prescribed habits and ceremonies had greatly increased in the Church; so that "the Queen," as Strype informs us, "had taken a great offence at many of the clergy, having information how remiss they were, both in the university and out of it, especially in the city of London, in wearing the habits appointed for the clergy to use in time of ministration and at other times; chiefly the square cap, the tippet, and the surplice." So far indeed were the consecrated vestments from being regarded with due reverence that they had become a jest and by-word with many both of the clergy and laity, who called them the "conjuring garments of Popery"; while the bishops themselves were dignified with the titles of "White-Coats, and Tippet Gentlemen." Some, moreover, had begun profanely to inquire: "Who gave them authority more over me than I over them, either to forbid me preaching, or to deprive me, unless they have it from their Holy Father the Pope?"* Her Majesty, therefore, in January 1564, directed her Archbishop and other bishops of the High Commission, "that orders might be taken whereby all diversities and varieties among the clergy and laity, as breeding nothing but contention and breach of common charity, and against the laws and good usage and ordinances of the realm, might be reformed and repressed, and brought to one manner of uniformity throughout the realm."

The Archbishop himself thought it now high time to look into these irregular proceedings, and to bring this free-spoken ministry into a wholesome subjection. The following list of the dangerous varieties in divine service then practised by clergymen, is quoted by Strype from a manuscript copy found among the papers of Secretary Cecil, dated February 14th, 1564.

"VARIETIES IN THE SERVICE AND ADMINISTRATION USED.

Service and Prayer.

Some say the Service and Prayers in the chancel, others in the body of the Church. Some say the same in a seat made in the church; some in the pulpit with their faces to the people. Some say it with a surplice, other without a surplice.

Table.

The table standeth in the body of the church in some places; in others it standeth in the chancel. In some places the table standeth altar-wise, distant from the wall yard. In some places in the midle of the chancel, north and south.

---

* Strype's Life of Archbishop Parker, p. 151.

In some places the table is joined ; in others, it standeth upon tressels. In some it standeth upon a carpet ; in others it hath none.

Administration of the Communion.

Some with surplice and cap ; some with surplice alone ; others with none. Some with chalice ; some with a communion cup ; others with a common cup. Some with unleavened bread ; some with leavened.

Receiving.

Some receive kneeling, others standing, others sitting.

Baptizing.

Some baptize in a font ; some in a basin. Some sign with the sign of the cross ; others sign not. Some minister in a surplice ; others without.

Apparel.

Some with a square cap ; some with a round cap ; some with a button cap ; some with a hat. Some in scholars' clothes ; some in others."

It has been objected to the Puritans that their grounds of dissent were trivial, and insufficient to justify a schism in the Christian body. Since God regards merely the heart and not the dress, or place, or posture, why, it is urged, could they not have sacrificed their own feelings in these indifferent points, to the preservation of Christian unity ? To this argument they replied, at the time, that things in themselves indifferent changed their nature when imposed on the Church of Christ as necessary, by a self-constituted power. They then became the test of a vital principle, viz., whether or not there resided in any individual, or in any body, ecclesiastical or civil, the competency of extra-Scriptural legislation for the Church ; in other words, whether the Bible were the sufficient and only authoritative standard for the Church in all matters, and as well in regard to her order and discipline as to her doctrine. Elizabeth and her Primate held the negative of this question. They maintained, that it was from the necessities of the time alone that the apostolic Churches received their peculiar form, which, therefore, was temporary and not to be accepted as the permanent model ; and that it belongs to the government of each country to settle the organization, rites, and observances, of that division of the Church lying within its territory, and to enforce them on all its subjects. The Puritans, on the contrary, held to the sufficiency and binding authority of the Scriptures in all respects ; and refused, by submission to ceremonies in themselves indifferent to acknowledge what they believed an unlawful and indeed fatal principle.

But they had a farther objection. What to the educated and enlightened were things indifferent, were not so to the people. In their eyes, the clerical vestments stood for the doctrines with which they had been accustomed to associate them. Some, we are told, now regarded the surplice with a superstitious reverence scarcely exceeded by that once felt for the monk's cowl, a fragment of which was looked on as the possessor's sure passport to heaven. The embroidered cross on the cope was to them the symbol of image-worship. The kneeling posture at the Supper, the chalice, and the hallowed wafer, to them recognized the Mass, a propitiatory sacrifice for sin. A still larger number viewed all these things with horror, as the badge of that cruel faith which had lighted the fires of Smithfield, and drank the blood of their nearest relatives, friends, and neighbors, and of the faithful ministers of Christ. While, therefore, the prelates were seeking to conceal the greenness of their new Church from the popular eye under this garb of antiquity, and to soften the shock of change to the adherents of Popery by retaining whatever was possible of the shows of the old faith, the nonconforming clergy felt themselves bound, by the New Testament law of brotherly love, to countenance nothing which might cause their weak brother to offend ; and claimed that the Church of Christ should be set forth before the eyes of the people, in sharpest outward contrast with the church of Antichrist.*

Thus, in regard to everything external, the Church planted itself at this crisis on the Romish ground of tradition and human authority ; the Puritans took their position no less firmly on the great Protestant principle—the Bible the only guide of faith and practice.

---

* It has always been the fashion with "liberal" historians, while they admit the great results to civil freedom from the position taken in this controversy by the Puritans, to sneer at the position itself as that of narrow-minded bigots. Even Mr. Macaulay seems not to have considered, in reference to their case, (Hist. Eng., vol. i., p. 50), that things trivial in themselves may become great by their relations and bearings. Eve's taking the apple was a very little thing in itself ; but as the exponent of a principle it decided the fate of a world. William Tell's refusal to take off his hat to Gessler's pole was a very little thing ; but it marked the dividing line between Swiss slavery and Swiss freedom. The Stamp Act was a very small grievance ; but as a test-measure on the part of England, resistance to it became the turning-point of American independence. Of precisely this character was the prescription of clerical vestments, and of a certain unalterable round of church forms ; and so was it regarded alike by those who urged and those who refused them. "Doth your Lordship think," thus writes Parker, on his death-bed, to Lord Burleigh, "that I care either for cap, tippet, surplice, wafer-bread, or any such ? But for the law so established I esteem them. For contempt of Law and Authority would follow and be the end of it, unless discipline were used."—*Strype's Life of Parker*, p. 492.

Fully awake to the alarming spirit of innovation and independence now manifesting itself in the Church, the Archbishop and his coadjutors in the Commission immediately prepared a set of Articles for the regulation of divine service, to which universal and unvarying conformity should be required. He then proceeded to cite many Puritan ministers before the Commission, and endeavored by admonitions and threats to induce compliance. Sampson and Humphrey were summoned from their duties at Oxford, and after being detained a year in attendance at court, at great expense and discomfort to themselves, were deprived of their offices and thrown into prison, where Sampson remained some months. In 1564, a royal proclamation enjoining uniformity in apparel having been obtained from the Queen, the Archbishop took a still higher tone, and fell to the task of compelling men to think alike, in a spirit more befitting a Papal legate or inquisitor than a Protestant bishop. This year he cited the entire body of the pastors and curates of London, and required from them a promise and subscription under their own hands, to comply with the apparel prescribed by law. The 24th of March, 1564, was a dark day to the London clergy. No remonstrance, no discussion was permitted. Beside the commissioners stood one Robert Coles, (a London minister who had once refused the habits, but afterward conformed), and arrayed in the prescribed vestments, square cap, tippet, and priest's robe, all according to statute. "My masters and ye ministers of London," said the Bishop's Chancellor, "the council's pleasure is that strictly ye keep the unity of apparel like to this man as you see him; that is, a square cap, a scholar's gown, priestlike, a tippet, and in the church a linen surplice; and inviolably observe the rubric of the Book of Common Prayer, and the Queen's Majesty's injunctions and the Book of Convocation. Ye that will subscribe, write Volo; ye that will not subscribe, write Nolo. Be brief. Make your words." When some of the unhappy men, many of whom had wives and children depending for support on their small stipends, attempted to speak—"Peace, peace!" cried the Chancellor. "Apparitor, call over the churches, and ye masters answer presently, *sub pœna contemptus.*" "By these resolute doings," adds the grave narrator, "were many of the incumbents and ministers present mightily surprised." Of the ninety-eight, sixty-one were induced, though with much difficulty, to subscribe; and we cannot doubt that of these many returned to their homes with a heavier load than a starving family on their hearts. Some cried out in the anguish of their spirits: "We are killed in the soul of our souls for this pollution of ours!" Thirty seven steadfastly refused to set their hands to a lie ; and were immediately suspended from all exercise of the ministerial vocation, and threatened with deprivation, if they did not conform within three months. These, by Parker's own admission, were the choicest members of the London clergy.*

These measures were followed by a set of injunctions for the London clergy, "such," says Neal, "as had never been heard of in a Protestant kingdom or a free government." Every clergyman who had cure of souls was obliged to swear obedience : " 1. To all the Queen's injunctions and letters patent ; 2. To all letters from lords of the privy council ; 3. To the articles and injunctions of the metropolitan ; 4. To the articles and mandates of their bishop, archdeacon, chancellors, somners, receivers, etc., and in a word to be subject to the control of all their superiors with patience." To forestall all possibility of evading these demands, from four to eight informers were appointed in each parish to watch over the conformity of both clergy and laity, and give their testimony accordingly, whenever required.

Could men with any conscience, with a spark of honor or self-respect, submit to a slavery like this? Miles Coverdale could not keep his little living on these terms ; but old and infirm as he was, being now eighty years of age, he preferred to risk the bread and shelter for his last days rather than soil his conscience. But he felt in his soul a commission as minister of Christ which no mortal could recall ; and he continued, though with much fear and caution, to preach the Gospel in and about London till near his death in 1567. It had been determined to make an example of John Foxe, by way of striking terror into his less distinguished brethren. But the sturdy old Puritan was more than a match for them. When required to subscribe, he drew his Greek New Testament from his pocket, saying : " To this will I subscribe." To the threat of deprivation he replied : " I have nothing in the Church but a prebendary in Salisbury, and much good may it do you if you take it from me." Their resolution failed, and they did not venture to touch a man so dear to the whole nation as the historian of the martyrs.

A letter addressed in 1566 by Coverdale, Sampson and Humphrey to several of the leading Swiss reformers, gives some idea of the state of distress then existing.

---

* Strype's Lives of Archbishops Grindal and Parker. The incidents of the above account are taken from the former work, where they are most fully given : the number of ministers present, and the proportion between the subscribers and non-subscribers, from the latter ; which being the later work, and the statement made on the authority of Archbishop Parker, who had the names before him, is undoubtedly correct.

"Our affairs," they write, "are not altered for the better, but, alas! are sadly deteriorated. For it is now settled and determined that an unleavened cake must be used in place of common bread ; that the communion must be received by the people on their bended knees ; that out of doors must be worn the square cap, bands, a long gown, and tippet ; while the white surplice and cope are to be retained in divine service. And those who refuse to comply with these requirements are deprived of their estates, dignities, and every ecclesiastical office ; viz., brethren by brethren and bishops, whose houses are, at this time, the prisons of some preachers ; who are now raging against their own bowels ; who are now imposing these burdens not only on their own persons, but also on the shoulders of others, and this too at a time when, in the judgment of all learned men, they ought to have been removed and abolished altogether."

But this is not the place for the details of that memorable conflict. The brief sketch just given of its incipient stages exhibits its grounds and the spirit in which it was conducted sufficiently for the purpose of our present history. As was inevitable, the breach continually widened. Multiplied exactions and increased rigor on the one side, rising at length to a denial of all the inborn rights of man, freedom of action, speech and thought, were met by increased firmness of resistance, and a bold questioning of the very foundations of the Church, from which the persecuted had at first only differed in some minor particulars. The weapons used by the two great parties in the conflict were in harmony with the fundamental principles on which they had respectively taken their stand. On the side of the ruling party, the forcible repression of discussion ; the limitation and rigid censorship of the press ;* the seizure of pious men and women who had met

---

* See the "Rules and Ordinances made and set forth by the Archbishop of Canterbury and Lords of the Privy Council, in the Star Chamber, for redressing abuses in Printing"; Strype's Life of Whitgift, Appendix No. XXIV. By this extraordinary instrument every printer was required to deliver within ten days from its date, an inventory of the number of his presses and of all his implements, on pain of their seizure and destruction, and twelve months' personal imprisonment "without bail or mainprize." No person should hereafter set up a press anywhere except in London and its suburbs, (one excepted in each University), nor within those limits except by leave of the Archbishop of Canterbury and Bishop of London, on the same penalty ; with the addition of being disabled forever from owning or managing a press, or being connected with the business in any way except as a journeyman for wages. No person should continue to use or occupy a press erected within the previous six months, on the penalty first named. No person should print a book not authorized by the Archbishop or the Bishop of London, on penalty of the loss of his instruments, six months' imprisonment without bail, and perpetual disability to exercise or derive any benefit from his trade. No person should sell, bind, stitch, or sew any book not thus authorized on pain of three months' imprisonment. All workshops and warehouses of printers, booksellers, and bookbinders, and all private houses were to

quietly to worship God ; the monopoly of schools ;* the inquisitorial tribunals which arraigned men on suspicion, and condemned them on their own forced confessions, or the testimony of secret informers,† to prison, exile, mutilation and hanging ; take us back to the days of Henry IV., and we ask with a bewildered feeling, "Is this the Reformation?" On the other side, in the measures of the Puritans we recognize those moral weapons with which the victories of truth have ever been won ; viz., the calm but unflinching exercise of the rights of conscience, and the steadfast passive endurance of the penalties thereby incurred. They preached, they wrote, they petitioned, and they suffered, through more than a generation, with a resolution and constancy which nothing could subdue. The usual result followed. The cause of the persecuted grew by being trodden on ; and before the scepter dropped from the hand of the aged Queen, not only a majority of the middle and lower ranks and of the House of Commons, but a powerful party in the Court itself, gave their entire sympathy to the advocates of religious freedom. The end of the battle was indeed yet far off ; but the moral convictions of the nation indicated with prophetic certainty what that end would be.

be open to search for books printed in contrariety to these ordinances, and all persons implicated in the printing, selling, uttering, binding, stitching, or sewing of the same, to be apprehended for trial before the High Commission, or three of its members, the Archbishop of Canterbury or Bishop of London being one. "For the avoiding of *the excessive number of Printers in this realm*," it is made unlawful for any printer, bookseller, or bookbinder in London to keep more than three apprentices, and for the printers at Oxford and Cambridge more than a single apprentice at one time. Under these regulations, the Press seemed likely to become a very dutiful handmaid of the monarchy and priesthood ; but the result reflects little glory on the sagacity of those who devised them.

* In 1591 it was made a pre-requisite to a schoolmaster's license, that he should take the oath of supremacy and subscribe the Articles of Uniformity ; a measure "thought convenient," says Strype, "to prevent the influence the Puritans might have on the minds of children."—Life of Whitgift, p. 377.

† When Udal, a nonconformist preacher, was, in 1590, tried for his life at the Court of Assize in Croydon, (having had a preliminary trial on the same charges before the Commission, and suffered a year's imprisonment uncondemned), no witnesses against him were brought into court, but the registrar merely swore to their examinations. When the prisoner, standing before his judges with his legs in irons, offered to produce witnesses in his defence, he was told that "because the witnesses were against the Queen's Majesty, they could not be heard!"—Neal, vol. i., p. 191.

CHAPTER XXVII.

THE BISHOPS' BIBLE CONTINUED.

It was near the close of the year 1565, just as the plans of Archbishop Parker for the repression of dissent were fully matured, and he had fairly entered on the work to which the remaining ten years of his life were devoted, when John Bodleigh made his application to Cecil in behalf of the Genevan Version.

With the events narrated in the preceding chapter before the mind, it is easy to see the relations of the course then adopted in reference to that version, to the general policy by which the Primate sought to secure universal conformity to the State Church.

The Bible "authorized to be read in churches," was Cranmer's Revision, the Great Bible, so-called, which had never been in high repute for its critical accuracy, and was now wholly eclipsed by the superior scholarship of the Genevan Version. The latter was the Bible of the Puritans. The associations of its birth were Presbyterian. It stood forth before the eyes of the nation as the symbol at once of Progress and of Dissent; while it was, at the same time, the most efficient agent in awakening the popular mind to the claims of religion, and planting therein the principles of godliness and virtue. And thus it happened that just in proportion to the extent of its usefulness was it dangerous to the peculiar interests of the Establishment. A Popish Bishop in the Primate's place would have laid his hands at once on this source of schism; neither hesitating to denounce it as unsafe for the ignorant and undiscriminating rabble, nor to dispose of it by the summary method of seizure and bonfires. This the spirit of Protestantism, a spirit created by the Bible itself, would no longer allow. Nor, indeed, have we any ground for supposing that Archbishop Parker would have resorted to violence, though he had been fully sustained by public opinion. Nevertheless, it was essential to his plans that the Church, which claimed to be the exclusive spiritual authority in the realm, should also be the exclusive spiritual teacher. To her, and not to any rival influence, must the people look for the supply of their religious wants, and for every privilege which they enjoyed as a Christian nation.

To the Protestant bishop two courses lay open for accomplishing this object; the one, by drawing the Genevan Version within the consecrated pale, and stamping it with episcopal patronage, to engraft on the popular favorite associations advantageous to the Church; the other, to supersede it by a new version, emanating directly from the Church.* The first was attempted unsuccessfully. Mr. Bodleigh did not accede to their proposal of pledging himself never to bring out an edition without their "advice, consent, and direction; and as the consequence, for more than ten years longer, or till 1576, the Family Bible of England was never printed on English ground, and the first English impression immediately followed the death of Archbishop Parker.† Public sentiment ascribed this delay, which of course much impeded its circulation, to the jealousy of the bishops; and it was thought a sore grievance that a version of the Bible which could be charged with no fault, should be thus arbitrarily kept from the multitudes who were hungering and thirsting for its instructions. The second course, that of preparing a new version, was within the Primate's own control; and at the time of Mr. Bodleigh's application measures were already in progress for this object. The result appeared in the year 1568, when the so-called BISHOPS' BIBLE was given to the public.

Strype, in his Life of Parker, thus speaks of the design, and of the method pursued in executing it:

"Among the noble designs of this Archbishop must be reckoned his resolution to have the Holy Bible set forth, well translated into the vulgar tongue, for private use, as well as for the use of churches; and to perform that which his predecessor, Archbishop Cranmer, endeavored so much to bring to pass, but could not, (the bishops in his days being most of them utterly averse to any such thing) that is, that the bishops should join together, and take their parts and portions in revising, amending and setting forth, the English translation of those Holy books. This our present Archbishop's thoughts much ran upon. And he had about this time (1565) distributed the Bible, divided into parts, to divers of his learned fellow-bishops, and to some other divines that were about him, who

---

* This, probably, was the ultimate design in any case. The Genevan Bible might be made to answer a good purpose till the new version was ready to be "set forth by authority," after which it would be at their own choice to suppress it at once, or to withdraw it gradually from public view, as should seem most judicious.

† Strype, in accounting for the failure of Bodleigh's application, remarks somewhat naively: "Whatever the cause were, it was not surely from any discouragement the translation received from the bishops. For they, by the fore-quoted letter, under their hands, like and approve it, and recommend the undertakers to the Secretary, to procure for them the Queen's license to reprint it. Unless the reason were that they were loath to subscribe to the terms that were demanded by the bishops."—Life of Parker, p. 207.

cheerfully undertook the work. . . . The Archbishop took upon him the labor to contrive and set the whole work agoing in a proper method, by sorting out the whole Bible into parcels, as was said, and distributing these parcels to the bishops and other learned men to peruse, and collate each, the book or books allotted them ; sending withal his instructions for the method they should observe ; and they to add some short marginal notes for the illustration or correction of the text. And all these portions of the Bible being finished, and sent back to the Archbishop, he was to add the last hand to them, and so to take care for printing and publishing the whole."

Fifteen learned men, most of them bishops, were employed on this work. The precise time when it was commenced is not known ; but it could not have been later than 1564, as we find Sandys, Bishop of Worcester, ready with his portion (Judges, Kings, and Chronicles) at the beginning of the next year. In a letter which accompanied it, he urges the prosecution of the revision in the most thorough manner ; "that it may be done in such perfection that the adversaries can have no occasion to quarrel with it. Which thing," he adds, "will, require a time. *Sed sat cito, si sat bene*"—[*but soon enough, if well enough*]. In accordance with this sound advice, the work seems to have been performed with praiseworthy diligence ; though, from causes presently to be mentioned, not with very satisfactory results. It was published in 1568.

Archbishop Parker's Preface to the new Bible contains many sensible and pious thoughts, and breathes a liberal Protestant spirit, widely in contrast with that displayed in his treatment of nonconformists. The remembrance of that treatment, and of his previous indifference to the cry of the nation for a more abundant supply of the Scriptures, does indeed much qualify the pleasure with which we should otherwise read it. Had he felt Cranmer's enthusiasm for the principles of the Reformation, and that its sheet-anchor was the Bible, his course would have been different. But it is too evident that episcopacy was still dearer to him than the Reformation, and that his reliance for its establishment was the sword of the magistrate rather than the word of God. And hence, while he was pursuing "*the precise brethren*" (his favorite designation of the dissenters) with deadly animosity, silencing faithful preachers, and imprisoning Christian people who sought spiritual nourishment elsewhere than from empty pulpits, or those filled by incompetent, worldly, or vicious men, by his own confession "*very many churches wanted Bibles.*" Nor can he be charged merely with neglect in this particular, when his influence was employed for the discouragement, against the earnest wishes of the people, of a version whose excellencies he could not deny. Yet with all these abatements, we cannot but rejoice over sentiments like the following, from the pen of the rigorous Primate ; for they indicate a public opinion in favor of the Bible, too deeply rooted and too full of life to be safely resisted or neglected by the highest in place and strongest in power.

"Antichrist must he be that, under whatsoever color, would give contrary precept or counsel to that which Christ did give us. Very little do they resemble Christ's loving spirit, moving us to search for our comfort, that will discourage us from such searching, or that would wish ignorance or forgetfulness of his benefits to reign in us, so that they might, by our ignorance, reign the more frankly in our consciences, to the danger of our salvation. Who can take the light from us in this miserable vale of blindness, and not mean to have us stumble in the paths of perdition, to the ruin of our souls ? Who will envy us this bread of life, prepared and set on the table for our eternal sustenance, and mean not to famish us, or instead thereof, with their corrupt traditions and doctrines of men, to infect us ? . . . Search, therefore, good reader, (in God's name), as Christ biddeth thee, the Holy Scriptures, wherein thou mayest find thy salvation. Let not the volume of this book, (by God's own warrant), depart from thee ; but occupy thyself therein in the whole journey of this thy worldly pilgrimage, to understand thy way how to walk rightly before Him all the days of thy life."

In reference to the cavils of the Romanists, who decried every existing translation into the mother'tongue, yet never themselves put hand to the work of supplying one which was more correct, he makes the pertinent inquiry :

"What manner of translation may men think to look for at their hands, if they should translate the Scriptures to the comfort of God's elect, which they never did, nor be not like to propose it, but be rather studious only to seek quarrels in other men's well-doings, to pick fault where none is ; and where any is escaped through human negligence, then to cry out with their tragical exclamations, but in no wise to amend by the spirit of charity and lenity that which might be more aptly put ?"

In apologizing for thus adding another translation to the many previously made, he quotes the words of Augustine, that "though in the primitive Church the late interpreters which did translate the Scriptures be innumerable, yet wrought this rather a help than an impediment to the readers, if they be not too negligent. For saith he, divers translations have made, many times, the harder and darker sentences the more open and plain." The Archbishop pleads, therefore, that no one should take offence at this new attempt at translation, inasmuch as it was neither intended to reflect on any other, or to claim perfection, " as that hereafter might follow no other that might see that which as yet was not understood." In these remarks, the Archbishop probably had one eye on those who opposed all change in the authorized version as a dangerous innovation ; and the other on the Puritans, whose attachment to their favorite version was not wholly free from party prejudice, many of them being unable, as was said, " to see the sense of Scripture, except through the Genevan spectacles."

And yet, with these liberal sentiments on the face of his translation, the Archbishop's first move after its completion was the attempt to obtain from the Queen an exclusive license for it as the one " to be *only* commended in public reading in churches, *to draw to one uniformity.*" This favor he requests, " not only as many churches want their books, but as that in certain places be publicly used some translations which have not been labored in this realm."* In other words, two grievances are to be redressed by her Majesty's countenance of the new version ; the churches destitute of Bibles are to be supplied, and the churches supplied with the Genevan version are to exchange them for the one furnished and authorized by her Majesty and the bishops.

The Bishops' Bible was, in some respects, an advance on that of Cranmer. The omission of the additions from the Vulgate was a marked improvement ; and many single passages were changed for the better (some also for the worse) by the substitution of the Genevan renderings. But it contributed little that was new to the stock of biblical knowledge. For this there were several causes. First and chiefly, the want of profound scholarship in the translators—learning being made subordinate to official position, in the selection of translators, by the object designed to be secured. The new Bible must be as good as bishops could make it ; but it must be a Bishop's Bible. England did not lack for scholars. The same men whose ripe learning had produced the Genevan version still lived in the prime and fullness of their powers, and there were other English scholars in all respects their equals. But it was the silent policy of the Church to recognize no merit in nonconformists ; and unfortunately the best talent and culture of the realm were thus buried from public use.

Another cause of the inferiority of the version was the rule laid down by Archbishop Parker, of deviating as little as possible from the old authorized version ; a rule which must necessarily produce an imperfect work, whatever may be the ability of the scholars by whom it is executed. To this rule there was, indeed, one remarkable exception. The uniform rendering of *ecclesia* by *congregation* formed one of the characteristic features of the earlier versions, and was ac-

---

* Parker's Letter to Cecil, quoted in Anderson's Annals, vol. ii., p. 333.

counted of primary importance, as representing to the English mind the generic idea of visible Christianity as a community of equals. This was the point in Tyndale's version against which Sir Thomas More directed his most powerful batteries. Coverdale, though allowing a false liberality to give a Popish tinge to his version in some other respects, never deviated in this from the Protestant principle. Cranmer, though his zeal for the Anglican Church was not scrupulous in its choice of means, maintained this feature of the English Bible in unimpaired integrity. In the "authorized version," as left by him and found by Archbishop Parker, *ecclesia* is rendered, in every instance without exception, "congregation." * It was therefore a very bold step, when the latter took the responsibility of a total change in this particular, by uniformly displacing "congregation," and putting "church" in its stead.† The controversy was no new one to him. He has himself recorded that this was one of the matters in debate when the Synod of Bishops, under Henry VIII., took into consideration the subject of a new translation. "There was then," says he, ‡ "a discussion [in the Synod] about the significance and force of certain words; as whether *Dominus* should be rendered from the sacred writings in English 'the Lord' or 'our Lord'; and whether *ecclesia* should be translated 'the congregation' or 'the church'; also, whether *caritas* should be expressed by 'charity' or 'love.'" He knew well which was the Protestant and which the Romish ground in this debate. His choice of the latter needs no explanation, except that furnished by the character of the rejected word, as indicating the original democratic constitution of the Christian body. The time had now come when Sir Thomas More's idea of The Church was to be realized in Protestant England; and the Primate saw, with Sir Thomas, that this could not be done so long as the true idea still lay on the face of the vernacular Bible. In this, King James' Revision followed that of the bishops; and thus the word for which Tyndale had so earnestly contended, the word which had stood on the sacred

---

* The word "church" occurs but once in Cranmer's Bible, and then as the translation of the Greek word for a *temple* or *sacred edifice*.

† With a remarkable exception in Matt. xvi., 18. There, the rendering of Cranmer's Bible was suffered to remain unchanged—"*And I say also unto thee that thou art Peter; and upon this rock I will build my congregation.*" The troublesome use of this passage by the rival Church of Rome sufficiently explains this silent deviation from uniformity. The only other instance is Hebrews xii., 23—"*And unto the congregation of the first born, which are written in heaven.*" The constitution of the Church militant was the object of the Primate's solicitude—not that of the Church triumphant.

‡ De Antiq. Britan. Eccle. p. 505; (Harvard Library).

page as an incorruptible witness against priestly usurpation, was thenceforward blotted from the English Scriptures. In this feature of the Bishop's Bible we find a motive for the undertaking, not less strong than the opposition felt to the general influence of the Genevan version.* We can now understand how this Bible, if established by authority as the only one to be publicly read in churches, might play an important part " in drawing to one uniformity."

It was but natural that Archbishop Parker should wish to secure to the English Church (to use the term in the Primate's sense) the advantage of furnishing the Bible both for public worship and for the private use of the people. Had he sought this object with a liberality suited to his vast income, and in a manner worthy of so difficult and so sacred a work ; employing the best scholars, furnishing them with the needed apparatus, and requiring from them nothing but a faithful rendering of the inspired original ; the good and wise of every age, and of every division of the Christian body, would have honored him as one of the world's benefactors. The savor of episcopal associations thus transferred to the English Bible, would have been fairly earned. But no man, no Church, has the right, for any purpose, to make God's word speak differently from itself ; † or to obscure its meaning even in the smallest particular, to the common eye. As the first English version undertaken for a less generous object than the extension of truth, and executed on the principle of making as little advance as the requirements of the age would permit, it must be regarded by the true Protestant rather with regret than satisfaction.

In 1572 a revised edition of the Bishops' Bible was published, to which Lawrence, a Greek scholar celebrated for his critical accuracy, contributed a number of emendations.‡ In 1584, under Archbishop Whitgift, the readings from the Vulgate, omitted by the first revisers, but which had been retained unmarked in the Book of Common Prayer, were replaced in the Bishops' Bible. It was important to

---

* The Genevan version used the words "church" and "congregation" interchangeably, and with about equal frequency. This variation from the practice of the previous versions had perhaps some connection with the State-church element of the Presbyterianism of that time ; but it at least respected the rights of the English reader, by giving, with the ecclesiastical term, the English term which clearly defined and explained it.

† A singular example of this is furnished by the suggestion of Guest, bishop of Rochester : viz., of conforming those passages in the Psalms, quoted in the New Testament from the Septuagint, to the readings there found—"for the avoiding," as he writes to Parker, " of the offence that may rise to people upon divers translations."—Strype's Life of Parker, p. 208.

‡ A list of these is given by Strype in the Appendix to the Life of Parker.

the Church that her Bible and her Liturgy should show no disagreement; and since the latter could not be altered without the concurrence of the Queen and Parliament, the old readings were quietly slipped back into the Bible; and, in order to complete the uniformity, they were left unmarked as in the Prayer Book. Seventeen of these interpolations occur in the Book of Psalms, one of them (in Ps. xiv.) including three entire verses. This is the most remarkable instance of deliberate imposition found in the history of Protestant Bible Translation.

This version passed through twenty-nine editions, most of them folios and quartos for public religious service, during the reign of Elizabeth; and it continued to hold its place in King James' reign, while his revision was in preparation. A few small-sized editions were printed for use in families; but it never became a popular favorite. The last edition appeared in 1608; and three years after, it was superseded, as the Bible of Churches, by the Common Version.

CHAPTER XXVIII.

THE RHEMISH, OR DOUAY BIBLE.

THE year 1582 witnessed a phenomenon in the history of English Bible translation ; viz., a version of the New Testament emanating from the Romish Church. This was not, however, the result of any change of principle in that venerable institution in regard to vernacular translation and the use of the Bible among the laity ; but merely a change of policy suited to the exigencies of the time. The work was executed by several English Catholics, all of whom had once been connected with the University of Oxford, but who, on Elizabeth's accession, had fled to the continent and found refuge in the Romish seminaries of Douay and Rheims. In their preface they explicitly declare :

"That they do not publish it upon an erroneous opinion of its being necessary that the Holy Scriptures should always be in our mother-tongue, or that they ought to be read indifferently of all, or could be easily understood of every one that reads or hears them in a known language ; or that they generally or absolutely judged it more convenient in itself or more agreeable to God's word and honor, or the edification of the faithful, to have them turned into vulgar tongues, than to be kept and studied only in the ecclesiastical languages. But they translated this sacred book upon special consideration of the present time, state and condition of their country, unto which divers things were either necessary or profitable and medicinable now, that otherwise, in the peace of the Church, were neither much requisite, nor perchance, wholly tolerable."

With regretful fondness, they look back to the happy days of the primitive Church, when, as they maintain, " it was not permitted even to those who understood the learned languages wherein the Scriptures were written, to read, reason, dispute, turn and toss the Scriptures ; nor might every schoolmaster that had a little Greek and Latin straight take in hand the Holy Testament ; nor were the translated Bibles put into the hands of every husbandman, artificer, prentice, boys, girls, mistress, maid and man." In those good times, the Bible was kept " in libraries, monasteries, colleges, churches, in bishops', priests', and some other devout principal laymen's houses and hands ; and the poor ploughmen, while tilling the ground, could sing the hymns and psalms either in known or unknown tongues, as they heard them in holy church, though they could neither read, nor knew the sense, meaning and mysteries of the same."

It cannot be claimed that the Rhemish and Douay translators represent, in this respect, merely the "obscurantists" of the Romish Church. The most distinguished members of her communion, illustrious by their own scholarship and by their zealous promotion of learning among the clergy, have spoken the same language in every age. We have already remarked this in regard to Cardinal Wolsey and Sir Thomas More. An equally striking instance is furnished by the policy of Cardinal Ximenes, after the conquest and "conversion" of Granada. Talavera, the benevolent bishop of the subjugated province, had much at heart the completion of a translation of the Scriptures into the vulgar Arabic for circulation among the Moorish converts. This purpose was sternly overruled by his superior. "It would be throwing pearls before swine," said Ximenes in reply to Talavera's arguments, "to open the Scriptures to persons in their low state of ignorance, who could not fail, as St. Paul says, to wrest them to their own destruction. The word of God should be wrapped in discreet mystery from the vulgar, who feel little reverence for what is plain and obvious. It was for this reason that our Saviour himself clothed his doctrines in parables, when he addressed the people. The Scriptures should be confined to the three ancient languages, which God, with mystic import, permitted to be inscribed over the head of his crucified Son; and the vernacular should be reserved for such devotional and moral treatises as holy men indite, in order to quicken the soul and turn it from the pursuit of worldly vanities to heavenly contemplation."*

And this was the man who founded and endowed the University of Alcala, for the education of the Spanish clergy; who projected that splendid monument of sacred learning, the Complutensian Polyglott, and defrayed the enormous expenses of the undertaking out of his own income! The aim in these and similar labors in the Romish Church was to increase and consolidate the power of the priesthood by raising it to an unapproachable height above the laity.

In what then consisted the necessity for so striking a deviation from the immemorial policy of the Church, as the publication of the New Testament for general distribution in the vulgar tongue? This the translators explain with equal frankness. It was the spreading poison of PROTESTANT VERSIONS; wherein, as they affirm, God's law and testament and Christ's written will and word are corrupted both in let-

* Prescott's History of Ferdinand and Isabella, ch. vi., last p. Note; and Hefele, Der Cardinal Ximenes, S. 63.

ter and sense, in order to make them agree with the false doctrines of their new religion. They say :

"In pure compassion, therefore, to see their beloved countrymen with extreme danger of their souls, to use only such profane translations and erroneous men's mere fancies, and being also much moved thereto by the desires of many devout persons, they had set forth the New Testament trusting that it might give occasion to them, after diligently perusing it, to lay away at least such their impure versions as hitherto they had been forced to use. . . . They had also set forth reasonable large annotations, thereby to shew the studious reader, in most places pertaining to the controversies of the time, both the heretical corruptions and false deductions, and also the apostolic tradition, the expositions of the holy fathers, the decrees of the Catholic Church and most ancient councils."

Thirty years after, 1609–10 the version was completed by the publication at Douay of the Old Testament, which had all this time been delayed by the want of the necessary pecuniary means—no very flattering index of the zeal of the infallible Church for the diffusion of the Scriptures.

The principles observed in the preparation of their work were worthy of the motives from which it was undertaken. It was made from the Latin Vulgate, in preference to the Greek and Hebrew Scriptures. "The Latin," they said, "was most ancient ; it was corrected by St. Jerome, commended by St. Augustine, and used and expounded by the Fathers ; the holy council of Trent had declared it to be authentical ; it was the gravest, sincerest, of greatest majesty, and the least partiality ; and in regard to the New Testament, was exact and precise according to the Greek ; preferred by Beza himself to all other translations, and was truer than the vulgar Greek text itself." This last claim, which might have been made with more reason in reference to the original text of the Vulgate (whose date was much older than the Greek manuscripts then in the possession of Protestant scholars), was made for modern copies of it, which embodied the mistakes and corruptions of its successive transcribers through more than a thousand years. Many attempts had been made for its restoration, but with confessedly little success. Such was the text to which the Rhemish and Douay translators appealed as the infallible representative of the inspired word.

Another characteristic feature of the work was the transfer of a multitude of words and phrases, untranslated, which by long usage had acquired a specific application to the doctrines, ceremonies, and discipline of the Romish Church. These, in their own words, "they kept exactly, as catholic terms." Many others also were retained, apparently for the purpose of throwing an air of mystery over the

Scriptures, as too profound and sacred to be understood by the common reader.

No more convincing evidence could be asked of the triumph of the great principle of Protestantism in England than the version thus forced from the reluctant hand of the Romish Church. It was not till an overwhelming public opinion demanded the free use of the Scriptures as the right of every individual, without respect to class or condition ; not till the sacred word was, as these translators conceded, in every man's hands in England, did she step forward, and with this version seek to tempt them from the more perfect Protestant translations.

The subsequent history of the Douay Bible is in full keeping with its origin. Were even so imperfect a version freely circulated among the Catholic masses speaking the English tongue, there would soon be witnessed among them the evidences of a new intellectual and religious life. But its office has ever been, and so continues in the present day, to stand as a barrier between them and the dreaded Protestant versions ; while between them and itself is interposed the general influence of the priesthood, and the secret inquisition of the confessional.

CHAPTER XXIX.

THE COMMON VERSION.

THE four or five years preceding the death of Elizabeth had witnessed a partial lull in the great contest between the Establishment and the Puritans. This was the effect of several causes, none of which however, contained the presage of permanent peace. The Queen, now yielding to the infirmities of age, could no longer maintain her prerogative over Church and State with the spirit and efficiency of former days. Archbishop Whitgift also, who had proclaimed "war to the knife" with nonconformists, on his elevation to the Primacy in 1583 and whose administration made that of Parker seem moderate and humane, was beginning to feel the weight of years. Meanwhile, the unwise and illegal severity of their measures had produced a corresponding reaction in public sentiment, which now affected all classes of society. It was no longer mere popular sympathy with the persecuted. The most thoughtful and far-sighted statesmen beheld with alarm the encroachments of a priesthood who, through their vast, undefined, ecclesiastical powers, and their coalition with the Star Chamber, had almost monopolized the administration of justice, and left to British subjects little more of liberty than the name. The courts of common law, provoked to resistance by long aggressions on their jurisdiction, now learned to check the action of the episcopal courts and of the High Commission by writs of prohibition, which could only be set aside by a tedious legal process, sometimes protracted through several years. This invasion of their prescriptive rights was hotly resented by the bishops; but in spite of their best endeavors, "the evil," says Strype, "increased more and more."*
Thus, in various ways, was the hierarchy crippled for the time, and disabled from that unrestrained use of its weapons to which it had been so long accustomed.

But that which contributed most of all to this state of comparative quiet, was the near prospect of a Puritan sovereign on the throne of England. James VI. of Scotland, Elizabeth's expected heir, had been educated a Presbyterian. He had publicly subscribed with his own hand the Solemn League and Covenant,† and on several occa-

---

* Life of Whitgift, Book IV. ch. xxvi. † Neal, Part I. ch. viii.

sions had reaffirmed his attachment to its principles. A marked instance of the kind had been witnessed in the General Assembly at Edinburgh, in 1590 ;* "when, standing with his bonnet off and his hands lifted up to heaven, ' he praised God that he was born in the time of the light of the Gospel, and in such a place as to be king of such a Church, the sincerest [purest] kirk in the world. The Church of Geneva,' said he, ' keep Pasche and Yule ; what have they for them ? They have no institution. As for our neighbor kirk of England, their service is an evil-said Mass in English ; they want nothing of the Mass but the liftings. I charge you, my good ministers, doctors, elders, nobles, gentlemen, and barons, to stand by your purity, and to exhort the people to do the same ; and I, forsooth, as long as I brook my life, shall maintain the same.' "

While therefore the Puritans, secure, as they supposed, of a speedy change in the government which would make them the administration party, were content silently to " bide their time," the bishops, dreading the reckoning which was to come, were quite willing to abstain from acts which might make a case, now sufficiently bad, quite irretrievable. " For indeed," says Strype, " he [the Archbishop] and some of the bishops, particularly the Bishop of London,† feared much that when this king came to reign in this realm, he would favor the New Discipline, and make alterations in the ecclesiastical government and liturgy."‡ The hopes of the one party and the fears of the other, both of which seemed so justly founded, were destined to a signal disappointment.

In 1603, the long career of the great Queen was closed by death, and the Scotch King succeeded to the English throne, under the title of James I. All eyes were now turned to the new monarch ; and his first movements were awaited by both parties with breathless interest. Messengers were promptly dispatched by both into Scotland to offer their congratulations and assurances of loyalty, and to bespeak the royal favor to their respective interests. His reply to the Bishops,

---

* Neal, Part II. ch. i.

† Richard Bancroft, who had been raised, in 1597, by the strenuous efforts of Whitgift, to the bishopric of London, owed the favor of that prelate to his long and active opposition to the Puritans. For many years previous he had been the Primate's right hand man in all measures for the suppression of that obnoxious party, and even surpassed him in the violence and cruelty of his proceedings. Since his elevation to the see of London, Whitgift's increasing age had thrown on Bancroft the active duties of the Primacy, and placed him foremost in the conflict. He had, therefore, more than any other man, reason to dread the expected new order of things.

‡ Life of Whitgift, p. 560.

that he would uphold the government of the late Queen as she left it, somewhat revived their courage. But he was also gracious to the agents of the Puritans. And thus, while he refrained from committing himself to any definite policy, each party was flattered with the idea of standing highest in his favor. Unsuspected by both, James had an object in view to which the settlement of the quarrel between the Prelates and the Puritans, in itself considered, was to him a mere trifle. Provided only his Prerogative were secured by the decision, he cared not which triumphed ; and to form a judgment on this point required time for personal observation. During several months succeeding his accession, he was engaged in a royal progress through his new dominions ; and though apparently absorbed in amusement, he diligently used the opportunity for watching the character and tendencies of the rival parties. Meanwhile, the war of opinion had broken out with renewed violence ; and the measures and publications, proceeding from both sides, developed still more palpably their characteristic views and aims.

James was at length ready to take a definitive position. On the 24th of October, a proclamation, issued under the royal seal, appointed a meeting of leading Churchmen and Puritans for discussing the ecclesiastical affairs of the kingdom. Thus originated the celebrated HAMPTON COURT CONFERENCE.

The terms of the proclamation left no room to doubt of his Majesty's decision to support the Established Church ; while the insulting arrogance of his tone toward the Puritans, his prohibition to them of all freedom of speech or of the press, and even of the right to join together in petitioning their sovereign on points of vital interest, taught them what treatment to expect in the appointed interview. The arrangements for the meeting corresponded to the style of the proclamation. Sixteen dignitaries of the Church, of whom nine were bishops, were designated to represent the prelatical party ; while only four Puritan ministers, and those selected by the King, were allowed to appear on the other side.

On Saturday, the 14th of January, 1604, the Conference held its first session. To this the Puritan ministers were not admitted. In Dr. Barlow's account of the Conference, drawn up by order of the Archbishop,* the occurrences of the first morning are stated as fol-

---

* " The sum and substance of the Conference which it pleased his excellent Majesty to have with the Lords Bishops and other of his clergy (whereat the most of the Lords of the council were present) in his Majesty's Privy Chamber at Hampton Court, Jan. 14th, 1603 [4]. Contracted by William Barlow, Doctor of Divinity, and Dean of Chester;" 301 pp. small octavo. It is of this document

lows. "All the deans and doctors attending my Lords the Bishops into the presence chamber, there we found sitting upon a form, Dr. Reynolds, Dr. Sparkes, Mr. Knewstubbs, and Mr. Chaderton, agents for the Millene Plaintiffs.* The bishops entering the Privy Chamber, stayed there till commandment came from his Majesty that none of any sort should be present but only the Lords of the Privy Council, and the bishops with five deans [naming them], who being called in, the door was close shut by my Lord Chamberlain."

The indignity thus put upon the reform party was followed by a meeting of the King and the bishops, in which they came to a perfect mutual understanding. It was opened by the King in an oration an hour long, whose key note was the sentiment expressed in the first sentence, that "Religion is the soul of a kingdom, and Unity the life of religion." It contained very severe reflections on that portion of the clergy who, by opposing conformity to the established doctrine and discipline, had bred dissensions now amounting almost to a schism, "a point," says the royal orator, "most perilous to the common weal as to the Church." They then proceeded to a consideration of the complaints against the Book of Common Prayer, as well as of alleged abuses in the administration of the service and discipline of the Church; which ended in an order from the King for a few verbal alterations in the titles of certain portions of the Prayer Book, "not," as he remarked, "in the body of the sense, and by way rather of some explanation than of any alteration at all."† His Majesty did

---

that Strype says in his Life of Whitgift, p. 571: "But that the very truth might appear [of the occurrences in the Hampton Court Conference], there was an authentic relation of it, written by one of the divines there present, viz., Barlow, Dean of Chester; and that by the Archbishop's own order, imposing this work upon him. Which then we may conclude to have been carefully revised by himself. And that it might be more exact and complete, it was compared and enlarged by the writer (before it was published), with the Notes and copies of the Bishop of London, the Deans of Christ's Church, Winchester and Windsor, and the Archdeacon of Nottingham."

The quotations from this tract, which has now become rare, have been made for the present work from the copy in the Harvard University Library. It has been accused of unfairness in representing the conduct of the Puritan divines at the Conference; its source leaves no room to suspect that James and the prelates are not presented in the most favorable light.

* In allusion to the so-called Millenary petition, signed by 750 Puritan ministers, and presented to the King soon after his arrival in England, praying for a reformation in the Church.

† Strype's Life of Whitgift, Appendix No. XLV: *Letter from the Bishop of Durham to the Archbishop of York, giving an account of the Hampton Court Conference.*

not allow the session to close without assuring the bishops that "howsoever he lived among Puritans, and was kept for the most part as a ward under them ; yet, since he was of the age of his son, ten years old, he ever disliked their opinions. As the Saviour of the world said, ' Though he lived among them, he was not of them.' "*

On Monday, the second day of the Conference, the Puritan ministers were called into the council chamber (the Bishops of London and Winchester being there already), and after them all the deans and doctors present which had been summoned. On this occasion, in the words of the Bishop of Durham,† his highness used more short and round speech." For five hours these learned and virtuous men (one of them, Dr. Reynolds, a distinguished Professor in the University of Oxford), were obliged to submit to a brow-beating from the king and prelates, which reflects deep disgrace on the cause that could need or use such weapons.

Mr. Knewstubbs having taken exceptions to the cross in baptism, on account of the offence to weak brethren, the King replied :‡ "How long will such brethren be weak ? Are not forty-five years sufficient for them to grow strong in ? Besides, who pretends this weakness ? We require not subscription of laics and idiots, but of preachers and ministers, who are not still, I trow, to be fed with milk, being enabled to feed others. Some of them are strong enough, if not headstrong ; conceiving themselves able to teach who last spake for them, and all the bishops in the land."

To the further inquiry of Mr. Knewstubbs, whether the Church were competent thus to add to the ordinance of Christ, and how far her authority is binding in such cases, his Majesty answered with great warmth : " I will not argue that point with you, but answer as kings in parliament, *Le roi s' avisera*. This is like Mr. John Black, a beardless boy, who told me the last Conference in Scotland that he would hold conformity with his Majesty in matters of doctrine, but every man for ceremonies was to be left to his own liberty. But I will have none of that. I will have one doctrine and one discipline, one religion in substance and in ceremony. And, therefore, I charge you never speak more to that point, how much you are bound to obey, when the Church hath ordained it."§

Dr. Reynolds objected to the apocryphal books, instancing, among other errors, *Ecclesiasticus* xlviii., 10. On this his Majesty said,‖ " with a pleasant apostrophe to the Lords : What, trow ye, makes these men

---

* Barlow's account of the first session of the Conference, closing paragraph.
† Letter, &c., as just quoted. ‡ Fuller, Ch. Hist. vol. iii., p. 186.
§ Barlow, p. 70. ‖ Barlow, p. 62.

so angry with *Ecclesiasticus?* By my soul I think he was a bishop, or else they would never use him so!"

Upon a proposition by Dr. Reynolds that the inferior country clergy might be permitted to meet together at stated times for the discussion of theological subjects,* James broke forth: "If you aim at a Scottish Presbytery, it agreeth as well with monarchy as God and the devil. Then Jack, and Tom, and Will, and Dick, shall meet and censure me and my council. Therefore, I say again, *Le roi s'avisera*. Stay, I pray you, one seven years, and then if you find me grow pursy and fat, I may perchance hearken unto you: for that government will keep me in breath and give me work enough." He then put the question to Dr. Reynolds, whether he knew of any "*who liked the present government ecclesiastical and disliked his supremacy?*" On his answering that he knew of none such, the King proceeded to relate his own and his mother's experience with the Scotch reformers, who cried up the supremacy of the monarch till the Popish bishops were put down, and then, "being illuminated with more light," as they professed, took in hand the supremacy also.† Then touching his hat to the bishops, he added :‡ "My Lords the Bishops, I may thank you that these men do thus plead for my supremacy. They think they cannot make their party good against you but by appealing unto it, as if you, or some that adhere unto you, were not well affected toward it. But if once you were out and they in place, I know what would become of my supremacy. No Bishop, no King, as I before said. Neither do I thus speak at random, without ground; for I have observed since my coming into England that some preachers before me can be content to pray for James, King of England, Scotland, France and Ireland, Defender of the Faith; but as for Supreme Governor in all cases and over all persons (as well ecclesiastical as civil), they pass that over with silence; and what cut they have been of I after learned." Then having asked if they had anything more to say, and being answered in the negative, the King rose from his

---

* Similar exercises under the name of prophesyings had been established by Grindal when Bishop of London, with a view to promote among the clergy of his diocese the spirit of preaching, which had almost died out in the Church. They were peremptorily suppressed by Elizabeth as savoring too much of the New Discipline, and Grindal's revival of them, as Archbishop, cost him the forfeiture of the royal favor, suspension from his office and banishment from Court, which harsh treatment broke the old man's heart. Freedom of thought was discouraged, no less among the inferior clergy than among the laity.—See Strype's Life of Archb. Grindal, Append. No. X. "*The Queen to the Bishops throughout England for the suppression of the exercise called Prophesying, &c.*"

† Fuller, vol. iii., p. 188.   ‡ Barlow, p. 82.

chair, saying as he passed to his inner chamber :* "If this be all they have to say, I will make them conform themselves, or I will harry them out of the land, or else do worse."

On the third and last day of the Conference, Wednesday, January 18, the Archbishop and other church dignitaries were present, together with many knights, civilians and doctors of the law. But the Puritan ministers were not admitted to any share in the discussion, being merely called in at the close of the meeting, to hear what had been decided. At this session the abuses of the High Commission were the chief subject of consideration. One of the Lords present affirmed that the proceedings in that court were like the Spanish Inquisition ; where men are urged to subscribe more than the law requireth ; and by the oath *ex officio*, forced to accuse themselves, being examined upon twenty or twenty-four articles on a sudden without deliberation, and for the most part against themselves." But the King defended the practice in a long speech, so entirely satisfactory to the prelates that the Archbishop of Canterbury, in a rapture of admiration exclaimed : ' Undoubtedly your Majesty speaks by the special assistance of God's spirit !" To this Bancroft, the Bishop of London, added, kneeling : I protest, my heart melteth with joy that Almighty God, of his singular mercy, hath given us such a King as since Christ's time, the like has not been !"†

This question and others proposed to the Conference having been settled, the four Puritan preachers were called in to hear the trifling alterations proposed to be made in the Liturgy. They ventured to beg for some little leniency and forbearance toward certain godly ministers in Lancashire, whose conscience did not allow them to conform in all particulars to the Church. To this application the King at first answered that it was not his intention, and he presumed it was not the bishops', presently and out of hand to enforce these things without fatherly admonitions, conferences, and persuasions" ; that he wished there might be inquiry made whether these ministers had converted any from popery, and were, withal, of blameless characters ; and if so, that the Lord Archbishop would write letters directing some favor to be shown them." But Bancroft promptly interposed with the suggestion that if such letters were granted, copies of them would fly all over England ; and then all nonconformists would beg for the same indulgence, and so no fruit would follow from the Conference, but things be worse than before. He desired, therefore, that a time might be limited within which they should be required to con-

---

* Barlow, p. 83.   † Fuller, Ch. Hist., vol. iii., p. 190.

form. To this his Majesty assented, and suggested that each bishop should see that it was done within his own diocese. At this point Mr. Knewstubbs, falling on his knees, prayed for the like forbearance to some honest ministers in Suffolk. But the King had now got his cue, and interrupting the Archbishop who was about to speak, he proceeded : "'Let me alone to answer him. Sir, you show yourself an uncharitable man. We have here taken pains, and in the end, have concluded on unity and uniformity ; and you, forsooth, must prefer the credit of a few private men before the peace of the Church. This is just the Scotch argument when anything was concluded which disliked some humors. Let them conform themselves shortly, or they shall hear of it.'"*

After a few more words the King, rising, dismissed the Conference. As he was leaving the council chamber the Bishop of London followed him with the benediction : " God's goodness be blessed for your Majesty, and give health and prosperity to your Highness, your gracious Queen, the young Prince, and all the royal issue !''

Thus closed the Conference of Hampton Court. On the day following, the royal Moderator thus described it in a letter to a confidential friend in Scotland, whom he addresses as " My honest Blake !"†

"We have kept such a revel with the Puritans here these two days as was never heard the like ; where I have peppered them as soundly as ye have done the papists there. It were no reason that those that will refuse the airy sign of the cross after baptism, should have their purses stuffed with any more solid and substantial crosses.‡ They fled me so from argument to argument, without ever answering me directly, *ut est eorum moris*, as I was forced at last to say unto them : That if any of them had been in a college disputing with their scholars, if any of their disciples had answered them in that sort, they would have fetched him up, in place of a reply ; and so should the rod—[here the royal pleasantry descends below ' the dignity of history.'] I have such a book of theirs as may well convert infidels ; but it shall never convert me, except by turning me more earnestly against them.

And thus, praying you to commend me to the honest Chamberlain, I bid you heartily farewell. JAMES R."

There can now be no room for doubt respecting the prime object and the *animus* of this memorable convention. The establishment of Episcopacy as the form of Church government most favorable to

---

* Fuller, vol. iii., p. 192.
† The whole letter, a curious if not very dignified specimen of royal literature, is contained in Strype's Life of Archbishop Whitgift, Appendix, No. XLVI.
‡ Coins stamped with the sign of the cross.

royal supremacy, and the extinction of Puritanism, as tending in the opposite direction, are written legibly in all its proceedings.

How then is the fact to be explained that in regard to one point of vital interest the wishes of the Puritan ministers received the prompt concurrence of the King, and that manifestly against the wishes of their opponents ; and that the realization of the measure thus inauspiciously commended to his notice became one of the chief objects of his royal care for several succeeding years, and the leading historical event of his reign ? This was the subject brought forward by Dr. Reynolds, at the second session of the Conference, of a NEW TRANSLATION OF THE SCRIPTURES. A careful attention to the circumstances of the case easily solves the problem.

This scene in the Conference is thus described by Barlow :*

"After that, he (Dr. Reynolds,) moved his Majesty that there might be a new translation of the Bible ; because those which were allowed in the reigns of Henry the Eighth and Edward the Sixth were corrupt and not answerable to the original. To which motion there was at the present no gainsaying, the objections† being trivial and old and already in print, often answered ; only my Lord of London well added, that if every man's humor should be followed, there would be no end of translating. Whereupon his Highness wished that some special pains should be taken in that behalf, for one uniform translation, (professing that he had never yet seen a good translation into English, but the worst of all he thought the Genevan to be), and this to be done by the best learned in both Universities ; after them to be reviewed by the bishops and the chief learned of the Church ; from them to be presented to the Privy Council ; and lastly to be ratified by his royal authority ; and so this whole Church to be bound unto it and no other. Marry, withal, he gave this caveat (upon a word cast out by my Lord of London), that no marginal notes should be added, having found in those annexed to the Genevan translation (which he saw in a Bible given him by an English lady), some notes very partial, untrue, seditions, and savoring too much of dangerous and traitorous conceits. As when from Exodus i., 19, disobedience to Kings is allowed in a marginal note ; and 2 Chron. xv., 16, King Asa is taxed in the note for only deposing his mother and not killing her. And so concluded this point, as all the rest, with a grave and judicious advice—First, that errors in matters of faith might be rectified and amended ; Secondly, that matters indifferent might rather be interpreted and a gloss added ; alleging from *Bartolus de regno* that, as better a King with some weakness than still a change, so rather a Church with some faults than an innovation."

It cannot escape the reader of this account that Bancroft's insolent

---

* Sum and Substance of the Conference, &c., p. 45. Comp. Fuller, Ch. Hist. Vol. iii., p. 182.

† Namely, to these versions, of the reigns of Henry VIII. and Edward VI. Dr. R. of course referred to a version for public use in the Churches. The one still in use was Cranmer's "authorized version," in the unsatisfactory revision of it by the bishops.

remark, thrust in with characteristic forwardness before the King had spoken, was a decided mistake. His Majesty's answer is based on a view quite different from that which had governed the policy of the Primate and his Lieutenant, the last twenty years ; while the sketch it contains of a specific plan for the execution of the proposed work looks much like the result of deliberate consideration and a previously settled purpose. The probability that such may have been the case will appear from a few facts.

The subject of an improved translation of the Scriptures was by no means a novel one. For many years before the death of Elizabeth, the question was frequently agitated of a thorough revision of the Church Bible which should bring it up in critical accuracy to the demands of the age. Hugh Broughton, the profoundest Biblical scholar of the time in England, and probably excelled by none elsewhere, wished to devote his own attainments to the task, and urged its claims with more enthusiasm than prudence on the great men both in Church and State. In 1595, he published a translation of a part of the Old Testament, with short explanatory notes, as a specimen of his proposed work, hoping thereby to secure the countenance and pecuniary aid necessary to its completion. Of this he sent a copy to Lord Burleigh, with a letter stating his plan and soliciting his lordship to be "chiefest in contribution toward the charge, which would be exceeding great." In another letter to the same distinguished person, he mentions that "sundry Lords, and among them some bishops, and others inferior of all sorts, had expressed the wish that his long studies in Hebrew and Greek might be bestowed on the improvement of the Bible's Translation. That they judged rightly that amended it must be. In what points, he thought it not good largely to tell in words till it were performed in work ; lest the Bible then in use be brought into unnecessary disgrace ; but that all persons of knowledge and conscience would grant that bettered much it might be." He reminds the Lord Treasurer that this subject had been presented to his notice two years before ; and that "her Majesty at that time sent word and message to Sir Francis Walsingham that it must be considered, which his Honor had intended to do, but was hindered by affairs of State." He then proposes that six of the most learned linguists, to be sustained by voluntary contributions, be employed in executing the work ; whose object shall be, on the one hand, not to alter where the translation is already well done ; and on the other, to spare nothing that carried open untruth against history and religion, or darkness, disannulling the writers. In which kind, Job and the Prophets might be brought to speak far better unto us."

But all his hopes were frustrated by the opposition of Whitgift and Bancroft, who disliked the man, and dreaded the inexorable honesty of his principles of translation. Their avowed objections to his plan were indeed of the most pious character, and seemed dictated by a holy zeal for the interests of truth. "They feared," says Strype, "that hereby an occasion might be given to the enemies of our religion, the Papists, of discrediting our common English Bible and the doctrines that were founded on it, and weaken the reputation of that former translation then used in the churches." Broughton, who despised their hollow cant, and was as hot-tempered as he was learned, denounced their cherished version as a disgrace to English scholarship; and charged their pretended reverence for it on their unwillingness "to lose their traps and pitfalls." This discouragement did not, however, cause him to remit his efforts for this great object; for in a letter to Lord Burleigh in 1596, he speaks of "having written to all the realm for the true Bible"; and he prays his Lordship to advise the Archbishop, whose opposition seems to have been generally recognized as the sole hindrance to the work, "to take heed lest he bring the realm to eternal shame in a matter the highest for religion." *

We see, from the foregoing, that the subject of a new version of the Scriptures was one familiar to English scholars, many years before it was proposed by Dr. Reynolds in the Hampton Court Conference; and that not a few churchmen as well as others acknowledged the absolute necessity of the work. How indeed could it be otherwise, with the fact staring them in the face that the common people were daily reading in their homes a version every way superior to that which was read to them 'by authority,' on Sundays in the churches? The comparison thus constantly forced on the popular mind, and converted by the warfare between Prelacy and Puritanism into a matter

---

* For the facts in this account of Broughton's efforts for a new translation, see Strype's Life of Whitgift, pp. 382, 432, 485, 489, 585, and elsewhere.

Broughton was one of those unfortunate geniuses who, with fine qualities and high aims in life, seem born to mar their own fortunes and ruin every cause they seek to promote through inability to govern their tempers and tongues. His resentment for affronts and injuries was invariably expressed in a way to help his enemy and hurt himself. Whatever might be the consequence, he could never deny himself the pleasure of using his sting; and every real or fancied wrong was proclaimed to the public with a heat and violence which gave his persecutors the advantage of seeming to be the injured party. His life was a series of cruel disappointments; and in most of them he had himself furnished his more crafty foes with the weapons by which they foiled him. So necessary in this world are prudence and temper, as well as merit and honesty!

of lively practical interest, could not have failed to become a fruitful source of discussion among all classes, greatly to the disadvantage of the State Church.

Now James, with all his mean and ridiculous traits of character, possessed an extraordinary amount of shrewdness in regard to everything which concerned his regal interests ; a faculty which he dignified with the name of KINGCRAFT, and exulted in as his peculiar gift and glory. With his eye fixed on the one object of confirming and extending the supremacy, he had in the course of his long reign attained no little royal expertness in detecting the bearings of whatever was passing in his dominions on this central point of interest. We have already observed, in his remarks on the prayers of the Puritan clergy, the keenness of his scent when on the track of popular tendencies. Can we doubt, then, that a subject so important in its relations, and so commonly agitated, as a new translation of the Bible, had been already subjected in the royal mind to the touchstone of prerogative ? As little does his speech in the Conference allow us to doubt that his sagacity had discerned what Whitgift and Bancroft had failed to see ; namely, that the demand of the age must be directed, not resisted ; converted if possible into an instrument of absolutism, not suffered to become an instrument of subverting it. Sent out with a *prestige* of scholarship which should silence the reproachful clamors of the Puritans and eclipse their favorite Presbyterian version, yet charged with conservative influences, and linked indissolubly with the Church and the Throne, the new version promised to become the chief agent in maintaining the established order. And hence it was, that though this measure was suggested by the obnoxious party he was resolved to crush, and was evidently relied on by the nonconformist leaders for the promotion of the New Discipline,* it was qietly appropriated by James and used for his own purposes.

* Their plan was both sagacious and liberal. While desiring to deprive Prelacy of the advantages which it derived from the Bishops' Bible, they did not ask that it might be superseded by the Genevan, though confessedly superior ; but, on the ground of its acknowledged corruptions and imperfections, prayed for a new translation, firmly believing that if executed on the principles of true criticism, it could not fail to sustain what they held as truth.

CHAPTER XXX.

THE COMMON VERSION—CONTINUED.

How strong a hold the project of a new version had taken of the mind of James, and how well he had considered the means for making it answerable to his ends, appears from the measures which he immediately adopted for carrying it into execution. Taking the matter into his own hands, he set on foot the necessary preliminaries without delay, and on a scale surpassing all that had been witnessed in England in connection with Bible translation. Bancroft, now fully won over to the King's policy, and appointed general overseer and final reviser of the work, pushed it forward with characteristic vigor and efficiency. Before the end of July fifty-four scholars had been selected as translators, and arranged into six companies, two of which were to meet at Westminster, and two at each of the universities. The heads of the universities were directed, moreover, to add to the number such others as they might deem qualified; and the bishops were exhorted to spare no pains for securing the suggestions and criticisms of the best scholars in their respective dioceses; " that so," in his Majesty's words, " our said intended translation may have the help and furtherance of all our principal learned men within this, our kingdom."

The maintenance and remuneration of the translators was the King's next care. The following letter, written by him to the Bishop of London, exhibits his plan for this object.*

"Right trusty and well-beloved, we greet you well. Whereas, we have appointed certain learned men, to the number of fifty-four, for the translating of the Bible, and that in this number divers of them have either no ecclesiastical preferment at all, or else so very small as the same is far unmeet for men of their deserts; and yet we of ourself, in any convenient time cannot well remedy it. Therefore we do heartily require you that presently you write, in our name, as well to the Archbishop of York as to the rest of the bishops of the province of Canterbury,† signifying unto them that we do will, and straitly charge every one

---

* From *Regist. III. Whitgift.* Copied from Wilkins' Concilia Magnæ Britan. et Hibern, vol. iv., p. 407 (Harvard Univ. library); also in Strype's Life of Whitgift, p. 950.

† Archbishop Whitgift had died in the preceding February, only a few weeks

of them, as also the other bishops of the province of York, as they tender our good favor toward them, that (all excuses set apart) when a prebend or parsonage being rated in our book of taxations, the prebend at twenty pound at the least,* and the parsonage to the like sum and upward, shall next upon any occasion happen to be void, and to be either of their patronage and gift, or the like parsonage so void to be of the patronage and gift of any person whatsoever ; they do make stay thereof, and admit none unto it until certifying us of the avoidance of it, and of the name of the patron, (if it be not of their own gift), we may commend for the same some such of the learned men as we shall think fit to be preferred unto it : not doubting of the bishops' readiness to satisfy us herein, or that any of the laity, when we shall in time move them to so good and religious an act, will be unwilling to give us the like due contentment and satisfaction : We ourselves having taken the same order for such prebends and benefices as shall be void in our gift.

"While We write to you of others, you must apply it to yourself; as also not to forget to move the said Archbishop, and all Bishops, with their Deans and Chapters, as touching the other point to be imparted otherwise by you unto them." [Then follows the direction referred to above for securing the voluntary criticisms of the learned clergy of each diocese.] " Given under Our Signet at Our Palace of Westminister, the 22d of July, in the second year of our reign of England, France, and Ireland, and of Scotland, xxxvii."

This letter the Bishop of London communicated to each of his brethren, as directed, accompanied by one from himself, dated July 31st, urging upon their attention " how careful his Majesty is for the providing of livings for those learned men." " I doubt not," he adds, " that your Lordship will have a due regard of his Majesty's request herein, as it is fit and meet ; and that you will take such orders, both with your chancellor, register, and such of your Lordship's officers who shall have intelligence of the premises, as also with the dean and chapter of your cathedral church, whom his Majesty likewise requireth to be put in mind of his pleasure herein ; not forgetting the latter part of his Majesty's letter, touching the informing of yourself of the fittest linguists in your diocese, for to perform, and speedily to return, that which his Majesty is so careful to have faithfully performed."†

---

after the Hampton Court Conference. His apprehension that the Puritan influence in the coming Parliament might undo what had been so satisfactorily settled in the Conference is supposed to have hastened his death. So well aware was he that the measures there carried through, with so high a hand, were in opposition to the wishes of the most substantial part of the nation !

* This, it will be recollected, would be equal to many times the same sum at the present time. Thus Fuller (vol. iii., p. 220) mentions, as an instance of Archbishop Hutton's munificence, that " he founded a hospital in the north and endowed it with a yearly revenue of thirty-five pounds."

† Wilkins and Strype, as quoted above.

To this letter was added a postscript explaining " *that other point* " in his Majesty's letter, which, being a matter of delicacy, seems to have been committed orally to Bancroft to be by him made known confidentially to the other prelates. It was, in substance, this : That the immediate support of such of the translators as were without livings, required a considerable sum to be raised without delay, " which his Majesty of his most princely disposition, was ready to have borne ; but that some of the Lords (as things then went) held it inconvenient."* A contribution for this object was therefore requested of the clergy, in his Majesty's name ; and as a stimulus to their zeal, the bishop mentioned that he was directed " to acquaint his Majesty with every man's liberality toward this godly work."

The following letter from Chancellor Cecil to the Vice-chancellor and heads of the University of Cambridge, bearing the same date as that of the King to Bancroft, suggests still another method of meeting this necessity, in order, as it seems, that the work might be taken in hand without delay :†

" After my very hearty commendations—Whereas his Majesty hath appointed certain learned men, in and of your university, to take pains in translating some portions of the Scripture, according to an order in that behalf set down (the copy whereof remaineth with Mr. Lively, your Hebrew lecturer) his pleasure and commandment is, that you should take such care of that work, as that if you can remember any fit men to join with the rest therein, you should in his name assign them thereunto ; and that such as are to be called out of the country may be entertained in such colleges as they shall make choice of, without any charge unto them either for their entrance, their chamber, or their commons, except it happen that any do make choice to remain in any of the poorer colleges that are not well able to bear that charge, and there such order will be taken by the Lord Bishop of London as that the same shall be defrayed. His Majesty expecteth that you should further the business as much as you can, as well by kind usage of the parties that take pains therein, as by any other means that you can best devise ;

* The royal finances were in a desperate condition, the officers of the household being driven to their wit's end to obtain either money or credit for his Majesty's weekly expenses. His persevering energy in pushing forward the new version under these embarrassments, is all the more worthy of notice. In 1607 the King thus speaks, in a letter to the Lords, respecting the better improving his revenue—" My Lords : The only disease and consumption which I can ever apprehend as likeliest to endanger me, is this eating canker of want ; which being removed, I could think myself as happy in all other respects as any other king or monarch that ever was since the birth of Christ. In this disease, I am the patient ; and ye have promised to be the physicians, to use the best care upon me that your wit, faithfulness, and diligence can reach unto."—Strype's Annals, Appendix, No. 297.

† Lewis' Hist. of Trans. of Bible, p. 313 (from the original in the Archives of Cambridge Univ.)

taking such order that they may be freed in the meanwhile from all lectures and exercises to be supplied for them by your grave directions ; and assuring them that he will hereafter have such princely care, as well by himself as by his bishops at his commandment, for the preferring of every one of them, as their diligence and due respect to his Majesty's desire in this so worthy an employment, shall (he doubteth not) very well deserve."

Under the same date as his letter to the bishops, Bancroft wrote to the Cambridge translators, informing them :*

"That his Majesty being made acquainted with the choice of all them to be employed in the translating of the Bible in such sort as Mr. Lively could inform them, did greatly approve of the said choice. And forasmuch as his Highness was very desirous that the same so religious a work should admit no delay, he had commanded him to signify unto them, in his name, that his pleasure was they should, with all possible speed, meet together in their university and begin the same ; that his Majesty's care for their better continuance together they might perceive by their Right Honorable Chancellor's letter to the Vice-chancellor and heads, but more especially by the copy of a letter written to himself for order to be taken with all the bishops of this realm in their behalf, which copy he had herewith sent them ; that he had desired Mr. Vice-chancellor to send to such of them as were not now present in Cambridge to will them in his Majesty's name that, all other occasions and business set aside, they made their present repair unto them that were at Cambridge. Upon whose coming, and after they had prepared themselves for this business, his Lordship prayed they would write presently unto him, that he might inform his Majesty thereof, who could not be satisfied till it was in hand. Since, he was persuaded, his royal mind rejoiced more in the good hope which he had for the happy success of that work than of his peace concluded with Spain."

His Lordship's letter to the Vice-chancellor, referred to above, is as follows :†

"After my very hearty commendations : Being acquainted with a letter lately written unto you in his Majesty's name by your right honorable Chancellor, and having myself received sundry directions from his Highness for the better setting forward of his most royal designment for translating the Bible, I do accordingly move you, that in his Majesty's name, agreeably to the charge and trust committed unto you, no time may be overslipped by you for the better furtherance of this holy work. The parties' names who are appointed to be employed therein Mr. Lively can show you ; of which number I desire you by him to take notice, and to write to such of them as are abroad, in his Majesty's name, (for so far my commission extendeth), that all excuses set aside, they do presently come to Cambridge, there to address themselves forthwith to this business. I am bold to trouble you herewith, because you know better who are absent, where they are, and how to send unto them than I do. And were it only, I suppose, to ease me of that pains, being myself not idle in the meantime, I am persuaded I might obtain at your hands as great a favor. You will scarcely conceive how earnest his

* Lewis, p. 314. † Ibid., p. 815.

Majesty is to have this work begun ; and therefore I doubt not you will, for your parts, in anything that is within your compass, as well in this moved now unto you, as for their entertainment when they come and better encouragement, set forward the same. And so, being always ready to assist you, if any difficulties do arise in the progress of this business, I commit you unto the tuition of Almighty God."

With this letter was likewise sent a copy of the KING'S INSTRUCTIONS TO THE TRANSLATORS, being a complete set of Rules devised and ordained by his Majesty for their guidance in the preparation of the work. As a statement both of the methods and the principles on which our Common Version was executed, they are worthy of the reader's most attentive consideration. They were as follows :*

1. The ordinary Bible read in the church, commonly called the Bishops' Bible, to be followed and as little altered as the original will permit.

2. The names of the prophets and the holy writers, with the other names in the text, to be retained as near as may be accordingly as they are vulgarly used.

3. The ecclesiastical words to be kept, namely, as the word *church* not to be translated *congregation*, etc.

4. When any word hath divers significations, that to be kept which hath been most commonly used by the most eminent Fathers, being agreeable to the propriety of the place and the analogy of faith.

5. The division of the chapters to be altered either not at all, or as little as may be, if necessity so require.

6. No marginal notes at all to be affixed, but only for the explanation of the Hebrew or Greek words, which cannot, without some circumlocution, so briefly and fitly be expressed in the text.

7. Such quotations of places to be marginally set down as shall serve for the fit references of one Scripture to another.

8. Every particular man of each company to take the same chapter or chapters and, having translated or amended them severally by himself where he thinks good, all to meet together, confer what they have done, and agree for their part what shall stand.

9. As any one company hath dispatched any one book in this manner, they shall send it to the rest to be considered of seriously and judiciously ; for his Majesty is very careful in this point.

10. If any company, upon the review of the book so sent, shall doubt or differ upon any places, to send them word thereof, note the places, and therewithal send their reasons ; to which, if they consent not, the difference to be compounded at the general meeting, which is to be of the chief persons of each company, at the end of the work.

11. When any place of special obscurity is doubted of, letters to be directed by authority, to send to any learned in the land for his judgment in such a place.

12. Letters to be sent from every bishop to the rest of his clergy, admonishing them of this translation in hand, and to move and charge as many as, being skillful in the tongues, have taken pains in that kind, to send his particular observations to the company, either at Westminster, Cambridge, or Oxford.

* Fuller's Ch. Hist., Book X., Sect. iii., 2.

13. The directors in each company to be the Deans of Westminster and Chester for that place, and the King's Professors in the Hebrew and Greek in each University.

14. These translations to be used when they agree better with the text than the Bishops' Bible; namely, Tyndale's, Matthew's, Coverdale's, Whitchurch's [Cranmer's], the Genevan.

Of the fifty-four appointed translators, only forty-seven actually engaged in the work. Among these it was apportioned in the following manner:

Of the three companies to whom was committed the Old Testament, the first—ten in number—met at Westminster, under the direction of Dr. Launcelot Andrews, Dean of Westminster. To them was assigned the Pentateuch and other historical books, as far as the end of 2d Kings.

The second—eight in number—with Edward Lively, regius Professor of Hebrew at Cambridge as President, met at that university. They had for their portion from the first of Chronicles to the end of Ecclesiastes.

The third met at Oxford, under Dr. John Harding, President of Magdalen College, and Professor of Hebrew. They took the remainder of the Old Testament, from Isaiah to Malachi.

Of the two companies on the New Testament, the first—consisting of eight translators—met at Oxford, under Dr. Thomas Ravis, Dean of Christ's Church. Their portion was the four Gospels, the Acts of the Apostles, and the Apocalypse.

To the second—seven in number—who met at Westminster, under Dr. Wm. Barlow, Dean of Chester, were assigned the Epistles.

The remaining company assembled at Cambridge under Dr. Dupont, Prebend of Ely, and Master of Jesus' College, consisted of seven scholars, devoted exclusively to the Apocrypha.

A disagreement having arisen among the Cambridge translators in regard to the application of the *third* and *fourth* rules, his Majesty, being informed of the same through the Bishop of London, added a new feature to the arrangements, viz.: a special Board, consisting of "three or four of the most ancient and grave divines, to be assigned by the Vice-Chancellor, upon conference with the rest of the heads, to be Overseers of the Translation, as well Hebrew as Greek, for the better observation of the rules appointed by his Highness, and especially concerning the third and fourth rules."*

---

* Lewis, p. 319.—In these rules and regulations, we find a sufficient explanation of the exclusion of Hugh Broughton from the list of translators. He would never have subjected his scholarship to such restraints, or yielded to the arbitrary

The exact time when the translation was commenced has not been ascertained. It has been currently supposed that the death, in May, 1605, of Edward Lively, the most distinguished Hebraist connected with the work, delayed even its commencement till considerably after that time. But it seems to be pretty clearly settled that the first revision was finished some time in 1607; and from a remark in the Preface, it appears that this had occupied not less than three years, which carries the beginning of their work back to 1604.

Their method of proceeding, in accordance with the King's directions, was as follows. The members of a company all took the same portion, which each first revised by himself; then all met together to make up a copy on which they could agree. The part thus completed was then submitted to the other companies for their criticisms; and if these were approved by the first revisers, they were adopted as permanent; if otherwise, they were reserved for the judgment of the final revisers.

The whole version being completed in this manner, three copies were made of it (one at each place) and delivered to a committee of twelve—six of whom were chosen by the translators from their own number—two from each company— and six, it is supposed, were selected by the King, according to his first intention, from his bishops and other learned ecclesiastics not previously connected with the translation.*

The work having received this second revision, passed into the hands of Bilson, Bishop of Winchester, and Dr Miles Smith (soon after made Bishop of Gloucester)†, who again revised the whole, and prefixed arguments to the several books. By the King's direction Dr. Smith also wrote a Preface for the work, which is chiefly occupied with a defence of its design and character against various classes of opposers.

---

decisions of men confessedly far inferior to him in learning. Strype tells us— Life of Whitgift, p. 589—that in the selection of translators, such were avoided "as should affect many alterations, and different readings from the former version, more than needed. Of which sort," he adds, "was the great linguist Mr. Broughton, whose mind the Archbishop knew full well, having divers years before condemned that translation, charging it with a great number of errors undeservedly, and treated very rudely those grave and learned bishops that were employed in it, as though they had translated from the Latin, and wanted sufficient skill."

* Introd. to Bagster's English Hexapla, p. 108.

† Next to Bancroft, Bilson had made himself conspicuous among the prelates of the Hampton Court Conference, in opposition to the Puritans. Dr. Smith's sentiments toward them are sufficiently manifest in the tone of his Preface, and in his speedy promotion to the Bench of Bishops.

Finally, the Bishop of London received it in charge, and bestowed such finishing touches as were yet needed to fit it for its destined position.

It was at length published in 1611, with a dedication to the King, in which flattery was carried to its culminating point. The title page proclaimed that it had been executed "by his Majesty's special commandment," and that it was "appointed to be read in churches."*

Thus have we traced the origin of our common version, and the principles and method observed in its preparation. It only remains to make a few remarks in regard to the character of the version, which was the product of so singular a combination of influences.

The breadth of the King's plan, as compared with that of Archbishop Parker, is worthy of special notice. It was the Primate's aim to advance the cause of Episcopacy by excluding all but bishops from a share in preparing the Bible to be used in Divine service; thus placing them before the people as a distinct sacred class, their authorized teachers and directors in matters of religion. This had, no doubt, some advantages; but, on the other hand, it divided them from the sympathy of the great body of English scholars, exposed their work and their own pretensions to unsparing criticism, and gave to the claims of the Genevan version the fairest chance of recognition. The plan of James, on the other hand, opened a field for the scholarship of England. Her chief schools of learning were invited to contribute to it their choicest sons. All classes of the clergy were represented in it. Even Puritan scholarship was welcomed to a distinguished place in the noble task. Its importance and dignity were further enhanced by the King's requirement that all other literary employment—even lectures in the university—should be relinquished for the time, and that the translators should be relieved of all care for their own support; while the royal employer pledged himself to reward their labor by honorable and profitable preferment for life. Nor was this all. The co-operation of every learned man in the kingdom, by suggestions and criticisms for the use of the immediate translators, was solicited with an urgency which would give compliance the grace of a favor to the King himself. Could a method have been

---

* "No evidence, however" (says Wescott, in his History of the English Bible, pp. 157-8), "has yet been produced to show that the version was ever publicly sanctioned by Convocation or by Parliament, or by the Privy Council, or by the King. It gained its currency partly, it may have been, by the weight of the king's name, partly by the personal authority of the prelates and scholars who had been engaged upon it, but still more by its own intrinsic superiority over its rivals."

T. J. C.

more skillfully devised for enlisting in the new version the universal interest of scholars, and for turning all eyes to it as a great national work? But it was also a Protestant work. Papists alone had no part in it. And thus it appealed to all good Protestants as a recognition of their common faith, and their common detestation of the corrupt and bloody Church of Rome.

So liberal, so catholic was the enterprise, when viewed on one side. Let us now look at it from another point—the principles to be observed in its execution. The first, third, and fourth of the King's rules for the translators furnish the answer on this point. The ordinary Bible read in the Church, commonly called the Bishops' Bible, is to be followed, and as little altered as the original will permit. The principle adopted in that version in regard to ecclesiastical words, as *church* for *congregation*, is to be still binding. Words with divers significations are to be translated according to the use of the Fathers, if agreeable to the propriety of the place and the analogy of faith. In other words, the appearance of change, which might throw discredit on the authority of the Church is to be cautiously avoided; the ecclesiastical terms which subserve the present constitution of the Church are to be retained, and not translated; the translation of doubtful words is to be decided by the doctrines of the Church.

If these rules have any other meaning, it must be shown on other testimony than that of the version itself. That they contained the pith and marrow of James' design is seen also in that committee of the "most ancient and grave divines," appointed for the express object of securing conformity to the King's wishes in these particulars. It is noticeable, moreover, that the prizes held out to the translators as a stimulus to their industry and ambition, were high positions in the Church; and of course not to be secured without subscription to its doctrines and discipline. Thus the accuracy of the version was to be made subordinate to considerations of expediency; and the scholarship concentrated on it was but to give new solidity and *éclat* to an ecclesiastical system which the majority of the English nation at that very time deemed at variance with the word of God.*

---

* "The following observation will confirm," says Hallam, "what may startle some readers, that the Puritans, or at least those who rather favored them, had a majority among the Protestant gentry in the Queen's [Elizabeth's] days. It is agreed on all hands, and is quite manifest, that they predominated in the House of Commons: but that House was composed, as it has ever been, of the principal landed proprietors, and as much represented the general wish of the community, when it demanded a farther reform in religious matters, as on any other

The same object is manifest also in the succeeding measures. The next step in the original plan was to subject it to the examination of the bishops ; and this seems to have been substantially followed in the third revision by a select committee consisting of six translators, and the same number of Church dignitaries not concerned in the translation. To this succeeded a fourth, by two high-churchmen ; and finally it passed into the hands of Bancroft, now Archbishop of Canterbury—a man without scholarship, without scruples, and with no power above him but the King, whose objects in this undertaking precisely coincided with his own. But though he gave account to no man of his proceedings in this matter, yet the whole body of the translators stood before the public as endorsers of all he might please to do ; and the Puritans were made to bear involuntary witness to the divine institution of the State Church, no less than the most zealous of her sons.*

The excellencies and the defects of the version thus produced are just what we should expect from its history. King James' third and fourth rules, while they decided its character in certain important respects, on principles as arbitrary and unsound as those adopted by the Rhemish translators, affected the expression only in single points. Portions of the work reflect the highest credit on the scholarship of the time. Bedell and Reynolds, and some other of the revisers, were undoubtedly masters of all that was then known of sacred criticism ; and that they bestowed their utmost pains on the work there can be no question. But all the translators were not scholars ; and consequently, other portions fall decidedly behind some of the previous

---

subject. One would imagine, by the manner in which some express themselves, that the discontented were a small faction, who, by some unaccountable means, in despite of the government and the nation, formed a majority of all parliaments under Elizabeth and her two successors."—*Constitutional History of England*, ch. iv., Note to p. 115 (Am. edition.)

* What use was made of this power by Bancroft is unknown. He was publicly charged with having altered the version in fourteen places. Dr. Smith is said to have admitted, in answer to complaints from previous revisers, that " he was so potent, there was no resisting him."

The reader of this history will find a remarkable coincidence between the rendering of 1 Peter ii., 13 in King James' Revision, (*to the King, as supreme,*) and the language used by him at the Hampton Court Conference (p. 238). This passage was rendered in the Bishops' Bible ; *unto the King, as having the preeminence.* Among the other versions to be consulted when that of the Bishops failed, it stood thus : Tyndale, Coverdale, Cranmer and Matthew's : *unto the King, as unto the chief head ;* Genevan : *unto the King as unto the superior.* To whom do we owe it that King James' Revision was the first among English translations which recognized in words the *King's supremacy ?*

versions. Passages are mistranslated which Tyndale and Coverdale and the Genevan—some or all of them—had translated right. As a whole, moreover, the work could not but exhibit the retrogressive tendency of that rigid conservatism which had made adherence to a defective version the fundamental rule of the revision, and deviation from it the exception, only to be allowed in cases of necessity. Under this pressure, much would be left untouched which an unshackled translator, aiming only to present the most perfect reflection of the divine original, would have changed for the better; and the changes that were ventured on would often be made with a timid hand. Its imperfection is, however, to be ascribed in part to the King's haste, which did not allow sufficient time for the ripening of the work. In the opinion of the learned Genebrard, a scholar as well qualified to judge on such matters as any of that age, the labor of thirty men for thirty years would not have been too large an estimate for the thorough execution of so great a work.* But James, while he wanted the best of versions, wanted it for a specific purpose; and that purpose could not be answered even by an immaculate version thirty years ahead. His anxiety for its completion is made the basis of the following high-flown compliment in the dedication of the work:

"Of the infinite arguments of a right Christian and religious affection in your Majesty, none is more forcible to declare it to others than the vehement and perpetuated desire of accomplishing and publishing this work, which we now present unto your Majesty. For when once your Majesty, out of deep judgment, had apprehended how convenient it was that out of the Original Sacred Tongues, together with comparing of the labors, both in our own and other foreign languages, of many worthy men who went before us, there should be one more exact translation of the Holy Scriptures into the English tongue; your Majesty did never desist to urge and to excite those to whom it was commended, that the work might be hastened, and that the business might be expedited in so decent a manner as a matter of such importance might justly require."

It has been objected, also, to the method prescribed by James, that decision by *plurality of voices* is not always the safest method of reaching philological conclusions. It is obvious upon reflection, moreover, that the plan of successive sets of revisers, though at first sight promising faultless accuracy, may prove, in practice, quite the reverse. For if the work should pass from the better into the worse hands, it would be marred rather than mended by the additional labor We have no evidence that among the revisers employed by James there

---

* He reckoned the necessary cost at 200,000 crowns.

were any more faithful or competent than those who performed the first revision ; and it is at least probable that had it been given to the public as they left it, it would have stood better the test of after times. That some of them were much dissatisfied with the arbitrary handling of their labor is beyond question. Both the Dedication and the Preface contain allusions to the Puritans, hardly to be explained except on the supposition of dissatisfaction in this respect among a part of the translators. In the former, after expressing the sanguine hope " that the Church of England will reap good fruit" by means of the new Bible, the writers petition that it may receive the royal support, both against those enemies of the faith, the Papists, and against the slanders of " self-conceited brethren, who run their own ways, and give liking unto nothing but what is framed by themselves, and hammered on their anvil." In the Preface they make particular mention that they have on the one hand " avoided the scrupulosity of the Puritans, who leave the old ecclesiastical words and betake them to others ; as when they put *washing* for *baptism*, and *congregation* for *church* ; as on the other side they shunned the obscurity of the Papists in their *azymes*, *tunike*, *rational*, *holocaust*, and a number of such like, whereof their late translation is full." At the very outset of this work, it will be remembered, disagreements of this kind occasioned the appointment of an extra Board of Overseers. Dr. Gell, who stood in an intimate relation to one of the translators, Dr. Abbott (afterward so disliked by James as the mild and liberal Archbishop of Canterbury), has said of its defects : " Yet is not all the blame to be laid upon the translators ; but part of it is to be shared with them also who set them at work, who by *reasons of state* limited them (as some of them have much complained) lest they might be thought not to set forth a new translation but rather a new Bible."* And he further asserts, that " many mistranslated words and phrases *by plurality of voices* were carried into the context, and the better translation was cast into the margin."

Such was the origin and history of our Common Version. The facts thus brought to view, by dissipating the mysterious halo which more than two and a half centuries have gathered round it, may diminish the blind fondness of our regard ; but they exhibit also its indisputable claims on our intelligent affection and veneration.

It is to be remembered with gratitude, not to James but to an overruling Providence, that the objects the King had in view required no

---

* Essay toward the amendment of the last Eng. Trans. of the Bible (1659), Preface, p. 29.

perversion or obscuration of the essential doctrines of our faith. The foundation still stood sure; the wells of salvation still gushed full and free, and all who would might drink and live. Even James' conservative narrowness was made the instrument of securing to the version one feature of inestimable value. We owe it to his anxiety for the credit of the Bible already sanctioned by the Church, that the English Scriptures still speak to us of these later days in substantially the same simple, noble, glowing phraseology in which Tyndale so long before had clothed the sacred oracles for the English people. That King James' revisers could not have changed its general manner for the better is sufficiently evident from the specimens of their ability which they have furnished in single cases. Whether in this respect it can ever be essentially improved, may well be questioned. It is at least certain that the English mind, thus long accustomed to a style so in unison with the simple majesty of the inspired original, will be slow to accept of any version conceived in a totally different spirit.

Nor must we forget that this version, though the immediate product of James' selfish ambition, was no less truly the offspring of English Protestantism. It owed its existence, primarily, to that deep-voiced popular demand for the word of God, and for that word in its purity, which had been so long one of the most striking as it was the noblest exponent of Anglo-Saxon piety. He seized upon this generous public sentiment, and used it for his own ends. But none the less was its life from the hearts of the people; none the less does it bear witness to that law of progress, which had already marked the course of English history for more than two centuries with successive vernacular translations.

In the opening chapter of this volume the Bible is claimed to be the true Magna Charta of the people. This has fully appeared in the facts of the preceding history. What else awakened in the bosoms of the down-trodden English masses those aspirations after light, that consciousness of manhood, that sense of moral obligation, which inspired and sustained their long struggle with tyranny? Through all the stages of this eventful story, embracing more than two centuries, the direct influence of the Bible in raising the common mind, in imparting to it a knowledge of its rights, and a fitness for enjoying them, is attested by facts so numerous and so striking that the wonder is they should ever have been overlooked. We have seen it giving birth in the fourteenth century, to religious inquiry and spiritual freedom, and in connection with these to the spirit of civil liberty. Under Henry VIII., under Bloody Mary, what numbers were strengthened by it to endure death, and shame worse than death, rather than submit to be enslaved in soul ! In the reign of Elizabeth these influences of the Bible developed themselves still more, as the use of it was more general and unrestrained. Who were then the advocates of a spiritual worship, as opposed to that of outward rites and garb and posture ; of equality among the ministers of Christ, and of the rights of the laity as members with them of the Christian body ? Who pleaded for the rights of conscience, for free discussion, and an unrestricted press ? None other than those who held to the Bible, as supreme and sole authority in religion.

Could we trace this great principle still farther down the stream of English history, we should find that the forewarnings of Whitgift and his predecessors had something of prophetic insight. The revolution of 1642 developed what they had so much dreaded, its dangerous leaning to " a Popularity."* The inspiration of the Puritan soldier was the " Soldier's Bible."† But the great crisis of 1688, when English nonconformists held the balance of political power, revealed in it a still nobler element. Then were seen Presbyterians, Independents, Quakers and Baptists, at the price of their own immediate freedom, emolument, and honor, taking their stand side by side with their ancient oppressor in defence of the constitutional liberties of England.

The natural and complete unfolding of this principle in its relations to the state was reserved for this western continent. The miniature commonwealth which sprang into being among the snows of Plymouth was its own immediate offspring ; and its mission was fulfilled when it had taught the empire developed from that feeble germ, that religion needs no other aid from the state than the guardianship of the rights of conscience ; and that the state needs no aid from religion, except what it derives from the virtues by her implanted in the individual citizen. These truths, though not yet fully recognized by our elder kinsmen, have largely infused their spirit into the old framework of English society ; softening its hard mediæval features with the beautiful light of progress and practical freedom. Alone among the nations stand these sister lands ; deriving whatever is noble and beneficent in their institutions, from the tendencies which the English Bible has imparted to the English mind. '

---

* Their common designation of a popular form of government.
† " *The Souldier's Pocket Bible :*" London, 1643. See Appendix, No. III.

CHAPTER XXXI.

DEMAND FOR A MORE THOROUGH REVISION.

WE have already seen that there was much dissatisfaction with some of the arrangements made by King James for the execution of the revision which bears his name. The haste with which the work was urged forward, "for reasons of state," made it impossible to do full justice even to the then existing materials for a thorough revision.* It is now conceded that the work would have been improved by a more thorough comparison of the earlier English versions and a closer conformity to them.† There were also among the revisers material differences of opinion on points of translation, to which the Dedication to the King alludes, and with scant courtesy invokes the royal support against views adverse to those expressed in the revision.

Accordingly the work was not received by the generation for whom it was prepared, with the unanimity its promoters had desired. It had not yet fairly established itself as the Bible for general use when measures were adopted for a new revision of the Scriptures. An order for this purpose was introduced in the Long Parliament in 1652, and again in 1656, and was made the subject of long and grave deliberation by a special committee of the House of Commons.‡ In 1659 Robert Gell published an "Essay toward the Amendment of the last English Translation of the Bible." But owing to the political agitations of the time, the design failed of execution. And from the restoration of the Stuarts to the first quarter of the reign of George III., a period of about one hundred and twenty years, the minds of men were so entirely occupied by great political events, or with purely secular and controversial literature that little attention was

---

* "Your Majesty did never desist to urge and excite those to whom it was committed, that the work might be hastened." *Dedication to the King.*

† With regard to the 14th rule ordained for the guidance of King James' revisers, Bishop Ellicott says in his treatise on "Revision of the New Testament," pp. 80-1 : "The rule was good, but it may be said generally that it was not very carefully followed, except perhaps in the case of the Genevan Version. Had they followed it more closely, they would have removed several errors which they left remaining, and have avoided some which they introduced."

‡ Journal of the House of Commons ; and Whitelocke's Memorials of the English Affairs. London, 1732, (Harvard University Library).

given to Biblical learning. King James' revision gradually came into general use, and although for nearly half a century the Genevan version competed with it in the esteem of Puritan readers, it ultimately became the Bible of the English-speaking race.*

But notwithstanding its universally acknowledged excellence, and its general fidelity to revealed truth, the Common Version has not held its place without remonstrance. It is not too much to say, that for more than two hundred years English scholars have had one Bible and the common people another. This has not been wholly the fault of the learned, though it must be admitted that the natural conservatism of true learning has had much to do with it.

In the last quarter of the eighteenth century renewed interest in the work of Bible revision was shown by individual scholars. In 1778 Bishop Lowth published his metrical translation of Isaiah. His notes are valuable, and the translation elegant, but the liberties he took with the Hebrew text make it worthless as a revision. A little later, Gilbert Wakefield, a distinguished English theologian, a Dissenter, brought out translations of parts of the New Testament, and in 1791 the whole of the New Testament with notes. Dr. George Campbell, President of Marischal College, Aberdeen, published "The Four Gospels, with Dissertations and Notes" toward the close of the eighteenth century. His preliminary dissertations and his notes are still useful; but his style of translation did not commend the proposal for a new revision. In 1785-8, Archbishop Newcome published his "New Critical Version of the Twelve Minor Prophets and Ezekiel;" in 1792 "An Historical View of English Bible Translation;" and in 1796 "An Attempt toward Revising our English Translation of the Greek Scriptures." These works were of value in their time; but no great progress had then been made in Biblical scholarship, and the translations are inferior in style to that of the Common Version.

Since the beginning of the present century, however, the advance in all branches of learning has been very great, and the facilities for undertaking the work of revision are now abundant. There is little probability, indeed, of much addition to them for a long time to come.

The modern era of textual criticism, commencing with the labors of Mill (*Greek Testament*, 1707), continued by Bengel (*Greek Testament*, 1734), and by Griesbach (*Greek Testament*, 1775-1806, the first

---

* It is an interesting fact that many copies of the Genevan Version were brought to New England by the Puritans—one of which, a precious heirloom, is now in the possession of the Rev. E. Kempshall, DD., of Elizabeth, N. J.

strictly critical Greek text), has culminated in the labors of Tischendorf and Tregelles in our own day. The Greek text of the New Testament, as known in the time of King James, was derived from a small number of Greek manuscripts of very modern date, which would now be regarded as of little weight in determining the true text of the sacred writers. Those now known, early and late, number little less than two thousand. The oldest Greek manuscript of the New Testament in England, the Alexandrine MS., was brought there in 1628. Only two ancient manuscripts, the Cambridge MS. of the Gospels and Acts, and the Claremont MS. of Paul's Epistles, were then known to Christian scholars, and these had not been critically examined. The celebrated Vatican manuscript, probably the oldest of the New Testament in existence, was not then accessible ; and the Sinaitic manuscript, nearly as old, has been discovered within a few years. The important Ephraem manuscript has but recently been fully brought to light, and was wholly unknown in the time of King James. Other ancient manuscripts of the New Testament, or of portions of it, have recently been added to them, till the whole number, including parts of manuscripts, amount to nearly a hundred.

These manuscript copies are only one class of the authorities relied on for ascertaining the true Greek text. Another class consists of extant manuscript copies of numerous ancient versions ; of the Old Testament dating from the first to the third century before Christ, and of the Old and New Testaments from the second to the eighth century after Christ. These are often helpful in determining contested points A third class are the quotations from the Holy Scriptures, found in the writings of the early Christian Fathers, from the second century onward ; and these are so numerous, that if the text of the New Testament were lost, it might be almost wholly recovered from their writings. These two classes of authorities were both inaccessible in the time of James ; either from want of knowledge of the languages in which they were written, or from want of correct editions of the text, which modern scholarship has supplied.

The Jews have been distinguished for their fidelity to the text of their Hebrew Scriptures. To them it was a sacred trust, and a cherished birthright. Their Scriptures were both the record and the sole relic of their once proud nationality. They saw in them the charter of their rights and privileges as the chosen people of the most high God, the Maker of heaven and earth. Of the many nations with whom they dwelt apart while among them, they saw none that could boast an origin, a history, and a destiny like theirs. Their present humiliation and its causes they found there described ; and with them the prophetic promise of future restoration and triumph. None of these nations could boast a literature like theirs; far surpassing in sublime eloquence and profound truths the highest efforts of human genius and intellect. Hence to no other people could its literature be what theirs was to them, and they guarded its text with jealous and ever watchful care.

In the early centuries of our era, learned Jewish scholars devoted their leisure to the laborious comparison of ancient manuscript copies of their Scriptures, in order to discover and correct errors of transcription, and to ascertain the genuine text of the sacred writings. Their labors resulted in the Masoretic text, so-called, leaving to modern investigators the plainer task of conforming to it the printed copies, under the principles and rules by which they were guided. This task has been prosecuted with great diligence and success; first by native Jews, and after them by Christian scholars, who have entered zealously into their labors.*

The present era of Hebrew learning dates from the issue, in 1810-12, of Gesenius' "Hebrew and German Lexicon," and in 1817, of his "System of Hebrew Grammar." His labors were supplemented by those of a host of eager toilers in Germany, America and England, the results of whose researches are now available for providing a more faithful English version of the Jewish Scriptures. The advance in Greek scholarship during the same period has more than kept pace with that in Hebrew. The grammars and lexicons of the present day are incomparably superior to any existing at the time our Common Version was made; and within the last half century equal progress has been made in the understanding of the peculiarities of the Greek and the New Testament.

The recent discoveries in archæology, in geography, and in the manners and customs of the East have also shed a flood of light upon the sacred page. Much that was unintelligible to the early translators, through their ignorance of these important sources of information, has been made clear to the modern scholar, who is now able, by their help, to give the exact sense of many passages hitherto obscure or meaningless to the ordinary reader. This is especially true with respect to the deciphering of the inscriptions upon the ancient Assyrian monuments—a marvellous example of patient and scholarly

---

* The Jews can claim the high honor of having first employed the art of printing to multiply copies of the Holy Scriptures.. After bringing out parts of the Old Testament, the Psalms in 1477, the five books of Moses in 1482, and the Hagiographa in 1487, they printed the whole Hebrew Scriptures in 1488; a hundred and twenty years before the first printing of the Greek New Testament.

research. The translator, as well as the interpreter of God's word, finds in these long-buried records of an extinct civilization material assistance in his work.

It was in order that the unlearned readers of the English Bible might share with scholars the benefit of these great advances in Biblical scholarship, that in 1853 the American Bible Union was formed with the avowed object of securing a thorough revision of the Common Version. The rules adopted for the direction of the revisers employed were as follows :

1. The received Greek text critically edited, with known errors corrected, must be followed.

2. The common English version must be the basis of revision, and only such alterations must be made as the exact meaning of the text and the existing state of the language may require.

3. The exact meaning of the inspired text, as that text expressed it to those who understood the original Scriptures at the time they were first written, must be given in corresponding words and phrases, so far as they can be found in the English language, with the least possible obscurity or indefiniteness.

The application of these rules is thus stated by the reviser of the Gospel of Matthew, in his Introduction :

" The version of the Gospel by Matthew, here presented to the public, is not a new translation. It is a revision of the common English version ; intended to bring that version to the present standard of critical learning, correcting its inaccuracies and its obscurities in English expression. In all these respects, the writer's object is the same as that of King James' revisers ; whose aim was not (to use their own words) ' to make a new translation, nor yet to make of a bad one a good one : . . . but to make a good one better, or out of many good ones, one principal good one.'

" In regard to the English style, the reviser has followed closely in their footsteps. The noble stock of English phraseology, which they found embodied in the earlier versions and revisions, and which they retained as the most fitting vehicle for the inspired thought of the original, forms the substance of the present revision. Where accuracy or clearness demanded a change, he has endeavored to make it in the same tone and manner ; selecting the expression from the simple, nervous Saxon vocabulary furnished by the English Bible itself in its successive revisions, and by the best writers contemporary with them."

The publications of the Bible Union awakened great interest in this country, where the supporters of the Society were numbered by thousands ; and the merits of the later revisions issued by the Union were acknowledged by scholarly critics in America, England and Germany. But the project of revision was vehemently opposed ; the great body of Christian people at that time regarding it as little short of sacrilege to make any, even the slightest, change in the Common Version.* Even scholars were not agreed as to the necessity or the propriety of attempting a new revision. The publication of these revisions, however, and their republication in England, undoubtedly did much to further the cause of Bible revision in both countries.

In 1857-58, the publication of a revision of the Gospel of John, the Epistle to the Romans, and the two Epistles to the Corinthians, by five clergymen, distinguished scholars of the Church of England, made a deep impression on the public mind, and prepared the way for further efforts in the same direction. These were soon followed by the learned and enthusiastic treatises on the subject of revision by Lightfoot, Trench and Ellicott (afterward republished in America by their permission, with an introduction by Dr. Philip Schaff), which fully proved at once that revision was a necessity, and that it ought not to be any longer delayed. Dean Trench, in his treatise, published in 1859, found himself compelled to say : " The question, shall we or shall we not have a new revision of the Authorized Version, is one which is presenting itself more and more familiarly to the minds of men."

Moved by these and similar discussions of the subject, the Convocation of Canterbury at length took decisive action for a revision of the common version.† At its session of May 6, 1870, a committee which consisted of eight bishops, the late Dean Alford, Dean Stanley, and several other dignitaries, reported :

1. That it is desirable that a revision of the Authorized Version of the Holy Scriptures be undertaken.

2. That the revision be so conducted as to comprise both marginal renderings and such emendations as it may be found necessary to insert in the text of the Authorized Version.

---

* A striking illustration of the popular feeling then prevalent is afforded by the signal failure of the effort to improve the common version made by the American Bible Society in 1851. " A committee appointed by the Society in 1848," says Dr. Schaff in his introduction to " The Revision of the New Testament," " found many errors and inconsistencies in the best English editions. . . . The Committee on Versions (including such scholars as Drs. Edward Robinson, Samuel H. Turner, and John M'Clintock) spent three years of labor and pains in correcting misprints, and improving the orthography, capital letters, words in italics, punctuation, and headings of columns and chapters. But the American Bible Society was induced, by a majority of its managers, to cancel the revised edition thus prepared (1852); on the ground of alleged want of constitutional authority, and popular dissatisfaction with a number of the changes made, especially in the headings of chapters, as substituting *Messiah* and *Sion*, in the Old Testament, for *Christ* and *Church*."

† For what follows see Dr. Schaff's Revision of the New Testament.

3. That in the above resolutions we do not contemplate any new translation of the Bible, or any alteration of the language, except where, in the judgment of the most competent scholars, such change is necessary.

4. That in such necessary changes, the style of the language employed in the existing version be closely followed.

5. That it is desirable that Convocation should nominate a body of its own members to undertake the work of revision, who shall be at liberty to invite the co-operation of any eminent for scholarship, to whatever nation or religious body they may belong.

The report was accepted unanimously by the upper House, and by a great majority of the Lower House. A committee was also appointed, consisting of eight bishops and eight presbyters, to take the necessary steps for carrying out the resolutions. At their first meeting, two companies of revisers were appointed from among the principal dignitaries of the English Church to have charge respectively of the revision of the Old and New Testaments. Distinguished scholars of the English Church, of the Catholic Church, and of the Protestant nonconformist bodies in England, were invited to join in the work.

The committee also, at the same session, adopted the following rules, to govern both companies in the execution of the work:

"1. To introduce as few alterations as possible into the text of the Authorized Version, consistently with faithfulness.

"2. To limit as far as possible, the expression of such alterations to the language of the Authorized and earlier English Versions.

"3. Each company to go twice over the portion to be revised, once provisionally, the second time finally, and on principles of voting as hereinafter is provided.

"4. That the text to be adopted be that for which the evidence is decidedly preponderating; and that when the text so adopted differs from that from which the Authorized Version was made, the alteration be indicated in the margin.

"5. To make or retain no change in the text on the second final revision by each company, except *two-thirds* of those present approve of the same, but on the first revision to decide by simple majorities.

"6. In every case of proposed alteration that may have given rise to discussion, to defer the voting thereupon till the next meeting, whensoever the same shall be required by one-third of those present at the meeting, such intended vote to be announced in the notice for the next meeting.

"7. To revise the headings of chapters and pages, paragraphs, italics, and punctuation.

"8. To refer, on the part of each company, when considered desirable, to divines, scholars, and literary men, whether at home or abroad, for their opinions."

The fifth resolution of the Convocation of Canterbury empowered the committee "to invite the co-operation of any eminent for scholarship, to whatever nation or religious body they may belong." In accordance with this resolution, Dr. Joseph Angus, President of Regent's Park College, London, and one of the English revisers, was deputed to proceed to America for the purpose of securing the aid of American scholars in the prosecution of the work. Dr. Angus arrived in New York in August, 1870. At his request, Dr. Philip Schaff prepared a draft of rules for co-operation and a list of names of Biblical scholars who would, in his judgment, best represent the different denominations and literary institutions of the United States. The suggestions were submitted to the British committee, and substantially approved. Dr. Schaff was empowered to select and invite scholars from non-Episcopal churches; and afterward, when the Bishops of the American Episcopal Church declined to nominate members, to fill out the list of Episcopal scholars.

In May, 1881, eleven years after the adoption of the resolution by the Convocation of Canterbury approving a revision of the English Scriptures, the New Testament was given to the public.

APPENDIX.

I. Specimens of the early English Versions.
II. The Immaculate Conception.
III. The Soldiers' Bible.

Note.—The Specimens of the early Versions in Part I. are given without change, except in the orthography, which is modernized. In Part II. a few additional specimens are given, as a matter of curiosity, with the original spelling retained. These are copied from very early editions; with the exception of the specimens of Tyndale's New Testament, which are from Offor's reprint of the first edition, 1526, and of Coverdale's Bible, which are taken from Bagster's modern reprint.

APPENDIX I.

SPECIMENS OF EARLY ENGLISH VERSIONS.

PART I.

WICKLIFFE.

EXODUS xx. 1–17.

And the Lord spake all these words: I am thy Lord God, that led thee out of the land of Egypt, from the house of servage. Thou shalt not have alien gods before me. Thou shalt not make to thee a graven image, neither any likeness *of thing* which is in heaven above, and which is in earth beneath, neither of the things, that be in waters under earth; thou shalt not herye [honor] tho; neither thou shalt worship; for I am thy Lord God, a strong jealous lover; and I visit the wickedness of faders into the third and the fourth generation of them that haten me, and I do mercy in to a thousand to them that loven me and keep mine hests. Thou shalt not take in vain the name of thy Lord God, for the Lord shall not have him guiltless that taketh in vain the name of his Lord God. Have thou mind that thou hallow the day of the sabbat; in six days thou shalt work and shalt do all thy works; forsooth in the seventh day is the sabbat of thy Lord God; thou shalt not do any work, thou, and thy son, and thy daughter, and thy servant, and thine handmaid, thy work beast, and the comeling [stranger] that is witnin thy gates; for in six days God made heaven and earth, the sea, and all things that

MATTHEW'S (TYNDALE).

EXODUS xx. 1–17.

And God spake all these words and said: I am the Lord thy God, which have brought thee out of the land of Egypt, and out of the house of bondage. Thou shalt have none other Gods in my sight. Thou shalt make thee no graven image, neither any similitude that is in heaven above, either in the earth beneath, or in the water that is beneath the earth. See that thou neither bow thyself unto them neither serve them: for I the Lord thy God am a jealous God, and visit the sin of the fathers upon the children unto the third and fourth generation of them that hate me, and yet show mercy unto thousands among them that love me and keep my commandments.

Thou shalt not take the name of the Lord thy God in vain, for the Lord will not hold him guiltless that taketh his name in vain. Remember the Sabbath day that thou sanctify it. Six days mayst thou labor and do all that thou hast to do: but the seventh day is the Sabbath of the Lord thy God; in it thou shalt do no manner work; neither thou nor thy son, nor thy daughter, neither thy man servant, nor thy maid servant, neither thy cattle, neither yet the stranger that is within thy gates. For in six days the Lord made both heaven

GENEVAN. EXODUS xx. 1–17.

Then God spake all these words, saying,

2. I am the Lord thy God, which have brought thee out of the land of Egypt, out of the house of bondage.

3. Thou shalt have none other gods before me.

4. Thou shalt make thee no graven image, neither any similitude [of things] that are in heaven above, neither that are in the earth beneath, nor that are in the waters under the earth.

5. Thou shalt not bow down to them, neither serve them; for I am the Lord thy God, a jealous God, visiting the iniquity of the fathers upon the children, upon the third [generation] and upon the fourth of them that hate me;

6. And showing mercy unto thousands to them that love me, and keep my commandments.

7. Thou shalt not take the name of the Lord thy God in vain; for the Lord will not hold him guiltless that taketh his name in vain.

8. Remember the Sabbath day, to keep it holy.

9. Six days shalt thou labor, and do all thy work.

10. But the seventh day [is] the Sabbath of the Lord thy God; [in it] thou shalt not do any work, thou, nor thy son, nor thy daughter, thy man servant, nor thy maid, nor thy beast, nor thy stranger that is within thy gates.

11. For in six days the Lord made the heaven and the earth, the sea, and all

APPENDIX I. (CONTINUED.)

COVERDALE.
EXODUS xx. 1-17.

And the Lord spake all these words, and said: I am the Lord thy God, which have brought thee out of the land of Egypt from the house of bondage.

Thou shalt have none other Gods in my sight. Thou shalt make thee no graven image, nor any similitude, neither of it that is above in heaven, nor of it that is beneath upon earth, neither of it that is in the water under the earth. Worship them not, and serve them not: for I the Lord thy God am a jealous God, visiting the sin of the fathers upon the children, unto the third and fourth generation of them that hate me; and do mercy upon many thousands that love me and keep my commandments.

Thou shalt not take the name of the Lord thy God in vain. For the Lord shall not hold him unguilty that taketh his name in vain.

Remember the Sabbath day that thou sanctify it. Six days shalt thou labor and do all thy work: But upon the seventh day is the Sabbath of the Lord thy God; thou shalt do no manner of work in it, neither thou, nor thy son, nor thy daughter, nor thy servant, nor thy maid, nor thy cattle, nor thy stranger that is within thy gates. For in six days the Lord made heaven and earth, and the sea and all that therein is, and rested

CRANMER.
EXODUS xx. 1-17.

And God spake all these words and said: I am the Lord thy God, which have brought thee out of the land of Egypt, out of the house of bondage. Thou shalt have none other Gods in my sight. Thou shalt make thee no graven image, neither any similitude that is in heaven above, either in the earth beneath, or in the waters under the earth. Thou shalt not worship them, neither serve them; for I the Lord thy God am a jealous God, and visit the sin of the fathers upon the children unto the third and fourth generation of them that hate me; and show mercy unto thousands in them that love me and keep my commandments.

Thou shalt not take the name of the Lord thy God in vain, for the Lord will not hold him guiltless that taketh his name in vain. Remember the Sabbath day that thou sanctify it. Six days shalt thou labor and do all that thou hast to do; but the seventh day is the Sabbath of the Lord thy God; in it thou shalt do no manner of work, thou, and thy son, and thy daughter, thy man servant, and thy maid servant, thy cattle, and the stranger that is within thy gates. For in six days the Lord made heaven and earth, the sea, and all that in them is,

BISHOPS'. EXODUS xx. 1-17.

And God spake all these words, and said,

2. I am the Lord thy God, which have brought thee out of the land of Egypt, out of the house of bondage.

3. Thou shalt have none other Gods in my sight.

4. Thou shalt make thee no graven image, neither the likeness of anything that is in heaven above, either in the earth beneath, nor in the waters under the earth.

5. Thou shalt not bow down to them, nor worship them; for I the Lord thy God am a jealous God, and visit the sin of the fathers upon the children, unto the third and fourth generation of them that hate me;

6. And show mercy unto thousands in them that love me, and keep my commandments.

7. Thou shalt not take the name of the Lord thy God in vain: for the Lord will not hold him guiltless that taketh his name in vain.

8. Remember the Sabbath day, that thou sanctify it.

9. Six days shalt thou labor, and do all that thou hast to do.

10. But the seventh day is the Sabbath of the Lord thy God; in it thou shalt do no manner of work, thou and thy son and thy daughter, thy man servant, and thy maid servant, thy cattle, and the stranger that is within thy gates;

11. For in six days the Lord made heaven and earth, the sea, and all that in

WICKLIFFE.

ben in tho, and rested in the seventh day; herefor the Lord blessed the day of the sabbat and hallowed it. Honor thy fader and thy moder, that thou be long living on the lond, which the Lord thy God shall give to thee. Thou shalt not slay. Thou shalt do no lechery. Thou shalt do no theft. Thou shalt not speak false witnessing against thy neighbor. Thou shalt not covet the house of thy neighbor, neither thou shalt desire his wife, not servant, not handmaid, not ox, not ass, neither all things than ben his.

MATTHEW'S (TYNDALE).

and earth, and the sea, and all that in them is, and rested the seventh day: wherefore the Lord blessed the Sabbath day and hallowed it. Honor thy father and thy mother, that thy days may be long in the land which the Lord thy God giveth thee.

Thou shalt not kill.
Thou shalt not break wedlock.
Thou shalt not steal.
Thou shalt bear no false witness against thy neighbor.
Thou shalt not covet thy neighbor's house; neither shalt covet thy neighbor's wife, his man servant, his maid, his ox, his ass, or aught that is his.

GENEVAN.

that in them is, and rested the seventh day; therefore the Lord blessed the Sabbath day, and hallowed it.

12. Honor thy father and thy mother, that thy days may be prolonged upon the land, which the Lord thy God giveth thee.

13. Thou shalt not kill.
14. Thou shalt not commit adultery.
15. Thou shalt not steal.
16. Thou shalt not bear false witness against thy neighbor.
17. Thou shalt not covet thy neighbor's house, neither shalt thou covet thy neighbor's wife, nor his man servant, nor his maid, nor his ox, nor his ass, neither anything that is thy neighbor's.

APPENDIX I. (CONTINUED.)

COVERDALE.
upon the seventh day ; therefore the Lord blessed the seventh day and hallowed it.

Honor thy father and thy mother, that thou mayest live long in the land, which the Lord thy God shall give thee.

Thou shalt not kill.

Thou shalt not break wedlock.

Thou shalt not steal.

Thou shalt bear no false witness against thy neighbor.

Thou shalt not lust after thy neighbor's house. Thou shalt not lust after thy neighbor's wife, nor his servant, nor his maid, nor his ox, nor his ass, nor all that thy neighbor hath.

CRANMER.
and rested the seventh day, wherefore the Lord blessed the Sabbath day and hallowed it.

Honor thy father and thy mother, that thy days may be long in the land which the Lord thy God giveth thee.

Thou shalt not kill.

Thou shalt not break wedlock.

Thou shalt not steal.

Thou shalt not bear false witness against thy neighbor.

Thou shalt not covet thy neighbor's house : neither shalt thou covet thy neighbor's wife, or his man servant, or his maid, or his ox, or his ass, or whatsoever thy neighbor hath.

BISHOPS'.

them is, and rested the seventh day ; wherefore the Lord blessed the seventh day, and hallowed it.

12. Honor thy father and thy mother ; that thy days may be long in the land which the Lord thy God giveth thee.
13. Thou shalt not kill.
14. Thou shalt not commit adultery.
15. Thou shalt not steal.
16. Thou shalt not bear false witness against thy neighbor.
17. Thou shalt not covet thy neighbor's house, neither shalt thou covet thy neighbor's wife, nor his man servant, nor his maid, nor his ox, nor his ass, nor anything that is thy neighbor's.

APPENDIX I. (CONTINUED.)

WICKLIFFE.
Luke vii. 36-50.

But one of the Pharisees prayed Jesus, that he should eat with him. And he entered into the house of the Pharisee, and sat at the meat. And lo! a sinful woman, that was in the city, as she knew that Jesus sat at the meat in the house of the Pharisee, she brought an alabaster box of ointment; and she stood behind besides his feet, and began to moist his feet with tears, and wiped with the hairs of her head, and kissed his feet, and anointed with ointment. And the Pharisee seeing, that had clepid [called, bidden] him, said within himself, saying, If this were a prophet, he should wite [know] who and what manner woman it were that toucheth him, for she is a sinful woman. And Jesus answered and said to him, Simon, I have something to say to thee. And he said, Master, say thou. And he answered; Two debtors were to one loaner: and one owed five hundred pence, and the other fifty; but when they hadden not whereof they shoulden geld [pay], he forgave to both. Who then loveth him more? Simon answered and said, I guess, that he to whom he forgave more. And he answered to him, Thou hast deemed rightly. And he turned to the woman, and said to Simon, Seest thou this woman? I entered into thine house, thou gave no water to my feet; but this hath moisted my feet with tears,

TYNDALE.
Luke vii. 36 50.

And one of the Pharisees desired him that he would eat with him. And he came into the Pharisee's house and sat down to meat. And behold a woman in that city which was a sinner, as soon as she knew that Jesus sat at meat in the Pharisee's house, she brought an alabaster box of ointment, and she stood at his feet behind him weeping, and began to wash his feet with tears, and did wipe them with the hairs of her head, and kissed his feet, and anointed them with ointment.

When the Pharisee which bade him to his house, saw that, he spake within himself, saying: If this man were a prophet, he would surely have known who and what manner woman this is which toucheth him, for she is a sinner. And Jesus answered and said unto him: Simon, I have somewhat to say unto thee. And he said: Master, say on. There was a certain lender which had two debtors; the one owed five hundred pence, and the other fifty. When they had nothing to pay, he forgave them both. Which of them, tell me, will love him most? Simon answered and said: I suppose that he to whom he forgave most. And he said unto him, Thou hast truly judged.

And he turned to the woman, and said unto Simon: Seest thou this woman? I entered into thy house, and thou gavest me no water to my feet; but she hath

GENEVAN. Luke vii. 36-50.

36. And one of the Pharisees desired him that he would eat with him. And he went into the Pharisees house, and sat down at table.

37. And behold, a woman in the city, which was a sinner, when she knew that Jesus sat at table in the Pharisees house, she brought a box of ointment:

38. And she stood at his feet behind him weeping, and began to wash his feet with tears, and did wipe them with the hairs of her head, and kissed his feet, and anointed them with the ointment.

39. Now when the Pharisee which bade him, saw it, he spake within himself saying, If this man were a prophet, he would surely have known who and what manner of woman this is which toucheth him, for she is a sinner.

40. And Jesus answered and said unto him: Simon, I have somewhat to say unto thee. And he said, Master, say on.

41. There was a certain lender which had two debtors: the one owed five hundred pence, and the other fifty.

42. When they had nothing to pay, he forgave them both. Which of them therefore, tell [me] will love him most?

43. Simon answered and said, I suppose that he to whom he forgave most. And he said unto him: Thou hast truly judged.

44. Then he turned to the woman, and said unto Simon, Seest thou this woman? I entered into thine house, and thou gavest me no water to my feet:

APPENDIX I. (CONTINUED.)

COVERDALE.
LUKE vii. 36–50.

And one of the Pharisees desired him that he would eat with him. And he went into the Pharisees house, and sat him down at the table. And behold, there was in the city a woman which was a sinner. When she knew that Jesus sat at the table in the Pharisees house, she brought a box with ointment, and stood behind at his feet and wept, and began to water his feet with tears, and to dry them with the hairs of her head, and kissed his feet, and anointed them with ointment.

But when the Pharisee which had called him saw that, he spake within himself and said: If this man were a prophet, he would know who and what manner of woman this is that toucheth him, for she is a sinner. And Jesus answered and said unto him: Simon, I have somewhat to say unto thee. He said: Master, say on. A certain lender had two debtors, the one owed five hundred pence, the other fifty: but when they had nothing to pay, he forgave them both. Tell me which of them will love him most? Simon answered and said: He, I suppose, to whom he forgave most. Then said he unto him: Thou hast judged right.

And he turned him to the woman, and said unto Simon: Seest thou this woman? I am come into thine house, thou hast given me no water unto my

CRANMER.
LUKE vii. 36–50.

And one of the Pharisees desired him that he would eat with him. And he went into the Pharisees house, and sat down to meat. And behold a woman in that city (which was a sinner) as soon as she knew that Jesus sat at meat in the Pharisees house, she brought an alabaster box of ointment, and stood at his feet behind him weeping, and began to wash his feet with tears, and did wipe them with the hairs of her head, and kissed his feet, and anointed them with the ointment. When the Pharisee which had bidden him saw, he spake within himself, saying: If this man were a prophet, he would surely know who and what manner of woman this is that touched him, for she is a sinner. And Jesus answered and said unto him: Simon, I have somewhat to say unto thee. And he said, Master, say on. There was a certain lender which had two debtors, the one owed five hundred pence, and the other fifty. When they had nothing to pay, he forgave them both. Tell me therefore, which of them will love him most? Simon answered and said: I suppose that he to whom he forgave most. And he said unto him: Thou hast truly judged.

And he turned to the woman, and said unto Simon: Seest thou this woman? I entered into thy house, thou gavest me no water for my feet; but she hath

BISHOPS'. LUKE vii. 36–50.

36. And one of the Pharisees desired him that he would eat with him. And he went into the Pharisees house and sat down to meat.

37. And behold, a woman in that city, which was a sinner, when she knew that Jesus sat at meat in the Pharisees house, she brought an alabaster box of ointment:

38. And stood at his feet behind him weeping, and began to wash his feet with tears, and did wipe them clean with the hairs of her head, and all to kissed his feet, and anointed them with the ointment.

39. When the Pharisee which had bidden him, saw it, he spake within himself, saying · If this man were a prophet, he would surely know who and what manner of woman is this that toucheth him; for she is a sinner.

40. And Jesus answering said unto him : Simon, I have somewhat to say unto thee. And he saith, Master, say on.

41. There was a certain lender which had two debtors; the one owed five hundred pence, and the other fifty.

42. When they had nothing to pay, he forgave them both. Tell me, therefore, which of them will love him most?

43. Simon answered and said : I suppose that he to whom he forgave most. And he said unto him, Thou hast truly judged.

44. And he turned to the woman and said unto Simon : Seest thou this

WICKLIFFE.

and wiped with her hairs. Thou hast not given to me a kiss; but this, sithen she entered, ceased not to kiss my feet. Thou anointedst not mine head with oil; but this anointed my feet with ointment. For the which thing I say to thee, many sins ben forgiven to her, for she hath loved much; and to whom is less forgiven, he loveth less. And Jesus said to her, Thy sins be forgiven to thee. And they that satten together at the meat, begun to say within themself, Who is this that forgiveth sins? But he said to the woman, Thy faith hath made thee safe; go thou in peace.

TYNDALE.

washed my feet with tears, and wiped them with the hairs of her head. Thou gavest me no kiss: but she, since the time I came in, hath not ceased to kiss my feet. Mine head with oil thou didst not anoint: and she hath anointed my feet with ointment. Wherefore I say unto thee; Many sins are forgiven her, because she loved much. To whom less is forgiven, the same doth less love.

And he said unto her, Thy sins are forgiven thee. And they that sat at meat with him, began to say within themselves: Who is this which forgiveth sins also? And he said to the woman: Thy faith hath saved thee; Go in peace.

GENEVAN.

but she hath washed my feet with tears, and wiped them with the hairs of her head.

45. Thou gavest me no kiss: but she, since the time I came in, hath not ceased to kiss my feet.

46. Mine head with oil thou didst not anoint: but she hath anointed my feet with ointment.

47. Wherefore I say unto thee: Many sins are forgiven her; for she loved much. To whom a little is forgiven, he doth love a little.

48. And he said unto her, Thy sins are forgiven thee.

49. And they that sat at table with him, began to say within themselves: Who is this that even forgiveth sins?

50. And he said to the woman; Thy faith hath saved thee: go in peace.

COVERDALE.

feet; but she hath watered my feet with tears, and dried them with the hairs of her head. Thou hast given me no kiss, but she, since the time she came in, hath not ceased to kiss my feet. Thou hast not anointed my head with oil, but she hath anointed my head with ointment. Therefore I say unto thee: Many sins are forgiven her, for she hath loved much. But unto whom less is forgiven, the same loveth the less.

And he said unto her: Thy sins are forgiven thee. Then they that sat at the table with him, began to say within themselves: What is he this, that forgiveth sins also? But he said unto the woman: Thy faith hath saved thee, Go thy way in peace.

CRANMER.

washed my feet with tears, and wiped them with the hairs of her head. Thou gavest me no kiss: but she, since the time I came in, hath not ceased to kiss my feet. Mine head with oil thou didst not anoint: but she hath anointed my feet with ointment. Wherefore I say unto thee: many sins are forgiven her, for she loved much. To whom less is forgiven, the same doth less love. And he said unto her: thy sins are forgiven thee. And they that sat at meat with him, began to say within themselves, Who is this which forgiveth sins also? And he said to the woman: Thy faith hath saved thee: Go in peace.

BISHOPS'.

woman? I entered into thine house, thou gavest me no water for my feet: but she hath washed my feet with tears, and wiped them with the hairs of her head.

45. Thou gavest me no kiss; but this woman, since the time I came in, hath not ceased to kiss my feet.

46. Mine head with oil thou didst not anoint; but this woman hath anointed my feet with ointment.

47. Wherefore I say unto thee, many sins are forgiven her, for she loved much; to whom little is forgiven, the same loveth little.

48. And he said unto her, thy sins are forgiven thee.

49. And they that sat at meat with him, began to say within themselves, who is this that forgiveth sins also?

50. And he said to the woman: Thy faith hath saved thee; go in peace.

TYNDALE.

Matt. xviii. 15. Moreover if thy brother trespass against thee, go and tell him his fault between him and thee alone. If he hear thee, thou hast won thy brother; but if he hear thee not, then take with thee one or two, that in the mouth of two or three witnesses, all sayings may stand. If he hear not them, tell it unto the congregation; if he hear not the congregation, take him as an heathen man and as a publican.

Acts ii. 47. And the Lord added to the congregation daily them that should be saved.

Acts viii. 1. At that time was there a great persecution against the congregation which was at Jerusalem.

Acts xi. 22. Tidings of this came unto the ears of the congregation which was in Jerusalem. 26. It chanced that a whole year they had their conversation with the congregation there.

Acts xii. 1. In that time Herod the King laid hands on certain of the congregation to vex them. 5. But prayer was made without ceasing of the congregation unto God for him.

Acts xiii. 1. There were at Antioch in the congregation prophets and doctors.

Acts xiv. 23. And when they had ordained them seniors* by election in every congregation.

1 Cor. iv. 17. Even as I teach every where, in all congregations.

Heb. xii. 22. But ye are come unto the mount Sion, and to the city of the living God, the celestial Jerusalem, and to an innumerable sight of angels, and unto the congregation of the first born sons.

* Afterwards, elders.

COVERDALE.

Matt. xviii. 15. If thy brother trespass against thee, go and tell him his fault between thee and him alone. If he hear thee, thou hast won thy brother. But if he hear thee not, then take yet with thee one or two, that in the mouth of two or three witnesses, every matter may be stablished. If he hear not them, tell it unto the congregation. If he hear not the congregation, hold him as an heathen and publican.

Acts ii 47. And the Lord added to the congregation daily such as should be saved.

Acts viii. 1. At the same time, there was a great persecution over the congregation at Jerusalem.

Acts xi. 22. This tidings of them came to the ears of the congregation at Jerusalem. 26. It chanced that a whole year they were there conversant together in the congregation.

Acts xii. 1. At the same time laid King Herod hands upon certain of the congregation to vex them. 5. But prayer was made without ceasing of the congregation, unto God for him.

Acts xiii. 1. There were at Antioch in the congregation, prophets and teachers.

Acts xiv. 23. And when they had ordained them elders by election, through all the congregations.

1 Cor. iv. 17. Even as I teach every where, in all congregations.

Heb. xii. 22. But ye are come to the mount Sion, and to the city of the living God, to the celestial Jerusalem, and to the multitude of many thousand angels, and unto the congregation of the first born.

GENEVAN.

Matt. xviii. 15. Moreover, if thy brother trespass against thee, go and tell him his fault between him and thee alone. If he hear thee, thou hast won thy brother.

16. But if he hear thee not, then take yet with thee one or two; that by the mouth of two or three witnesses, all the matter may be confirmed.

17. And if he will not vouchsafe to hear them, tell it unto the congregation. And if he refuse to hear the congregation, let him be unto thee as an heathen man, and as a publican.

Acts ii. 47. And the Lord added to the church daily such as should be saved.

Acts viii. 1. And at that time, there was a great persecution against the congregation which *was* at Jerusalem.

Acts xi. 22. Tidings of these things came unto the ears of the congregation which was in Jerusalem.

26. And it chanced that a whole year they had their conversation with the church there.

CRANMER.

Matt. xviii. 15. Moreover, if thy brother trespass against thee, go and tell him his fault between him and thee alone. If he hear thee thou hast won thy brother. But if he hear thee not, then take yet with thee one or two, that in the mouth of two or three witnesses, every matter may be stablished. If he hear not them, tell it unto the congregation. If he hear not the congregation, let him be to thee as an heathen man and as a publican.

Acts ii. 47. And the Lord added to the congregation daily such as should be saved.

Acts viii. 1. And at that time, there was a great persecution against the congregation which was at Jerusalem.

Acts xi. 22. Tidings of these things came unto the ears of the congregation which was in Jerusalem. 26. And it chanced that a whole year they had their conversation with the congregation there.

Acts xii. 1. At the same time Herod the King stretched forth his hands to vex certain of the congregation. 5. But prayer was made without ceasing of the congregation unto God for him.

Acts xiii. 1. There were in the congregation that is at Antioch, certain prophets and teachers.

Acts xiv. 23. And when they had ordained them elders by election in every congregation.

1 Cor. iv. 17. Even as I teach every where, in all congregations.

Heb. xii. 22. But ye are come unto the mount Sion, and to the city of the living God, the celestial Jerusalem; and to an innumerable sight of angels and unto the congregation of the first born sons.

BISHOPS'.

Matt. xviii. 15. Moreover, if thy brother shall trespass against thee, go and tell him his fault between thee and him alone; if he shall hear thee, thou hast won thy brother.

16. But if he will not hear thee, then take yet with thee one or two; that in the mouth of two or three witnesses, every word may be stablished.

17. If he will not hear them, tell it unto the church: if he will not hear the church, let him be unto thee as an heathen man and a publican.

Acts ii. 47. And the Lord added to the church daily such as should be saved.

Acts viii. 1. And at that time there was a great persecution against the church which was at Jerusalem.

Acts xi. 22. Then tidings of these things came unto the ears of the church which was in Jerusalem. 26. And it came to pass that a whole year they had their conversation with the church there.

Acts xii. 1. At the same time the King stretched forth his hands to vex certain of the church. 5. But prayer was made without ceasing of the church unto God for him.

Acts xiii. 1. There was also in the church that was at Antioch, certain prophets and teachers.

Acts xiv. 23. And when they had ordained them elders by election in every church.

1 Cor. iv. 17. As I teach every where in all churches.

Heb. xii. 22. But ye are come unto the mount Sion, and to the city of the living God, the celestial Jerusalem, and to an innumerable company of angels.

23. And unto the congregation of the first born.

GENEVAN.

Acts xii. 1. In that time, Herod the king stretched forth his hands to vex certain of the congregation.

5. But prayer was made without ceasing of the church unto God for him.

Acts xiii. 1. There were in the congregation that was at Antioch, certain prophets and teachers.

Acts xiv. 23. And when they had ordained them elders by election in every church.

1 Cor. iv. 17. Even as I teach every where in all congregations.

Heb. xii. 22. But ye are come unto the mount Sion, and to the city of the living God, the celestial Jerusalem; and to the company of innumerable angels,

23. And to the congregation of the first born sons.

PART II.

PSALM xix.

MATTHEW'S.

The very heauens declare the glory of God and the very firmament sheweth his handy worcke.

One daye telleth another, and one nyght certifyeth another. There is neyther speach ner language, but their voices are hard among them.*

Their sounde is gone oute into all landes, and their wordes into the endes of the worlde. In them hath he sette a tabernacle for the Sunne, whych commeth forthe as a brydegrome out of his chamber, and reioyceth as a giaunt to runne his course.

It goeth forth from the one ende of the heauen, and runneth aboute vnto the same ende agayne, and there maye no man hyde hymselfe from the heate therof. The lawe of the Lorde is a perfecte lawe it quickeneth the soule.

The testimonye of the Lorde is true, and geueth wisdome euen vnto babes.

The statutes of the Lord are ryght, and reioyse the hert : the commaundement of the lord is pure, and geueth lyght vnto the eyes.

The feare of the Lorde is cleane, and endureth for euer : the iudgementes of the Lord are true and ryghtuous altogether. More pleasaunt are they then golde, yea then much fyne golde : sweter then hony and the hony combe. These thy seruaunt kepeth, & for kepynge of them there is great reward.

* *Marg, or rather*, there is no voyce amonge them.

BISHOPS'.

1. The heauens declare the glorie of God : and the firmament sheweth his handie woorke.
2. A day occasioneth talke thereof vnto a day : & a nyght teacheth knowledge vnto a nyght.
3. No language, no woordes, no voyce of theyrs is hearde : yet theyre sounde* goeth into al landes, and theyr woordes into the endes of the worlde.
4. In them he hath sette a tabernacle for the sunne, whych commeth foorth as a brydegrome out of his chamber, and reioyceth as a giant to runne his course.
5. His setting foorth is from the vtmost part of heauen, & his circuite vnto the vtmost part therof : and there is nothing hid from his heate.
6. The law of God is perfect, conuerting the soule : the testimonie of God is sure, and geueth wysdome vnto the simple.
7. The statutes of god are ryght, and reioyce the hart : the commaundement of god is pure, and geueth light vnto the eyes.
8. The feare of god is sincere, and endureth for euer : the iudgementes of god are trueth, they be iust in al pointes.
9. They are more to be desired then golde, yea then muche fine golde : they are also sweeter then hony, and the hony combe.
10. Moreouer, by them thy seruant is wel aduertised : and in keping of them there is a great rewarde.

* v. 3, *marg*. rule, *or* line.

GENEVAN.

1. The heauens declare the glorie of God, & the firmament sheweth the worke of his hands.
2. Day vnto day vttereth the same, and night vnto night teacheth knowledge.
3. [There is] no speach nor language, [where] their voyce is not heard.
4. Their line is gone forth through all the earth, and their wordes into the endes of the world : in them hath he set a Tabernacle for the sunne.
5. Which commeth foorth as a bridegrome out of his chamber,* [and] reioyceth like a mightie man to runne [his] race.
6. His going out [is] from the ende of the heauen, and his compasse [is] vnto the endes of the same, and none is hid from the heate thereof.
7. The Lawe of the Lorde is perfit, conuerting the soule : the testimonie of the Lorde is sure, and giueth wisedom vnto the simple.
8. The statutes of the Lorde [are] right and reioyce the heart : the commandement of the Lord [is] pure, and giueth light vnto the eyes.
9. The feare of the Lorde [is] cleane, and indureth for euer : the iudgements of the Lorde [are] trueth : they are righteous all together.
10 And more to be desired then golde, yea, then much fine golde : sweeter also then honie and the honie combe.
11. Moreouer by them [is] thy seruant made circumspect, [and] in keeping of them there [is] great reward.

* v. 5. *marg. or* vaile.

MATTHEW'S.

Who can tell how oft he offendeth: Oh clense thou me from my secrete fautes. Kepe thy seruaunt also from presumptuous synnes, lest they get the dominion ouer me: so shall I be vnde fyled and innocent from the greate offence.

Yea the words of my mouth and the meditacion of my herte shalbe acceptable vnto the, O Lorde, my helper and my redemer.

BISHOPS'.

11. Who can knowe his owne errours: Oh, cleanse thou me from those I am not priuie of.

12. Kepe thy seruant also from presumptuous (*sinnes*) let them not raigne ouer me: so I shalbe perfect & voyde from al heynous offence.

13. Let the woordes of my mouth and the meditacion of my hart be acceptable in thy sight, O God, my strength and my redeemer.

GENEVAN.

12. Who can vnderstand [his] faults; clense me from secrete [faultes].

13. Keepe thy seruant also from presumptuous sinnes: let them not reigne ouer me: so shall I bee vpright, & made cleane from much wickednesse.

14. Let the wordes of my mouth, and the meditation of mine heart be acceptable in thy sight, O Lord, my strength, & my redeemer.

APPENDIX I. (CONTINUED).

DANIEL vii. 9.

MATTHEW'S: I loked tyl the seates were prepared and tyll the olde aged sat hym doune.
COVERDALE and CRANMER the same.
GENEVAN: I beheld, till the thrones were set vp, & the Ancient of dayes did sit.
BISHOPS', same as Genevan.

THE LORD'S PRAYER.

IN MATTHEW vi.

TYNDALE.

O oure father which arte in heven, halowed be thy name. Let thy kyngdom come. Thy wyll be fufilled as well in erth, as hit ys in heven. Geve vs this daye oure dayly breade. And forgeve vs oure treaspases, even as we forgeve them which treaspas vs. Leede vs not into temptacion, but delyvre vs from yvell, Amen.

COVERDALE.

O oure father which art in heauen, halowed be thy name. Thy kyngdome come. Thy wyll be fulfilled vpon earth as it is in heauen. Geue us this daye oure dayly bred. And forgeue us oure dettes, as we also forgeve oure detters. And lede vs not in to temptacion : but delyuer vs from euell. For thyne is the kyngdome, and the power, and the glorye for euer. Amen.

BISHOPS'.

9. O our father which art in heauen, halowed be thy name.
10. Let thy kyngdome comme. Thy wyl be donne, as wel in earth, as it is in heauen.
11. Geue vs this day our dayly bread.
12. And forgeue vs our dettes, as we forgeue our detters.
13. And leade vs not into temptation, but delyuer vs from euyl: for thyne is the kyngdome, and the power, and the glorie, for euer. Amen.

IN LUKE xi. 2-4.

TYNDALE.

Oure father which arte in heven, halowed be thy name. Lett thy kyngdome come. Thy will be fulfillet even in erth as it is in heven. Oure dayly breed geve vs this day. And forgeve vs oure synnes : for even we forgeve every man that traspaseth vs, and ledde vs not into temptacion, Butt deliver vs from evyll. Amen.

MATTHEW'S. (N. T. Tyndale's.)

O oure father whiche arte in heauen, ha'owed be thy name. Thy kyngedome come. They will be fulfylled euen in earthe as it is in heauen. Geue vs our daylye breade euermore. And forgeue vs oure synnes : for euen we forgeue euery man that trespasseth vs. And ledde vs not into temptacyon. But deliuer vs from euyll.

COVERDALE.

O oure father which art in heauen, halowed be thy name. Thy kyngdome come. Thy wil be fulfilled vpon earth as it is in heauen. Geue vs this daye oure daylie bred. And forgeue vs oure synnes, for we also forgeue all them that are detters vnto vs. And lede vs not in to temptacion, but delyuer vs from euell.

CRANMER.

O our father whiche art in heauen halowed by thy name. Thy kyngdome come. Thy will bee fulfilled, euen in earth also as it is in heauen. Our dayly breade geue vs this day, and forgeue vs oure synnes : For euen we forgeue euery manne that trespasseth vs. And leade vs not into temptacion. But delyuer vs from euyll.

BISHOPS'.

2. O our father whiche art in heauen, halowed be thy name. Thy kyngdome comme. Thy wyl be donne, euen in earth also as it is in heauen.
3. Our dayly bread geue vs this day.
4. And forgeue vs our sinnes : for euen we forgeue euery man that trespasseth vs. And lead vs not into temptation, but deliuer vs from the euyl.

1 CORINTHIANS xiii. 1-3.

TYNDALE.

Though I speake with the tonges of men and angels, and yet had no love, I were even as soundynge brasse : and as a tynklynge Cynball, and though I coulde prophesy, and vnderstode all secretes, and all knowledge : yee, if I had all fayth so that I coulde move mountayns oute of there places, and yet had no love, I were nothynge. And though I bestowed all my gooddes to fede the poore, and though I gave my body even that I burned, & yet have no love, it profeteth me nothynge.

CRANMER.

Though I spake with the tongues of men and of angels, and haue no loue, I am euen as soundyng brasse : or as a tinklinge cimbal. And thoughe I coulde prophecye and vnderstode all secretes & all knoweledge ; yea, yf I haue all faythe, so that I can moue mountaynes oute of theyr places, and yet haue no loue, I am nothyng. And though I bestow al my goodes to fede the poore, and though I geue my body euen that I burned, and yet haue no loue, it profyteth me nothyng.

GENEVAN.

1. Though I speake with the tongues of men and Angels, and haue not loue, I am (as) sounding brasse, or a tinkling cymball.
2. And though I had the (gift) of prophecie, and knewe all secretes and all knowlcdge, yea, if I had all fayth, so that I could remoue mountaines and had not loue, I were nothing.
3. And though I feede the poore with all my goods, and though I giue my body, that I be burned, & have not loue, it profiteth me nothing.

BISHOPS'.

1. Though I speake with the tongues of menne and of Angels, and haue not charitie, I am [as] sounding brasse, or [as] a tincklyng Cymbale.
2. And though I haue prophecie, and vnderstande al secretes, and al knowledge : yea, yf I haue al fayth, so that I can remooue mountaynes, and haue not charitie, I am nothing.
3. And though I bestowe al my goodes to feede the poore, and though I geue my body that I should be burned, and haue not charitie, it profiteth me nothing.

APPENDIX II.

THE IMMACULATE CONCEPTION.

As this doctrine is of late claimed to have been the universal sense of the Holy Catholic Church in all ages, though not recognized by formal act,* it may be interesting to hear Sir Thomas More's testimony on the point. It is contained in a letter from Margaret Roper to her sister-in-law, detailing an interview with her father in the Tower She thus gives his words :

"For an ensample of some such manner of things, I have I trow before this time told you, that whether our blessed lady were conceived in original sin or not, was sometime in great question among the great learned men of Christendom. And whether it be yet decided and determined by any general council, I remember not. But this I remember well, that notwithstanding that the feast of her conception was then celebrated in the church (at the least wise, in divers provinces), yet was holy St. Bernard, which, as his manifold books in the praise and laud of our lady do declare, was of as devout affection toward all things sounding toward her commendation that he thought might well be verified or suffered, as any man living ; yet, I say, was that holy devout man against that part of her praise, as appeareth well by an epistle of his, wherein he right sore and with great reason argueth there against, and approveth not the institution of that feast neither. Nor was he not of this mind alone, but many other well learned men with him, and right holy men too. Now there was on the other side, the blessed holy bishop St. Anselm, and he not alone neither, but many very well learned and very virtuous also with him."—*More's English Works, p.* 1439.

APPENDIX III.

THE SOLDIER'S BIBLE.

An account of this Bible, prepared in 1643 by Cromwell's order for the use of his army, has been published by the late George Livermore, Esq., Cambridge, Mass., from which the following particulars are quoted :

"The selections from Scripture are divided into eighteen chapters, each with an appropriate heading to indicate the class of Scriptures contained therein. A few examples of these headings or titles will sufficiently show their general character.

1. A Souldier must not doe wickedly.
2. A Souldier must be valiant for God's cause.
3. A Souldier must pray before he go to fight."

Mr. Livermore refers to the remarkable fact, " that the success of Cromwell's army commenced immediately on the publication of The Souldier's Pocket Bible; and they never after lost a battle !"

* On December 8th, 1854, it was defined by Pope Pius IX. as an article of faith of the Roman Catholic Church.

THE SOULDIERS Pocket Bible:

Containing the most (if not all) those places contained in holy Scripture, which doe shew the qualifications of his inner man, that is a fit Souldier to fight the Lords Battels, both before he fight, in the fight, and after the fight:

Which Scriptures are reduced to severall heads, and fitly applyed to the Souldiers severall occasions, and so may supply the want of the whole Bible, which a Souldier cannot conveniently carry about him:

And may bee also usefull for any Christian to meditate upon, now in this miserable time of Warre.

Imprimatur, *Edm. Calamy.*

Jos. 18. This Book of the Law shall not depart out of thy mouth, but thou shalt meditate therein day and night, that thou maist observe to doe according to all that is written therein, for then thou shalt make thy way prosperous, and have good successe.

Printed at *London* by *G. B.* and *R. W.* for *G. C.* 1643.

Only two copies of this curious work are now known to be in existence, one of which, at the time this volume was written, was in the possession of Mr. Livermore. The other had but recently come to light in England. In a letter written by Mr. Livermore, he says on this point : " It is quite remarkable, that the question concerning the ' Souldier's Bible' should be answered on this side of the Atlantic. English Bibliographers have never been able, till the past year, to decide what *edition* of the Bible was furnished to Cromwell's army ; and the existence of ' The Souldier's Bible' was unknown, until I had sent a description of it to Rev. Dr. Cotton, George Offor, Esq., Henry Stevens, Esq., and other eminent English Bibliographers. This little work was entirely unknown to them. After a long and diligent search in various public and private libraries, only one other copy has been found, and that is in the British Museum."

On another point of interest, in reply to an inquiry of the writer, he says : " The selections from Scripture are, *in almost every instance*, taken from the Genevan Version ; but in some cases, a very few, King James' Version has been used. In a few cases, the phraseology varies slightly from all the English Versions which I have examined."

This is an interesting corroborative testimony to the preference of our Puritan forefathers for the Genevan Version (see p. 204), so late as 1643.

Note.—During the late Civil War, a Special Pocket Bible was presented and widely distributed among the Union armies, containing the same passages as the above, but in the language of the common version.

www.ingramcontent.com/pod-product-compliance
Lightning Source LLC
Chambersburg PA
CBHW050338230426
43663CB00010B/1906